FRAY

R
AY

JULIA
BRYAN-WILSON

art + textile politics

FRAY

THE UNIVERSITY OF CHICAGO PRESS
Chicago & London

Publication of this book has been aided by a grant from the Neil Harris Endowment Fund, which honors the innovative scholarship of Neil Harris, the Preston and Sterling Morton Professor Emeritus of History at the University of Chicago. The fund is supported by contributions from the students, colleagues, and friends of Neil Harris.

The University of Chicago Press, Chicago 60637
The University of Chicago Press, Ltd., London

Published 2017
Printed in China

27 26 25 24 23 22 21   4 5 6

ISBN-13: 978-0-226-07781-9 (cloth)
ISBN-13: 978-0-226-36982-2 (e-book)
DOI: 10.7208/chicago/9780226369822.001.0001

Publication of this book has been aided by a grant from the Millard Meiss Publication Fund of the College Art Association.

MM

Library of Congress Cataloging-in-Publication Data
Names: Bryan-Wilson, Julia, author.
Title: Fray : art and textile politics / Julia Bryan-Wilson.
Description: Chicago ; London : The University of Chicago Press, 2017. | Includes bibliographical references and index.
Identifiers: LCCN 2016058305 | ISBN 9780226077819 (cloth : alk. paper) | ISBN 9780226369822 (e-book)
Subjects: LCSH: Fiberwork—Political aspects. | Art—Political aspects—Case studies. | Homosexuality and art—United States. | Handicraft—Political aspects—United States. | NAMES Project AIDS Memorial Quilt. | Vicuña, Cecilia. | Textile crafts—Political aspects—Chile. | Feminism and art. | Art, Modern—20th century—History.
Classification: LCC N7433.9 .B79 2017 | DDC 746.08—dc23 LC record available at https://lccn.loc.gov/2016058305

∞ This paper meets the requirements of ANSI/NISO Z39.48-1992 (Permanence of Paper).

To Mel Y. Chen

Contents

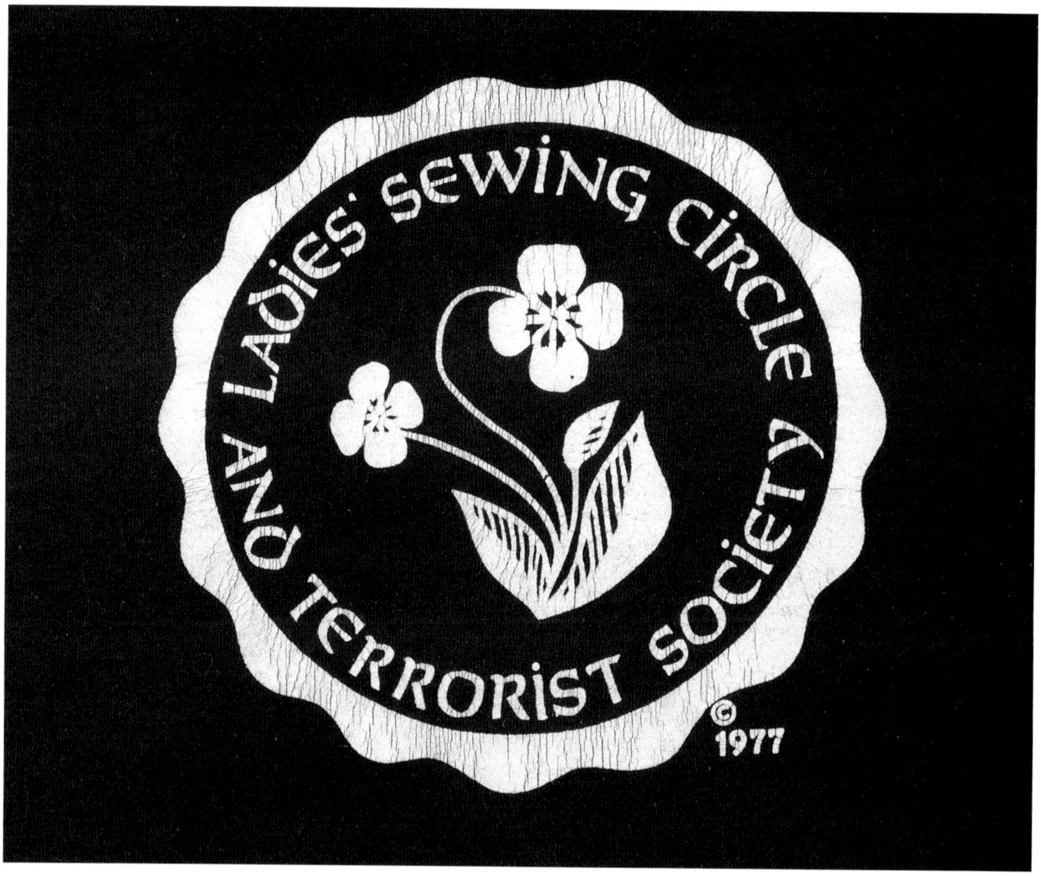

Fig. 0.01.
Ladies' Sewing Circle and Terrorist Society T-shirt, detail, designed by Sally-Jo Bowman, 1974 (copyright 1977). Collection of the author.

Introduction

TEXTILE POLITICS

Around 1974, the mock organization Ladies' Sewing Circle and Terrorist Society emerged out of conversations within a small feminist consciousness-raising group in Eugene, Oregon. The women in the group laughed among themselves about putting their faux moniker onto a T-shirt, but none took concrete action until writer Sally-Jo Bowman drew up a design. She based her sketch on an embroidery pattern that included a stem of flowers with open petals and striated leaves, hoping the sweetness of the motif would drive home the stark juxtaposition between the presumed harmlessness of the sewing circle and the menace of the terrorist society.[1] The resultant logo, with its deceptively innocent flower motif and a crypto-Celtic-meets–art nouveau typeface, came to be emblazoned not just on T-shirts but also on coffee mugs, stickers, and buttons (fig. 0.01). The circularity of the design functions conceptually as well as formally: it breaks the phrase into two grammatical and visual parts, leading to greater payoff as you first read the prim top portion—"ladies' sewing circle"—and then your eyes swing down for the surprise of the punch line—"and terrorist society."

What does it mean to imagine the sewing needle as a dangerous tool and to envision female collective textile making as a process that might upend conventions, threaten state structures, or wreak political havoc? The joke relies upon assumptions about the very impotence of textiles and the assumed absurdity of decorous "ladies"—not "women" but their more dainty or polite counterparts—fostering violent unrest. Made within the context of a specific historical moment in the United States (as the women's liberation movement of the 1970s was nearing its crescendo and the Vietnam War was coming to its bitter end), the slogan captures a bit of wry feminist humor regarding the unlikelihood of textile groups fomenting illegal, dangerous action.

Bowman took her design to a local T-shirt company (known for making sports shirts) and had two dozen shirts silkscreened. They were a hit with the consciousness-raising group, so Bowman shopped them around to women's conventions, where according to her "they sold like hotcakes." Casting a sewing circle as insurrectionary might be the engine of the design's comedy, but the shirt's immense popularity points to a sober desire to rethink feminist collectivity as world-changing. For about a decade, Bowman, based in Fall Creek, Oregon, sold the T-shirts through mail order, advertising primarily through small print classifieds in the back of *Ms.* magazine. "You're sure to entertain and invite comments too," stated one version of the ad.[2] Bowman placed her design under copyright in 1977, and though she never made anything close to a living with the shirts and stickers and buttons, it became an iconic item within 1970s feminist material culture.

Bowman sold the copyright in 1986 after the T-shirt business dwindled, but in recent years the logo has been revived and placed on an array of objects by younger feminists cashing in on its enduring cleverness, as well as its nostalgia for a different era, one in which women's rights might be taken seriously while at the same time terrorism might be invoked lightly. In the intervening years, the connotations affiliated with the label "terrorist" have changed. Then it signified homegrown radicals such as the Weather Underground, whose manifesto *Prairie Fire* urged armed struggle against US imperialism and advocated for militant anticapitalist, antiracist, and antisexist politics—causes endorsed by many on the Left, even if their tactics were controversial.[3] Published in 1974, contemporaneous with Bowman's T-shirt, *Prairie Fire* includes a section on feminist liberation and describes undervalued textile and garment labor as "the traditional work of women;" these and other traditions were to be shattered.[4] Some revolutionary feminists embraced the very rhetoric of extreme violence that was satirized by the Ladies' Sewing Circle, demonstrating that there was not as much dissonance at that time as is felt today by the alignment of feminism and so-called terrorism (the Weathermen themselves rejected that term). But in recent years, "terrorists" have shifted away from being seen as New Left agent provocateurs to being constructed as demonized Others by the US government's post-9/11 "war on terror," and have been largely understood to promote regressive gender politics; implausibly, George W. Bush declared the wars on Afghanistan and Iraq to be crusades for women's rights.[5]

I know the "Ladies' Sewing Circle and Terrorist Society" T-shirt intimately, because my mother bought one in 1977 after seeing the ad in *Ms.*—she was an early subscriber—when I was a young child in Texas. While I was growing up, the T-shirt was in steady rotation in her wardrobe, and I have somewhat mortified memories of her wearing it, provoking consternation and stilted smiles among a few less-than-amused storekeepers, church members, and schoolteachers. I badly wanted to include a photograph of my mom in the T-shirt from those years, but no such image exists. ("I was a single parent, Julia!

I was always the one *behind* the camera," she reminded me after she looked through her photo albums.) As a committed feminist, my mother considered the "Ladies' Sewing Circle" T-shirt especially funny because she was also a dedicated sewer who had an ingenious knack for textiles. Throughout the 1970s and 1980s, she handmade many of my family's clothes, because it was far cheaper than buying new things and because she was good at it. In other words, she sewed for reasons of class-based expediency rather than ideology. She taught me how to sew the summer I turned thirteen; under her guidance I made a few awkward outfits. Though I was never very good, this exposure made me curious about textiles from the perspective of making.

When I was in high school and coming into my own feminist politics, I borrowed the T-shirt from my mother so frequently that she finally gave it to me. Like her, I reveled in the puzzled looks it elicited. I wore it, too, because it felt palpably "vintage" and as such it signaled my ironic affiliation—akin to what Elizabeth Freeman has called "temporal drag"—with the outdated or bygone era of my mother's generation, who, unlike my friends or me, might have earnestly self-identified as sewers.[6] (Though she was sincerely and proudly a sewer, I did not quite grasp that she would have considered "sewing circles" anachronistic.) Wearing it as a teenager circa 1990 signaled my absolute allegiance to feminism while at the same time distancing me from what seemed to me to be a time long past: 1970s women's liberation, which to me existed in a murky realm between the familiar and the strange, as the quaint flowery design was transmuted into near-cultic paraphernalia.

But not every woman who wore Bowman's design in the 1970s and early 1980s necessarily identified with progressive feminist politics. An article on the Republican Party national field director Maxene Fernstrom from 1981 recounts that "she turns heads when she bursts into a room wearing a mink coat over a sweatshirt that says, 'Ladies' Sewing Circle and Terrorist Society.'"[7] With its evocation of a clash between luxurious fur and workaday sweatshirt, the description of Fernstrom as a Republican head-turner illustrates how the logo was open-ended enough to appeal to those from across the political spectrum. The T-shirt itself embodies a tension within textiles: they occupy a central place in traditionalist histories while they also erupt as potential sites of resistance to that very traditionalism, claimed by competing factions at once as hegemonic and counterhegemonic.

It is exactly such tensions that this book explores, for expectations about textiles are thwarted depending on which histories, and which objects, one examines. The first scholarly book of its kind, *Fray* takes up key moments from the 1970s, 1980s, and 1990s in which textiles were put to work in a range of circumstances (often intertwining activist and artistic purposes) and sometimes tattered, or tore, under the pressure. I attend closely to the forms, processes of making, materials, and aesthetics of the following subjects: the campy, crafty costumes of the Cockettes, the braided rag-rug sculptures of Harmony Hammond, the ephemeral threads of Cecilia Vicuña, the burlap-backed tapestries of Chilean *arpilleristas*, and the hand-sewn panels of the AIDS Quilt. As will be made clear, this close looking constitutes both my art-historical methodology and my political project.

In the Fray

This introduction defines some of my terms and provides a genealogy of my approach. More focused background on the various intellectual and geographic loci taken up in the body of the book—gay liberation, the Pinochet dictatorship, and the dawn of the HIV/AIDS crisis—is found in the individual chapters. Throughout, I use *fray* in several senses: the material wearing out of textiles, the undoing of threads, the pulling apart of fibers through strain and repeated use. Edges—or borders—are more prone to fraying, as they are subject to more friction. I am theoretically indebted to Roland Barthes's understanding of the "fraying" of textual meaning; he eloquently described the shared etymological roots of *textiles* and *texts* (from the Latin *texere*—to weave) as "at once interwoven and unfinished"; Theodor Adorno's concept of the fraying boundaries between artistic genres (*Verfransung*), or even an infringement into nonart, has also been a touchstone.[8] Often used as tactile forms of communication or kinds of writing, textiles offer themselves as objects to be understood, but as with any system of language, they are dense with multiple meanings and are available for a range of readings and conflicting interpretations.

Textiles are thus also "in the fray" of heated disputes, controversies, and disagreements, and have been at the center of arguments about the materiality of gendered labor. Those debates are often about the limits or boundaries between high and low, since textiles, not least because of their constant use in and affiliation with the everyday, trigger suspicions that such boundaries might not exist. Nerves, and tempers, also fray. While it is said that one should "rise above the fray," this book choses to dwell in its sometimes uncomfortable place of forceful confrontation, for I take as my central subject fractious disputes about what and how textiles mean, where they should live institutionally, and where they belong politically.

As with the many definitions of *fray*, I also consider the term *textiles* in its most capacious sense, to refer to everything from needle-based techniques like appliqué to mass-produced clothing, while maintaining important distinctions between various processes and their effects. The word *textiles* and terms denoting their constitutive elements, fibers such as *cords*, *twine*, and *yarn*, are sometimes used interchangeably: within the practices I am investigating, those classifications are not always rigidly defined and are sensitive to purpose. At times fiber is organized into fabric, but often it remains as a skein, a coil, or a jumble. Some of the objects in this book are only marginally "handmade"; they integrate commercial factory-fabricated items along with string or cloth scraps as they probe the various thresholds of textiles (between hand and machine, or between states of becoming and processes of unmaking).

In *Fray* I discuss select instances in which textiles from the 1970s to the 1990s—in art as well as nonart contexts—have been marshaled for their specially tensile properties, that is, their capacity to be pulled, stressed, and withstand tension, sometimes to their breaking point. The book is episodic and makes no claims for encyclopedic or global coverage; instead I elaborate on a handful of potent moments of textile making in the United States and Chile. Organized around a series of focused case studies that examine both amateur practices and those destined for fine art audiences, *Fray* considers the classed, raced, gendered, and sexualized formations that have surrounded, and critically produced, textiles since the 1970s.

For me, by far the most important, ambitious, and risky aspect of the book is its organizational structure, in which chapters are broken into two parts, giving consideration to hobbyist and fine art practices while also undoing the logics of the categorizations of "high" and "low." Rather than adopt a binary scheme in which amateurism is defined, oppositionally, against professionalism, I understand these as ever-mobile terms in a broader, flexible matrix that admits a range of individual and collective production by all kinds of self-proclaimed textile makers. This book structurally asserts how, in the case of textiles, fine art and amateur practices are mutually coconstitutive, constantly informing each other and viewed radically differently depending on context. As Stephen Knott cogently articulates, "Amateur craft is inherently dependent on the routines of everyday life . . . the division of labour, entrepreneurship, the adulation of productivity, and the accumulation of capital. Yet it simultaneously constitutes a spatial-temporal zone in which these structures can be stretched, quietly subverted, and exaggerated."[9] Though I employ words such as *amateur* and *artist*, I also aim to pick at, worry, and put pressure on their mutual borders until they, too, unravel.

Amateur textile craft in the main falls outside the scope of contemporary art, which is increasingly comfortable with assessing the exceptionalism of self-trained or "outsider artists" such as Judith Scott (evermore folded into the apparatus of auction houses and art magazines) but is less able to critically account for the tremendous amount of making generated by those termed, in a telling phrase that equates amateurism with nonremunerative leisure time, "Sunday makers." In recent decades, textiles have provided a unique challenge to these divisions as more self-trained crafters are absorbed into the art market; the traveling exhibits and coffee table books featuring the African American quilters of the rural Alabama hamlet Gee's Bend are a signature example. Yet such instances expose some of the fault lines of fine art / non–fine art dynamics, bringing to the fore extraordinarily fraught questions about race, cultural appropriation, valuation, and class disparity.[10] And the institutionalization of the Gee's Bend quilts, which are now displayed in art museums alongside abstract painting and sculpture, is the most striking exception to the still generally intractable separation of objects not originally created for museums from the self-appointed realm of contemporary art (this division is far less stringently maintained in other periods). Despite such ruptures within the field of the contemporary, I believe art history offers crucial theoretical tools with which to theorize the elastic weaving together of the registers of high and low—and what lies outside that binary—within recent textile making.

This book includes occasional moments of autobiographical disclosure, because accounting for textiles—objects that are in close physical contact with us at virtually every minute of the day—demands alternative methodologies, ones that extend from shared bodily knowledge. Regardless of specialized education or technical vocabulary, by virtue of wearing garments, sleeping among linens, and sitting on upholstered surfaces, we are all de facto experts in textiles, attuned to subtle distinctions in their variable heft, durability, and breathability. Before children reach school age, they know which fabrics itch, which are smooth, which are warm. I honor the lay expertise, personal proficiency, and tacit intelligence abundantly displayed every time I see people perform the simple but effective gesture of rubbing cloth between their fingers to distinguish texture, thickness, suppleness. We undergo a lifetime of training that makes us keenly attuned to the material properties of textiles, and when I write about my own encounters with these objects I affirm the importance of "amateur" methods.

At the same time, because some of the textile objects discussed in this book no longer exist, I am reliant upon photographs and descriptions by both makers and wearers as I attempt to recapture, however partially, their tactile nature.

Textured Politics

Bowman's T-shirt makes an argument, which is that the affective politics fostered in sewing circles might be akin to those within terrorist groups, and longer histories show that she was not the first to connect textiles to threats to the social order or use them as a means of dissent. Over the following few pages I offer a schematic overview of a handful of these moments. Necessarily compact, it is meant as the sparest of evocations to introduce well-known instances of textile politics. With the phrase *textile politics* I mean not only to suggest how textiles have been used to advance political agendas but also to indicate a procedure of making politics material: *textile* as a transitive verb. Drawing on another word with the Latin root *texere*, in this book I claim that to textile politics is to *give texture* to politics, to refuse easy binaries, to acknowledge complications: textured as in uneven, but also, as I will show, as in tangibly worked and retaining some of the grain of that labor, whether smooth or snagged.

Even before the Industrial Revolution, crafting textiles was capable of registering a polemical message; Laurel Thatcher Ulrich has chronicled how anti-British spinning bees performed by women in New England during the immediate pre–Revolutionary War period were taken as a form of "political resistance."[11] Such resistance is notable because it simultaneously promoted ideals of femininity, in which women's organizing communicated "sacrifice, self-discipline, and personal piety"—a reminder that textile politics are frequently double-edged, as disruptive causes can be promulgated by actions or methods that serve a regulatory function to cement normative gender roles as well as nationalist agendas.[12] Textiles have been central both to histories of capitalism and to organized resistance against its ruthless systems of production. Some of the first acts of workplace sabotage took place when textile workers—mostly men but also women—of early nineteenth-century England destroyed mechanical looms and lacemaking machines in the beginning moments of the Industrial Revolution.[13] Friedrich Engels's and Karl Marx's theorizations about the division of labor that governs capitalism and shapes laborers, and the urgent need for a workers' revolution, were rooted in their observations about class stratification and textile fabrication.[14] In fact, Engels's father was a cotton textile manufacturer, and many of Marx's examples about labor power in volume 1 of *Capital* revolve around the spinning of thread and the conversion of raw linen into a coat.

Textiles suffuse Marx's theories about use value and the commodity; while yarn, loom, tailor, and weaver function as paradigmatic examples of broader processes of labor, they are much more than metaphorical. These materials and procedures were at the contested heart of industrial change and the concomitant emergence of the notion of craft. Glenn Adamson's *The Invention of Craft* crucially illuminates how handicraft as a category emerged in relation to, and remains inextricable from, industrial procedures.[15] Within the knotted history of textile politics, women's labor as such has not always been acknowledged as a distinct force in the transition of work from the home to the factory but is subsumed under other economic categorizations, yielding fissures and blanks regarding the complex relationship between class and gender within some Marxist theories of production. In addition, this labor force has been racialized; the interlocking mechanisms of patriarchy, waged and unwaged labor, racism, and global inequality are strikingly evident in the current realm of textile making (in particular the garment industry).

At the same time, since the rise of industrialization, textiles have been central to many passionately anticapitalist movements and artistic initiatives, including within the workshop of nineteenth-century British Arts and Crafts leader William Morris.[16] (Indeed, Bowman's font for the "Ladies' Sewing Circle" logo seems to echo some of Morris's typography.) Utilizing a socialist framework, Morris championed craft as a gratifying form of production in which a maker could produce something from beginning to end and hence counteract what Marx described as the deadening effects of the wage labor system. Fabric design was at the core of Morris's utopian theories of work and of his decorative arts company, founded in 1861, even though his textiles were never made consistently available to the working-class population with whom he proclaimed solidarity.

Just as textiles have stretched between art, craft, and industry, they have also oscillated between being defined as leisure and as labor. One well-known image from the history of handmaking that brings together depictions of race, gender, and textiles is a photographic portrait, dated 1864, of the African American abolitionist Sojourner Truth knitting with a ball of light-colored yarn in her lap as a thread unfurls across her skirt (fig. 0.02). (This carte de visite is one of many she arranged to have taken and then sold to support her lectures.) As Darcy Grimaldo Grigsby has brilliantly argued, this self-aware image of the former slave in the act of making does not signal Truth's gentility or pursuit of a feminine hobby but connotes "industry, skill, and work."[17] The knitting stands in, Grigsby argues, not only for respectability but also for mindful and strategic self-authentication, akin to a hand-drawn or scribbled signature that registers her masterful, and bodily, presence across the surface of the mechanically reproduced photograph. Truth might have so carefully deployed knitting *because* it could be seen several ways, as a nonthreatening demonstration of her aptitude for domestic work, a reassuring sign of her femininity, *and* as an assertion of her strident activism and creative self-production. That a former slave would so carefully position yarn on her lap further signals a basic fact about textile production: it is grounded in racialized, gendered systems of labor. Truth's scrawled yarn functions as a model, for it evidences the text embedded in textiles, a line that twists between illegible fiber and signifying utterance.

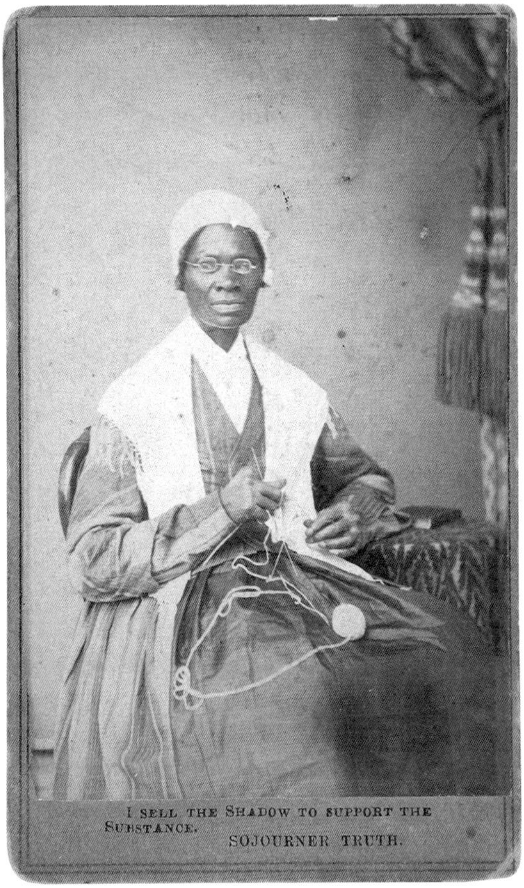

Fig. 0.02.
Sojourner Truth knitting, carte de visite, 1864. Collection of the Berkeley Art Museum and Pacific Film Archive. Gift of Darcy Grimaldo Grigsby.

This capacity of textiles to mean in multiple directions is evident in another oft-cited moment of politically motivated craft—the embroidered and appliquéd suffragette banners that were paraded through the streets during right-to-vote demonstrations in England in the early twentieth century. Lisa Tickner points out that like the colonial spinners before them, suffragettes used embroidery specifically because of its Victorian associations with chaste femininity, as the banners "dignified womanly skills while making unwomanly demands."[18] Theorizations of the ability of textiles to simultaneously shore up and undo codes of femininity have been most influentially articulated by Rozsika Parker, who writes that handwork like embroidery "has been the means of educating women into the feminine ideal . . . but it has also proved a weapon of resistance to the constraints of femininity."[19] She suggests that the matrilineal transmission of textile making instructs women about what their proper place should be as well as produces a set of knowledges that can be utilized for alternative purposes.

In the twentieth century many advanced artists and designers turned to textiles as ways to integrate populist politics within usable objects that were literally made for the masses. While William Morris looked to handmaking as one way to resolve the problem of estrangement that attends the division of labor, artists working outside the frame of capitalism understood textiles as a site for modeling socialist forms of transparent making. For instance, in 1923–24 Liubov Popova and Varvara Stepanova made forays into textile design, and their constructivist patterns in postrevolutionary Russia were manufactured for popular use in garments and household goods like curtains. As Christina Kiaer has written, "A conscious retrieval of fabric design as a typically feminine practice was emphatically *not* how Popova and Stepanova articulated their practice." Instead, "their stated goals at the textile factory were precisely the scientific and technical ones usually associated with Constructivism," including "to see their work enter the process of mass industrial production."[20] Despite these goals, Stepanova, reflecting on her experience at the First State Cotton-Printing Factory some years later, felt she had been "forced to remain a mere applied artist, a handicraft decorator."[21] This disappointment stemmed in part from the intransigently feminized associations that clung to textiles across the spheres of applied art, everyday fashion design, and industry.

Textile making is often represented iconically as a stand-in both for tradition and for defiance against the reigning order. Along with the knitting Sojourner Truth, a widely reproduced example is the photograph of Mahatma Gandhi, taken by Margaret Bourke-White in 1946, sitting next to his spinning wheel—a picture that evokes the meditational qualities of spinning as a form of "spiritual, ennobling labor."[22] Gandhi's push for a widespread return in India to making and wearing khadi (undyed, handspun, hand-woven cloth) was a means to both morally and economically undermine British rule. He advocated for the increased use of this tool of textile self-sufficiency as part of his larger anticolonial project, and local fabric making—coupled with the halting of reliance on foreign imports—was a major component of his plan for India's economic independence. Gandhi's emphatic embrace of spinning disrupted long-standing classifications of it as a primarily female task.[23]

Along with their shifting definitions as "women's work" and as activating an anticolonial politics, knitting, sewing, and quilting have been historically mobilized in moments of stabilizing pro-war nationalism. For instance, a US propaganda poster from World War II exhorts women to "remember Pearl Harbor" as they, in a groan-worthy pun, "purl harder" (a purl is a type of knitting stitch; fig. 0.03). Against a saturated lemon-yellow background (which signals, through the distorted logic of racialized hues, the "yellow peril" of the Japanese), a pale, slender hand brandishes two knitting needles, cocked together to suggest a *V* for victory. The yellow also serves as a graphic contrast to the presumed whiteness of the single hand, its dimensionality clumsily rendered in two blotchy tones that suggest shadow and light; the gender of this phantom figure is suggested, but not entirely secured, by the womanly slimness of the fingers. Severed at the wrist, this one hand is incapable of actually knitting; rather than show the actual process of purling, a single disconnected strand of black thread wraps around the index finger and snakes up between the needles. People sometimes tie strings around their fingers as an aide-mémoire, and the image connects that practice of remembering with the exhortation to knit "harder"—but what does that mean, exactly? Knit more? Knit difficult or "hard" objects? Knit ferociously? The rhetorical force of the image and its command rests on the adamant conjunction of female domestic activity with anti-Japanese sentiment; to knit, it seems to say, is to necessarily insert oneself into this racist discourse.

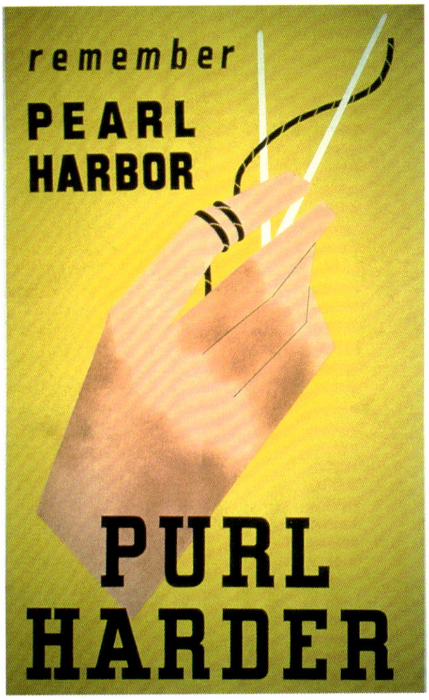

Fig. 0.03. *Remember Pearl Harbor—Purl Harder*, poster, New York City WPA War Services, 1942. Courtesy of the Division of Political History, National Museum of American History, Smithsonian Institution.

This poster is part of a long legacy in the United States, beginning with the Civil War, of women being urged to knit while their husbands are away at war, ostensibly as a way to provide necessary goods for the war front but also as a way to channel their anxiety or keep lonely hands occupied. More than that, as the poster suggests, it became a way to perform one's support of wider wartime efforts. These performances of handmade labors were cultivated over many decades; during World War I, the Red Cross distributed over a million pamphlets and held instructional sessions throughout the United States to teach young girls to knit. Yarn companies unsurprisingly embraced the declared "national knitting phenomenon" as a way to sell more of their product, advertising their goods with slogans like "Uncle Sam wants you to knit." World War II witnessed a similar knitting frenzy as women organized to knit military supplies like gloves and helmet liners. But as historian Anne Macdonald recounts, in a time of widespread industrial production and availability there was far less need for homemade objects, and "many women knit[ted] because women had *always* knit in wartime."[24] In other words, textile handmaking had become more a symbolic, nostalgic custom and ritual than an actual material necessity. In these instances, textiles were utilized to maintain patriotic ideologies and to reinforce the boundaries of "natural" or "appropriate" behavior for women, particularly in the wake of wartime crises about masculinity.

Recent scholarship has chronicled the use of textiles during military conflicts around the world, including Afghan war rugs, Hmong embroidered story cloths, and other objects that grow out of many ideological perspectives and serve functions that include the memorial and the oppositional.[25] While these and other instances establish a persistent theme in which women's textile handmaking has been wielded strategically as an attribution of political avowal, with sometimes conflicting valences to those politics, the photo of Gandhi is a reminder, too, that textile production has not been uniformly considered feminized labor in all cultural contexts; some of its procedures have gendered associations that differ throughout history and across regions. In seventeenth-century New England, for instance, weaving was done primarily by men and was considered "a skilled occupation"; by the twentieth century, due to occupational segregation and the feminization of such labor, much textile work became strongly identified with women.[26] Some queer male Latin American artists in the 1960s and 1970s, including Peruvian artist Jorge Eielson and Brazilian artist Hélio Oiticica, used cloth and fiber; Oiticica, along with fellow neo-concretists Lygia Clark and Lygia Pape, experimented with string and fabric as a means of bodily activation in the face of dictatorial repression, though this work has only begun to be comprehensively discussed specifically in terms of textiles.[27] In other geographic locations, for example in some countries in Africa, textile techniques like weaving are not only associated with women; certain looms are operated exclusively by men. While *Fray* focuses on sites and times with strong associations between textiles and women's handiwork, it also looks at how multiple genders have engaged with procedures like sewing and quilting.

No one book—and certainly not the slight introductory sketch of the past few pages—could possibly account for the ways that textiles have been used across history for both pacifying and radical causes. Given that textile handicraft has played a significant role both in the consolidation of national identities, especially in moments of turmoil or upheaval, and in agitational actions and anti-authoritarian protest cultures, it can be difficult to reconcile frequently diametrically opposed uses or incompatible interpretations. *Fray*, with its focused case studies, attempts to give specific texture to particular moments that have been too often generalized. Those generalizations can be hard to shake, especially because textiles saturate and structure everyday life—they surround us intimately, night and day, often delimiting the boundary between what is individual and what is collective—and they are used in various contexts (from medicine to religion to fashion) for functions that can be utilitarian, ritualistic, or ornamental. As the editors of the anthology *The Object of Labor: Art, Cloth, and Cultural Production* write: "The physical and intimate qualities of fabric allow it to embody memory and sensation and become a quintessential metaphor for the human condition."[28] Textiles do not solely *metaphorize* the human condition so much as fabric itself helps create what we think of as "the human." What is more, textiles are temporally pervasive, significant for each chronological period in history, and transcultural, laden with meaning in every site around the globe, in a way that few other modes of production are. Like food and shelter, textiles organize how we understand "culture" itself. Janis Jefferies's 2015 book *The Handbook of Textile Culture* makes the case that textiles *as* culture are implicated in virtually every sphere of life, including technology, identity, and architecture.[29]

In fact, textiles have inspired a colossal literature scattered across disparate fields that includes (to name just a few) anthropology, decorative arts, economics, history, sociology, and material culture. Conceptual art curator and dealer Seth Siegelaub, who endeavored to create the first truly comprehensive bibliography of textiles, observed that this dispersed literature is a result of the fact that they are "an art, handicraft, and a business too, the first big capitalist industry, in fact."[30] It is thus not sufficient to approach cloth, or its constitutive fibers, primarily as an artistic "medium." Though art historians since the consolidation of the discipline such as Alois Riegl have looked to textiles for, among other things, theories of pattern and style, within the arena of contemporary art history, I must emphasize, it was the activism of feminists that brought textiles more prominently into the conversation.[31]

Feminist Craft

Textiles have been central to—indeed have a tendency to dominate—conversations about handmaking; yet the term *textiles* is not equivalent to *craft*, or vice versa. (There are other realms of handicraft unrelated to fabric or fiber, and since industrialization, not all textiles are understood to have been "crafted.") *Fray* deliberately focuses on this frequent elision by examining the fertile territory where textiles overlap with handicraft, though I do not treat them as completely coterminous. Within contemporary art history, craft has occupied a very specific place, as it is often defined in relation to utility and crafted objects are understood to have functions or use values. This is one of the distinctions that, arguably, separates it from "art." Within the twentieth century, art has constantly tested and refined itself against a series of ostensible opposites, such as "work," "life," or "craft"; the history of recent art is in part the narration of what happens when those divisions collapse or bleed into each other (from the Russian constructivists to Rosemarie Trockel). Many types of craft have long migrated out of the studio and into the gallery, as art institutions have embraced fine-art textiles and exhibit them alongside other kinds of objects.

But if within contemporary art the art-versus-craft divide has more or less eroded, there persist classed, raced, and gendered distinctions between "high craft" meant for institutional display (works made by Trockel or Louise Bourgeois, for instance) and the "low craft" of hobbyists that is often cited or directly appropriated by such artists but is not meant to, and might not ever, travel beyond a living room and is sometimes stained by "bad taste." While it is necessary to interrogate the studio craft-versus-art divide, it is also imperative to dismantle the false binary between highly trained skilled professional craft and amateur efforts from across the twentieth century. Some of the most vital interventions regarding how textiles bring together corporeality, materiality, community building, history making, race, class, and gender have come from female visual artists and writers of color, whose contributions to this field are immeasurable, including Amalia Mesa-Bains, bell hooks, and Alice Walker.[32] In addition, texts in recent decades by art historians, cultural theorists, and material culture specialists Adamson, Elissa Auther, Maria Elena Buszek, Bridget R. Cooks, Jessica Hemmings, Laura E. Pérez, T'ai Smith, Freida High W. Tesfagiorgis, Michele Wallace, and Judith Wilson have addressed these issues within specific histories of art and handmaking; I am profoundly indebted to each of them.[33]

I also build on the pioneering and intelligent works of those art historians and critics who wrote about the feminist reclamation of handicrafts in the United States and United Kingdom during the 1960s and 1970s and who continue to be leading voices for the development of critical discourse around craft, including Jefferies, Parker, Tickner, Griselda Pollock, and Lucy Lippard.[34] It was during those decades that textile handicraft, along with many other forms of handmaking, was seized upon by feminists—both those who identified as artists and those who did not, including those who drafted off the popular craze for such techniques as crochet. Heralded anew as encompassing significant tasks that had long been unfairly denigrated, domestic female labor was resignified as central to women's lives and integrated into feminist art practices as a challenge to sexist, racist, and classist "standards."

I turn now to a few touchstones within this broader reclamation. Within the US context, African American artist Faith Ringgold was one of the earliest feminists to incorporate textiles into her practice; in her Feminist Series from 1972, she took inspiration from portable Tibetan Buddhist *thangka* paintings, which are made on silk and hung from dowels and whose lack of a rigid stretched frame allows them to be packed up and moved around easily. Bordered with elaborately patterned fabrics, Ringgold's series also follows the form suggested by the *thangka* with its braided cords hanging from each upper corner. Each is inscribed with a short quote by a black woman thinker and activist such as Amy Jacques Garvey or Shirley Chisholm. For *And Man Is So Selfish: The Feminist Series #16*, from 1972, Ringgold transcribes a 1867 quote

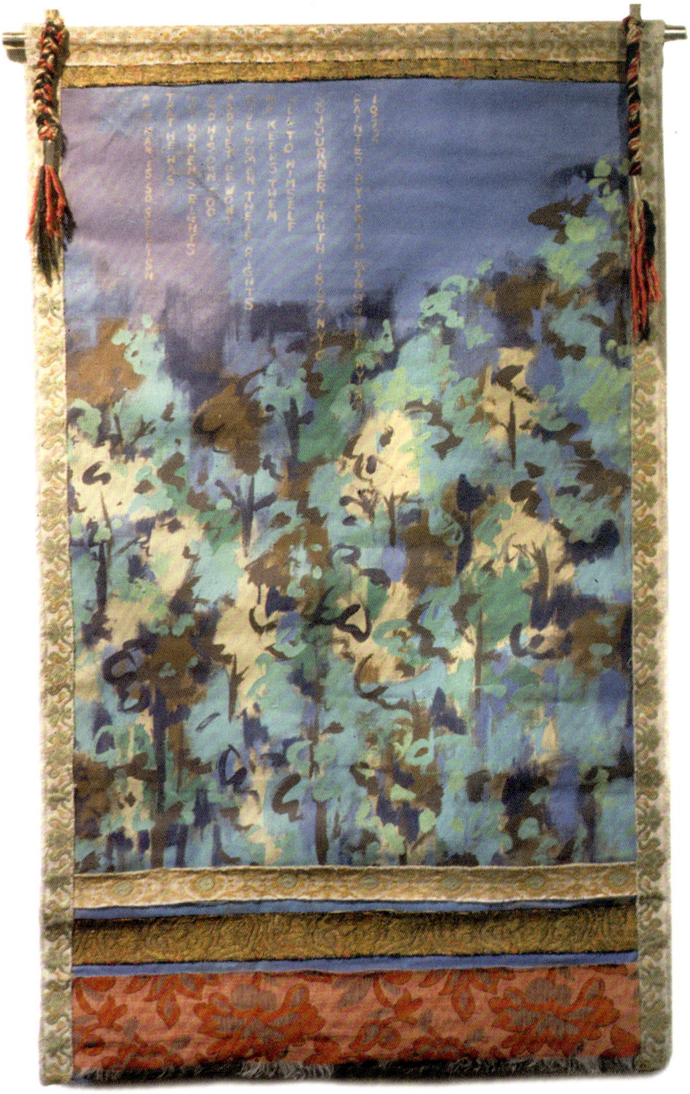

Fig. 0.04.
Faith Ringgold, *And Man Is So Selfish: The Feminist Series #16*, 1972, acrylic on canvas *thangka* with printed, pieced, and embroidered fabric. Faith Ringgold © 1972.

from Sojourner Truth, written as vertical columns (echoing Chinese text) in the blue space and bleeding into the flourish of brushstrokes whose gestures compose a tree-filled landscape: "And man is so selfish that he . . . won't give women their rights. He keeps them all to himself"[35] (fig. 0.04).

With its placement of Truth's name directly next to her own artist's signature, Ringgold's fabric-based piece harks back to the photo of Truth with her knitting needles poised at the ready, and affirms both herself and the abolitionist as black women textile makers. An African American female artist who was involved in a number of political causes related to combating the overwhelmingly white- and male-dominated New York art world in the late 1960s and early 1970s, Ringgold, whom I return to in chapter 3 in relation to quilts, has played a major role in both the Black Arts Movement and feminist art.[36] In her textile work of the early 1970s she thematized hybridity, assertively mixing Eastern and Western cultural forms with African American traditions and flirting with abstraction as her brushstrokes dissolved into the fabric, its thicket of trees becoming nearly formless.

Ringgold's *thangka* paintings also hybridized art and craft, though, as Auther has written, her insistence that the fabric-backed works were *paintings* meant that "the goal of overcoming or breaking down the barriers between art and craft important to a given work's formal and political significance could only be carried out in the name of art."[37] Ringgold's subsequent forays into "folk" art forms such as African-inspired masks, dolls, and quilts throughout the 1970s and 1980s reveal that she was eager to admit the fluidity of the categories of high and low and, what is more, to transgress them. The Feminist Series, with its conjunction of landscape, cloth, and cord, also importantly uses *text* as a key compositional element—and this explicit, prescient incorporation of language makes Ringgold's series a crux of text/iles and a groundbreaking forerunner of US feminist fabric-based art and conceptualism.

Judy Chicago's *The Dinner Party* (1974–79) has become one of the most prominent examples of the US feminist reclamation of handicrafts in the 1970s. For this project, some four hundred volunteers skilled in ceramics, weaving, and needlework worked with Chicago to make woven banners and thirty-nine place settings—hand-painted porcelain plates featuring her signature vaginal "central core" imagery, chalices, earthenware cutlery, linen napkins, and embroidered runners—dedicated to historical and mythic women. Some volunteers accused her of exploiting their labor by vastly undervaluing their time and expertise.[38] This accusation focused with special intensity on the textile work; the embroidery was extraordinarily painstaking and Chicago set exacting standards, yet the artist herself was inexperienced with textiles. In a 1979 article for *Craft Horizons*, written as the piece was on display at the San Francisco Museum of Modern Art, Chicago commented that this model of production was akin to the work of nuns in a cloister or of medieval guilds: "the artist needs more resources than can be achieved working alone. . . . *The Dinner Party* is really a throwback to the Middle Ages."[39] By casting her use of volunteers as a "throwback" to earlier labor practices, Chicago at once demolishes and upholds the distinction between fine art and non-art craft making.

Though involving craftspeople was meant to be part of its innovation, that blurring also made it a controversial object, as the entire piece became tainted for its associations with the low, as when Hilton Kramer dismissed it as "very bad art" and, even more damningly, "kitsch."[40] Unlike Ringgold's series, which integrates Sojourner Truth into a long lineage of black feminists, Chicago singles her out, on the piece's one plate honoring an African American woman, for an oddly different compositional treatment, showing faces rather than the central core motif found on every other plate. Alice Walker wrote: "It occurred to me that perhaps white women feminists, no less than white women generally, cannot imagine black women have vaginas. . . . Sojourner Truth certainly had a vagina, as note her lament about her children, born of her body, but sold into slavery."[41] Walker's words are among the most salient responses to *The Dinner Party*. It has received necessary criticism for its deeply troubling racial politics, yet it is still granted institutional attention (it now occupies an entire specially built wing of the Brooklyn Museum of Art) disproportionate to that given to women artists of color such as Ringgold, Theresa Hak Kyung Cha, Senga Nengudi, and Howardena Pindell, all of whom made work with textiles from needlework to pantyhose to banners to stuffed canvases in the 1970s.[42] At the same time, often overlooked in *The Dinner Party* is the textile aspect of the project; though the runners constitute an important visual and material frame for the porcelain plates, they are usually relegated to the background. The embroidered runner with interlocking triangles around the edge hints at other aspects of Truth's legacy—her teaching of domestic skills—and gestures to the racialized histories of quilting in the United States, including slaves' integration of African strip-weaving techniques with European piecework.

Just as US feminist art critics and artists were starting to take seriously crafts such as textiles and their gendered and racialized histories in the 1970s, that decade also witnessed a specific turning point in the wider museum institutionalization of "folk art"—a designation that often encompasses much amateur textile making and can serve as a shorthand for work by men and women of color, poor people, and untrained white women. The "folks" of folk art, that is, are "outsiders" not only to the art world but within structures of stratification and privilege. In 1970 the Museum of American Folk Art in New York launched its widely seen *Twentieth-Century Folk Art and Artists* exhibit, accompanied four years later by a companion volume; it included needlepoint projects alongside paintings, sculptures, and drawings.[43] However, while the volume's authors emphasized the folk makers' personal, "private" visions, feminists understood textile practices as fraught with political and social consequences that rippled out beyond the realm of the "personal."

In 1971 the Whitney Museum show *Abstract Design in American Quilts* proposed a dialogue between modern abstract art and the handiwork of quiltmaking.[44] This was one of a triad of exhibitions at the Whitney that year that featured textile objects; the others were *Two Hundred Years of North American Indian Art*, which did not include any contemporary work and consigned

Native making to history, and *Calder's Tapestries*. (The three shows were reviewed on successive pages in the December 1971 issue of *Craft Horizons*.)[45] Some exhibits during the early 1970s emphasized folk art not as belonging to the past but as a contemporary practice, including *Folk Art in America: A Living Tradition* at Atlanta's High Museum of Art in 1974. Like many texts in this period that attempted to elevate "folk" craft practices through their formal association with Western fine art, publications and exhibitions about Native American textiles, including the 1975 book *Navajo Pictorial Weaving*, described Navajo weaving technique as differing "in no vital way from that of the fine tapestries of Europe."[46] At this time of growing institutional attention to Native, self-taught, and folk art—categories that name their alterity from fine art with assumptions about race, education, class, and gender—museums were also exhibiting studio-based fiber art, but these practices were not always seen in relation to folk textiles and were often explicitly contrasted to such work.[47]

The 1970s return to handmaking in the United States was extensive enough to be deemed a trend, and many publishers encouraged it, riding the wave of its popularity by churning out an unprecedented array of textile how-to books, magazines, and kits. One high-profile figure in this realm was the British-born needleworker Erica Wilson; she published over a dozen instructional books and in the early 1970s had a televised show that broadcast techniques like cross-stitch and crewel embroidery into homes across the country. "With the recent upsurge of interest in handcrafts and homemade items, quilt-making has become a very popular, 'in' pastime," states the jacket of Ann-Sargent Wooster's 1972 book *Quiltmaking: The Modern Approach to a Traditional Craft*.[48] With its suggestion to consult the canvases of Barnett Newman and Paul Klee for inspiration, echoing the Whitney show that had launched the previous year, Wooster's text is notable for its integration of twentieth-century white male artists (whose belonging to the loose category of "modern" is surely uncontested), as well as its mention of Harriet Powers, a nineteenth-century African American quilter, whose inclusion under that rubric is more unexpected. Powers's *Bible Quilt* (ca. 1886) is not only illustrated and described as "lively, original, and subtly balanced" but also called a groundbreaking example of the "modernity" of quilt design.[49]

Though bell hooks has noted that "the work of black women quiltmakers needs special feminist critical commentary which considers the impact of race, sex, and class," such connections go unelaborated within Wooster's celebration of formal innovation.[50] Yet her inclusion of Powers is instructive, for the 1970s also witnessed the publication of books dedicated to examining traditional African American crafts, folk art, and decorative arts.[51] Some of these texts emphatically connected black American craft to African making; for instance, John Michael Vlach opens *The Afro-American Tradition in Decora-*

tive Arts (1978) with a map of Africa and considers Powers's approach to be "especially African."[52] Vlach's book does not articulate a specifically feminist motivation for documenting these craft histories, which is one reason that Ringgold's textile work—a primary origin moment for this story as it elucidates African American (and other cultural) traditions within a feminist context—is especially vital.

A Matrix of Making

Even during the heyday of handicraft reclamations in the 1970s, feminist critics noted that acute ambivalence accompanied the return to such work. As Parker wrote in 1977, "On one level the use of craft validates women's traditional skills and emphasizes how much pleasure there is in, for example, crocheting. On another level it draws attention to the way our time and energy has been absorbed by our massive contribution to the domestic economy: knitting, sewing, and furnishing the home."[53] Textile making was viewed as affirming of women's labor and skill but potentially complicit with antifeminist regimes of domesticity. The 1978–79 documentary television and book project *Anonymous Was a Woman* (which grew out of that decade's feminist art and hobby interest in handmaking) drew together historical images and archival materials about "traditional American art" like needlework; though largely celebratory, it is tellingly full of nineteenth-century complaints about the toil of textile efforts. A diary entry in 1851 by Ellen Birdseye Wheaton recounts that she "made an effort to get on my much talked of quilt, but with no assistance, it was very laborious, and I was almost sorry I undertook it."[54] (*Almost* sorry, but not quite.)

Hoping for a widespread dismantling of high and low that might be catalyzed if serious consideration were granted to handmaking, Lippard wrote in 1978, "It seems all too likely that only in a feminist art world will there be a chance for the 'fine' arts, the 'minor' arts, 'crafts,' and hobby circuits to meet and to develop an *art of making* with a new and revitalized communicative function."[55] The dream of a "feminist art world" in which hobby and fine art objects are given equal attention has not yet been fulfilled, but as I have mentioned, *Fray* places these forms of making side by side, stitched together as necessary halves of a greater whole. By arguing that all these registers of textiles matter and that they must be seen in conjunction, this book attempts, however modestly, to confront this hierarchy. Along with case studies of nonfine art formations since 1970, I focus on two women who identified themselves explicitly as artists—Hammond and Vicuña—both of whom were very much part of the feminist art movement's return to craft, yet who were not always fully embraced by critics precisely because of their use of textiles. I place their work in conversation not only with feminism but also with other social movements, including queer liberation in the United States (in the case of Hammond) and struggles for human rights during the Pinochet dictatorship in Chile (in the case of Vicuña). Throughout, the seams show and the often irreconcilable gaps between these differently valued spheres are made evident, as I am interested in the *contingency* of many textile practices. Their meanings are conditional, dependent on context, shifting over time, open to rereadings and misreadings; as I argue, these threads of reception can be difficult to decipher as they tangle, snare, knot, twist, double back, tear, and snap while they stretch between the most elite sites and the most ordinary.

The pervasive idea that craft might be utilized for strategic or polemical purposes (whether as a vehicle for the Right or for the Left) has been shadowed by an even more prevalent story within the twentieth century regarding textile techniques such as sewing, knitting, or quilting, which is that they are fundamentally *trivial*. In fact, "hobbyist" methods of textile handmaking have long been castigated as inconsequential, particularly because they have traditionally been gendered female. As Simone de Beauvoir wrote in 1949, "With the needle or the crochet hook, woman sadly weaves the very nothingness of her days."[56] If Bowman's "Terrorist Society" T-shirt represents one end of the spectrum of thought about textiles in the 1970s as "terroristic" or potentially inciting (however playful that suggestion may have been), the then-ubiquitous, and now widely ridiculed, macramé home projects represent the other end.

In the popular imagination, macramé evokes the dilution or mainstreaming of hippie culture, divorced from the advanced environmentalism that was also understood as intrinsic to handmade countercultural lifestyles. Trade books such as *Macramé: The Art of Creative Knotting* (1967) and *Macramé: Creative Design in Knotting* (1971) were part of a flood of instructional publications geared toward home crafters in the late 1960s and through the 1970s in which terms like *art* and *creativity* freely intermingled with words like *hobby* in their step-by-step instructions.[57] A how-to magazine from 1975 featuring macramé owls and plant hangers is enthusiastically titled *Mad about Macramé* (fig. 0.05). With its series of decorative and functional macramé projects for the home, *Mad about Macramé* calls the knotting technique "one of the world's oldest crafts" but does not elaborate on those roots (Arabic, Turkish, and French) nor its more immediate precedents in the fiber-based sculpture of the studio craft movement in the United States.[58]

When I show materials like *Mad about Macramé* to my students, they invariably laugh. What stirs this titter of amusement—or shudder of shame—that now, decades later, attends the reception of these textiles? The objects the

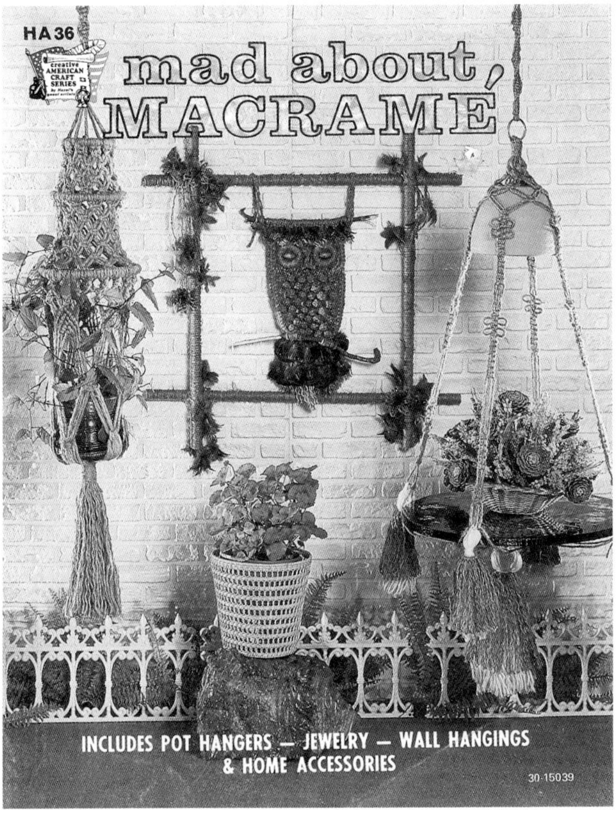

Fig. 0.05. *Mad about Macramé* magazine cover, published by Hazel Pearson Handicrafts, 1975. Collection of the author.

magazine promotes are more than just outmoded and ungainly: they are also gendered and evidently classed, as the interiors represented in the magazine bespeak a decisively middlebrow and largely white milieu. Very few such publications feature any women of color or acknowledge macramé's indebtedness to non-Western cultures.[59] (One notable exception to the mostly white female world of craft instructional guides at this time is *Rosey Grier's Needlepoint for Men* from 1973, featuring the African American football star.)[60] The macramé enthusiast magazine represents an adamantly homespun strand of textile making in the 1970s; in keeping with other structuring contradictions, this blossoming of handicraft was dependent upon the mass distribution of standardized patterns. Yet despite their seeming inconsequence, in the 1970s it was these sorts of publications, and all the proliferating owls, that helped create a groundswell of support for fine art textile exhibits, nurturing broad audiences for such shows and kindling communities of crafters.

Other projects from that period demonstrate how insistently the interest in textile crafts like knitting, crochet, and macramé spoke to multiple makers, including those decorating their own domestic spaces and those more experimentally motivated and publicly oriented. In the early 1970s, weaver,

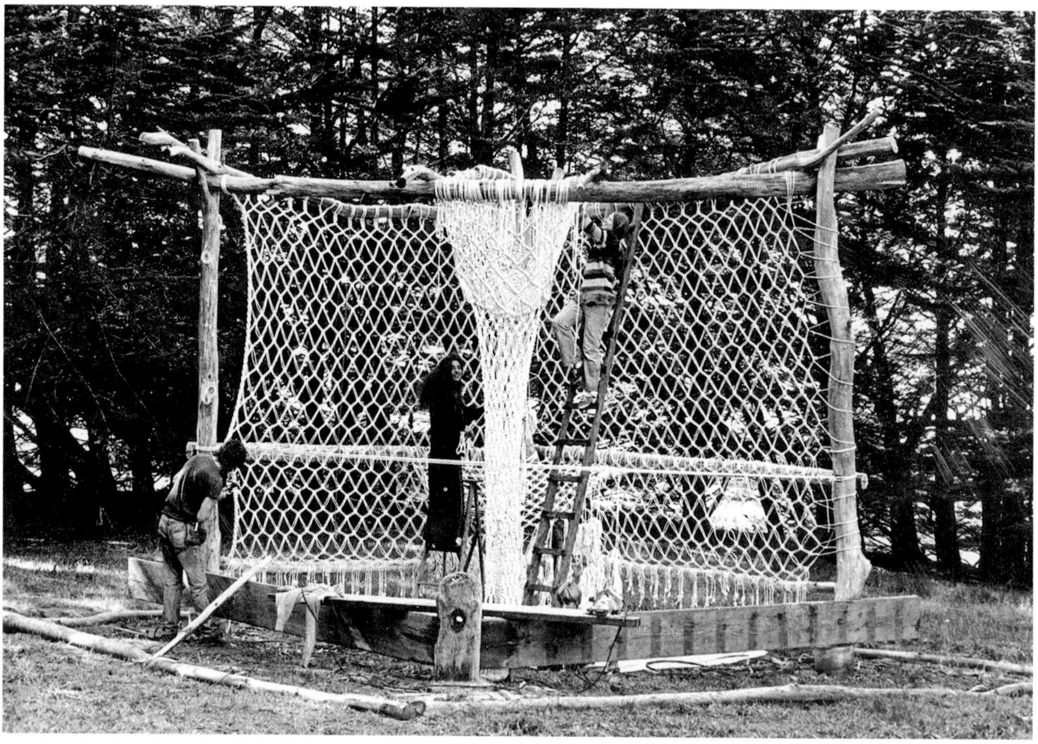

Fig. 0.06. Alexandra Jacopetti Hart, *Macramé Park*, Bolinas, California, in process with apprentice Selena Heron and carpenter John Barrow, 1973. Dacron rope and wood. Photograph by Jerry Wainwright. Courtesy of Alexandra Jacopetti Hart.

embroiderer, and textile artist Alexandra Jacopetti conceived of an outdoor macramé jungle gym. Completed in 1974 and known colloquially as *Macramé Park*, it resided on a lot adjacent to a public utility building in the coastal town of Bolinas, California (fig. 0.06). This was not a commission but was generated by Jacopetti's own initiative. It took many months to secure the necessary permits, gather enough donated rope (more than 12,000 feet of it), and satisfy insurance company queries before she began to actually construct the intricate, shiplike form. Huge webbings of rope were suspended from a wooden frame to create several levels of play space on which children could hang and climb, including a rope slide and a "crow's nest" at the top.[61] For the scaffolding, she scavenged large eucalyptus logs from the beach; for the rope, she chose to use ¼-inch Dacron sailmaker's lay rope from a boat supply store, as it would be soft on tender young hands and firmly held its knots. A woodworker assured her that the driftwood logs "had the tensile strength of steel."[62]

She worked hard to make sure the loops were just the right size (the entire project was braided and hand-knotted, using double half-stitches and square knots, by Jacopetti and others in her crafts guild): big enough to grab easily but not so large that a small head could inadvertently be snared. Jacopetti's guild used paid apprenticeships and funded their organization through

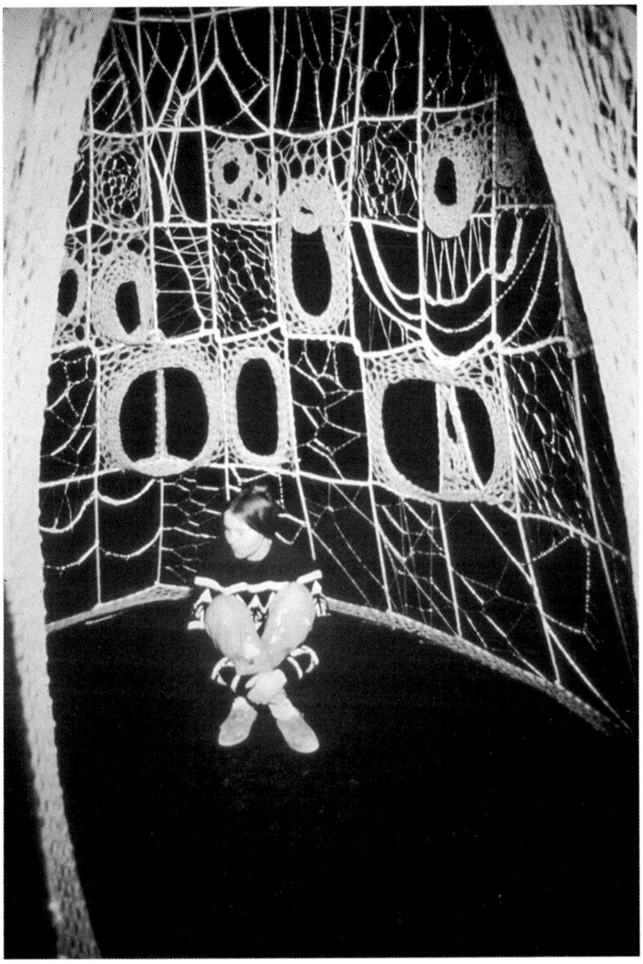

Fig. 0.07.
Faith Wilding, *Crocheted Environment (Womb Room)*, 1971–72, installed at *Womanhouse*, Los Angeles. Rope, wool, twine. Courtesy of Faith Wilding.

selling their wares in fairs and stores, effectively mixing, to quote *Newsweek*, "medieval crafts" with "modern economics."[63] According to Jacopetti, children played on this fiber vessel, and the occasional adult slept on it, for around fifteen years, and *Macramé Park* became both a community landmark and a touchstone for hippie crafts in Northern California.[64]

Around the time Jacopetti was convincing Bolinas residents to support her textile playground, in Southern California a different fiber environment was taking shape. From January 30 to February 28, 1972, Faith Wilding, a member of the Feminist Art Program at the California Institute of the Arts, led by Chicago and Miriam Schapiro, exhibited her signature *Crocheted Environment (Womb Room)* within the larger *Womanhouse* installation in Los Angeles[65] (fig. 0.07). The entire collective project of *Womanhouse* was meant to exaggerate, in order to exorcise, legacies of domestic women's work, such that "the age-old female activity of homemaking was taken to fantasy proportions. *Womanhouse* became the repository of the daydreams women have as they wash, bake, cook, sew, clean, and iron their lives away."[66] Wilding's piece was one of the only abstract elements in *Womanhouse*, and it created the effect of architecture as its scale moved crochet away from the realms of décor and utility to suggest excess and fantasy. Using crochet to create porous "walls," *Crocheted Environment* utilizes the grid as a loose structure punctured by circles and half-circles; Wilding's complex patterning becomes a play of negative and positive space (indeed the word *fabric*, from the Latin *faber*, signals its resonance with fabrication, construction, building). In one photograph of the original installation, Wilding sits cocooned by her handiwork, hugging her knees, as the light-colored webs of lines envelop her within an otherwise darkened room. Though Wilding considers the piece "an anomaly" in her practice and has been at times "embarrassed when people claim me for the craft movement," she did have a background as a weaver, and she acknowledges the work's importance within feminism.[67]

Both projects are now gone, so we must rely upon documentation to see how they related to the sites for which they were created. Wilding's entire piece was stolen from *Womanhouse* during its month-long run, the cords cut off at their base where they were nailed to the floor. (Wilding told me she heard that a fish restaurant in Malibu had a net on its wall, dotted with seashells, that looked suspiciously like her crocheted work, but this story remains apocryphal. When the piece is now exhibited, it is a re-created version.)[68] Bizarrely, as with Wilding's work, someone took a blade to *Macramé Park*—in this case, before it was fully completed, a man attacked it with a penknife (Jacopetti does not know why), but because the macramé knots did not unravel in a way that would compromise the overall structure, it was easily repaired.

Though *Macramé Park* and *Womanhouse* emerged simultaneously and have some formal parallels, Jacopetti and Wilding were not aware of each other's work. Differently oriented toward different kinds of publics, the two projects could be taken to represent starkly distinct approaches to textiles: one meant for children to scramble around in, the other aimed at feminists and fellow artists as an arena of visual contemplation and political reflection. But even the clear bifurcations that appear to sort the works into two distinct spheres, such as interactive versus optical, or functional versus aesthetic, break down. In addition, the care of children, along with housework, was increasingly politicized by feminists as a form of women's labor; both projects thus speak to textiles as a site of unremunerated female work.

Placing Jacopetti and Wilding next to each other—and in close proximity to the *Mad about Macramé* magazine—is meant to emphasize, again, my insistence on a matrix of terms that does not depend on the high–low, or art–craft, axis but rather activates some other, polyvocal set of identifications in which a committed network of textile makers of many orientations found their place. Jacopetti's participatory *Macramé Park* was not begun as an artwork, nor was it an amateur project, nor was it an example of studio craft; it occupies yet another territory, that of countercultural community practice. It would not have been out of place in the *Whole Earth Catalog*, as an example of how we might use tools to "shape [our] own environment"; the *Catalog* featured, in its section "Industry and Craft," listings for macramé and "progressive knitting."[69] Though these two projects were produced in distinct realms, in the intervening years their fates have intertwined: Wilding's piece (maybe) ended up in a seafood restaurant, and documentation of *Macramé Park* has been exhibited in museums (most recently at the Oakland Museum of California, in 2014), exemplifying the permeability and persistent crossing of "high" and "low" sites.

Craftivism Skepticism

Beyond my interest in probing the background of Bowman's sewing circle T-shirt, this book has another origin moment: my growing sense that the championed "rediscovery" of handmaking in the 2000s—unfolding as I was beginning to think about textiles theoretically—was accompanied by rather extreme claims. Starting around the turn of the twenty-first century, a proliferation of websites, publications, and conferences began to insist upon the progressive nature of textile handmaking. Books called *Subversive Cross Stitch* (2006) and *Subversive Seamster* (2007) extolled the "subversive" potential of cross-stitching samplers with curse words or sewing your own gauchos.[70] At first glance, these titles could be citing the influential feminist literature about how craft has been marshaled as a form of socialization, particularly Parker's pivotal book *The Subversive Stitch* from 1984. Parker's gender- and class-based analysis, together with a deep history of embroidery technique and the labor formations it engendered, provide a model for thinking through how craft methods have been coded, deployed, and politicized over time.

But Parker's precedent is generally unacknowledged within the more recent books, many of which are hipster how-to guides complete with irreverent patterns and practical sewing tips. Other texts from the 2000s asserted that textile handmaking might be itself a method of direct protest action—including books titled *Knitting for Peace* and *Quilting for Peace*.[71] Betsy Greer is widely credited with popularizing the term *craftivism* in 2004, a snappy neologism that grafts craft onto activism to suggest that handmaking

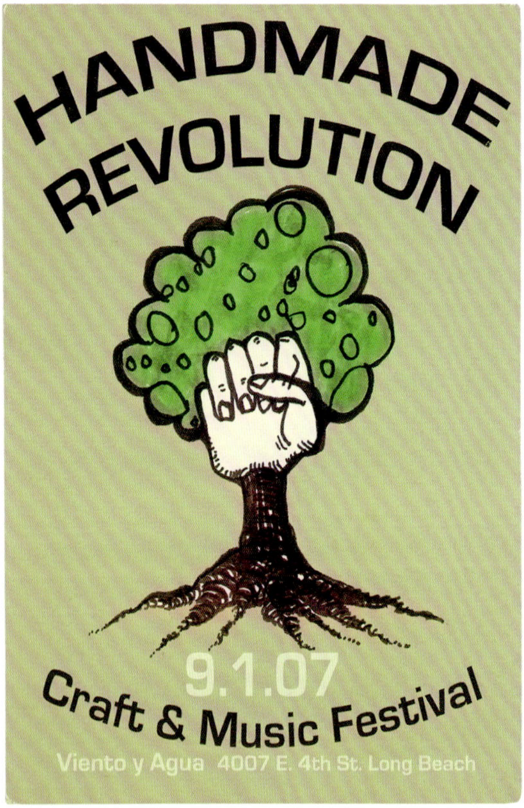

Fig. 0.08. Handmade Revolution craft and music festival flyer, 2007, Long Beach, California. Collection of the author.

(especially the domestic "female" crafts like knitting and sewing) have become—or are even implicitly—a form of resistance.[72] Greer herself has been circumspect, and indeed forthright about her suspicions that craftivism as a political concept has become inflated.[73] Nonetheless, the renaissance of craft was optimistically trumpeted—or at least cannily marketed—as a way to create "personal, social, and political change stitch by stitch," to quote the subtitle of Greer's *Knitting for Good*.[74] The craftivist movement of the early 2000s, which advocated knitting and crocheting as ethical practices, consisted primarily but not exclusively of younger white women who formed stitch-and-bitch groups, blogged about craft, and sewed Bowman's design on messenger bags.

A 2005 video by artist Renée Green titled *Knitting* includes interviews with art students who extol the do-it-yourself nature of knitting, discussing the "sense of empowerment" that comes from handmaking scarves and hats. But as Green's video also explores, here one cliché was easily replaced by another: if craft was formerly the territory of the amateur, the low, the decorative, or even the blatantly kitschy, as in the stereotypical macramé owls from the 1970s, in the early 2000s it became a glib, uncontested shorthand for alternative politics. (Against consensus, one skeptical student in Green's *Knitting* asserts that, rather than an act of protest, it is a "definite escape activity.")[75] Within the craftivist rhetoric, handmaking was proclaimed "revolutionary." A 2007 flyer announces an event called "Handmade Revolution" at a café in Long Beach, California. Notice how, as in the World War II "Purl Harder" poster, the graphic features a disembodied hand (fig. 0.08). Here a hybrid tree/hand signifies solidarities between resistance movements and environmentalism, but the Power to the People gesture (commonly known as the Black Power fist) has been deracinated, turned ever whiter as it thrusts upward from its dark tree-trunk roots. The fist morphs into a kind of face—the designer has drawn the leaves around it in a vague echo of an afro—but the image displaces blackness with "greenness," the color of earth-friendliness. Interestingly, though insistently racialized as white, the disconnected hands in this flyer are somewhat gender ambiguous, which could indicate the significant queer faction involved in craftivism.

Craftivism aimed to bestow fresh relevance on textile handmaking in the early twenty-first century. Some of this "revolutionary" craftivist rhetoric reflects long-standing desires to link handmaking to left politics, following the socialist legacies of William Morris. If craft has historically been rallied for patriotic or sexist or conformist causes, as in the US government's knitting-for-war campaigns, the craftivist movement sought to resist those narratives, to contradict them with proliferating examples of leftist, antinationalist, or innovative handmaking. In addition, young crafters' understanding of the do-it-yourself imperative was fueled by the dominance of corporate, factory-made products within consumer capitalism. Beginning in 2008, US consumers were asked to boycott big-box chain stores as part of the online campaign buyhandmade.org; the call was signed by over fifty thousand people. Pointedly, however, the slogan urged you to *buy* handmade, not to make things yourself. And this is one of the most paradoxical aspects of craftivism—just as in Morris's day, when his fabrics became upholstery for the wealthy—which is that so much of the purported handmade revolution is really about individualized niche shopping, a way to guarantee the value and originality of a bespoke purchase.

Many of the items for sale in these handmade venues barely qualify as craft, in that they are altered or customized by textile techniques rather than produced by them. The Handmade Revolution event in Long Beach, like many Maker Faires and I-Made-It markets, was full of people hawking store-bought baby clothes that had been hand-embellished with stitched animals. The conflict generated by craft's anticonsumerist consumerism has become increasingly evident not only in the craft fairs proliferating around the country but also within the online retailer Etsy, which began by selling mostly handmade items and whose slogan is "Shopping for meaning in a sea of stuff." Beginning in 2014, Etsy faced accusations that some of its high-volume sellers were outsourcing their work to mass-produce objects. But as craft scholar Nicole Burisch points out, the lines between handcrafted things and manufactured ones are increasingly unclear, "a false distinction . . . unless you are digging your own clay, weaving your own cloth, raising your own sheep."[76]

As this demonstrates, the "buy handmade" pledge overlooked one significant fact: mass-manufactured goods (especially those with textile elements) are also often in large part made by hand. Figure 0.09, a stock photograph from the image service Corbis, depicts working conditions in the shoe industry (a highly visible focus of activist organizing around unfair corporate labor practices in the 1990s) and provides a glimpse of how much significant bodily effort goes into factory production. Though the picture emphasizes the rows of work stations that recede, as if endlessly, into the distance, it also shows

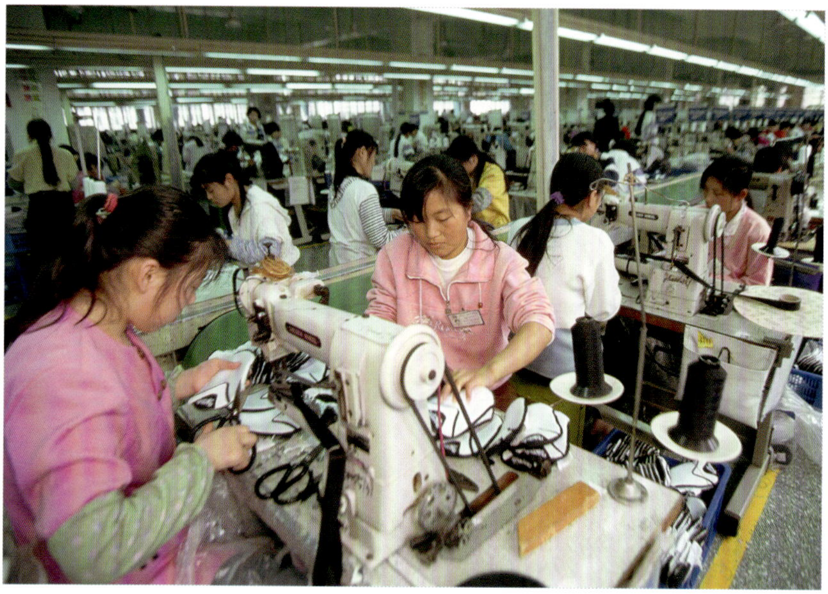

Fig. 0.09. Employees making shoes at Reebok factory, Zhongshan, Guangdong Province, China, 1996. Photo by Michael S. Yamashita. © Michael S. Yamashita / Corbis.

women engaged in the detail-oriented tasks of textile construction (stitching, sewing, piecing, trimming) using sewing machines, bobbins of thread, and scissors. Photos like this, most often featuring Asian or Latin American women, have become overdetermined in their relentless circulation, and they have become problematically schematic shorthand illustrations of the insistent feminization and devaluation of globalized outsourced labor performed by what Lisa Lowe calls "racialized working women."[77] Yet in the context of early twenty-first-century discussions about the supposed evaporation of handmade things, it is essential to ask questions about whose handiwork, exactly, is at issue: some is vastly undervalued but central to the mechanisms of capitalism, while some is triumphed as "revolutionary" and posited as a form of economic refusal. I return to these issues in my afterword.

The chapters of *Fray* unfold amid two major shifts: one, the emergence of gender and sexuality liberation movements, and two, widespread global economic shifts as they pivot around neoliberal capitalism, marketing, and consumerism. This book begins just as 1969 turns into 1970, with the spontaneous formation of the Cockettes at a midnight show. Two of my three chapters consider queer material, and in chapters 1 and 3 I discuss how inversions of high–low have the capacity to register queerly. But I do not argue that there is something *inherently* queer about textiles, which is far too sweeping a claim; nothing is inherently meaningful across the entirety of textiles (or, it should be said, any other kind of matter or method of making).[78] Material specificities such as pliancy and flexibility might suggest a set of political or affective affinities, but we must be attentive to how those affinities are themselves pliable and shift depending upon how a material is used and received. In certain moments textiles have been viewed as a disruption to norms of straight sexuality, while in others they are submerged within and productive of those very conventions. Rather, I think about the instability of textiles' relationality, which in some instances might be felt to be queer—that is, how they propose different sorts of bodily orientations and create volatile interfaces between public and private selves.

Fray homes in on some much-discussed touchstones in the realm of contemporary textile studies, including Chilean *arpilleras* and the AIDS Quilt. In part I decided to write about them *because* they have been so often invoked—they verge on becoming a "craftivist canon"—as I aim to tease out their complexities and attend to their forms and means of making. Though they have been mentioned in passing, they are little examined within the context of contemporary art history. In addition, by investigating practices that were rooted in the United States and Chile but that circulated widely and internationally, I want to complicate how we think of "American" art (which, unlike many other subfields of art history, has long incorporated folk art as one of its proper objects of inquiry).

I have also selected these case studies because both Chile and the United States have, arguably more than other nations, championed, struggled with, and been reshaped by neoliberalism; the two countries, and their textile practices, were closely linked starting in the 1970s. In fact, since the 1970s Chile and the United States have been at the forefront of free-market policies and privatization; during the Pinochet regime, Chile functioned as a test case for the "Chicago Boys" (economists trained at the University of Chicago under Milton Friedman) and their theories of neoliberalism. Carlos Huneeus, in his *El régimen de Pinochet*, outlines how the economists often personally benefited from the restructuring of Chile, and how the dictatorship and neoliberal policies functioned in close concert.[79] As Juan Gabriel Valdés writes, Pinochet's authoritarianism was essential for implementing neoliberalism, as it was "an efficient mechanism for the drastic transformation of the Chilean economy."[80] Many of these transformations took hold first within the sphere of textiles; indeed, from the Industrial Revolution until today, textile making has been the bleeding edge of manufacturing, modeling new modes of factory efficiency and production. One consequence of neoliberalism is, according to Valdés, the diffusion of "cultural models of economic individualism in society as a whole."[81] Textiles, on one hand emblematic of global manufacturing, and on the other typical of domestic unpaid labor, are frequently in the middle of these debates. And neoliberal hallmarks such as entrepreneurialism and self-branding are especially pronounced in the case of much textile production. While a detailed economic comparative analysis falls outside the scope of this project, my chapters touch on these processes in the United States and in Chile. By no means do I equate these sites of production; rather, I attend to local geographies and circumstances when I discuss the conflicts and contradictions generated around textiles.

Following Wendy Brown, I do not assume a monolithic neoliberalism but take it to be an "economic policy, a modality of governance, and an order of reason" that is "inconstant, differentiated, unsystematic, impure."[82] The twin developments of feminism and neoliberalism in the 1970s form the backdrop to my book, and recent thinkers have posited that these movements should not be theorized as independent developments. Silvia Federici has argued that women have disproportionately shouldered the burdens of neoliberalism—motored by overwhelming economization and monetization of every social relation—and that dismantling it is an urgent feminist project.[83] A countervailing view is offered by Nancy Fraser, who asks, in her 2009 article "Feminism, Capitalism, and the Cunning of History": "Was it mere coincidence that second-wave feminism and neoliberalism prospered in tandem? Or was there some perverse, subterranean elective affinity between them?"[84] She argues that 1970s women's liberation, with its focus on "the personal" and "female empowerment" understood narrowly within the scope of capitalist accumulation, among other things, has contributed to the widespread embrace of neoliberal attitudes. But Fraser's analysis has been critiqued for its broad-brush, homogenizing approach to feminism, ignoring the many important anticapitalist contributions of third-world feminisms, particularly in the global South.[85] By detaching from a strict US focus, I attempt to account for other economies, other political geographies, and other feminisms.

Hands On

It is this terrain—the unsteady and tenuous entwining of textiles, labor, art, and politics within the United States and Chile—that *Fray* seeks to explore and also historicize. It evolved out of my long-standing concern with process and is motivated by my interest in examining how things are made and how such methods are imbricated in wider economies and social movements. This research ramifies into questions about class, gender, race, effort, and materiality as I seek to examine both "higher" fine-art utilizations of craft techniques and "lower" or amateur methods of production. As mentioned, it is an archival project that offers a corrective to the presentist focus of craftivism, especially since the galvanizing roles played by women's liberation and other social movements were often effaced in the parade of books on craft published in the 2000s.[86] Some of these books do envision longer histories. For instance, Faythe Levine and Cortney Heimerl's *Handmade Nation: The Rise of DIY, Art, Craft, and Design*, from 2008, though focused on its contemporary moment, included a timeline of handmaking in the United States, proposing that the "new wave of craft" began with the publication of the *Venus Zine* in 1994.[87] A different origin moment for the upsurge in craft might be posited for this exact year—namely, the implementation of the North American Free Trade Agreement. Though I do not go back as far as, say, William Morris's fabrics (or hand-sewn suffragette banners) to include the sweep of textile politics since the nineteenth century, my starting point of 1970 is meant as to acknowledge handicraft's relation to the emergence of some feminisms in that moment as well as to contemporaneous economic shifts in global manufacturing.

For Marx and Engels, textile manufacturing was a precipitating event in the history of capitalism; since their time, crafts like knitting and sewing have been posited as a resolution to the crisis of commodity manufacturing and the crisis of alienated labor. Handmade textiles have been heralded as materials that could resist the mass standardization of everyday life by visibly and affectively reinscribing the intimate and personal procedures of their making. More recently, amateurism has been heralded anew given the "artisanal" culture of individualism in which commodity objects are all the more valued when they are visibly made by hand and in which *professionalism* has become a dirty word that signifies cold, faceless corporatization. But if figures like Morris looked to handmaking as a contrast to the alienation of the assembly line, hoping to demystify industrial labor processes with a return to making in which one person completes an object start to finish, craftivism arguably remystified craft by proclaiming for it special, and romanticized, powers of disruption. Again, my focus on contingency and ambivalence stresses that textile-based techniques, like any others, have no particular immanent politics. Many handmade textiles are adamantly not "revolutionary": alongside pro-choice crafters crocheting handmade wombs, for instance, there are anti-choice knitters inspired by biblical passages about being "knit" in the womb by God.[88]

In addition to the hip craftivist how-to guides discussed above, many trade crossover books published since 2000 announced a return to handiwork for the privileged classes in the face of the (largely psychic) devastations wrought to the wealthy and white by late capitalism. These include Jean Zimmerman's *Made from Scratch: Reclaiming the Pleasures of the American Hearth*; Shannon Hayes's *Radical Homemakers: Reclaiming Domesticity from a Consumer Culture*; and Matthew Crawford's *Shop Class as Soulcraft* (which was published in England under the title *The Case for Working with Your Hands*). Such books indicate a groundswell in the 2000s of neo-Luddite, "back-to-the-hand" sentiment.[89] These texts recycle tiresome conservative gendered tropes: women "reclaim the hearth" while men tinker with motorcycles. Their claims of inventiveness in reviving the lost rewards of handicraft demonstrate a collective amnesia about the enduring paradoxes of craft, since handmaking, a site of perpetual struggle in our relation to the past, frequently oscillates between being forgotten, then reclaimed, then denigrated, and then once again vaunted within the churning cycles of taste and trend.

Along with the return to handmaking proclaimed in the popular press, textiles (and, to a somewhat lesser extent, ceramics) have also been subject to much greater art-institutional attention since around 2001. Artists who work with textiles have been featured in major international biennials and high-profile surveys of mostly studio crafts like *Fiber: Sculpture 1960–Present*, at the Institute of Contemporary Art in Boston in 2014.[90] But the medium-specific presentations of studio craft in many museum exhibits diminish the specifically political history of textiles for some feminists, in which textiles became the arena in which gatekeeping notions of "quality" could be suspended. The modernist argument for handcrafted textiles has largely relied upon abstract fiber work and posits such aesthetic achievements as distinct from the rangy, homegrown efforts that many feminists in the 1970s embraced.

This recent art-institutional embrace not only has occurred in tandem with, but more fundamentally has been in large measure *propelled by*, the hobby and popular embrace of craft in the 2000s—such non-"star" makers constitute what Gregory Sholette calls the unacknowledged "dark matter" that subtends the art world.[91] Careful attention to this dynamic is instructive, as, no less than in the 1970s, it was the fanatic knitters and crocheters who helped spur the more recent art-world rediscovery of textiles. What is more, handmaking has had increased visibility within academic scholarship in the last fifteen years, including texts by many of the art, craft, and textile theorists previously mentioned.[92] In some respects there has never been a better time to write about handicraft, as a wealth of scholarship has generated a vibrant array of textured analyses, including those published in venues like the *Journal of Modern Craft*, which launched in 2008, and important books focusing on handiwork and nation building across the Americas, including Rick A. Lopéz's *Crafting Mexico*.[93] Research projects like Rike Frank and Grant Watson's exhibition and edited collection *Textiles: Open Letter* continue to keep the subject alive within critical discourse, persuasively making the case that textiles are "a fulcrum . . . that have transformed relations between subject and object, the material and the immaterial, artistic and artisanal labor."[94]

At the same time, textiles—understood not as a singular artistic "medium" but as a field of cultural production or matrix that moves nimbly between and beyond high and low—continue to be underrepresented within contemporary art history. During the many years I have researched this book, I have been showered with a dizzying array of examples whenever I state my subject. I have been alerted to dozens if not hundreds of emerging textile-based artists and have been told many stories about, and shown samples of, people's own textile creations, or been handed fiber-based objects made by members of their families. I have thoroughly enjoyed working on a topic about which so many feel expert, and personally invested in, and I have learned a tremendous amount from these interactions. I doubt that I would have been presented with so many *but what about X?* queries if I were writing about, say, sculpture. I take these irrepressible offerings as a sign of how much work remains to be done regarding textiles from recent decades, and I hope that this book can be a place of departure for future scholars and makers of all kinds.

These legions of hobby quilters, sewers, and weavers are in some measure responsible for the current academic and art-world interest in textiles, but despite their keen eyes, enthusiastic blogs, and museum admission dollars, their actual work is often considered too mundane, uninteresting, generic—that is to say, too amateur—to itself cross the threshold of institutional visibility. Even if technically these makers conform to the dictionary definition of the word *amateur* by pursuing craft not as a profession but rather for pleasure or gratification, it is still a word associated with lack of skill. The term *amateur* has curdled into an insult, rather than maintaining its original meaning, which stemmed from the word *love*. Many of the ostensibly "amateur" objects I describe in this book are full of finesse and demonstrate mastery of challenging techniques. Within *Fray*, the category "amateur" is not fully sufficient to describe the mourning makers of AIDS Quilt panels, many of whom came to sewing out of rage and despair, or the arpilleristas who made a living selling their tapestries. Yet I maintain it, uneasily, as well as the term *hobby*, rather than rely on a term like *folk* or *vernacular*, to signal how these types of activities have existed in complex relation with employment and labor. (I mostly avoid the word *vernacular* because the objects examined were often created in distinctly unordinary moments and resulted in quite uncommon things.)

Within contemporary culture, the term *hands-on* (as in "hands-on learning") signifies becoming active by bodily involving oneself in some manner. It links the work of the hand to a broader experiential process of interacting with the world, and thus implicates handmaking in a wider body—that is, the social body or the body politic. To further explore these relations, *Fray* focuses insistently on textiles. Though other handmaking methods (such as pottery) can register fluctuating political meanings and exist across the high–low divide, textiles are understood to play a central role in everyday life and have long been afforded unique cultural significance. In part, this is because sewing, quilting, weaving, and knitting are specialized forms of making and communicating. But it also bears repeating that cloth has the ability to traverse the line between public and private as it travels with us on our bodies as we shift from the domestic realm to the street.

Textiles as dense and multivalent sites of inscription help define our relationship to interiors and exteriors; they shape how we move through space, and they alert others to our sense of self and signal our attempts to collectively belong. In many respects they map the coordinates of social status, including our allegiances and disidentifications with categories of gender, race, class, sex, age, ethnicity, subcultural stylistic affiliation, and much more. As Janet Berlo writes, "Textiles are eloquent texts, encoding history, change, appropriation, oppression, and endurance, as well as personal and cultural creative visions."[95] We utilize fabric in our daily lives far more than we do, say, hand-blown glass, as we have a profound somatic connection to cloth material (wrapped around bodies when waking and sleeping, underfoot on floors, cushioning our furniture) that mediates many of our encounters. Textiles thus have distinct meanings as structure, covering, marker of space, attire, interior element, and social signifier.

Beyond the fact that we constantly use cloth, textile making is also distinct from craft processes such as throwing pots in that it is frequently *portable*—it can be carried around as lap work—and can be made in a range of fluid circumstances. Much of this work is small scale and requires no extensive equipment (unlike, say, a pottery wheel); hence it is often performed in public to create new forms of social space, from early feminist quilting bees to contemporary activist groups like the British knitting club Cast Off, which held major "knitting for peace" events in the London Underground during the wars against Iraq and Afghanistan.[96] Knitting's flexible transportability has allowed it to be pressed into service in the activist group the Granny Peace Brigade, whose members took their needles to the streets during antiwar demonstrations with signs (placed in clear plastic sleeves to protect them from rain) around their necks declaring, "I am knitting stump socks for amputees" (fig. 0.10). Conjuring the history of female wartime craft by employing knitting to register dissent, the Granny Peace Brigade uses textiles to express political anger as well as to transform that anger into what seem to be inarguably useful objects.[97]

Proclaiming themselves "grannies," the knitters make links between sexism, ageism, and ableism.[98] Yet the Granny Peace Brigade's sign relies upon a presumed shock or discomfort around figuring disability in public, as if the

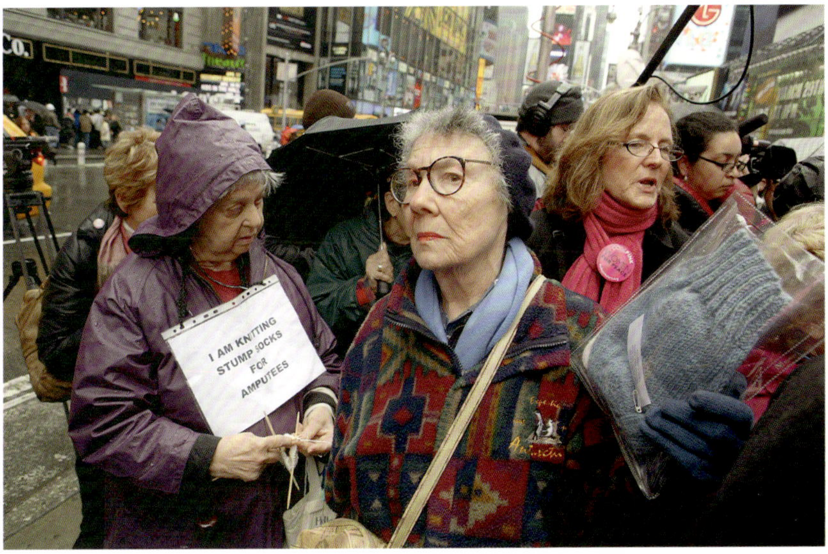

Fig. 0.10. Granny Peace Brigade, March 19, 2008. Photo by Tyler Hicks. © Tyler Hicks / The New York Times / Redux.

registration of these injured bodies—invoked by the sign as existing in the realm of the out-of-sight elsewhere, awaiting needed garments from beneficent charities—were in itself a scandal. The sign does not specify whether the women are knitting for US war veterans, or for Iraqi soldiers, or for Afghan civilians wounded by the US military; the disabled are summoned but not named. (It takes more research to discover that the Granny Peace Brigade has made socks destined for the Middle East and also donated them to the New York Department of Veterans' Affairs.)[99] The gesture raises questions about whose damages are assumed to matter and how such injuries might be cared for. Brigade members' act of public making reminds us that, historically, textile craft has been capable of addressing lacunae in the sphere of commercial production. But, as with gloves for men on the front lines of World War II, stump socks today need not be hand-knitted for all who need them—in the United States at least, they are manufactured and available for purchase to those who can afford them. And this is not the only story of knitting to erupt during recent US military conflicts; alongside these antiwar knit-ins, there were many promilitary crocheted yellow-ribbon campaigns, promoting a starkly different understanding of the utility of textiles.[100] From Sojourner Truth with her needles to the terroristic Ladies' Sewing Circle to "support our troops" knitting groups, the tools of textiles are wielded to contradictory ends. It matters whose hands hold the needles, and under what circumstances.

Craft has traditionally been associated with skill and careful attention; we need to bring similar skilled scrutiny to thinking about textiles as they appear both within and, crucially, outside of museum contexts. As my chapters detail, we must not assume political homogeneity; I plumb moments when artists and activists have turned to textiles and as a result have been received as reactionary rather than progressive. The first two chapters, "Queer Handmaking" and "Threads of Protest," are split into two halves, each taking on distinct but related practices that are thematically connected: first, the Cockettes's garments are placed alongside Hammond's work, and then Vicuña's sculptures are considered next to the arpilleras. The paired case studies mean that the chapters move across the amateur–fine art divide while respecting the differences between these objects. While these two chapters establish this rule, the third, "Remains of the AIDS Quilt," violates it. Because the Quilt is so pivotal, and because aspects of it both encompass and dissolve the high–low spectrum, I have chosen to focus the entirety of my final chapter on it. Further, this intentionally tips the balance of the entire book toward non–fine-art making, serving as a corrective to the recent spate of contemporary art interest in studio-based fiber sculpture. My afterword, "The Currency of Cloth," considers textile projects since the popularization of the term *craftivism* in the early 2000s.

The irreverent humor and circular design of Bowman's 1974 "Ladies' Sewing Circle and Terrorist Society" T-shirt emblematizes the shuttling of textiles between ideological poles. By conjoining seeming opposites with a simple *and*, it asks us to take seriously the logic of both-at-once. Likewise, this book attempts to think different realms together with an insistent *both/and*, as so many of its examples span—depending on circumstances of production and reception—high *and* low, untrained *and* highly skilled, conformist *and* disobedient, craft *and* art. It also sometimes rejects those terms altogether with a defiant *neither/nor*. In the elucidations of *Fray*, textiles permute the politics of materiality and exchange in all their labors, pains, and pleasures.

QUEER HANDMAKING

1

even you, fellow creature, sister
sitting across from me, dark with love,
working like me to pick apart
working with me to remake
this trailing knitted thing, this cloth of darkness,
this woman's garment, trying to save the skein.

Adrienne Rich, "When We Dead Awaken"[1]

In a poem from Adrienne Rich's 1973 collection *Diving into the Wreck*, she metaphorizes same-sex desire as a "trailing knitted thing," a cloth that might be collectively undone and remade, a garment perpetually in process. In this Rich suggests a resonance between textile making (especially needlework) and crafting a self in relation to other selves—or what has been termed worldmaking. As they work to re-create themselves and actualize new forms of consciousness, the figures in Rich's poem envision themselves as fiber workers alongside mythic knitters, crocheters, and sewers like Penelope of Greek legend, who endlessly weaves and unweaves her shroud.

A more sexually explicit invocation of queer craft in the 1970s is found in Dorothy Allison's memoir *Skin: Talking about Sex, Class, and Literature*. In an essay about sex toys used by lesbians, she narrates her first experience using a dildo with a female lover. She describes the pleasure that it brought to her as well as her surprise upon discovering that the toy was not a purchased object, but rather handmade by her butch lover Marty—"a large-sized glove finger stuffed with cotton." As Allison recounts, the "ingenuity impressed me but clearly embarrassed" Marty, who did not necessarily want Allison to see and hence demystify this erotically charged appendage.[2]

The year was 1973, and though commercially made dildos had been produced in the United States starting in 1966 (shaped in a factory in North Hollywood and sold by mail order),[3] this was decades before mass-manufactured sex toys would be widely available in well-lit, women-owned emporia. In the US South, where Allison was living, resources for alternative sexualities were scarce, and lesbians often had to go north to buy their sex toys or, like Marty, invent and construct their own versions. Allison goes on to describe how another lover, Carey, made her own harness in the 1970s, "stitched . . . up out of a couple of old belts and carpet thread."[4] Frustrated with the ill-fitting mechanism that came with her mail-order dildo, Carey had "sat down with her old belts and begun to put together the lesbian equivalent of the wheel." Notes Allison with admiration, this makeshift design "worked better than any harness I subsequently discovered."[5]

The stuffed phallus and sewn-together harness arose from a combination of need and resourcefulness—truly *crafty*, to invoke several senses of that word, both cunning (and possibly devious or deceitful) in design and crafted by hand. These objects are also craft*y*, to use the suffix in its diminutive, in that they are craftlike, or craftish, not always hewing to classic traditions of skilled manual effort but rather approaching the category of craft elliptically, or at an angle—that is, queerly. One says something is "arty" when it is not quite art and may or may not aspire to be considered such; similarly, these crafty textile-based creations take direction, but also definitively stand at some remove, from conventions of craft.

This chapter considers the centrality of textile craftiness within queer culture in the early 1970s in the United States, homing in on two case studies that unfold on each coast. I opened with the memories of cotton-filled gloves and hand-stitched harnesses because Allison's anecdotes gesture to a crucial aspect of making things oneself, even in a late capitalist era when almost everything—almost—can easily be bought. Though the 1970s were awash in an abundance of fabricated commodities, handmaking remained a creative and necessary act for some subcultural groups, a key part of forging queer identities and the enabling of queer sexual practices, such as the fashioning of custom dildos for lesbians in the southern United States. Crafting was a resource to physically bring objects, and new forms of representation and self-expression, into the world in a time when the marketing of queerness and its accoutrements, and the molding of gay and lesbian subjects as a demographic of consumers worth targeting, had not yet taken hold.

In these years around and just after the explosion of gay liberation in the United States, hybridized and unexpected techniques of fiber-based production such as stitching, sewing, and braiding (and, yes, cotton-stuffing) were the vehicles by which many queer subjects enacted their desires.[6] To say that handicraft textiles became a queer resource in this moment is not to generalize (all forms of making are resources, by definition) but rather to emphasize its urgencies—and its eccentricities—with respect to queer countercultural economies. I mean this both symbolically and materially: these techniques are used to make the tangible things that surround bodies and that organize, structure, and lend meaning to the contours of everyday life.

In what follows, I consider two formations of textile making in the early 1970s vis-à-vis the historical emergence of the queer liberation movement in the United States—first, the elaborate handmade (and not so handmade, semi-skilled, or "crafty") costumes of the Cockettes and the Angels of Light, San Francisco–based countercultural theater troupes, and second, lesbian artist Harmony Hammond's braided rag-rug paintings (the *Floorpieces*), which she began in 1973 while living in New York City. (Though there is some overlap, I recognize that *queer* and *lesbian* are by no means interchangeable terms; I deploy *queer* to gesture to a broad spectrum of nonnormative sexualities, practices, and subject positions, while keeping alive the specificities of lesbianism.) Thus this chapter is organized around two discrete but conceptually or thematically related case studies: one that grew out of regional, hippie performance formations and one that is more firmly ensconced within fine arts discourses. At some level this distinction is based on presumed audience—the Cockettes stitched together their outfits for each other and for their initially slapdash productions, while Hammond was making her works for a gallery or museum context. Yet both fit within their respective categories uncertainly, as they consistently challenge high–low assumptions; indeed, intended venue of reception only goes so far in indicating how these crafted objects circulated differently. At the same time, both partook of larger dialogues around fabric, piecing together, and queer making in this moment.

Throughout the book, I aim to suggest that low–high divisions within textile handicraft are insufficient and faulty, as it frays these neat binaries. By juxtaposing two registers of making, I suggest that these spheres are crucially coconstitutive, feeding each other in a multitude of ways, as the perpetually intersecting realms of the amateur and the fine arts motor a greater visibility for textiles more generally. I do not mean to imply causality, or even mutual awareness, between my two case studies—rather, I hope to illuminate how different makers were working through questions of queerness *through textiles* at around the same time. On the face of it, this is a highly unlikely pairing: one, lavish but rough-hewn drag wear; the other, abstract art that is euphemistically nonrepresentational. Yet by looking first at the Cockettes and their artful self-ornamenting and then turning to Hammond's process of making the fabric-based *Floorpieces*, I emphasize that these textile-based projects both craftily comment on consumerist excess, overflow, waste, and the queer vitality of reuse. In addition, campy decoration and décor—in the sense of embellishing domestic space as well as theatrical settings—threads throughout these case studies. As theorized by Susan Sontag, camp is a conversion operation that transmutes low into high, and here I place camp's procedures alongside textile craft's related ability to transgress the line between the everyday and the refined.[7]

The Cockettes' Crafty Genders

In 1974 Alexandra Jacopetti's book *Native Funk and Flash: An Emerging Folk Art* chronicled the resurgence of traditional craft techniques within alternative hippie subcultures in California.[8] Amongst its colorful pages, which included documentation of intricate embroidery, hand-carved woodwork, and Jacopetti's own macramé children's park (discussed in the introduction), sit photographs of what the book refers to as "Glitter Boys"—gender-bending performers who were affiliated with San Francisco–based groups the Cockettes and its offshoot the Angels of Light in the 1970s. These collectives were equal parts experiments in communal living, theater troupes, and active promoters of radical new modes of queer and feminist self-fashioning. Category-defying in every sense, the Cockettes and the Angels of Light were known for their outrageous performances wearing handmade outfits both in the theater and in the street. One vivid picture from *Native Funk and Flash* features Pristine Condition ("known as Prissy to her friends"), bedecked in a pink dress with cascading tiered sleeves, a large headdress of gathered fabric and silk flowers, and an appliquéd apron (fig. 1.01). Scraggly threads drip from the skirt's uneven hemline. A diamond-shaped piece repurposed from a granny-squares blanket is affixed to the bodice, and the ensemble is festooned with long ragged streams of lace trim. The overall effect, with Prissy perched in pink high heels on a quilt and framed by a light pink wall decorated with a giant rose (made by Billy Orchid and sprinkled with glitter), is fantastic excess.

Yet it is a form of excess marked not by wealth but by thrift: outfits such as these were made from scavenged materials and trash-picked treasures and relied upon the inventiveness of scarcity to achieve their distinctive glamour. The caption for Prissy's photograph states, "As she hitched up his dress, s/he said, 'I'm a firm believer in safety pins!'"[9] Such text not only points to the thrown-together, impromptu style that was integral to the "Glitter Boys" but also underscores their fundamental gender indeterminacy. Within this one brief sentence, three gendered terms are used in rapid succession in reference to Prissy—first female ("she"), then male ("his"), then bigendered ("s/he"). It is as if no one singular pronoun could encapsulate the ever-morphing iden-

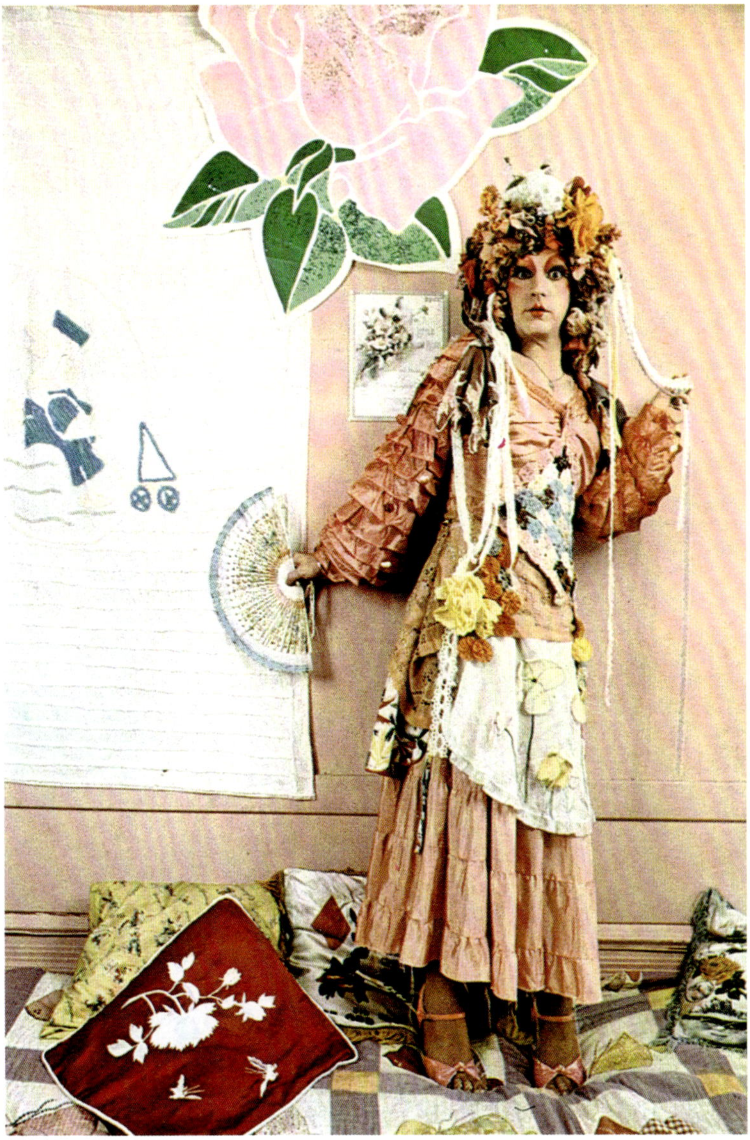

Fig. 1.01. Pristine "Prissy" Condition in *Native Funk and Flash*, Scrimshaw Press, 1974. Photograph by Jerry Wainwright. Courtesy of Alexandra Jacopetti Hart.

tities Prissy is taking up, playing with—or perhaps *putting on*—as with the exaggerated headdress and bright red eye shadow.

These garish getups could be situated within long-standing traditions of *camp* and *drag*; within the academy these two dense, related, but distinct terms have been productively circulated, debated, and revised by thinkers such as Susan Sontag, Esther Newton, and Judith Butler.[10] Sontag's influential 1964 essay theorizes camp as a mode of interpretation, sensibility, and taste: "Camp is a certain mode of aestheticism. It is one way of seeing the world as an aesthetic phenomenon."[11] For Sontag, camp serves a destabilizing function, as it obviates distinctions between good and bad, flippantly erasing the lines between the morbid and the merry. At the same time, she demarcates her own binary categories, most notably drawing a line between "naïve and deliberate" camp, with the latter, self-aware version dismissed as "usually less satisfying."[12] As I discuss, the extravagant plumage of the Cockettes fits unevenly into the realm of what she calls deliberate "camping," while other aspects of camp articulated by Sontag apply to the group somewhat more clearly, as when she writes: "To perceive camp in objects is to understand Being-as-Playing-a-Role. It is the farthest extension, in sensibility, of the metaphor of life as theater."[13]

Drag was a word used frequently by members of the Cockettes; rather than narrowly designating a modality of gender inversion, they understood drag as their daily process of getting dressed. It was how they referred, generically, to their clothes, in an acknowledgment that their outfits jumbled the norms and codes of legibility of the "straight" world. Butler's work on drag reminds us that the notion that gender might be like a metaphoric change of clothes—worn and then discarded at will—is highly problematic, as it disregards the punitive, regulatory force of the law to maintain and uphold compulsory gender conventions. As she clarifies in *Bodies That Matter*, "I never did think that gender was like clothes," arguing that drag is not "unproblematically subversive," as it can entrench and augment heterosexuality's hegemonic reach.[14] For the Cockettes and Angels of Light in this historical moment, however, gender *was* treated like clothes, as handmade outfits were part and parcel of a utopian vision in which smashing gender binaries seemed to them entirely possible. They wanted to devise their own discourse of drag, one whose iterative daily momentum might ignite a total transformation of the self. That they did not dress "as men" or "as women" did not shield them from the expectations and lived realities of gender, but their daily experimentations with sartorial codes quite earnestly endeavored to suspend those realities.

I investigate the handmade costumes of the Cockettes and the Angels of Light to propose that the upsurge in crafting in the late 1960s and early 1970s overlapped in provocative ways with a simultaneous emergence of some gay and feminist cultures in Northern California in the post-Stonewall era. I focus on the specific material practices that went into constructing these garments and ornamentations and how the Cockettes and Angels of Light, like many in the California alternative craft movement, aligned handmaking with countercultural worldmaking—as an individualist practice of differentiation but also within a larger, if somewhat inchoate, communalist project. (In the end, this utopianism had its limits, as ruptures around race and sexuality disproved their fervent beliefs that their riotous dress allowed them to step outside of enforced categories of identity.)

In his book *Ways of Worldmaking*, published in 1978, philosopher Nelson Goodman claimed: "We start, on any occasion, with some old version or world that we have on hand and that we are stuck with until we have the determination and skill to remake it into a new one."[15] Goodman was not the first to theorize worldmaking; earlier in the twentieth century, Hannah Arendt importantly connected labor (defined by her in relation to both work and political activity) to bringing the material and affective conditions of the world into existence.[16] Yet Goodman's ideas about worldmaking as essentially a method of recycling or repurposing—that is, making do—resonate with wider 1970s ecological rhetorics of the "enoughness" of consumer culture and the political importance of salvaging. As he notes, "Worldmaking as we know it always starts from worlds already on hand; the making is a remaking."[17]

More recently, Lauren Berlant and Michael Warner, among others, have turned to worldmaking with regard to the formation of queer counterpublics. For them, queer subjects have been denied a world and must conjure one into being, by virtue primarily of intimacies that are outside the normative realms of heterosexual coupling. They write, "Queer and other insurgents have long striven, often dangerously or scandalously, to cultivate what good folks used to call criminal intimacies. Making a queer world has required the development of kinds of intimacy that bear no necessary relation to domestic space, to kinship, to the couple form, to property, or to the nation."[18] As will be discussed, the Cockettes forged their queer intimacies—the knowing of others and the knowing of oneself—in part through their garments, handcrafting their outfits as they simultaneously handcrafted new conceptions of ownership and the proper boundaries of the body.

Genderfuck

The Cockettes were born in San Francisco on New Year's Eve 1969–70 and lasted for a little more than two years, staging regular theatrical extravaganzas at the Palace Theater that garnered an avid cult following.[19] These performances, rowdily embellished by their flamboyant, gender-bending costumes, showcased irreverent parodies of Hollywood musicals and integrated solo numbers, music, group reviews, and dance as they flaunted their general disregard for traditional codes of sexuality. Though the troupe included a diverse assortment of characters, including soon-to-be disco celebrity Sylvester, the Cockettes circled around one primary charismatic figure, Hibiscus, who wore makeup on his face and glitter in his long beard, and innovated in his dress style with evocative sartorial flair. In figure 1.02 Hibiscus is transformed into a luminous peacock from the production of *Myth Thing*, in a costume designed by fellow Cockette Martin Wong, with flame-colored cardboard feathers arrayed around the upper torso to augment and enhance a glitter-encrusted beard.[20] (Wong later moved to New York and became central to the New York queer art scene.)[21] A wide sash around Hibiscus's chest holds the splashy feather-fan in place on his back, and his sparkly lamé dress is cinched at the waist with more sashes. His skin glows in the light of the stage like an ember, shining with the glitter that covers the surface of his body and his outfit.

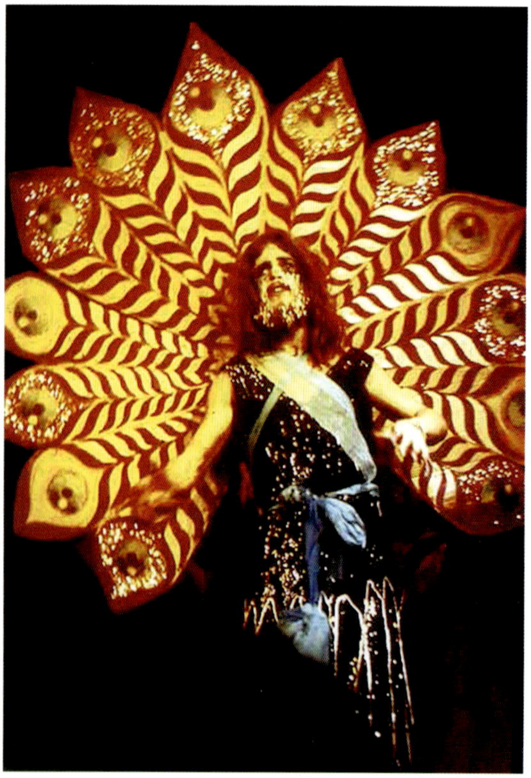

Fig. 1.02. Hibiscus as a luminous peacock in *Myth Thing*, in an outfit designed by Martin Wong, ca. 1972. Photographer unknown. Courtesy Estate of Martin Wong and the Martin Wong Foundation.

Anarchic in both spirit and practice, the Cockettes made little distinction between stage and street or between public and private, as they wore their fantastical regalia as much in everyday life as they did at the Palace Theater, such that Hibiscus would pass out flyers for their shows wearing layers of skirts, a veil shrouding his face, and a tall headdress. Jewelry and other ornaments were worn constantly, even in bed, as in a photograph showing Sylvester seemingly naked but for a large metal necklace, wrapped in sheets and eating next to his lover/husband Michael Lyons (they had a marriage celebration in Golden Gate Park), a cat resting at their feet (fig. 1.03). Despite the seclusion implied by such a bedroom scene, the couple and the cat gaze directly into the photographer's lens, and indeed the Cockettes became increasingly used to being watched, and documented, even while not on stage.

Audience member and poet Allen Ginsberg wrote of their performances: "Their productions were transvestite-glitter-fairie-theatre masques. Trans-

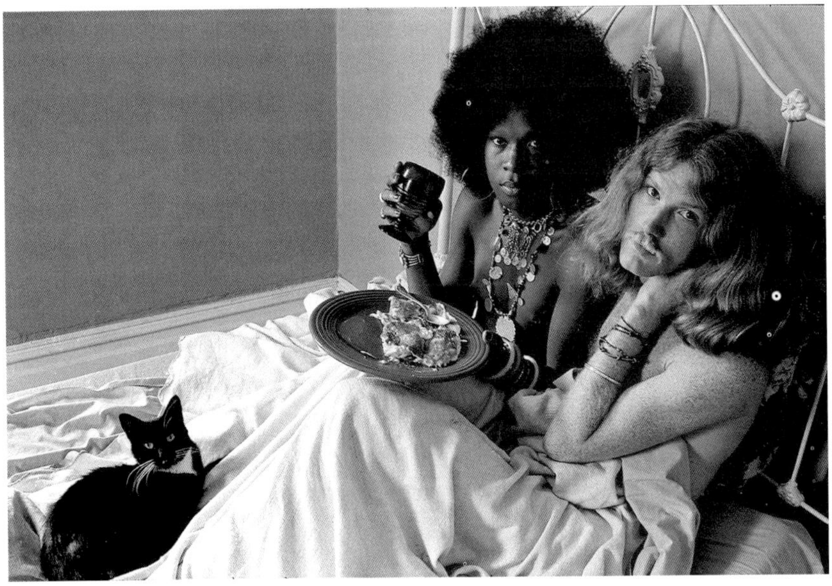

Fig. 1.03. Sylvester in bed with his husband Michael Lyons, ca. 1970. Photograph by Bud Lee. © bud lee / budlee.net.

sexual dressing is a gay contribution to the realization that we're not a hundred percent masculine or feminine, but a mixture of hormones—and not being afraid of that natural self which the hormones dictate. The Cockettes brought out into to the street what was in the closet, in terms of theatric dress and imaginative theatre."[22] With his reference to hormones, and his quick switch between "transvestite" and "transsexual" and "gay," Ginsberg appears to speak to a biological basis for several versions of transness and gayness. His remark highlights the crucial role of the imagination and of dress in attempting to push open a space for fluid sexual openness—or what is now called genderqueer, though that was not the term used at the time. Instead, Hibiscus was a touchstone for a nascent neologism—*genderfuck*.

Encompassing a wide spectrum of queer, trans, and assertively nonnormative sexualities, the term *genderfuck* was first used in reference to phenomena such as the Cockettes in a 1974 article in the magazine *Gay Sunshine*.[23] Its author, Christopher Lonc, wrote that to clad oneself with accretions of accessories that scrambled the gender binary was to transform into a "one-person guerilla theater" and a "revolutionary army attacking the entire straight structured world."[24] If there is an implied violence evoked by this attacking army, akin to the feminist terrorist society T-shirt, it is one aimed not at bodies but at social norms. Another key precedent for this kind of West Coast psychedelic drag/genderfuck was Cyclona (Robert Legorreta), the queer Chicano performer who was active in East Los Angeles beginning in 1966, though Cyclona had a more gothic sensibility and a more pointed critique of racism than did Hibiscus.[25]

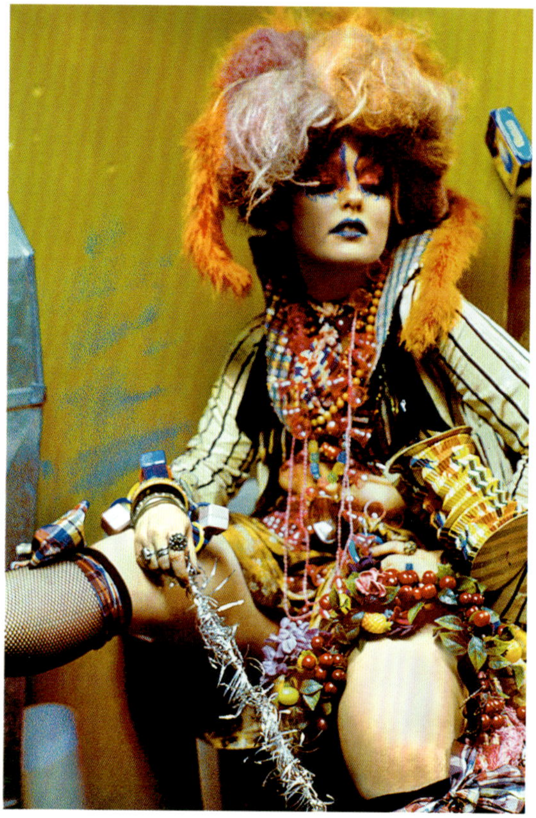

Fig. 1.04.
Fayette Hauser with feathers and beads, 1972. Photograph by Roger Arvid Anderson.

For those affiliated with the Cockettes, the theatrical outfit that "comes out of the closet"—never has that wardrobe metaphor been so appropriate—was one that had been lovingly emblazoned with broken jewelry, Mardi Gras beads, silk tassels, glitter, and detritus from the street. At its core, theirs was a transformative rag-picking enterprise, part of what Susan Strasser calls "trashmaking," that involved elaborate procedures of gathering, sorting, and reusing.[26] "We'd take acid and go to the Alameda Flea Market and the magical elements of drag would just come to us," explains former Cockette Fayette Hauser, whose limbs in a photo from the era are garlanded with beads and strands of plastic cherries such that it is hard to distinguish what are clothes and what is adornment, as a fountain of fake feathers crowns her head and crimson outlined with cobalt rings her eyes[27] (fig. 1.04).

Venturing far outside purely gendered frames of reference, these costumes blended animal/human/machine/myth: papier-mâché horse heads sprouted manes of rubber dildos, and flowing biblical robes were worn with headdresses of fresh calla lilies. In contrast to Allison's memoir of constructing a dildo out of materials on hand (an object that is kept secret, meant to give pleasure but remain unseen), here readymade sex toys are incorporated into disorienting and perverse garments. However embraced by admirers of their theatrical productions, their outfits also courted rage and hostility. "People became angry at us for looking so different," recalled Beaver Bauer, noting that sometimes on the street passersby would throw objects at them.[28] They also faced resentment from older members of the drag community who were more eager to pass or to comport themselves according to conventional genderings.

In 1971 an ideological rift led to the formation of a splinter group, the Angels of Light, which was dedicated to free performances and was active throughout the 1970s. Several of the Cockettes became Angels of Light members; in contrast to the tenuous, ad hoc organization of the Cockettes, the Angels established many tenets of collectivity, lived together in a communal house that had no locking doors, espoused the eradication of private property, and shared all their resources. The Angels' group house was part of a larger social movement of alternative living that was in full bloom across the United States in the 1970s.[29] While there are important distinctions to be made between these two groups, I am primarily interested in the common ground they shared—namely their investment in and pioneering of handcrafted clothing, worn both at home and in their theatrical presentations. Both believed they embodied the revolutionary edge of a new society that began with such textile crafting. As former Angel Beaver Bauer says, "How we lived and what we made were part of what we wanted to see the world become."[30] By all accounts, the communal Angels' group house had its personality clashes, logistical problems, and petty infights, but it was also an attempt, however compromised, to create an idealistic projective space—the world of *what-if*.

As a photo from the 1973 Years Ahead Fashion Show demonstrates, both the Cockettes and the Angels were defiant about nonconformity and self-fashioning on many axes, not least gender (fig. 1.05). Here a Cockette known as Wally—pictured on the far right—is adorned from head to toe in hot pink

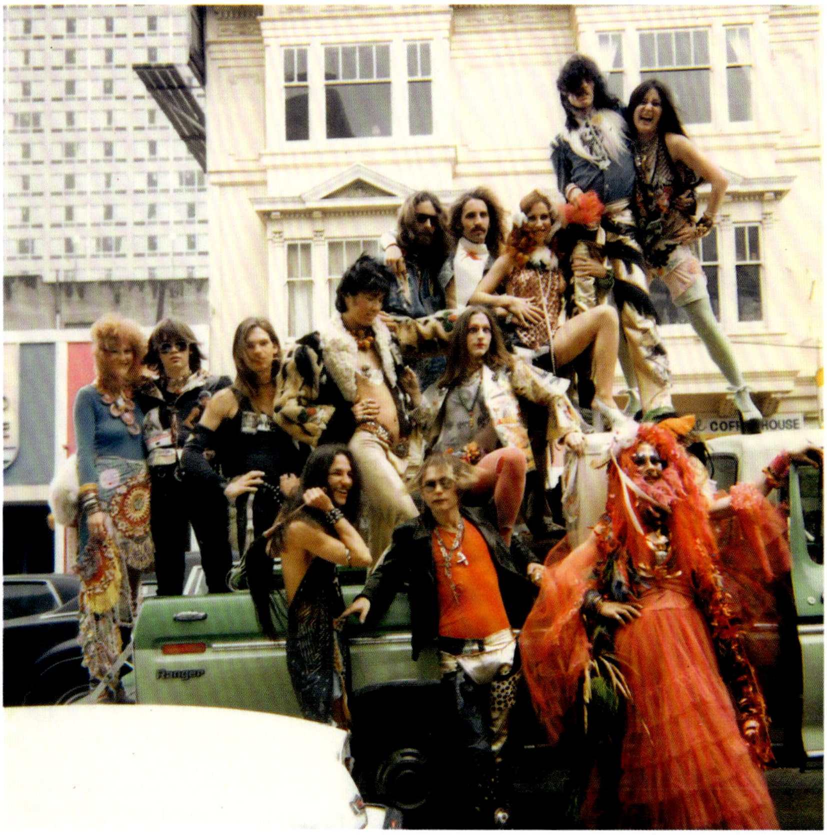

Fig. 1.05. Models from the Years Ahead Fashion Show, San Francisco, 1973, modeling Billy Bowers's clothes and their own ensembles; Wally in a self-made outfit on far right, bottom. Photograph © Wendy Mukluk.

and red. Sporting a feather boa, a bird perched atop a red wig, a beard dyed pink, and a flowing gown trailing swaths of sheer material, this ambiguously gendered figure is a vision of extreme fashion confection. According to Hauser, Wally "spent hours on his gear, then he'd be gone for days tripping around the city, and when he came back it would be in shreds."[31] Such costumes were not always recognizable within the usual rubric of drag's gender inversion. In an interview in 1980, Hibiscus said: "Instead of dressing in drag, I was dressing more as gods. We were all creating mythic figures."[32]

As the Cockettes garnered their own particular brand of groupies, they became a source of fascination for both national and local press. They were featured in *Rolling Stone* in October 1971, described as "more than a drag show, a tribe of outrageous cockflapping transvestites, but more than just a stageful of swishy fellas camping it up in ratty old dresses from the Goodwill."[33] Contrasting the Cockettes with their gender plurality to old-school queens ("swishy fellas" in thrift-store dregs), the article heralded the former as "true freaks" whose ostentatious costumes allowed them to "*live out* fantasies" in what were described, in awe, as "rags. Capes. Dresses made out of curtains."[34] In 1971 a book of paper dolls based on the Cockettes was issued by Last Gasp Eco-Funnies in San Francisco, selling for two dollars a copy.[35] It featured photographs by Clay Geerdes of various members striking glam poses in their skivvies next to some of their actual outfits, complete with little paper tabs that one could cut around to dress up and stylistically recombine (fig. 1.06). The figures are inserted into scenes drawn by John Flowers, with the members' names above in a hand-rendered show-light font and a catchphrase below. Conceived by Flowers and Hauser, who grew up surrounded by paper dolls, the book was like an expanded program for the Cockettes shows in which they were able to be depicted in more than one costume, showcasing their multiple identities with the kinetic ingredients of their clothing. "We brought gobs of drag to the photo shoot in huge shopping bags," recalls Hauser. "We filled a truck."[36]

The paper dolls emphasize the importance of outfits in their self-fashioning and extend the process of playing dress-up out to the viewer. In the page featuring Wally, the "before" figure is already depicted in an improbable mix of genitally affixed balloons, fishnet stockings, and a cone-shaped bikini top made of what looks like mounds of tinsel. A small cross dangles delicately between the two breasts. In the accompanying "after" outfit that is meant to be superimposed on the "before," Wally's human shape is obscured by a massive headdress of large plumes, fabric flowers, and strips of fabric with pinked edges that tumble down to the taffeta and tinsel skirt. One arm is outstretched, holding out a bespangled cape fringed with shiny tinsel, and the upper figure is ringed with small balloons. With sketchy palm trees in the

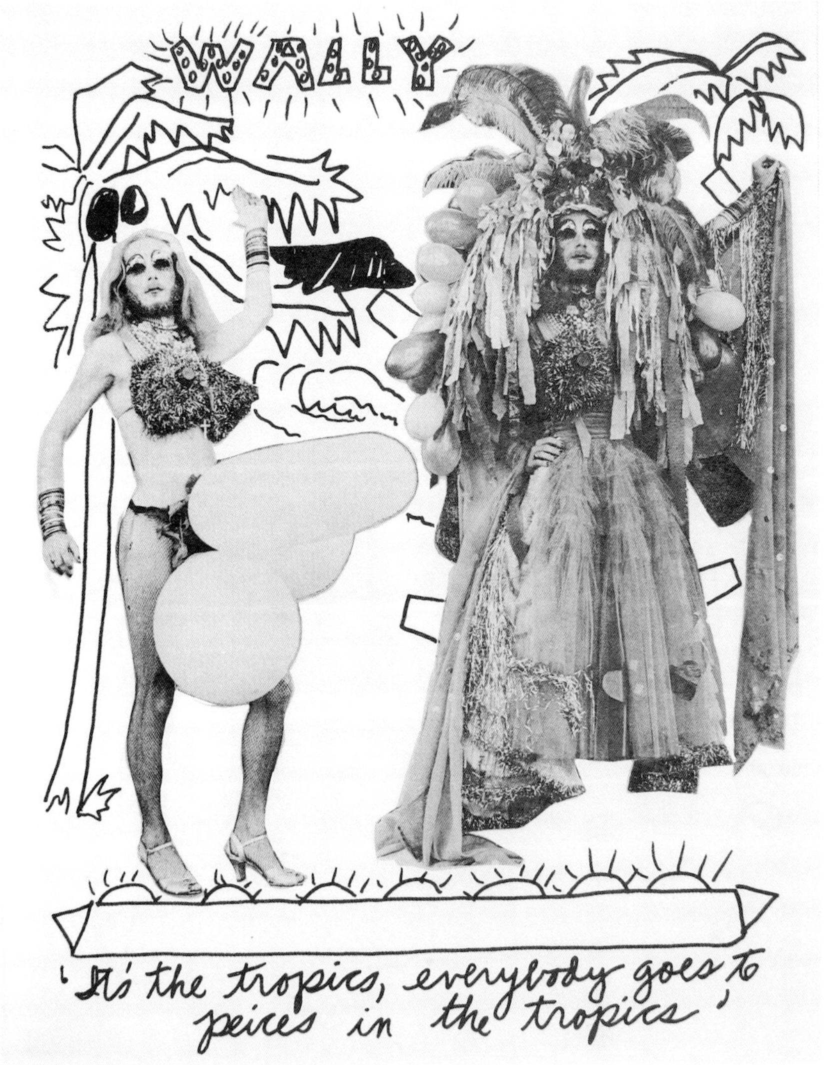

Fig. 1.06. Wally, featured in *Les Cockettes: The Official Cockettes Paper Doll Book*, 1971. Art by John Flowers, photography by Clay Geerdes.

background, the slogan "It's the tropics, everybody goes to pieces in the tropics" suggests an abandon that accompanies the "exoticism" of a faraway locale.

The newsprint paper doll book, the only official publication produced by the Cockettes, has the feel of an instant collector's item and does not seem genuinely intended be sliced up by the owner. It utilizes photomontage and collage as imaginative queer strategies, ones that build upon the crafting techniques of sewing, cutting, gluing, and rearranging so familiar to their outfit production. It also invites the holder of the book to participate conceptually in the process of chopping up and recombining, as it implies that the cut-out garments can be swapped between the different figures. Placing outfits on the "wrong" bodies to produce a comic mismatch is one of the standard amusements of paper dolls, for one delights in the clashes made possible by a switch in clothes and the incongruities of scale and shape (a big vest on a tiny torso!). The paper dolls also emphasize the importance of the make-believe in dressing the Cockettes, since playing with the outfits does not have to take place materially, with scissors actually curving around the outlines, but can unfold in the mind.

Finding and Making

The aesthetic of the San Francisco queer counterculture put a great emphasis on dazzle: you were to make a stunning first impression with an overload of eye-catching detail and leave a trail of spangles in your wake. A ruling mantra was "Glitter covers a multitude of sins."[37] These sparkly surfaces were built up by hand using glue, staples, and whatever else was available. Sometimes an outfit might require little more technique than draping linen in a togalike form, accessorized by toys that were safety-pinned on. Some, like Scrumbly Koldewyn of the Cockettes, owned their own sewing machines and knew how to use them; Koldewyn had been taught by his mother growing up and was accomplished in designing his own pants and shirts.[38] Others, like Wally, could not sew and relied more on assemblage and accretion—affixing plastic Halloween jack-o'-lanterns to his chest, for instance, to punctuate the shock of tall pale feathers erupting from his headdress, and carrying both a polka-dotted paper parasol and a tambourine to augment his rustling garb with a further, distinctly audible, component (fig. 1.07). This kind of making

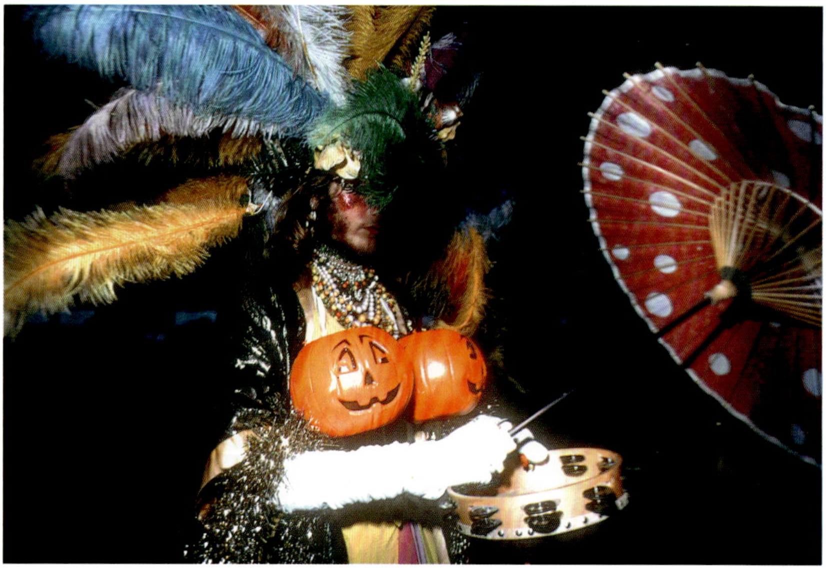

Fig. 1.07. Wally with jack-o'-lanterns, ca. 1970. Photograph by Bud Lee. © bud lee / budlee.net.

was untrained, and such gathering of unlikely objects together is amateur "handmaking" in its most loosely defined, crafty sense. In the Angels' group house there was only sporadic access to one used (frequently broken) sewing machine. Former Angel Jessica Copen recalls many drug-fueled all-nighters gluing rhinestones into place.[39] Most were defiantly uninterested in professional polish; in fact, their New York theatrical premiere, chronicled in the documentary *The Cockettes*, was disastrous precisely due to the perceived disgrace of amateurism.

Since everyone was in charge of their own costumes, and skill sets varied widely, many improvised their methods of crafting with little care for how things "should" fit the body. In fact, especially in the beginning years, there was an overarching disregard for the natural shape of the figure.[40] For example, the red outfit from 1973 turned Wally's human form into a bright pyramid of color and texture, aspiring to living statuary. This disregard for pattern or precedent, combined with a sense that anything at all—from taffeta to tattered curtains—might be used as potential material, promoted experimentation. Within the space of the theater, too, the sets were cobbled together from castoffs and found objects such as painted sheets, cut-out cardboard shapes decorated liberally with glitter, and lights stuck in coffee cans. Background and foreground often merge in these production shots, as the patterned figures and the cardboard shapes among which they stand blur together in an optical flickering (fig. 1.08).

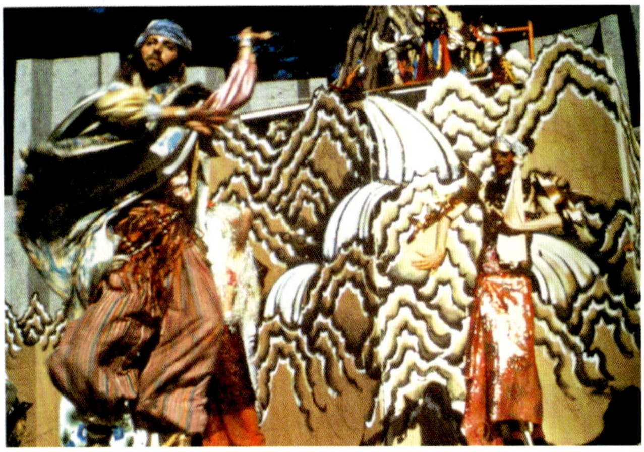

1.08.
Martin Wong, stage set for an Angels of Light performance of *Paris Sights under the Bourgeois Sea*, ca. 1971. Courtesy Estate of Martin Wong and the Martin Wong Foundation.

Many of their base garments were recycled—dumpster-dived, stolen from costume shops, or found in cheap thrift stores, where used clothes from the 1930s and 1940s were still prevalent. Marshall, one of the few Cockettes who earned a paycheck, worked at a store called the Third Hand and set aside choice pieces for his friends. Vintage boas, velvet gowns, and grungy ripped-up castoffs alike all became part of communal "drag rooms" where piles of other fabrics, scraps, and possible accessories were stored. In fig. 1.09 Wally, naked but for bracelets and a headdress, crouches to assess his visage at the mirror propped against the wall, perhaps before deciding what next to put on. Occasionally they would make a pilgrimage to Lew Serbin's Dance Art Company, a boutique of "party beads, marabou feathers, strips of sequins, and boxes of turquoise and emerald rhinestone. Located downtown on Pow-

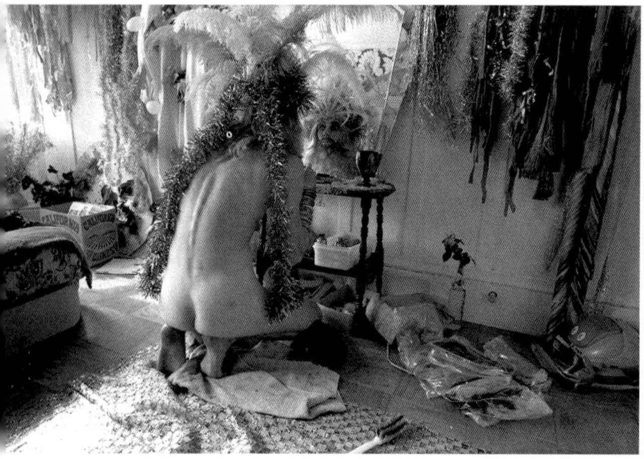

Fig. 1.09.
Wally, nude with headdress, ca. 1970. Photograph by Bud Lee. © bud lee / budlee.net.

ell Street, the place housed more fantasy clutter than a Hollywood five-and-dime and was revered in our circle as a holy shrine."[41] As Bauer put it, making a trip to Lew Serbin's to rummage through its collection of boas, fabric, sequins, and faux jewelry was like "going to the promised land."[42]

Because they had to either make their outfits themselves or beg/barter someone else to do it, they learned quickly how to take shortcuts and to create the most effect from the least expense. Adrian Brooks's memoir *Flights of Angels: My Life with the Angels of Light* recounts the minimal means that they lived on—few had jobs, and they lived primarily from a fund of pooled welfare checks. "In 1973, San Francisco reveled in the Glitter Age, its prevailing style coming from retro fashions found in thrift stores or salvaged from 'free boxes.' . . . [A] new culture was inventing itself."[43] No one found it paradoxical that the new was being refashioned from the old; they relied on the anachronistic as well as the futuristic, borrowing especially heavily from the deco drawings of Erté and the ethos of art nouveau, its sweeping organic lines as well as its problematically orientalizing tendencies (including heavy use of yellow-face in productions like *Pearls over Shanghai*; fig. 1.10).

Indeed, when considering the seemingly casual racism that accompanied many of the Cockettes productions, we might ask: whose world, exactly, is being made here? The claim to worldmaking is bound up in questions of identity that are inevitably unevenly articulated. Here it is instructive to return to Jacopetti's *Native Funk and Flash*, which documents a regionally specific phenomenon in the 1970s—the rebirth of what was called in her subtitle "an emerging folk art" in the San Francisco Bay Area. Jacopetti's inclusion of the Cockettes folds them into the rubric of folk art, which she elaborates from a white American viewpoint that emphasizes yearnings toward cultural otherness and "authenticity." As she writes in the book's introduction: "Many of us have hungered for a cultural identity strong enough to produce our own version of the native costumes of Afghanistan or Guatemala, for a community life rich enough for us to need our own totems comparable to African and Native American masks and ritual objects. The native funk and flash in this book tell us something of that hunger and what we are doing to fill it."[44] But who is the "we" here? The book is filled with examples of ethnic annexation as a way to "fill" this hunger, including crafting traditions that integrate motifs and techniques from historical sources and non-Western customs; her language of ingestion partakes of larger tropes of presumably unmarked white

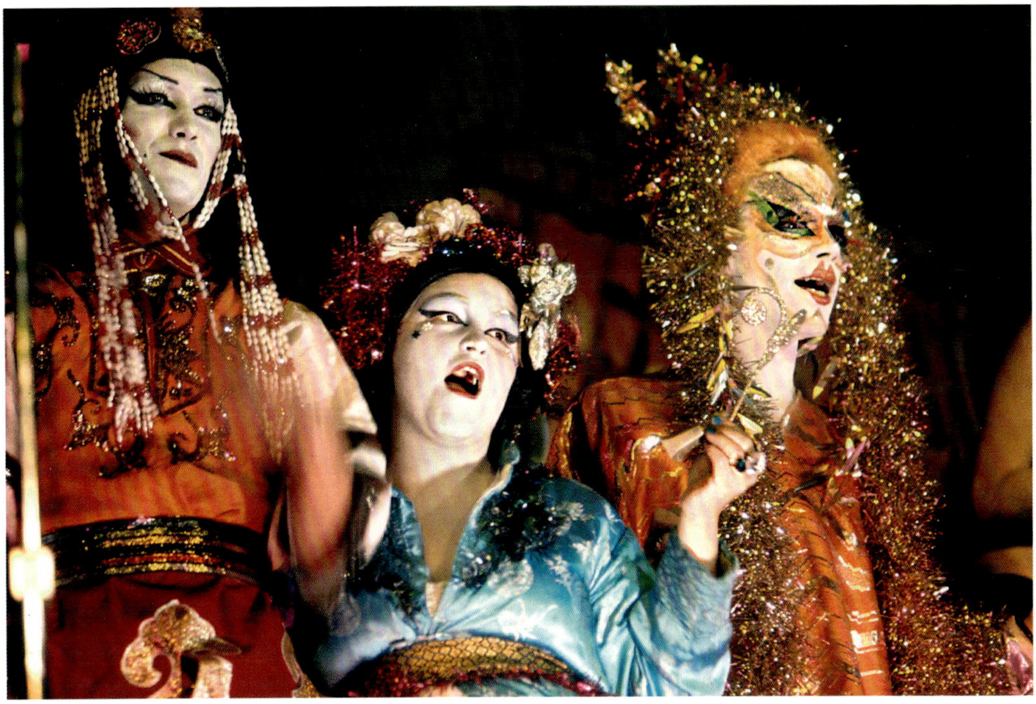

Fig. 1.10. Cockettes in *Pearls over Shanghai*, 1970. Photograph by Bud Lee. © bud lee / budlee.net.

populations "hungrily" consuming "foreign" cultures.[45] Jacopetti was in this respect responding to larger trends of the 1960s and 1970s, including debates in the US studio craft world about its contested connections to global "folk" or "native" art. One key moment in this history was the formation in 1964 of the World Craft Council, whose institutional formation exacerbated many tensions between non-Western craftspeople (whose work, in shows sponsored by the council, was frequently exhibited as anonymous artifacts) and non-Native makers from nations like the United States and Canada (whose work was displayed accompanied by the artists' names).[46]

Jacopetti was inspired by a range of heritages and tribal traditions that included Native American, African, Asian, Middle Eastern, and Eastern European crafts, and in 1974 she cofounded a clothing pattern company, Folkware Patterns, which provided "ethnically inspired" designs such as Syrian dresses and Romanian blouses for the at-home sewer. This version of worldmaking is a hybrid affair, as it exists within and among ideologies of international incorporation while also insisting on the specificity of locale. Jacopetti has recently emphasized that the use of the word *native* was not a specific invocation of indigeneity or Native Americanness (though there are many mentions of Native American crafts throughout *Native Funk and Flash*)—but rather was meant to convey a sense that this resurgence of folk craft was "native to this ground, native to who were are. We were yearning for a sense of our own roots. It was not about stealing things from elsewhere."[47] Others are more frank about the appropriations that fed new styles, including Hauser, who claims that "the essence of the hippie" look came from the Michoacán peoples of Mexico, transported via the wives of rock groups who traveled there for marijuana.[48] Native American ritual dress is also evoked in some of the feather headdresses worn by Hibiscus, Hauser, and Wally.

Like *native, funk* was a racialized term in the early 1970s, with its associations with black funk music (though the mostly white funk art movement and ceramics of the Bay Area were Jacopetti's more likely connection).[49] What is more, *flash* had African American connotations in the early 1970s. In a 1971 *New York Times* review of Melvin van Peebles's musical *Ain't Supposed to Die a Natural Death*, African American writer, professor, activist, and actor Clayton Riley explains that "flash, as a register of Black American life, is style gone beyond, behavior, and appearance taken past the perimeters of respectability, taken outside. Brother glitters on the weekend. . . ."[50] He describes a Sister with "spectacular clothes and freakish shoes to match or not, knowing how to use the word *fly* as an admiring adjective . . . flash—all flash" (ellipses in original). Riley emphasizes that while "flash" pushes the boundaries of respectability with clothes, shoes, and style—qualities that much of the work in *Native Funk and Flash* demonstrates, especially photos of the "Glitter Boys"—it is a distinctly African American phenomenon, related to a political sense of self that relishes taking up space in a white world. Despite the prominent use of *flash* in the title, no visibly black makers are depicted in Jacopetti's book.

No less than in *Native Funk and Flash*, questions of racial appropriation are central to the story of the Cockettes. *Pearls over Shanghai* was angrily denounced by some Asian American commentators for its racist stereotyping when it was restaged in San Francisco in 2009. It was apparently also seen as offensive in its own day by some, as when it was performed on the UC Berkeley campus and a woman jumped up and screamed, "This is the most sexist, racist piece of shit I've ever seen!"[51] In response to the 2009 criticisms, when the musical was revived five years later by the Thrillpeddlers theater troupe, Koldewyn wrote an open letter directly addressing the issue, and it was posted on the theater's wall. He explains that Link Martin, who wrote the script, was fascinated by the absurd and distorted clichés of China he had received in popular culture as a child. Koldewyn states that Martin grew up in San Francisco, "which had the largest Chinese origin population anywhere outside of China, and [he,] of mixed race himself, dismissed this all as camp."[52] (Martin was partly of Cherokee heritage.) This invocation of camp as a way to defuse politically charged material treats it as a conversion operation or a translation machine, permitting the most repellent aspects of society to be switched into something more lighthearted—though of course this reinterpretation is wholly contingent on reception.

When I went to see the restaging of *Pearls over Shanghai* at the Hypnodrome in San Francisco in May 2014—it featured some of the original cast members—what struck me was how generic the comedy was, reliant on old-fashioned bawdiness and predictable plot turns. The costumes, designed by Billy Bowers and Tahara, were the most interesting part of the production; with liberal use of dragon motifs, fishnets, and corsets, they drew inspiration from the opulence of Chinese opera and the grungy make-do look of gutter glamour. The inventiveness of some of the gravity-defying headpieces kept my interest in the show, suggesting that the production was in part a vehicle for the costumes rather than the other way around. Rumi Missabu, playing Madame Gin Sling, was outfitted in a dress of green sequins with a matching tasseled headdress; large fake breasts protruded from the chest, covered with a bikini of dollar signs. Examined up close, they looked like much theatrical garb—in order to be durable enough for the stage, the garments had to be overconstructed and evidenced many clunky junctures. Yet they were also underconstructed in the sense that what appeared finessed from the stage was in fact fairly rough edged—rough edges that ramify into the play itself. Did the grafting of drag conventions onto Asian "dragon lady" clichés undermine those clichés? In the end, the exaggeration of stereotypes did not for me lessen their sting.

The lingering controversy about *Pearls* is just one instance of widespread indifference toward structures of racism among the Cockettes. As mentioned, Chinese American Cockette Martin Wong designed many Cockettes and Angels of Light costumes and sets, including for some of the very plays accused of being anti-Asian, raising questions about his own relation to the productions' orientalizing. And though there were a small handful of black Cockettes (including Anton "Reggie" Dunnigan and Lindon "Bebe" Mbutu), Sylvester felt that the group held him at a distance and ultimately "wouldn't let me in, and I thought it was because I was black."[53] A rare photo that shows two of the black Cockettes together captures Mbutu and Sylvester, along with Martin Worman and others, at the airport in 1971 (flying to New York for their much-touted East Coast premiere). In a festive invocation of group identity, Mbutu, wearing a turban, holds a handmade cloth pennant reading "COCKETTES"; he or Worman (it is not clear who) is also clutching a garland of tinsel, redefining what we think of as travel-related necessities to include—why not?—Christmas decorations in one's carry-on (fig. 1.11).

Sylvester's statement about perceiving his own exclusion stands in sharp contrast to statements by many white Cockettes that "we didn't look at differences."[54] In the paper dolls book only one black member is depicted: Mbutu

Fig. 1.11.
Lindon Bebe Mbutu, Martin Worman, and Sylvester at the airport, 1971. Photograph by Clay Geerdes. Courtesy the Estate of Clay Geerdes.

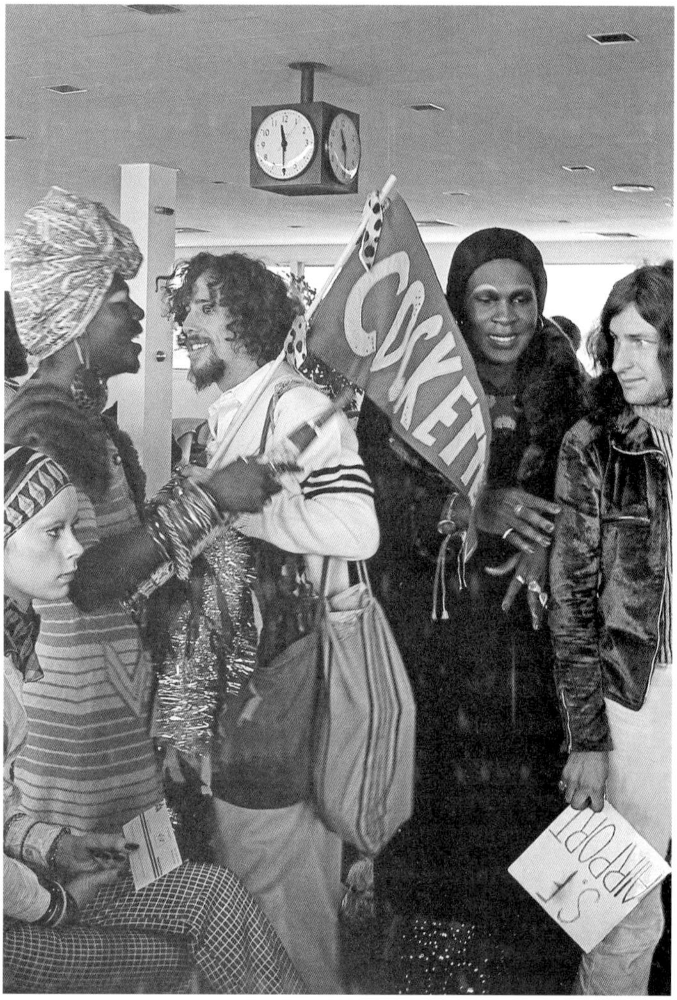

(whose first name is here spelled Lendon), encircled by a feather halo and by tiered skirts on his lower half. His caption, the only one in the book that makes any direct mention of race, is "Black Fire," and he is surrounded by hand-drawn flames (fig. 1.12). It is a privilege of whiteness to ignore racial distinctions, and it is crucial to note that in the grab-and-steal aesthetic of their countercultural practice, the Cockettes were racially inclusive in their membership while generating racist fantasies in their productions and in their everyday dynamics. The Cockettes fostered the interracial closeness depicted in the previously illustrated photo of Sylvester and Lyons in their conjugal bed (fig. 1.03) and encouraged the talents of artists like Wong, but the stereotypical and abrasive racial characterizations in their productions continue to draw condemnation.

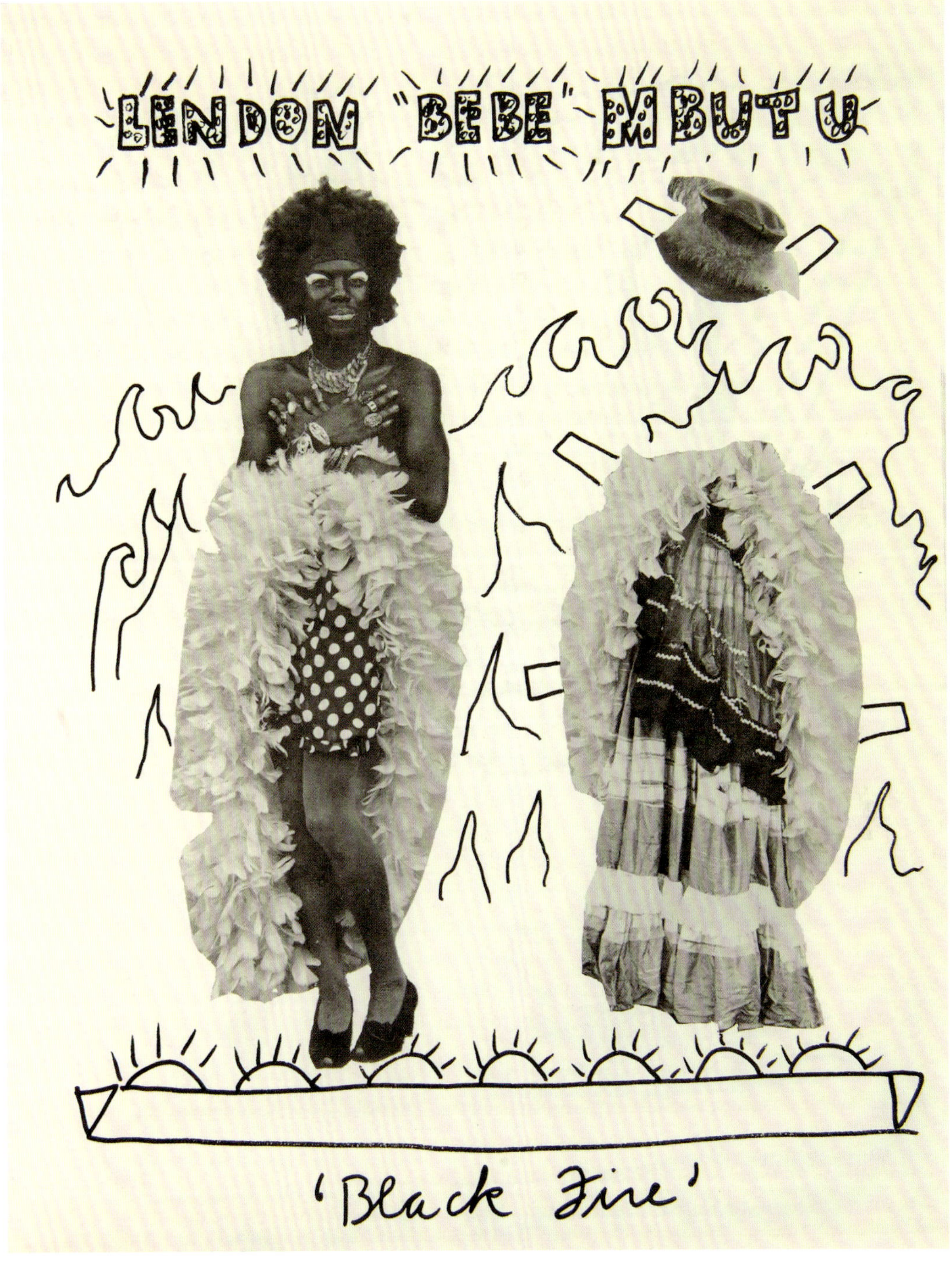

Fig. 1.12. Lindon Bebe Mbutu, featured in *Les Cockettes: The Official Cockettes Paper Doll Book*, 1971. Art by John Flowers, photography by Clay Geerdes.

As stated, many came to the Cockettes and the Angels with no background in craft or sewing at all; Bauer reports having previously only made an apron in her Ohio middle-school home economics class, and it was, she told me, "a tragedy."[55] Learning by making on the spot, she went on to create some of the Angels' most memorable outfits, including costumes for the 1978 production *Sci-Clones* (fig. 1.13). Here the space aliens wear gowns of transparent shower curtains and extraterrestrial helmets fashioned from plastic champagne flutes found at Community Thrift for an effect that was equal parts Aubrey Beardsley drawing and Fritz Lang's *Metropolis*.[56] In another example of reusing surprising materials, Bauer took from a garbage pile a wad of the sticky material that goes under rugs to keep them from skidding to make an elaborate frog outfit complete with psychedelic patterning. The bubbly texture of the industrial material perfectly suited her character's reptilian skin. Bauer transformed trash to become a resplendent creaturely princess, fully upending the legend of lowly frog that turns into a prince.

Indeed, queer drag and textile craft could be considered closely aligned, parallel practices—historically, non-gender-conforming folks like drag queens, drag kings, butch lesbians, and femmy fags (as well as transgendered folks who aim to pass "seamlessly," to invoke a sewing metaphor) have had to make their own clothes, significantly tailor garments, and invent body-altering modifications like breast binders and packing cocks. Jennie Livingston's 1990 documentary about black and Puerto Rican ball culture in Harlem, *Paris Is Burning*, tracks a generational change between older drag queens hunched over sewing machines making their own spangled dresses and younger ball-walkers who state that they would much rather buy or shoplift name brands from department stores.[57] The reality TV show *RuPaul's Drag Race*, which premiered in 2009, has insisted upon sewing as fundamental to drag, and making clothes is as vital to the competition as lip-synching; many contestants have been ousted due to their inability to create outfits from scratch, whether with a hot-glue gun or with a needle and thread.

Larger shoulders, poorly scaled sleeves, ill-fitting crotches, or the simple desire to amp a garment up and make it one's own: alterations for non-normative bodies—whether too big, too small, or otherwise "wrong"—necessitate a kind of skilled invention, design sense, and improvisational skill that, like artisanal knowledge and tradition, is often learned by doing and passed down through mentorship, example, and demonstration. The logic of crafted production—and of reproduction—is not hereditary or heteronormative but is instead managed within the queer kinship of counter-

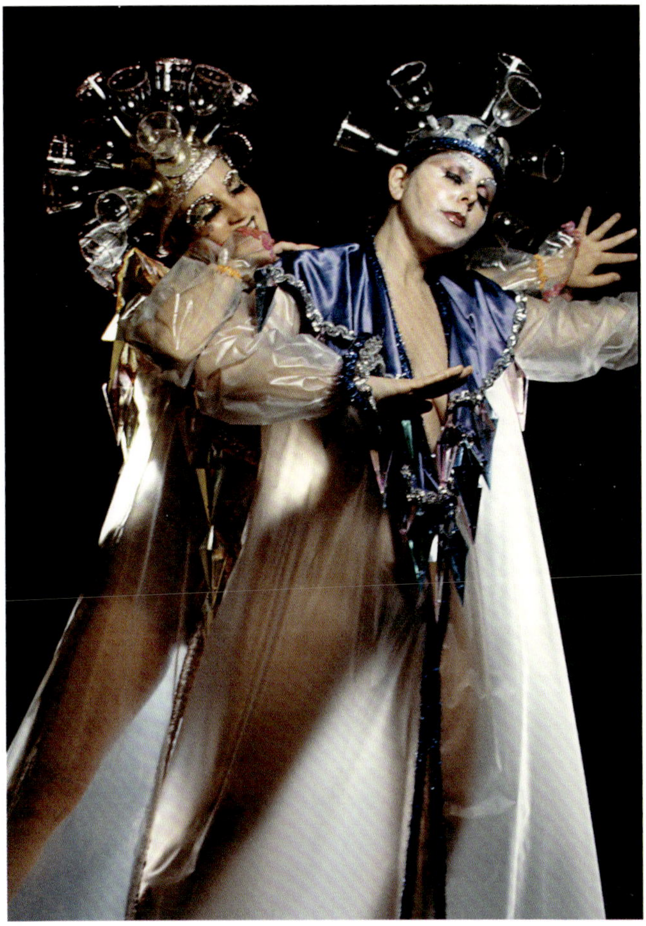

Fig. 1.13.
Beaver Bauer and Jessica Copen in *Sci-Clones*, an Angels of Light performance, 1978. Photograph © Daniel Nicoletta.

publics forged through shared affiliation and activity. In one photograph, some of the Cockettes are lounging in the group house on Oak Street, with every possible surface rippling with fabrics and other materials. As a child is being nursed in one corner, in another corner, at left, someone is working at a sewing machine—the act of textile making is fully integrated into the bustle of daily life (fig. 1.14).

None of the outfits created by the members of the Cockettes and Angels were ever considered purely *theatrical*, taken in its most basic definition to mean "destined for the stage."[58] Ensembles were not exclusively meant for performances but assembled to be worn around town, for instance, as Hibiscus stood on a street corner and passed out handmade flyers promoting upcoming shows. Yet even when at home popping popcorn or making dinner or hanging out in the backyard, group members elaborately enrobed themselves *for themselves* and for each other (they never missed a chance to pose for the camera; fig. 1.15). They were interested in creating personas unveiled first

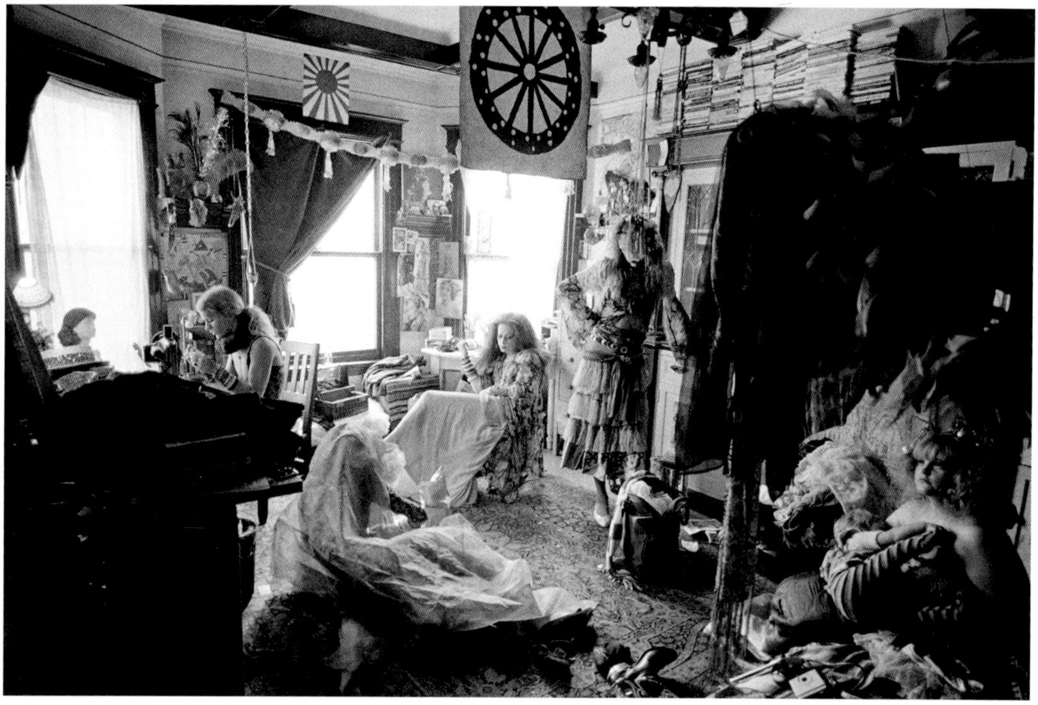

Fig. 1.14. Cockettes at home, 83 Oak Street, with sewing machine, ca. 1970. Photograph by Bud Lee. © bud lee / budlee.net.

at home or on the street and later rehearsed and integrated into a show—an "urban carnival" in which the viewers were as richly attired in rhinestones as the performers.[59] As their own best and first audience, they dressed to outdo and impress each other, as well as to command attention within the vibrant tapestry of San Francisco. The outfits were understood as outward manifestations of their mutable inner lives. There was little investment in an "authentic" or stable self; instead, "what resonated deep beneath the glitter," as one memoir puts it, was a constantly shifting "spirit."[60] Distinctions like natural versus artificial were dissolved and made irrelevant within the unfolding theater that the Cockettes and the Angels of Life attempted to embody.

If, as Sontag writes in "Notes on 'Camp,'" "the essence of Camp is its love of the unnatural: of artifice and exaggeration," then these outfits might not be properly called camp—some saw them instead as sincere manifestations of complex internal landscapes.[61] On the stage, masks and costumes were used to obviate the division between reality and fantasy, but they were also charged with the special power of psychic illustration. Especially in the early years of the Cockettes and, later, the Angels, the shows were only loosely scripted, and everyone more or less designed their own costume based on who or what they wanted to become that day. Because they were conceived by each person for each show, individual outfits gave form to each distinctive personality. By extension, they were meant to embolden the spectator to see a range of possibilities for how life could be lived at its most extreme and imaginative. "We believed," states Bauer, "in the transformative power of our masks and outfits and costumes, to change us but also to change the people who saw us."[62] Such crafting was a social sphere; members would together scavenge, staple, and hand-sew their outfits, or make jewelry that might be given away spontaneously on the street. Over time, the Angels experimented with elastic headdresses and masks; their main mask-maker, Tony Johnopoulous, also worked with other alternative theater groups such as Bread and Puppet and the Living Theater. As productions became more organized and coherent in later years, the Angels also made preliminary sketches to unify the design themes and would develop these concepts communally.

For some the *process* itself of handmaking was a forceful means of individual expression and communication. For instance, after a drug-induced episode of psychosis in which she became unable to speak, Cockette Hauser invented her own intricate visual language of crafted scraps. "The aesthetic was 'more more more,' and every layer conveyed meaning as we created eclectic mystical collage on our bodies. With my drag, I was collaging myself together," she recalls.[63] Unlike many others, Hauser had an art background as a painter and had learned to sew as a child from her grandmother. Handmade textiles, especially the quilts that she surrounded herself with, became a potent metaphorical, almost cosmic vehicle for Hauser; for example, shredded red velvet upholstery layered against an ochre gold tablecloth came not only to signify but to potentially reorder her own blood and flesh. ("I don't really know how to express it now," she confessed to me.)[64]

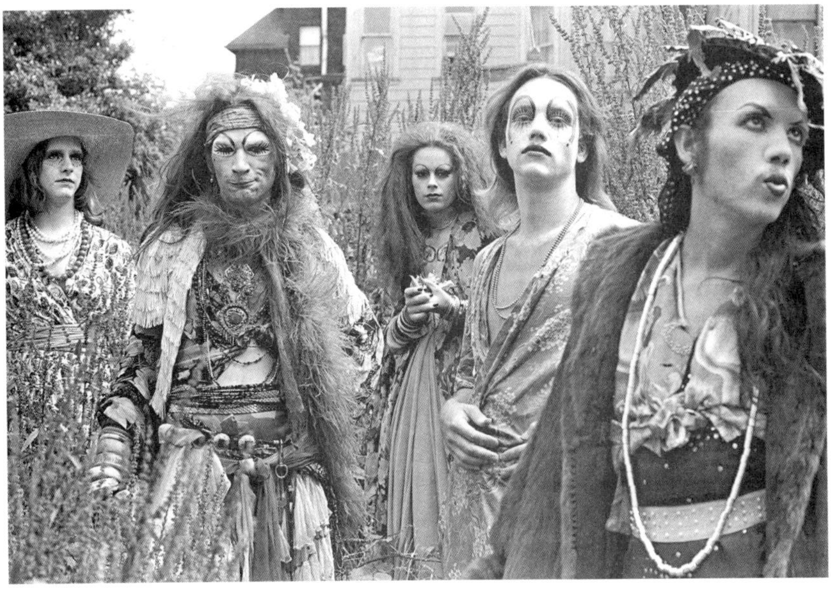

Fig. 1.15. Cockettes in a field of lavender, San Francisco, 1971. Left to right: Pristine Condition, Marshall, Bobby, Danny Isley, Link Martin. Photograph by Fayette Hauser.

This nonverbal sign system, pieced together from colorful fabrics, was not necessarily readable by others but had a logic through which she was able to communicate with herself, as she surrounded herself with fabrics in "an organic swirl of color and objects that came together like a Sufi flame."[65] As Pam Tent (aka Sweet Pam) recounts, "Her mind was so fragmented that assembling her drag became her only focus—a kind of psychological puzzle to help her put herself back together."[66] In other words, crafting drag was not about dissembling (or falsity) but about assembling an earnest, if provisional, self by which she could engage in a conversation with herself. The knowing archness that is a hallmark of drag (and of "deliberate" camp) does not quite fit in the case of Hauser, who used it not as a self-aware wink to the world but as a route to a sort of fugitive authenticity.

Folk and Flash

Let me return to the appearance of the "Glitter Boys" within the specific context of Jacopetti's *Native Funk and Flash*. Next to the picture of Prissy, Koldewyn is featured in his intricate doily outfit (fig. 1.16). Koldewyn, like Nikky Nichols and a few others, was skilled at constructing garments out of unconventional materials due to his long experience with sewing, and he felt, as they all did, that the impetus was to "display trash as treasure."[67] With his "panoply of frou-frou" and over twenty doilies that he recalls cost no more than fifty cents each, he collaged together pants, a top, and a jacket of thin metallic fabric with chubby pink chenille trim. (He sometimes sold similar tops at the Third Hand.) Sewn together with a "quick and dirty zigzag stitch," the crocheted doilies with their loose diamond net are pulled at the body's side, revealing flesh. The outfit has no underlayer, as the skin was meant to show through, though the doilies are strategically placed around the crotch for more coverage (in the fig. 1.17 detail, the outfit is modeled by someone wearing striped boxers). A back pocket made of solid material—a table scarf—is adorned with silk flowers and affixed with a button, as the pants were pulled on and closed using a few buttons to hold it all in place. Modeling his outfit for *Native Funk*, Koldewyn stands in his bedroom, itself a showroom of textiles and pattern, with his drapery fabric behind him, Chinese scarves hung like molding, a heart-shaped pillow he made himself, a found plaid bedspread, and a pile of doilies and blankets at the foot of the bed, just out of reach of the viewer.

This series of photos is notable, and not only because of the book's casual, unassuming incorporation of radically undefined gender identities within what is an otherwise fairly heteronormative framework. Jacopetti chronicles

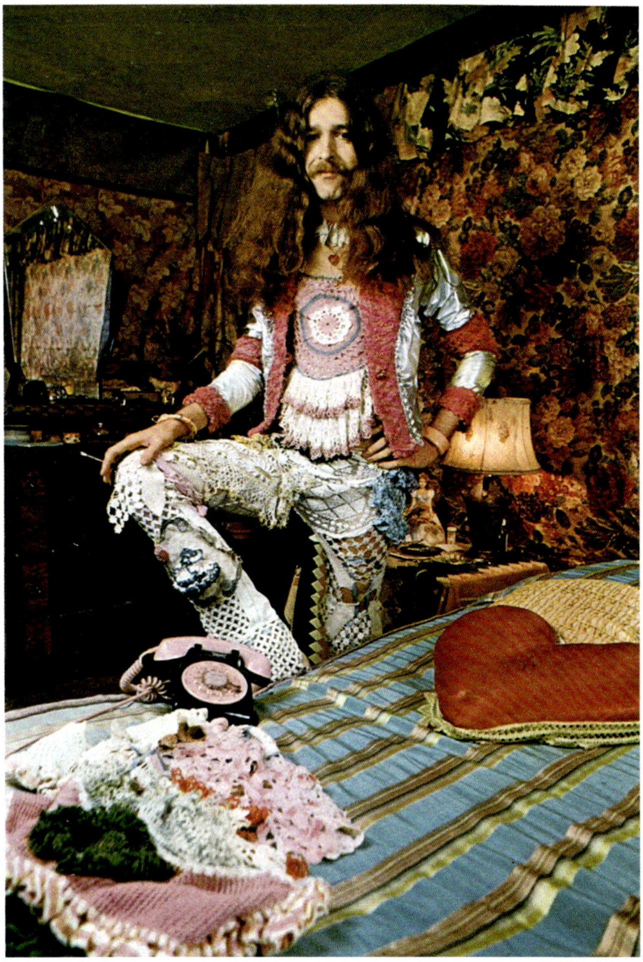

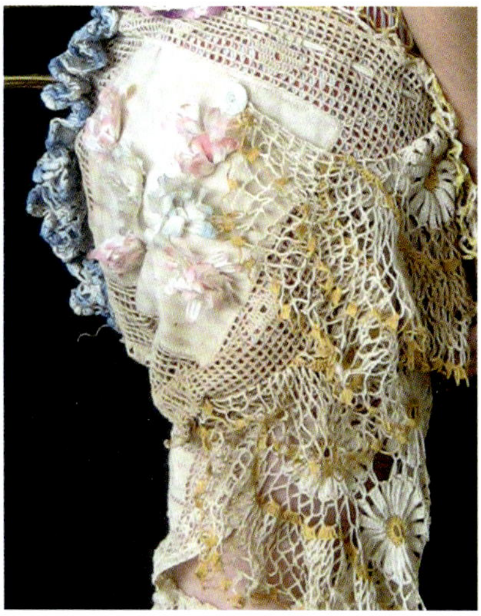

the revival of traditional folk arts by mostly San Francisco–area crafters, including everything from neoprimitive jewelry to stitched-together dolls to hand-decorated denim shirts, with a decided interest in showcasing finely done work, emphasizing the time, care, creative inspiration, and effortful labor of the hand—what we have come to think of as "craftsmanship."[68] Her inclusion of Scrumbly's doilies and Prissy's dress therefore legitimizes them as *craft*—with some significant disclaimers. Though she celebrates these raw, lively outfits, Jacopetti's explanatory captions also state: "So here's the art of costuming, not craftsmanship, and the use of common elements like patchwork pieces and old doilies. It's all joined with a fantastic ability to achieve an effect, rivaling the scary shamans of past times for sheer outrageous impact."[69] The book thus makes a distinct differentiation between these hodgepodge, safety-pinned concoctions and the intricate, precise work in the rest of the book—Prissy's costume is heralded for its lack of finesse, its *disregard*

Fig. 1.16.
Scrumbly Koldewyn in *Native Funk and Flash*, Scrimshaw Press, 1974. Photograph by Jerry Wainwright. Courtesy of Alexandra Jacopetti Hart.

Fig. 1.17.
Detail of Koldewyn's doily outfit. Photograph by Scrumbly Koldewyn.

for skill. Though *Native Funk and Flash* draws a line between "costuming" and "craftsmanship," in fact, some of the outfits documented here were early designs by Cockette Billy Bowers, who went on to be a legendary fashion designer for the stars, heralded for his handcrafted work using nontraditional materials that was featured in Italian *Vogue* and *Women's Wear Daily*.

The resurgence of folk art that Jacopetti records, like hand-thrown ceramics, leather tooling, and woodworking, was broadly connected to the concomitant growing environmentalism in the late 1960s and early 1970s and was seen as a path to a "gentler" lifestyle.[70] Thus it was loosely part of a countercultural politics of anticommercialism and a rejection of mass production that would pave the way to a living with more integrity. The term *counter culture* was put into wide circulation by Theodore Roszak in 1969; he theorized that the turn to "cultural" modes of protest such as hippie living was a response to the imperious face of industrialization, mass production, and the destruction wreaked by the Vietnam War.[71] At the same time, some of those documented in *Native Funk and Flash* saw handmaking as adjacent to consumer culture rather than a complete opting out. A two-page spread in the book features the Berkeley Telegraph Avenue crafts market, where vendors sell their goods, including batik shirts that cost $5 each, rainbow pillowcases, and jewelry. The text explains that many but not all of the items for sale are made locally: "some stuff has been brought back from travels across the borders and seas, but much of it is homegrown."[72]

Indeed, the Telegraph Avenue craft market was one of many markets that sprang up in the United States during the early 1970s as the handmaking ethic became more mainstream. According to a small book that sketches the history of the Telegraph market, vending permits to sell crafts in Berkeley surged in 1974 (just around the time of the publication of *Native Funk and Flash*).[73] Along with woodcuts that depict some of the vendors and their goods, the book includes an illustration of what the market looked like before the city instituted its licensing process. A man who appears to be Native American, with two long braids framing his face, stands in front of a table full of moccasins as a woman with a fringed bag bends to inspect his wares; this could be an acknowledgment of the growing Native crafts market being officially promoted across the United States, but perhaps hints at even deeper histories of handmaking in an area once populated by the Ohlone peoples.[74] The caption describes this as a scene of selling "viable, usable crafts" (fig. 1.18). Rather than being regarded as a space apart from consumerism, these markets were understood as *models* of neoliberal capitalism, which was then taking hold as a dominant economic and ideological system with its emphasis on individual marketing, business savvy, the monetization of social transactions, and self-promotion. "Craftspersons and the street vending tradition are good examples of a small-scale free enterprise system at work," states the book approvingly.[75]

Obviously the "free enterprise" entrepreneurialism of the craft market was at odds with the self-made costumes and handcrafted gift economy promoted by the likes of Hibiscus. (For his part, Hibiscus left the Cockettes to found the Angels because they "got too commercial.")[76] Thus while the ideals promoted by craft markets could be seen as in accordance with the utopian dreams of the Angels, there were also significant divergences. For instance, the imperative to make as much as you could by hand was violated when the Angels' costumes freely incorporated cheaply made consumer goods like plastic glasses and jack-o'-lanterns. Their craft practices and politics were much more heterodox, and due to the pressures of putting shows together quickly and with very little money, they were unabashed about using whatever they could find (or steal).

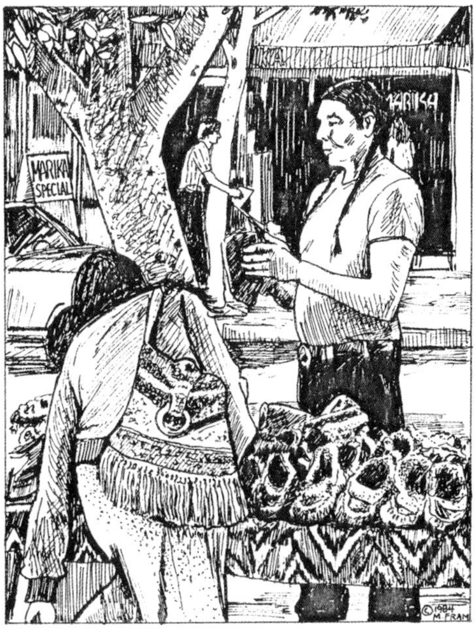

In the early 1970's, before any of the street merchants had to be licensed, there were craftspeople and importers of crafts. They all sold viable, usable crafts.

Fig. 1.18. Page from *Telegraph Avenue Craft Market*, text by Claudia Levin, drawing by Michael Fram, 1984. Courtesy of the Bancroft Library, University of California, Berkeley.

In the 1970s, strict divisions between handmade and store-bought within the craft scene were dissolving. Writing in 1975, folklorist Michael Owen Jones connects skills sharing in textile work to storytelling and oral histories but does not discount the role played by mass-produced kits and instructions. For instance, he describes "contemporary urban tie-dyeing" as an example of the rich mix of standardization and individual innovation. He writes: "A young college educated housewife in Los Angeles learned to tie-dye T-shirts; she relied in large measure on the instructions that accompanied a bottle of commercial dye, though other sources of information about textile work were available."[77] This "young housewife" goes on to make her own discoveries as her knowledge and skills grow in part through printed instructions and in part through face-to-face interactions and through purchasing objects at craft fairs like the one on Telegraph Avenue. Owens writes that the spread of technique happens in part via "small interactional networks, each with its own special identity and set of values."[78] Cultural transmission is understood not as generational (passed down from mother to daughter, for instance) but rather as reliant upon promiscuous circuits of exchange both store-bought and informal.

Though women's liberation and gay male liberation have often been historicized as parallel yet somewhat separate movements sometimes pitted against each other, the Angels of Light provide a crucial, different narrative.[79] As discussed in the introduction, the upsurge in traditional textile techniques (sewing, embroidery, quilting, knitting, crocheting) in the early 1970s was integrally related to feminist art's reclamations of previously denigrated "women's work." In fact, feminism is vital to this story—not least because it drove much of the return to craft within both the art world and in the hobbyist countercultural movement.

Koldewyn sought to recognize and dignify women's work when he used doilies in his handmade creations. And openly feminist participants like Bauer and Copen advocated for strong female roles in the performances and for gender parity in the labor of the communal house. They even made an all-female film (now lost) to showcase their talents and to emphasize that they were sick of "playing second fiddle to the men," according to Copen.[80] As Bauer states, "We didn't want to be fan-carriers for drag queens making a grand entrance." Perhaps because fashion design is gendered female and coded homosexual, one place where equality was relatively easily established within the Angels was in the creation of costumes—in other words, textile handmaking was a sphere where female and gay male labors could be equally valued.

Decadent Décor

In the 1960s and 1970s, California in particular was a space where the revitalization of handicraft fed on and into gay liberation, feminism, and communal living. The literature on the decade's craft revival details the regional blossoming of local artisan communities.[81] The fact that the Cockettes and the Angels surfaced in the Bay Area is significant, reflecting certain economic and architectural circumstances such as the availability of rambling, low-rent Victorian houses that were well suited to large groups.[82] The formation of the Cockettes in late 1969 demonstrates that despite the widespread assumption that the June 1969 Stonewall rebellion (just six months earlier) was the singular origin point of gay liberation in the United States, the genderfuck movement had a unique formation in the hippie counterculture of California.[83]

Furthermore, the turn to handmade fashion, dripping with sequins and beads, resonates with negative stereotypes of California as a place obsessed with “the superficial” and with appearance—politics as style, rebellion reduced to aesthetics. One of the signature features of genderfuck groups and their costumes is decorative flourish. *Decoration*, of course, is a charged word within the history of art and design. In the 1950s Clement Greenberg warned that decoration was the “specter that haunts modernist painting,” threatening to devolve art into kitsch.[84] Earlier in the century, Adolf Loos in his 1900 essay “Ornament and Crime” cast self-decoration as “criminal” and “degenerate,” writing that “the evolution of culture marches with the elimination of ornament from useful objects.”[85] Loos was especially disgusted with the art nouveau style that so enchanted the Cockettes and the Angels of Light—its hyperbole, its disregard for the categories of high and low, and its mixing of art, design, and craft. In his important reconsideration of Loos, Hal Foster notes that Loos’s terror of art nouveau is related to his revulsion for how it “commingles subject and object”—just the sort of fantasy of the ecstatic hybridized merging the Cockettes and Angels celebrated.[86] (For her part, Sontag believed art nouveau to be “the most typical and fully developed Camp style.”)[87] What Loos saw as degradation and decadence, they understood as an emotionally charged remaking of both self and society as they draped their bodies and their sets in boas in every color and shining lamé.

Though decoration is never explicitly queered in either Loos or Greenberg, Richard Dyer in his book *The Culture of Queers* discusses the negative association of homosexuality with the decorative and the superficial.[88] The Cockettes and the Angels reveled in extending the self with florid, oversized headdresses and trailing garments, pleasuring in artifice and showing little concern for the difference between surface and depth. Or, better, they demonstrated what it might look like when those terms converge to become, to quote a phrase sometimes attributed to Andy Warhol, “deeply superficial.”[89]

There was sometimes a more explicit politics to their dress-up, as in 1971, when Hibiscus, painted gold and wearing an enormous shredded-paper headdress, picketed Varig Airlines (a Brazilian company) to protest the Brazilian dictatorship’s mistreatment of members of the Living Theater.[90] A benefit for the Living Theater members “busted and behind bars” was held in August 1971 at the UC Berkeley Pauley Ballroom, featuring Allen Ginsberg, Lawrence Ferlinghetti, and the Cockettes (fig. 1.19). Such a protest demonstrates how these groups identified themselves not only as regional freaks whose mission was entertainment but as crucially participating in bigger social movements, following the radical precedents set by groups such as the Living Theater. Whatever class or race background they might have had growing up, some Cockettes understood themselves to be “poor gays—oppressed people,” and “the ragtags and rejects of society.”[91] However overstated, this language connects their scrapwork aesthetic to their own sense of marginalization, suggesting that when the low meets the low, transformation is enacted: garbage for garbage, made ecstatic.

When Memory Surfaces

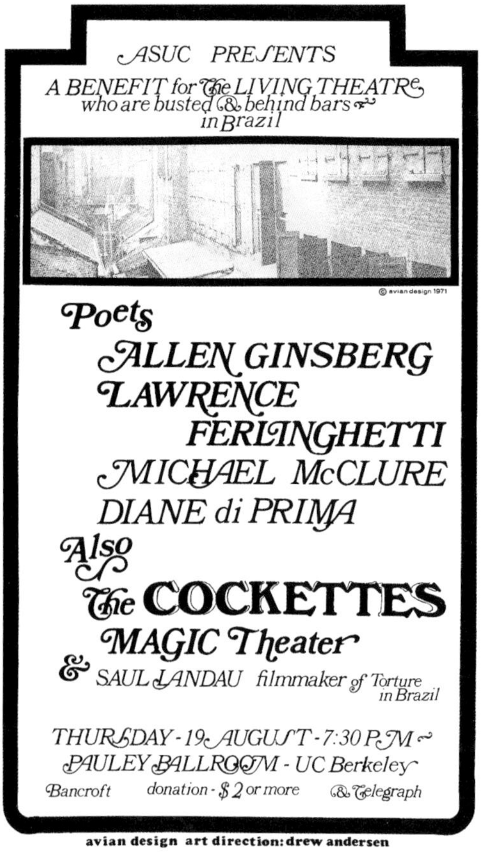

Fig. 1.19. ASUC [Associated Students of the University of California] Presents a Benefit for the Living Theater, UC Berkeley, poster, 1971. Designed by Drew Andersen at Avian Design.

In the late 1960s, not everyone saw utopian potential beneath the sparkles and the makeup in San Francisco. Joan Didion's famous 1967 account of Haight-Ashbury, "Slouching towards Bethlehem," registers a numbed discomfort with drug culture and a free-wheeling hippie approach to living: "We were seeing the desperate attempt of a handful of pathetically unequipped children to create a community in a social vacuum."[92] Didion, riffing on a poem by William Butler Yeats, bleakly asserts that all these art-into-life experiments were proof that American society was rotting from within: "The center was not holding."[93] The writer of a 1971 feature in *Rolling Stone* likewise saw something ominous in what the Cockettes portended: "We are seeing the beginning of the 21st century, and it feels like sitting ground zero during an explosion of sexuality and hedonism and dope and sensation-seeking unparalleled in American history."[94] Indeed it is important not to overly nostalgize or romanticize groups like the Cockettes and Angels of Light, which, along with schisms around racism and sexism, had their share of jealousies, infighting, overdoses, and the like. Yet for the Angels the center did hold together for almost a decade—they lived and worked together until the early 1980s. That decade saw a further devastation as gay men began to contract HIV. Hibiscus—inspiration and figurehead—became an early casualty of AIDS in the United States when he died in 1982. Many other men involved in the Cockettes and the Angels also died of AIDS-related illnesses, including Sylvester, Reggie Dunnigan, Martin Wong, Wally, and Prissy.

Art and design historian Christopher Reed has declared, "There is something queer about archives."[95] That statement has been borne out in this research project in unexpected, and unsettling, ways. When interviewing Bauer, for example, I asked to see some of her photographs of her time with the Angels. "I'll need to think about that," she responded. "To be honest, dredging up that past is very painful for me. When I look at those pictures, I am reminded of tremendous loss and death." Talking with former members constantly reminded me of the fragmented, piecemeal nature of history itself, the unraveling fabric of time. Some of their stories were detailed and precise; other times they confessed to large gaps in memory. Tent's memoir emphasizes the communally crafted nature of recalling this heady era; its first sentence describes the book as a "collective memoir, and much like a Cockettes show, [it] was pasted together from scraps in our closets and our shared experiences."[96] She is quick to acknowledge holes in the narrative. Likewise, Brooks interrupts his memoir with the phrase "memory fails."[97] Lost films, missing photographs, vanished costumes: it is easy to lose the thread.

In the wake of the Cockettes documentary and the publication of memoirs by former members, this history (and, to a lesser extent, that of the Angels of Light) is being rediscovered for a new generation.[98] Unfortunately, the majority of the costumes made by the Cockettes and the Angels did not survive. Though they made spectacular first impressions, many of the outfits were in constant states of disrepair, and some of them were disassembled and reused to make other garments. The performers shed sequins as they staggered offstage. Sylvester rhapsodized that "you lived in glitter and you ate glitter—the whole thing was glitter."[99] Tent says, "We ate and even pooped glitter."[100] With these handmade costumes, outside decoration was incorporated inside, ingested and excreted, traversing the porous membrane between exterior surface and what lies beneath. In a time and place that seemed ripe for social revolution, these groups dreamed of a queer and feminist politics of handmaking, worldmaking, and self-making that would eradicate the lines between performing theatrical numbers and performing a new way to live. They used their outfits as a laboratory site to craft multiple skins.

Handmade costumes—not to mention radical queer culture—are still considered somewhat marginal within art history, perhaps rightly so. Yet despite this marginalization, and despite the destruction and loss of many of these outfits and stage sets (as well as the deaths of many former members), the residue of this textile craft stubbornly lingers. For example, Wong is represented in a 2008 textbook on Asian American art history for his Angels of Light stage designs (seen in fig. 1.08)—an important recognition of the cross-racial nature of this group that was at the same time internally riven by racism.[101]

I conclude this section with one last anecdote: in the early 1970s, Allen Ginsberg had a sexual liaison with Hibiscus. Ginsberg later commented that the erotic encounter was less than comfortable: "His bed was a little gritty because he had a lot of sequins in it. And it was difficult to sleep on the sheets because there was sort of like difficult glitter stuff there."[102] It is a peculiar conjunction: glamour so excessive that it can admit and embrace its own decrepitude. This is one lesson of the queer textile handmade aesthetic—it exists where grit and glitter meet, ostensibly right on the surface of things, yet also profound.

In what follows, I continue to consider questions of surface and depth, remaking and queer worldmaking, examining a very different kind of textile—braided abstract rag-rug paintings made in New York City in the early 1970s. Turning from the West Coast hippie genderfuck costuming to East Coast lesbian-feminist reclamations of amateur "women's work" within the fine arts, I explore how such reclamations were in dialogue with thrift and waste. While the Cockettes and Angels of Light perverted, frayed, or transformed high-art traditions of theater and costume with their exuberant campiness, Harmony Hammond, with a more muted form of camp, dragged crafted rags from the low hobby arena into a fine arts realm.

Fig. 1.20. (*facing, top*) Harmony Hammond, *Floorpiece II*, cloth and acrylic, 46" diameter, 1973. Art © Harmony Hammond / Licensed by VAGA, New York, NY.

Fig. 1.21. (*facing, middle*) Harmony Hammond, *Floorpiece III*, cloth and acrylic, 65" diameter, 1973. Art © Harmony Hammond / Licensed by VAGA, New York, NY.

Fig. 1.22. (*facing, bottom*) Harmony Hammond, *Floorpiece V*, cloth and acrylic, 59" diameter, 1973. Art © Harmony Hammond / Licensed by VAGA, New York, NY.

Harmony Hammond Goes Down

In 1973, US artist Harmony Hammond came out as a lesbian. That same year, she created a series of watershed artworks—her *Floorpiece* sculptures (figs. 1.20, 1.21, 1.22). Made using traditional braided-rug techniques, the circular, spiraling *Floorpieces* recycled cloth found during Hammond's rag-picking excursions in New York City's Garment District. These industrial cast-offs were braided together, tightly coiled, stitched to a heavy cloth backing, and then selectively painted with acrylic paint. Hammond has called the *Floorpieces* her "most radical works."[103] The term *radical* invokes its Latin origins—a rooting or return to foundations—while it also suggests a strident politics. I consider the *Floorpieces'* radicalism anew within two related contexts: Hammond's craft-based textile process and the concurrent emergence of her queer identity as a form of worldmaking. (To be clear, Hammond did not use the word *queer* in the 1970s, as the term had not yet been reclaimed; like most gay women of the time, she called herself a lesbian. In recent years she has identified as queer, and throughout this section I frequently interchange these words.) However, one need not have recourse to the biographical to make claims, as I do, about the queer orientations of her *Floorpieces*.

To understand the *Floorpieces* as queer craft is to assert a feminist art history that is defiantly lesbian as well as sensitive to class. Few artists in 1973 were as dedicated as Hammond was to bringing art down while also bringing textile craft up. In a statement for her solo show in 1973 at AIR (Artists in

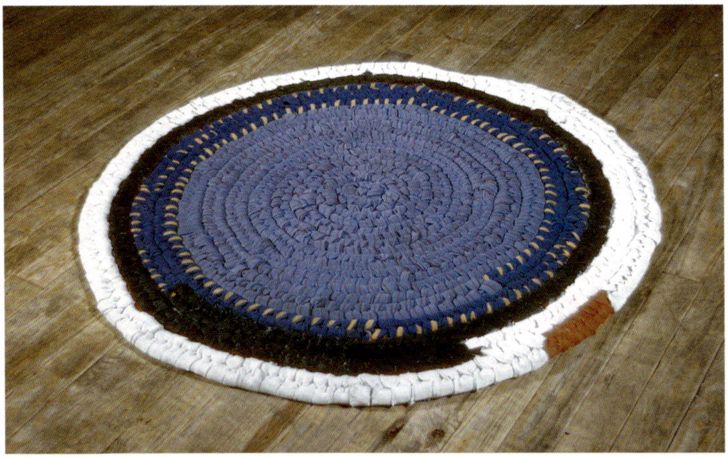

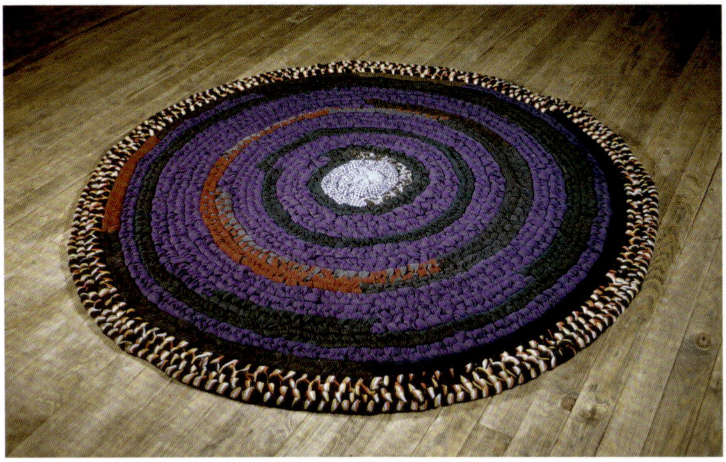

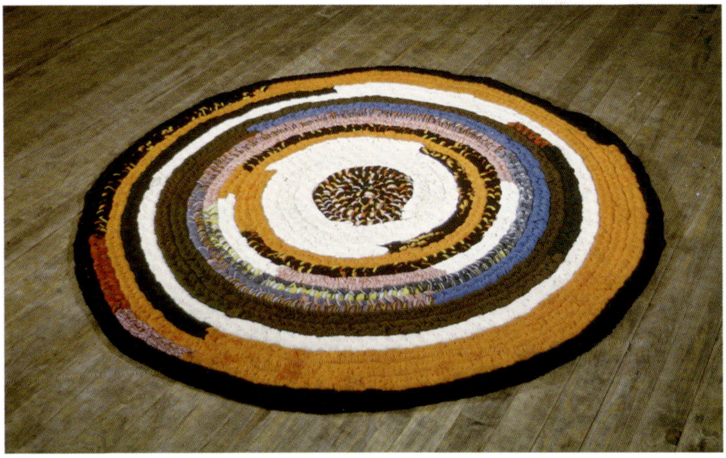

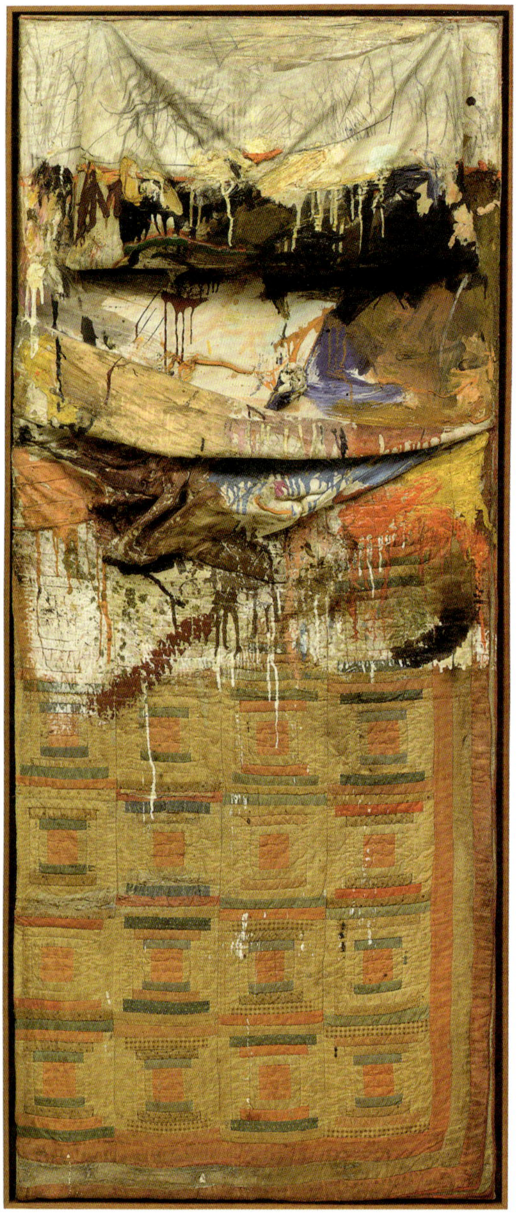

Residence), the women-only alternative cooperative gallery of which she was a cofounder, Hammond wrote of her "desire to break down the distinctions between painting and sculpture, between art and women's work, and between art in craft and craft in art."[104] Many other textile craft-based fine arts rely upon a spatial shift from horizontal to vertical as they are institutionally framed and legitimized as art—think of Robert Rauschenberg's *Bed* (1955; fig. 1.23). Leo Steinberg might have famously categorized Rauschenberg's use of the horizontal as a "flatbed picture plane," but *Bed* is importantly not meant to be displayed on the ground.[105] Rauschenberg's *Bed* with its prominent quilt—which had belonged to Dorothea Rockburne—as a foundation or base for his messy painting (invoking a sexualized site of bodily fluids and gestural expressions), like Hammond's work, highlights the fact that textiles often exist at the intersection between public and private, a queer place that transgresses the border between the sites of erotic activity and artmaking.

Yet Rauschenberg's move to the wall cancels out the quilt's utility; such use-value, of course, is one standard dividing line between craft and art. As Susan Bernick snappily comments regarding Rauschenberg's work and its effortless acceptance into the realm of high art, "A quilt is an art object when it stands up like a man."[106] Hammond's *Floorpieces*, however, stubbornly resist that change in orientation. They are rugs laid on the floor as rugs—insistently low, although any functionality they have in that capacity is partial and is intentionally compromised. They may exist on the ground, but they are also fragile paintings that require carefully considered conditions of display. If you owned one, you would not put it in your living room with a coffee table over it. Rauschenberg's *Bed*, with its copious drips, evident handiwork, vertical orientation, and wooden frame, insists upon its status as art—and not only that, *as painting*, which is given pride of place in the hierarchy of artistic genres. Hammond riskily, and confidently, forgoes such blatant markers, as her careful, nearly camouflaged application of paint on top of the braided textile threatens to obscure her artistic intervention.

Hammond's work is positioned within several overlapping art-historical movements. The *Floorpieces* have been exhibited alongside other gendered handmade art (*Division of Labor: "Women's Work" in Contemporary Art*, curated by Lydia Yee at the Bronx Museum of Art, 1995), as well as seen as expanding the definition of painting in the late 1960s and early 1970s (*High Times, Hard Times: New York Painting 1967–1975*, curated by Katy Siegel, 2006). While these are relevant critical contexts, Hammond's work also exceeds them, bringing together feminist politics, avant-garde abstraction, queer sensuality, and "middlebrow" hobbyist crafting. As Elissa Auther has argued, fiber crafts and fine arts, while sharing common ground aesthetically, were often segregated in this era and subject to hierarchical divisions.[107] Some of this separation was challenged by feminism, and the *Floorpieces* reference a range of 1970s feminist concerns: namely, the elevation of the domestic arts, the dismantling of gendered hierarchies of art and craft, and the dignifying of historically feminized labor.

They also key in to other social and political issues of that decade; Hammond's use of remnants from garbage dumpsters had an ecological component, for instance, resonating with the nascent environmental and do-it-yourself anticapitalist movements. And the braided pieces are embedded in a kind of feminist primitivism of the time that attempted to link women's art cross-culturally and transhistorically with indigenous and traditional craft practices. Like the *Native Funk and Flash* invocation of "native" production, the *Floorpieces*' spiraled forms cite Native American pottery and basketmaking, which are based on similar coiling, and Hammond immersed herself in research about coiling techniques across time.[108] In addition, Hammond has long been concerned with the ritualistic stitching of much women's work, drawing connections between her process and the repetitions intrinsic to domestic fiber-based chores like sewing and mending.

Fig. 1.23. (*facing*) Robert Rauschenberg, *Bed*, 1955. Oil and pencil on pillow, quilt, and sheet on wood supports, 6′3¼″ × 31½″ × 8″. Collection of Museum of Modern Art, New York. Art © Robert Rauschenberg / Licensed by VAGA, New York, NY.

The Labors of Handmaking

Within art history, the *Floorpieces* are most often retrospectively understood as being in dialogue with other 1960s and 1970s floor-based artworks, primarily the metal sculptures of Carl Andre. Much has been made of the differences between Hammond and Andre, in language that is routinely and hyperbolically gendered: circular versus square; soft, warm fabric versus hard, cold metal; saturated applied color versus neutral inherent tones; and hand-crafted domestic surfaces versus found industrial material. Hammond's integration and braiding together of her cloth strands to create a unified spiraled rug is at odds with Andre's placement of individual units that remain separate even when subsumed within his precise grids. Yet such easy dichotomies disregard the fact that these two artists shared an interest in flatness, baselessness, and the phenomenological activation of the viewer's space. In addition, according to Rosalind Krauss, the grid has been endlessly returned to by modern artists in part because of its ability to evoke the spiritual as well as the logical; the form also echoes the material basis of the canvas with its woven (that is, gridded) cloth—one could conjecture, then, that Andre's sculptures are from the outset haunted by textiles.[109]

What is more, Hammond's materials—strips from the end cuts of large bolts of machine-knit fabric—are just as industrial as Andre's metals. Andre's grids were in oblique dialogue with the late capitalist urbanization of New York and the closing of its factories; meanwhile textile manufacturing in New York was undergoing its own transformation in the early 1970s. Long associated with an immigrant workforce, the feminization of labor, and attendant injustices (as in the 1911 Triangle Shirtwaist Factory fire), apparel production in New York peaked in 1970 and then went into rapid decline.[110] In a photograph from the era, a man pulls a cart full of bolts of cloth through the intersection of Seventh Avenue and West Thirty-Sixth Street (the area where Hammond would gather her scraps), straining with all his weight to move the heavy load; his bandaged thumb registers some of the bodily costs of this type of work (fig. 1.24). Though Manhattan in general had undergone a widespread "deindustrialization" starting in the 1950s, textile and garment manufacturing was still evident in the early 1970s, reaching a high of some quarter-million workers in the industry (many of them unionized).[111] That number saw a steady decline throughout the late 1970s as factories fought unionization and moved to the US South, or overseas, where wages were lower and workers had far less protections.[112]

It was in these years that Hammond turned to textile leavings for her materials. She lived at 87 Bowery Street just off Canal, south of the Garment District, and found the cotton and synthetic knit cloth in garbage bags and dumpsters in the form of one- to four-inch-wide strips (the end cuts of bolts of knit fabric rolled around cardboard centers). Her loft's proximity to these workspaces that employed low-paid women and her use of their waste materials were significant to her project. As she has written, "This work must be considered in relation to labor and the geographic and social spaces of lower Manhattan garment districts being colonized by artists, such as myself, as we began to live and work in these neighborhoods. . . . Using this discarded fabric . . . I was able to reference the women working in the sweatshops and

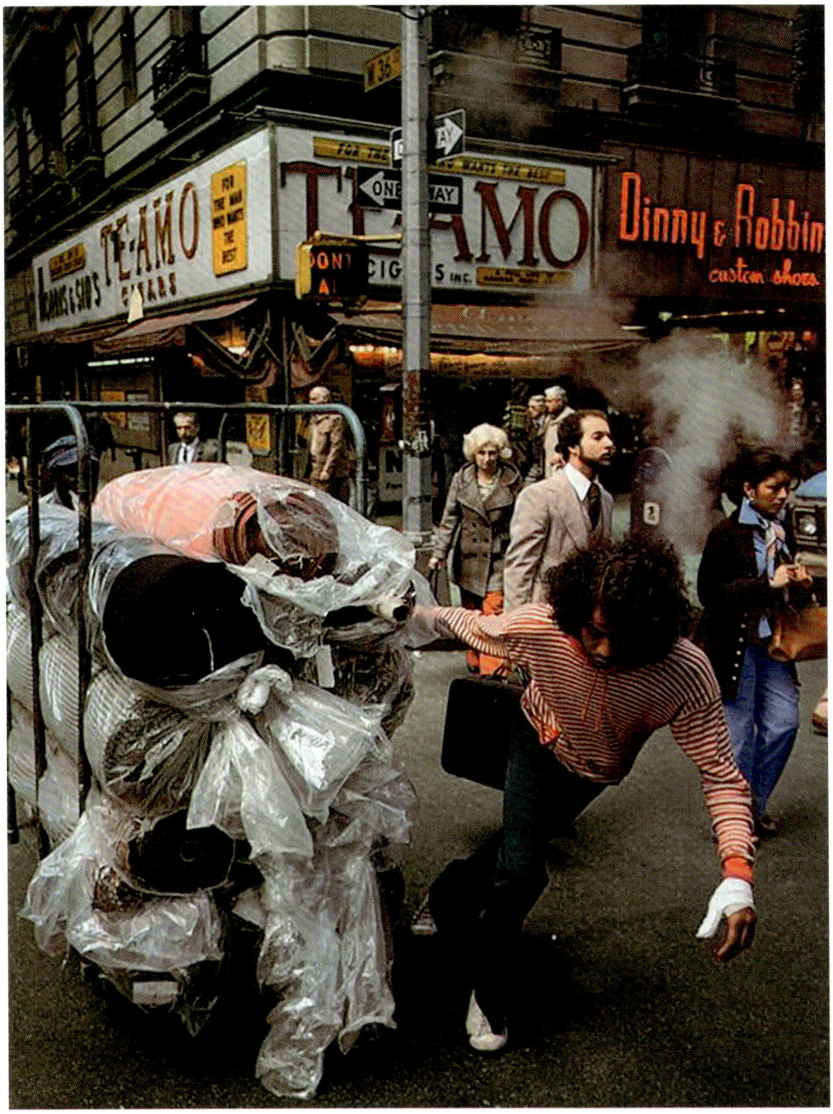

Fig. 1.24.
Man pulling cart with rolls of fabric, Garment District, New York, 1970s. Photograph by Ozzie Freidman.

myself—a woman and an artist in a capitalist patriarchal culture—with what I called an 'esthetic of survival.'"[113] Hammond attempts to reckon here with the gentrifying presence of artists, the gendering of textile work, and the manufacturing procedures from which she was culling her supplies, though one cannot equate these incommensurable labors—that of an artist in her studio and that of an underpaid worker in a factory. Her 1977 declaration that "art is essentially work" does not fully account for the discrepancies of valuation and privilege embedded in these categories, especially as the contours of industrial textile labor were being reorganized in that moment of neoliberal restructuring.[114]

Perhaps the most important difference between Andre's grids and Hammond's *Floorpieces*, which she views as "lateral paintings," is that the latter are not meant to be walked on. Andre's metal pieces—stepped onto and trod upon—are in clear dialogue with utilitarian floor coverings, but the artist himself was strongly opposed to this reading, as it pushed his sculptures dangerously close to the long-dismissed realm of textile craft. Phil Leider referred to them as "rugs" in his 1968 review of Andre's solo show at Dwan Gallery in New York, a terminology that had wide circulation despite Andre's objections.[115] In a letter to the editor in *Artforum* in 1973—the same year that Hammond made her floor-based sculptures—Andre asserted, "My work derives from the working-class crafts of bricklaying, tile-setting, and stonemasonry. I have pointed this out over and over again and yet my works are described as 'rugs.'"[116] Andre's insistence that his art derives from (masculine) artisanal labor ignores the fact that rug making might as easily be considered a "working-class craft." *Rug* becomes a pejorative term—all the more so because it is a textile—and Andre distances himself from its low feminine origins. Andre's class and his masculinity were especially at issue in the late 1960s and early 1970s, a time when he was a vocal member of the Art Workers' Coalition and proclaimed his identity as an "art worker" by sporting a daily uniform of worker's overalls.[117] What Andre's letter does not mention is that rugs, too, are in dialogue with labor. Hammond's *Floorpieces* are feminist, class-conscious comments on work—floors are, after all, loaded sites of women's housekeeping.

If Andre is one "father" of floor-based art, Lynda Benglis might be considered a "mother." Starting in the late 1960s, Benglis poured pigmented latex directly on the ground in large colorful swaths. Benglis also used industrial materials such as polyurethane foam to create droopy, bulbous forms on floors. With their almost fluorescent, intentionally vulgar colors and debased materials, Benglis's "fallen" paintings were, like Hammond's work, meant to challenge fine art hierarchies. Though Benglis was similarly interested in tactility and the registering of the body in her art, her process was distinct from Hammond's investment in handwork. A *Life* magazine article from 1970 titled "Fling, Dribble and Dip" famously placed Benglis's art on a continuum with Jackson Pollock's actions[118] (fig. 1.25). The photographs accompanying the article depict the artist at work, wielding a bucket of latex with gloves on. Keeping such materials at arm's length, Benglis was clearly divorcing her actions from the presumed preciousness of the hand. By contrast, with the *Floorpieces*, Hammond deftly integrated the modernist fixations on support, flatness, and edge seen in both Andre and Benglis with an investment in touch and traditional women's fiber crafts.

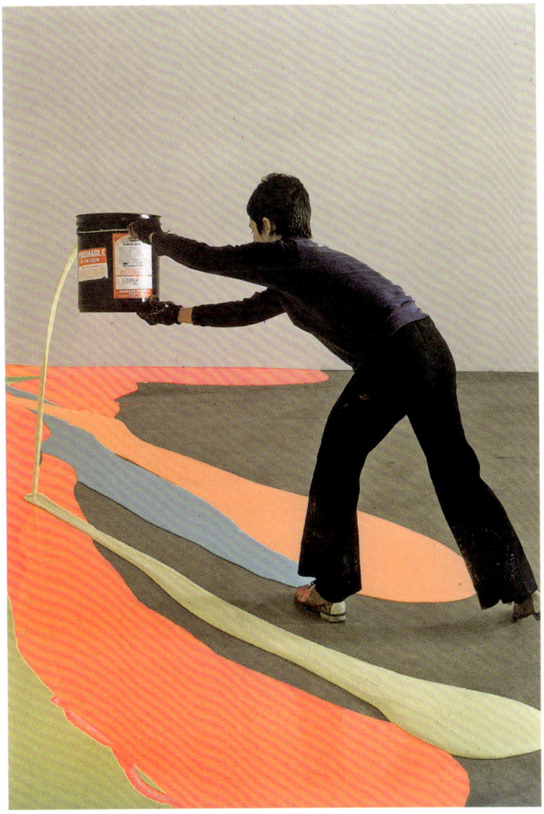

Fig. 1.25.
Lynda Benglis at work pouring latex, University of Rhode Island, 1969. Art © Lynda Benglis / Licensed by VAGA, New York, NY. Photograph © Henry Grosinsky / The *Life* Picture Collection / Getty Images.

How to See the Floorpieces

Because Hammond's work troubles the line between art and craft, it does not sit easily within strict categories. More recently the *Floorpieces* have been understood almost as conceptual works or assisted readymades—fairly straightforward appropriations of the traditional form of the braided rag rug. This reading proposes that Hammond is performing a Duchampian act, injecting inappropriate objects into a fine art context, as if the *Floorpieces* are exactly what they resemble—barely altered rag rugs that have been moved from the domestic sphere into the art institution.[119] This misreading is due in part to the fact that the works are somewhat difficult to read in reproduction; their vividly painted passages, which make them quite unlike actual rag rugs, are evident only when viewed in person. Especially since much of the paint has soaked into the fabric, their surfaces rely on subtle textural contrasts not clearly visible in photographs. Hammond let the patterns of the found rags guide her painting and mimicked their colors, using paint

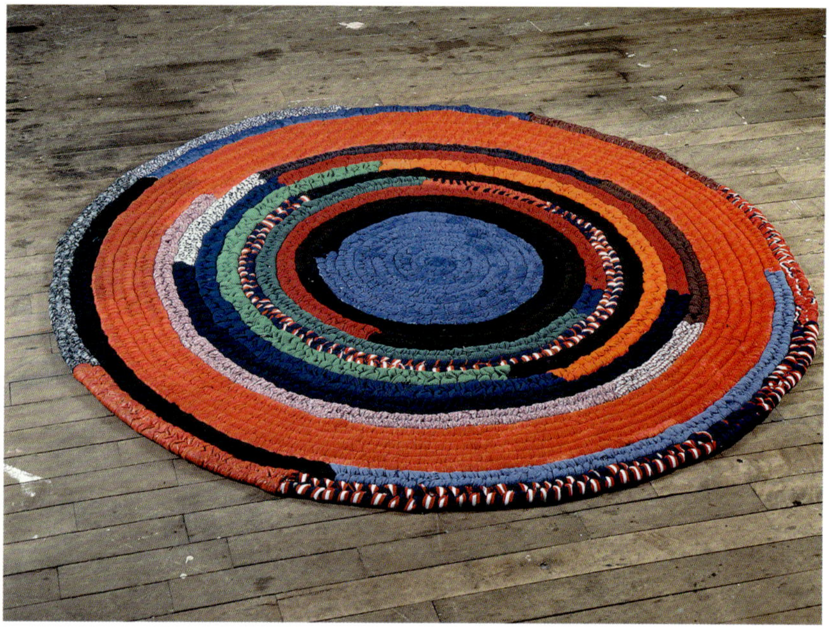

Fig. 1.26.
Harmony Hammond, *Floorpiece VI*, cloth and acrylic, 65″ diameter, 1973. Art © Harmony Hammond / Licensed by VAGA, New York, NY.

to only slightly brighten or intensify the fabrics' hues. In some respects the works are also produced via the operations of chance and contingency, for as she braided and spiraled the knit fabric strips together, unexpected patterns were created, which she responded to with her selective painting (some areas remained untouched; fig. 1.26).

In *Floorpiece VI*, which has more paint on its surface than some of the earlier works, Hammond has over time repainted some areas that had faded or become besmirched; this process maintains the color choice of the original work as she mends and repairs the painted portions as well as redresses the piece's frailty and aging process. Its bright blue center, which is ringed by a black circuit (the name for a length of braid going once around the circumference of the rug) like an iris, is dynamically set against the orange-red that dominates the middle rows of the spiral. Patterned sections—which braid together complementary colors orange and blue—interrupt the solid colors at the very outer edge and again about one-third of the way in. The central blue "pupil" is saturated, but the paint is slightly mottled and not totally uniform. And though you can see a bit of the crusting of paint on the outer red band, these tactile aspects are hard to discern in photographs.

This fugitiveness, characterized by their difficult-to-see quality as well as their resistance to singular interpretations, is central to the *Floorpieces*, as Hammond insists on the importance of the spectator's presence, and skirts the border between visibility and invisibility. They are precisely *not* readymades; Hammond did not purchase these rugs but made them herself as a basis for her painterly interventions. In addition, Hammond pointedly used acrylic pigment, not fabric dye, to apply color, because for her the braided rug was a support for the painting; this refusal to adopt rug-making techniques whole cloth further hybridizes the works as craft, painting, and sculpture.

Their large scale (another quality hard to capture in a photograph) makes them different from "real" rag rugs in other ways. It is crucial that the *Floorpieces* are exaggerated and outsized. Hammond's tight coiling method has rendered them firmer and more rigid than actual rugs, and at about five feet in diameter each and almost two inches in height, they are too thick to comfortably walk upon. To step from the bare floor onto one of these awkwardly elevated surfaces would cause a slight stutter in gait. In photographic documentation, the works shift from circular in shape to oval—they are difficult to comprehend *as round* unless one is standing directly on them looking down, which is not permitted by the protocols of the work. One cannot see them head on but rather must view them obliquely; they thus skew or bend perception.

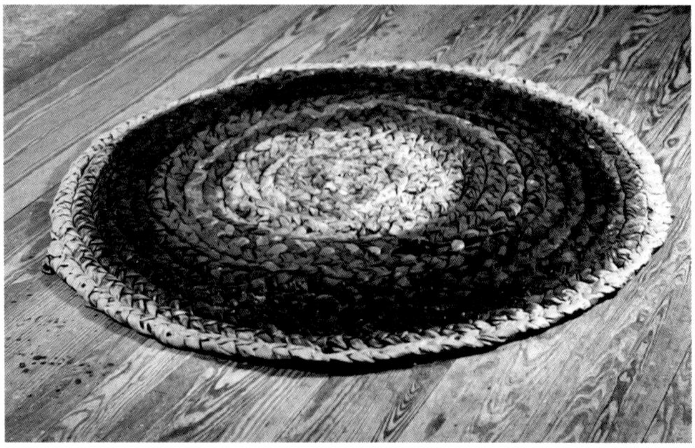

Fig. 1.27. Harmony Hammond, *Floorpiece I*, cloth and acrylic, 52" diameter, 1973. Art © Harmony Hammond / Licensed by VAGA, New York, NY.

Hammond's first *Floorpiece*, which the artist considers transitional and has not shown publicly, illustrates somewhat more clearly how her sculptures differ from regular rag rugs (fig. 1.27). Still experimenting with an earth-toned palette, she painted this piece with the same muted tans and browns used in her 1972 *Presences* series, the large-scale cloth bodies that immediately preceded her move to the floor (she has described her textile work from these few years as increasingly succumbing to gravity as it dripped down from the *Presences* to yield to the plane of the ground).[120] In *Floorpiece I* the acrylic paint is stiff, almost leathery, as it is heavily layered on top of the fabric, and the form has been unified by the allover color into a series of concentric circles. By contrast, in the remaining, fully realized five works of the series, Hammond respected the patterns of the found rags themselves—the way her spiraling misaligned the various rows of fabric, the arbitrary designs made by braiding.[121] After *Floorpiece I* Hammond began to only selectively paint the surfaces of the works, using the pigment to accentuate the fabrics' colors or to clarify their edges or boundaries; each has surfaces marked by painted and unpainted passages.

Thus it is not quite right when Blake Gopnik writes in his 2006 review of the *High Times, Hard Times* exhibit that Hammond's works "borrowed intact" techniques of fabric art, as they were "laid out on the gallery floor rather like a circular rag rug." He continues, "Almost exactly like a rag rug, in fact. Folk art gave Hammond access to an informality and modesty that earlier, prissier abstraction had avoided . . . [as she was] making objects that barely register as more than slight conceits, modestly realized."[122] "Almost exactly like a rag rug"—the painted passages and the thickness register here as very subtly taking the forms away from their utilitarian cousins, to the point of near disappearance. Note the coded gendered language of Gopnik's review: the word *modest* is used twice—not to mention *prissy*. To the contrary, immodesty, shamelessness, and vulgarity are flaunted in these works, especially as they exist in tension with their own restraint and handcrafted "hominess." Hammond's insistence on fusing art and textile craft and her repositioning of painting at ground level are strident, not modest, gestures—assertively feminist and complexly queer. She contests the primacy of verticality by insisting on horizontality as active rather than passive.

What did the horizontal composition of the *Floorpieces* mean to Hammond? Her description of her process—"I would literally sit on the floor in the center of one of the pieces, coiling the fabric, pushing it out from the center to fill a space and create a circular boundary"[123]—reflects, first of all, her growing interest in martial arts. She took up aikido in 1973, the same year she made the *Floorpieces*, and the discipline's emphasis on channeling spirals of energy has been central to her work ever since. Like the work of many feminists of the time, who were concerned with reclaiming space, the braided works grew larger to mark out an ever-wider area. Further, this creation of a circular space drew upon her contemporary investment in feminist consciousness-raising, a process she describes as going around "the proverbial circle."[124] In fact, the *Floorpieces* were first shown in January 1974 in the show *A Woman's Group* at the Nancy Hoffman Gallery in New York. The exhibition included work made by women in Hammond's feminist art and consciousness-raising group, including Louise Fishman, Patsy Norvell, and Jenny Snider, although little of it had direct reference to the issues they discussed.

In figure 1.28, an installation shot from that 1974 show, *Floorpiece IV* with its large white center is seen in relation to wall works by Hammond that explored methods of weaving and interlacing, including her oil-on-canvas work *Oval Braid*. Each artist had her own delimited area of the exhibition; though the artists had created their pieces in awareness of each other's art, the art itself did not intermix in the show. The exhibition was framed within the context of feminist politics, but those politics were far from obvious. As Hammond has reflected, "Like the early work of many women my age my work was personal. But we learned to hide this aspect for fear that the work would be ignored or ridiculed. . . . So we hid our sources and disguised the

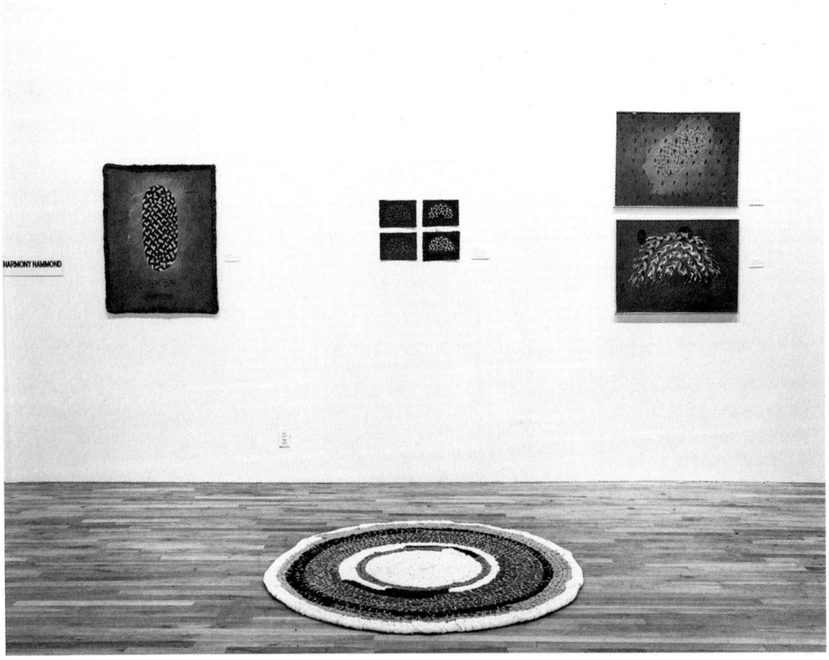

Fig. 1.28. Installation of Harmony Hammond's *Floorpiece IV*, cloth and acrylic, 56" diameter, in *A Woman's Group*, Nancy Hoffman Gallery, New York, 1974. Art © Harmony Hammond / Licensed by VAGA, New York, NY.

meaning of our imagery in formal concerns."[125] One result of this "disguising" was an engagement with abstraction that is thick with metaphor and layered with shades of meaning. Hammond's investments in formalism—and in metaphor—help untangle how the *Floorpieces* are bound up in queerness, even if that queerness was not overtly legible.

Some of the earliest reviews of the *Floorpieces* took them to be unproblematic instances of "mere" craft, ignoring their painterly verve, or described them (incorrectly) as "circular hooked rugs."[126] They are only briefly mentioned, rarely described or analyzed. One of the longer considerations of them came when Carter Ratcliff wrote in 1976:

> Some of Harmony Hammond's recent works—her *Floor Pieces* [*sic*] in the form of rag rugs, for example—looked very much like the products of women who hadn't arrived at a feminist self-consciousness. These "rugs" were, of course, rescued from being seen that way by the artist's choice to exhibit them in art galleries during a period when the art world was filled, as it still is, with discussions of feminist issues.[127]

He went on to declare, "Not everyone recognized Hammond's ironies." As this passage demonstrates, textile politics in the early 1970s were fraught around gendered issues of the denigration of craft and high–low hierarchies, which were inverted in what Ratcliff refers to as Hammond's "ironies." Because the *Floorpieces* were not seen as different enough from their source material of rag rugs, they could only be "ironic," rather than genuine homages to a material form that has been significantly altered. Feminist writers too were critical of Hammond's project, as when Judith Barry and Sandy Flitterman-Lewis discussed how the "valorization of crafts . . . can be seen as an essentialist position" and dismissed Hammond as a "pattern painter" whose work was not as "tough," or as theoretically advanced, as that of Jackie Winsor.[128] Rather than applauding her use of textile craft, such critics believed that the structural sexism intrinsic to domestic handmaking could not be overcome or resignified. These responses demonstrate how Hammond's use of textiles was often perceived as nostalgic, regressive, or essentializing.

Queer Spaces

Hammond has written: "I came out as a lesbian artist—meaning the two are connected and affect each other."[129] Created as Hammond was beginning to realize her lesbianism and proclaim it (to herself and to others), the *Floorpieces* are now widely acknowledged as her breakthrough pieces. The tactility of the works and the act of physically making them were crucial to this breakthrough; she had to bodily enact the various handiworks of braiding, spiraling, stitching, and painting. Hammond writes, "I find that materials which suggest direct hand manipulation . . . seem to carry with them sexual references."[130] This new exploration of bodily processes connected her work to onanistic sensuality, as she aligned making by hand with "touching oneself" and reveled in the "heightened erotic sense" she felt in her studio.[131] The corporeal process of making the works in 1973 was aligned, then, with the simultaneously deepening awareness of her own desires, desires that included same-sex attractions.

Importantly, the *Floorpieces* are not hooked—nor knit, woven, or crocheted—but *braided*. The braid for Hammond is a potent carrier of queer identity; as she wrote in the introduction to her book *Lesbian Art in America*, "I like to think of lesbian art as a braid with three strands, gender, sexuality, and art, though from time to time other stands, such as history or identity, are woven in and out."[132] The three strands of the braid invoke what I want to argue is for her a radical queer "third space"—an orientation beyond the heteronormative binary.[133] So, too, does braiding evoke for Hammond a kind of power in collectivity; she writes, "The strands remain discrete, but the final braid is stronger than any one strand—how's that for metaphor!"[134] For Hammond, the braid is a multifaceted symbol for lesbian community formations, which are famous for their enmeshments and entanglements.

Unconnected to any head and lying flat on the ground, the *Floorpieces* suggest piles of cut-off braids. According to Paul Eli Ivey, "In 1974, after a devastating fire in the her Bowery loft, [Hammond] cut off her long hair. Her new crew cut was a cleansing, a visual sign of chance in her life, and a proclamation of her gender and lesbian sexuality."[135] Hammond has continued to use hair as a substitute for bodies as well as words. In *Speaking Braids*, from 2000–2002, a hemp braid emerges from the mouth of a bronze woman's head, projecting like a tongue, an elaborately woven sentence (fig. 1.29). The braid tumbling onto the ground in a loose circle connects this work back to the coiled *Floorpieces* as it heaps up around a sculptural element that resembles a book. As charged bearers of sexual codes, the braid, the crew cut, and the bald head all signify or "speak."

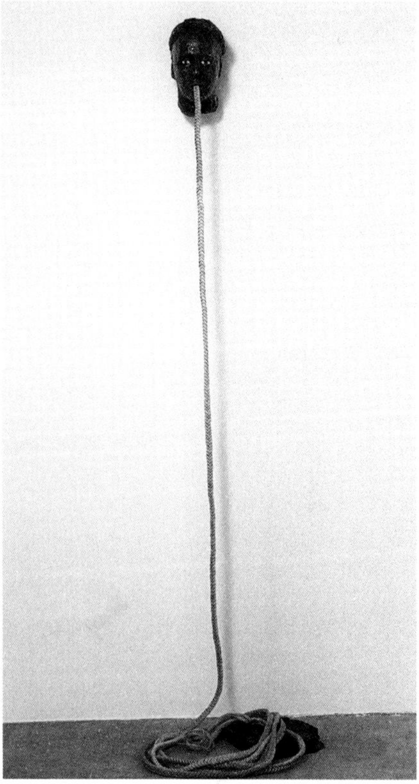

Fig. 1.29. Harmony Hammond, *Speaking Braids*, bronze, acrylic, hemp, and wax. 83 × 22 × 22", 2000–2002. Art © Harmony Hammond / Licensed by VAGA, New York, NY.

For Hammond, the spiral form of the *Floorpieces* was also significantly gendered, and in later works it became an animated female figure. In her 1982 painting *My Little Fan Lady*, the spiral is a woman, and the artist has referred to this motif as a "spinning spinster"[136] (fig. 1.30). As this phrase indicates, Hammond is a keen wordsmith who frequently employs double meanings. The Fan Lady encapsulates Hammond's use of spirals and braids as erotic female stand-ins, as well as her irreverent wordplay: "A woman who whirls and twirls and turns things upside down. Wrapping/spiral. The spiral of the oval braids and floorpieces is the spiraling of the wrapped shapes. The spiral becomes Fan Lady's body . . . Insidious. Outrageous. She goes where she wants and opens herself up. She does not take herself too seriously."[137]

Beyond the queer indeterminacy of the "third term" of the lesbian braid, Hammond suggests that a spiral is suggestive of female sexuality, as it is one continuous line that autoerotically folds back in on itself, a formulation that mirrors French feminist Luce Irigaray's theory of the "two lips" of the female "sex which is not one."[138] As mentioned, the gratifications wrought by the spiraling action were integral to Hammond's process of making and related to other pleasures; as she has written, "I think it is highly significant that in private conversation many women artists will mention that they frequently masturbate and enjoy masturbating in their studios and in the process of working."[139] The braided spiral becomes a metaphor for self-touching as well as for touching a realm beyond the distinctions

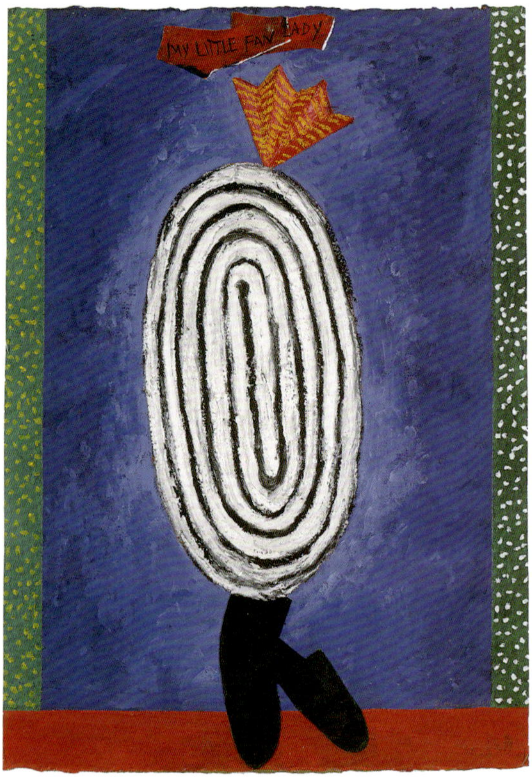

Fig. 1.30.
Harmony Hammond, *My Little Fan Lady*, acrylic and oil crayon on paper, 30 × 20¼", 1982. Collection: Jo Ann Teter. Art © Harmony Hammond / Licensed by VAGA, New York, NY.

between self and other. While Hammond was coming out, she began seeking models that moved beyond binary divides. She was drawn to the work of French feminist Monique Wittig, in particular her novel *The Lesbian Body*.[140] Written in 1973 in vividly corporeal language, Wittig's experimental novel plays with language and dismantles the rigid boundaries between its subjects, to suggest an indeterminacy between the *I* and the *you* as well as the *he* and the *she*. Hammond's spiraling three-strand braids indicate that she was formally drawn to the imaginative possibilities opened up by this queer thirdness.[141]

It is worth noting that braiding itself has long had gendered connotations. In Sigmund Freud's 1933 lecture on femininity, he discussed what he singled out as the premiere women's contribution to the history of civilization—indeed, the "one technique which they may have invented"—the processes of weaving and plaiting. These activities stemmed, in his thesis, from penis envy, as women's shame—what he called "a feminine characteristic *par excellence*"—drove them to try to braid their pubic hair together to conceal their "genital deficiency."[142] (Women's textile activity was further connected to their "pliancy," a kind of bodily teachability, which Freud saw as endemic to femininity.)[143] While positing braiding as an anxious compensatory activity for the lack of the penis is ludicrous, for many lesbians the notion of a stand-in phallus is not necessarily offensive (recall Allison's lover with her stuffed glove finger). Hands, tongues, and dildos can be eagerly pressed into service as queer surrogates; they do not imply replacement or substitute penises in place of "lack" but rather indicate the invention of new tools. Maybe Freud was onto something with his sexualization of women's textile handwork: one definition of craft is "skill in making or doing things, especially by hand." This could be a line from a women-seeking-women personal ad; many lesbians take pride in their dexterity in erotically "doing things" (that is to say, to other women) "by hand."

Might the *Floorpieces* be understood as *burlesques* of rag rugs—or better, rugs in drag, like a partially made-up queen whose fabulous makeup sits somewhat unevenly on the surface of her face? Like that of the Cockettes, this drag exaggerates in order to undo, highlighting the "rugness" of the hybrid sculptural object. Think of how the paint on the rugs, like drag makeup, emphasizes, limns, or edges; in fact, Anna Chave has called the *Floorpieces*' bright reds and blues "gaily colored."[144] Sontag understands one mode of camp as a way of seeing the world in quotes: "It's not a lamp but a 'lamp'; not a woman but a 'woman.'"[145] Similarly, the *Floorpieces* are "rugs," not rugs. Understanding Hammond as camp puts a different, queer spin on the presumed essential femininity taken for granted in the comparisons between her and Carl Andre. The *Floorpieces* parodically inhabit that feminine stereotype to such excess that any suggestion of essence collapses. Hammond heightened some clichés of women's art to the point of ultimately triumphant absurdity, as if to say: if you think what we do is crafty and low, I'll show you just how crafty and low I can be. By performatively citing the rag rug but then skewing it and thwarting its utilitarian purpose, the works point to a new understanding of the queer potential of textile craft as practiced by Hammond, to transgress the oppositions of "authentic" versus "sham," functionality versus decoration, private versus public, furniture versus art.

In the catalogue of the 2007 exhibition *WACK! Art and the Feminist Revolution*, curator Helen Molesworth writes about the marginalization of feminist abstraction, while artist Catherine Lord discusses the invisibility of lesbian art within feminism.[146] Despite the recent smattering of attention given to Hammond's *Floorpieces*, the works still hover beneath the sightline of most histories of art—not only because they are feminist abstractions (Molesworth), or because they are lesbian (Lord), but also because they are indebted to vocabularies of textile craft. Hammond's crafty lesbian abstraction, that is, faces a triple erasure compounded by her use of widely denigrated folk techniques. By recuperating the *Floorpieces* as flat sculptures or as pure citations of domestic objects, critics have ignored the subtle distortions (including use of paint and outsized scale) that make them both craft and noncraft.

The works themselves thematize and trope that invisibility. Lesbian writer Jill Johnston wrote in 1972, "Recently a prominent feminist told me 'we want to sweep the lesbian issue under the rug.'"[147] This metaphor crops up again in a review of Hammond's groundbreaking survey book *Lesbian Art in America*, published in 2000: "Lesbian artists have been swept under the rug of history—but a thought-provoking new book seeks to give them their due."[148] Hammond's *Floorpieces* literalize the metaphor of the rug as a secret place where dirt is gathered and hidden. The language of sweeping things "under the rug" activates a sense of domestic space and invisibility that is similar, perhaps, to the metaphor of the closet (also a dark enclosed place where things are meant to be kept out of sight). Closets and rugs and other queer domestic sites—with the *Floorpieces*, the spatial dimension of the sculptures matters, as they delineate an area or an arena for action; this is worldmaking as placemaking.

Speaking Euphemistically

The *Floorpieces* are polyvalent utterances, as all artworks are, and one thing they might propose is a coded "talking back" to a straight feminist aversion to emerging lesbian sensibilities. Lesbian handiwork explodes one persistent assumption about craft as rooted in the primarily straight, domestic sphere and made in relation to "men's" work. Lesbian art critic Laura Cottingham critiqued the 1995 exhibition *Division of Labor*, which included Hammond's work, for the way that it "heterosexualizes the feminist art movement"; its overarching representation of women thematizing housework meant that they were exclusively "cast as men's domestic servants, housekeepers, and wives."[149] What happens, Cottingham asks, when craft is removed from that connotation, when the domestic is not predicated on a male–female divide? She raises important questions about the marginalization of lesbians from a feminist art history that has become increasingly consolidated. While most lesbians in the 1970s were feminists, some straight feminists saw themselves at odds with lesbian concerns. Betty Friedan was quoted in the *New York Times Magazine* in 1973 as saying that lesbians were at the center of a CIA plot to infiltrate and discredit the National Organization for Women, in an article titled "Up from the Kitchen Floor" (suggested movement away from and against the lowly domestic).[150] The so-called lavender menace threatened at times to splinter the feminist movement.

These are conditions under which the *Floorpieces* were made—a time not long after the 1969 Stonewall rebellion when declarations of lesbianism could be treated with suspicion or outright hostility, when announcing one's homosexuality could have negative repercussions in one's family life and workplace. Yet Hammond's coming-out story is not dominated by secrecy or repression. Beginning in the early 1970s, Hammond has played an active, vocal role in shaping both feminist and lesbian art history. To list just some of her artistic activism: she was a founder of the alternative women's co-operative gallery AIR and was one of the first AIR members to come out; she was also one of the openly lesbian board members of the collective that published *Heresies: A Feminist Publication on Art and Politics*. Since the 1970s she has advocated for lesbian visibility, and she curated the first US lesbian art exhibition, in 1978, at 112 Green Street, called *A Lesbian Show*, which consisted mostly of abstract work. The show was in some respects difficult to organize, as many lesbian artists were too afraid of discrimination and stereotyping to participate; in the introduction to the exhibit's accompanying publication (a photocopied and stapled compilation of artists' statements), Hammond wrote that due to "the attitudes in this society towards lesbians, there were some women who felt that they could not participate, and some were forced to withdraw."[151]

Hammond's own contribution to this publication continues her work with the braided form: a drawing of an elongated oval is placed in the center of a page dense with handwritten notes. The text states, in part, "I know that . . . being a lesbian is connected to my art making. I also know I don't understand it. Perhaps I am afraid of it. It is not simply a matter of imagery . . . more likely its [sic] our approach to making art" (fig. 1.31). She has conjectured that throughout *A Lesbian Show*, explicitly sexual content may have been rechanneled into allusion and abstraction along with a direct and bodily engagement with materials. As she wrote in 1978, "I believe there is something as yet undefinable in my work, and other work that we might call 'lesbian sensibility,' but for the most part it is hidden."[152]

Queer codes and gossip have long been important for queer epistemologies.[153] With Hammond's "undefinable" sensibilities in mind, I suggest that along with gossip, the related concept of *euphemism* is a vital way of spreading queer knowledge: gay men and lesbians were forced to speak in code among ourselves, for example, indicating lesbian relationships with terms like *sisters*, *dear friends*, or *companions*. Queerness often employs sexual puns, and an in-language flourishes within communities bracing themselves against hostility. Since Hammond's floor-bound works treat horizontality as a different, sexualized orientation, the *Floorpieces* could be euphemistic for "going down"—oral sex between women—thus resonating as visual lesbian slang, one not meant to be visible to the entire population but made legible within specific subcultural contexts.

Hammond has said that museums often want to show her works hung on walls, but she is insistent that they stay on the ground. *Going down*, *rug licking*, *carpet munching*, and other coded lingo for oral sex between women render this horizontality and lowness specifically lesbian. Given the unofficial, "underground" nature of such lingo, it is difficult to know exactly which of these terms were in circulation in the early 1970s; "going down" certainly was.[154] Lesbian language has been even less documented than gay male slang, which was collated into the first queer English dictionary, *The Queen's Vernacular: A Gay Lexicon*, published in 1972.[155] That dictionary is not an ideal resource for researching lesbian-specific terms, because, as was noted at the time, "one must speak of a 'gay community' with caution, since only the most fragile bonds link the lives of lesbians with those of gay men."[156] Hammond's "rugs"—also slang for the female pubic region—exemplify the sexual vulgar-

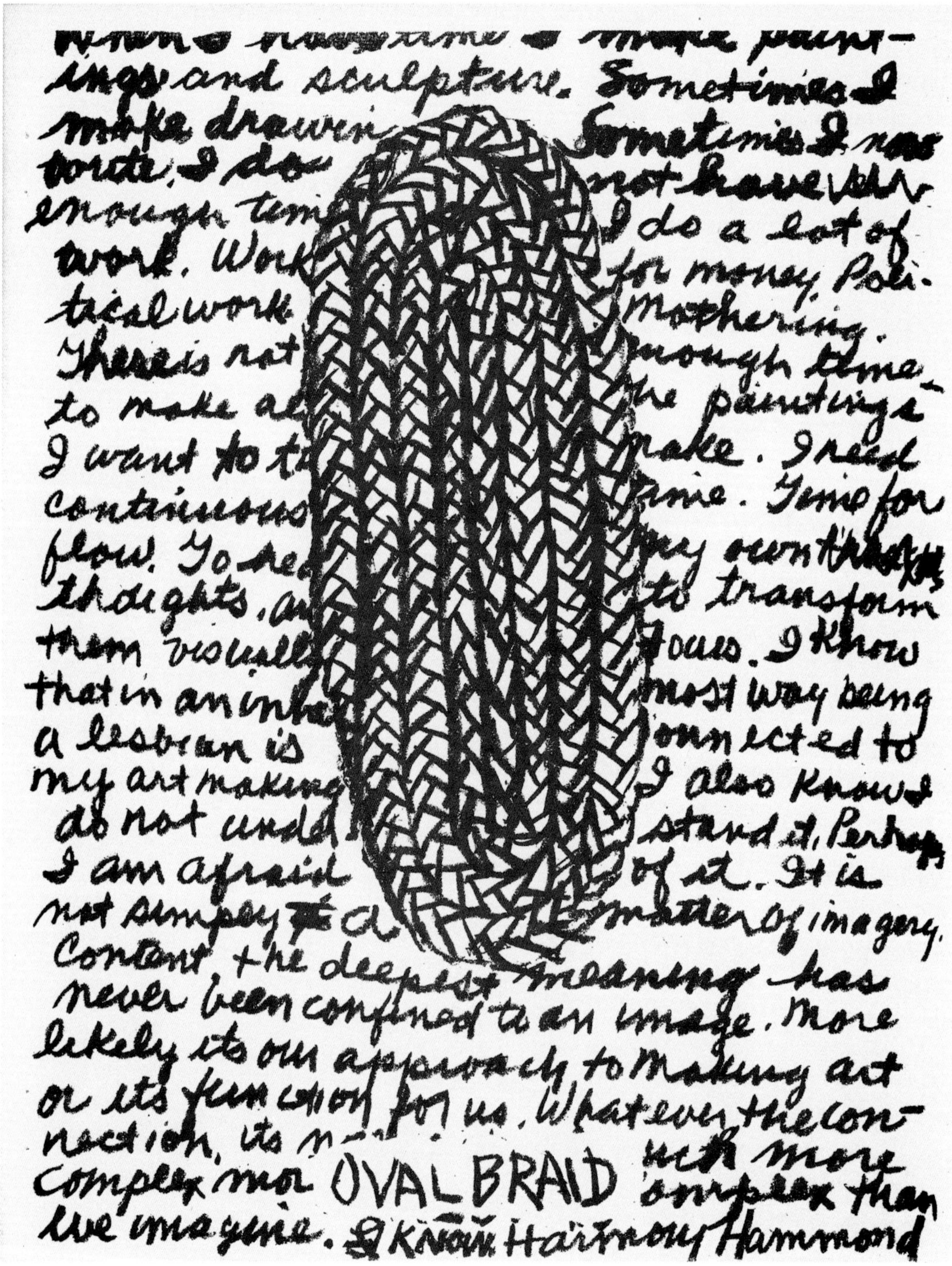

Fig. 1.31. Harmony Hammond, contribution to *Statements by Lesbian Artists*, exhibition catalogue for *A Lesbian* Show, 112 Greene Street Workshop, New York, 1978. Image courtesy of the artist and White Columns, New York. Art © Harmony Hammond / Licensed by VAGA, New York, NY.

ity of much "central core" imagery in feminist art. (Judy Chicago's *The Dinner Party*, with its elaborately designed cunts on plates, has likewise been seen as reference to "eating out" a woman.)[157] The slang could be seen as derogatory or demeaning but is also cunningly reclaimed and resignified.

Hammond's abstractions thus operate on some level as dense and elaborate visual puns; in her hands, nonfiguration becomes queer euphemism. These rag rugs have an understated yet wicked and knowing humor. The *Floorpieces* could function as jokes about embarrassing female bodily processes: being *on the rag*, for instance, is a euphemism for menstruation. They also slyly burlesque the alignment of women with passivity and floor-based textiles. Horizontality is not just lesbian-specific; it is the primary position of women in art history, as evidenced by the ubiquity of the odalisque or reclining nude. With their defiant, even shameless lying down, the *Floorpieces* also prefigure the flip in orientation suggested when the feminist journal *Off Our Backs* spawned a counter publication, *On Our Backs*, in 1984. The upright stance implied by the title *Off Our Backs* was sassily laid low by the lesbian porn magazine, which implied that horizontality need not be a position of powerlessness.

Class Matters / Race Matters

While Hammond's *Floorpieces* are inextricable from issues of sexuality, they are also bound up in economic questions and questions of race. Hammond's decision to leave her artwork-cum-rug on the floor took place within a wider reconsideration of the place of women's textile craft, one that is fundamentally connected to class and race. Hammond herself broached these connections in her 1977 article "Class Notes," published in the "Lesbian Art and Artists" issue of *Heresies*. In this text she puts her "lower middle class background" in dialogue with her queerness. She argues, contentiously, that since lesbians often (but not universally) have less access to capital and have less class privilege than do straight women, who can "marry up" to men who earn higher wages, few have had the time or resources to make art. Of course, a number of out lesbian artists who preceded the era of gay liberation were independently wealthy; not so Hammond, and her lower-middle-class status was implicated in her use of found rags. As a white single mom in the 1970s with limited funds, she scrounged for materials, enacting her own version of trashmaking.

"Class Notes" calls for the explosion of "esthetic hierarchies" such as good and bad taste.[158] As Lucy Lippard has commented, traditional handiwork like quiltmaking is not just at the bottom of the high–low, art–craft division, for "there are also 'high' crafts and 'low' ones," freighted with different levels of respectability.[159] For instance, the rhythmic opticality produced by the *Floorpieces'* integration of form and pattern recalls the target-like colors of Sonia Delaunay, as seen in the tapestry *Syncopé* from 1970 (fig. 1.32). Beginning in the early twentieth century, Delaunay was at the forefront of artists blurring the line between fine art and crafts such as textiles, rugs, and costume design. Yet Delaunay's crafts were always dignified by their association with her painting and other fine art practices. Destined for decorative arts museums or a collector's walls, such woven Aubusson tapestries are examples of "high craft." "Low craft," by contrast, is classed as "middlebrow" and usually put into service as a functional object. It is often gendered female (though craft can be gendered at both high and low registers, depending on medium, format, etc.).

While Hammond's use of the braided rug form stemmed in part from genuine practicality, it is reductive and anachronistic to think of the *Floorpieces* simply as manifestations of thrift. The 1970s were not the pioneer days, or even the 1940s, when the expediencies of wartime economy led to a national obsession with frugality. In the World War II era, countless newspaper and magazine articles urged women to recycle used stockings or discarded neckties into braided rugs. But by the early 1960s it was just as cheap, and definitely quicker and more convenient, to buy a factory-made rug than to make one. Sylvia Plath's *The Bell Jar*, published in 1963, makes this point:

> Once when I visited Buddy I found Mrs. Willard braiding a rug out of strips of wool from Mr. Willard's old suits. She'd spent a week on that rug, and I had admired the tweedy browns and greens and blues patterning the braid, but after Mrs. Willard was through, instead of hanging the rug on the wall the way I would have done, she put it down in place of her kitchen mat, and in a few days it was soiled and dull and indistinguishable from any mat you could buy for under a dollar in the five and ten.[160]

Plath notes a generational shift away from utilitarian handmaking to the emerging field of hobbyist craft. Such a generational shift was already afoot in the years before second-wave feminism. Postwar industrialism, with its surplus of cheap manufactured material goods at the five and dime—or what Mike Davis calls the "overconsumption" stage in late capitalism—started in the early 1960s.[161] It was this economic shift, even more than second-wave feminism, that made it increasingly unlikely that well-off white women such as Plath's narrator would make a rag rug out of necessity.

In the immediate postwar decades, such handiwork began to signify a leisure-time activity whose product would be admired on the wall, rather

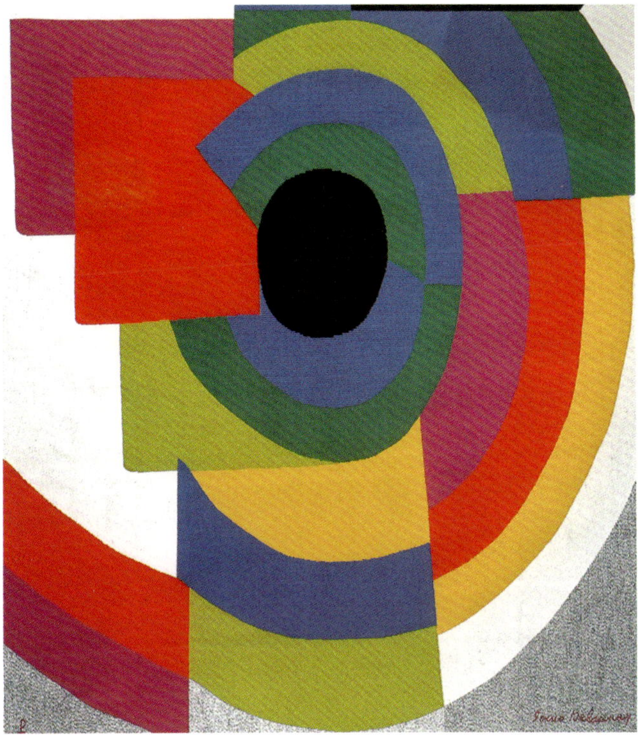

Fig. 1.32.
Sonia Delaunay, *Syncopé*, woven Aubusson tapestry, 77½ × 68⅞", 1970.

than the grind of domestic labor resulting in something to be dirtied underfoot. The women who would make such objects were increasingly unlikely to be working-class women who worked to make necessary goods for the home, and the domestic crafts become a middle-class free-time pursuit—in other words, a hobby. These years saw an upsurge in mass-market store-bought "make it yourself" kits—manufactured instructions and tools to assist with, simplify, or speed up the making of handmade objects. The kit-ification of "spare time" making has been referred to as the "deskilling" of craft, with a consumer base of presumably "heterosexual females living in a nuclear family unit."[162]

Paradoxically, as women entered the work force, many turned to domestic activities formerly coded as chores (such as knitting or rug making) not out of duty but for pleasure. For instance, the packaging for a hobby kit by the Henry Seligman Company gives its users the tools to make everything from hot pads to handbags using the traditional three-strand braiding technique (fig. 1.33). The instructions claim that if followed correctly, they will provide "hours of fun" at a great time saving over previous methods of making, which might require days or weeks. The graphic rendering of the rug-in-progress curiously echoes Hammond's Fan Lady, as the metal folders—wildly out of scale—become little legs that animate the braided form as if it might scurry

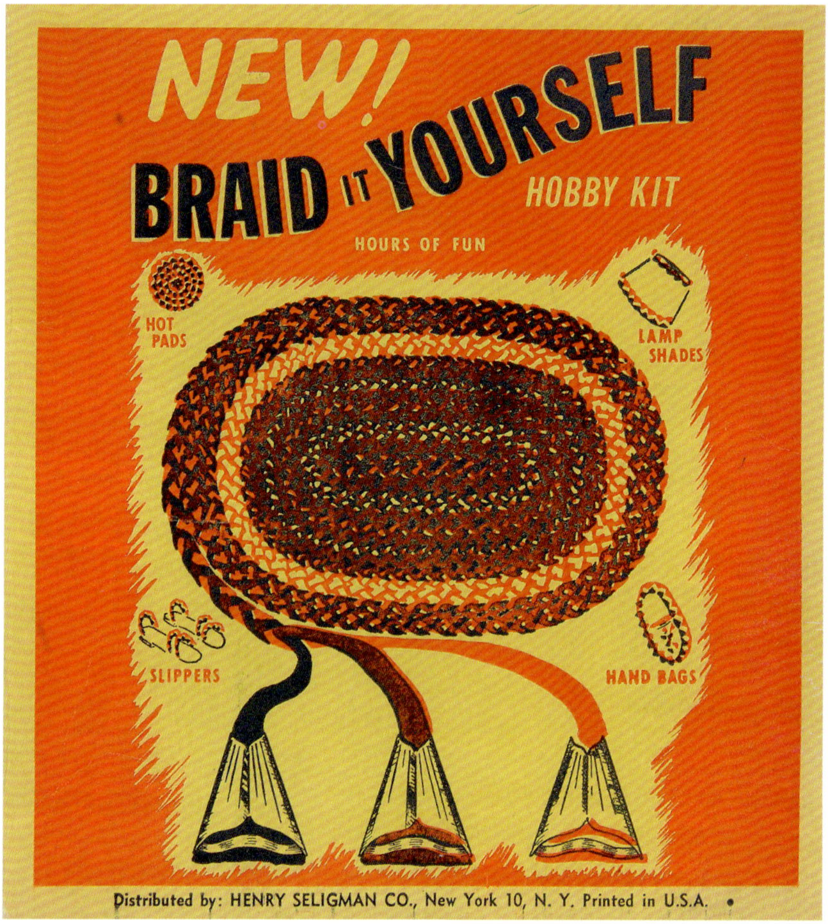

Fig. 1.33.
New! Braid It Yourself Hobby Kit, Henry Seligman Co., ca. 1950. Collection of the author.

away. Another kit, distributed by the Braiding Post in Atlantic City in 1948, advertises that with its "braid-eze" folders—called "marvelous new machines" though they are not remotely mechanical—it is "easy" to make a rug in a day. (The braiding, however, is the quickest work in making such rugs, as one must first assemble uniform strips of fabric and then, as the rug is in process, periodically stitch the coiling strands together with strong thread so that the rug lies flat.) In other kits and instruction books in the 1940s and 1950s, braided rugs both oval and round are shown with names such as the Florissant (a town in Missouri and French for *flourishing*), emphasizing their regional and aspirational flavor.

Because making rag rugs has been considered a "mundane" activity for children, women, and the infirm, it has fallen somewhat out of traditional accounts of history, though it is well documented in material culture studies.[163] As the 1973 short publication *The Braided Rug: Our American Heritage* announces, braided rag rugs were understood as a distinctly American formation, dating back to the colonial era (but were not, in these accounts, necessarily connected to Native craft traditions).[164] However, braiding likely emerged slightly later than that, between 1830 and 1850, and became common both in America and in England, though "more braided rugs were made in North America than the British Isles."[165] By the mid-nineteenth century, easily movable rugs (as distinct from larger carpets) were found in homes throughout most of the United States, and rag rugs made of scraps by women "adorned the hearths and hallways of even the poor."[166] Important to this history is the Colonial Revival within the United States, which started around the 1876 Centennial International Exhibition in Philadelphia and peaked in the 1920s, canonizing the spinning wheel and other domestic handmade textiles as symbols of Americana.[167] Handmade rugs surged in popularity along with the rise of the textile industry, and newly available store-bought fabric meant a sudden surplus of cloth for garments as well as for rugs.[168]

In the 1930s the Great Depression created national pressure to salvage and reuse materials, including textiles. Yet these pressures were exerted somewhat differently, inflected by region and race. A photograph taken in 1938 at the Lakeview Project in Arkansas shows four young African American women braiding rag rugs with a pile of rags snaked together on a wooden table and braided rounds already begun on the left-hand side (fig. 1.34). (The Library of Congress labels this image "Pupils at school making rag rugs.")

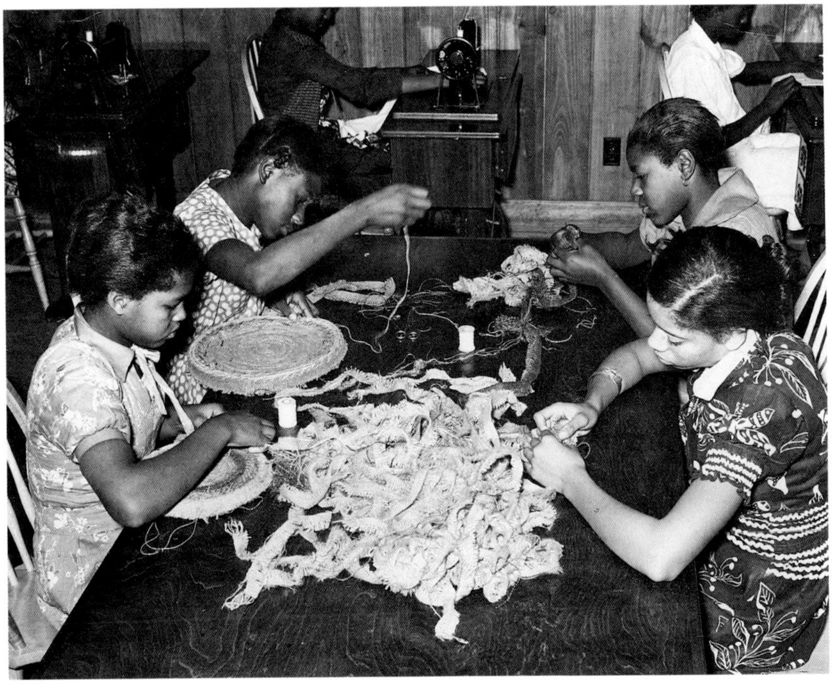

Fig. 1.34. Russell Lee, *Rag Rug Making, Lakeview Project, FSA*, 1938. Courtesy of the Drapkin Collections.

Absorbed in their work, they attend to thread, strip, and coil, while behind them other students sit at a row of sewing machines. The photograph depicts an atmosphere of diligence and focus, with much visual interest provided by the patterned elements on the makers' cotton-shift dresses. Taken by white photographer Russell Lee under the auspices of the Farm Security Administration, the image was carefully framed to show the Lakeview Project—a site of forced relocation in which black farmers and sharecroppers were collectively "resettled" to maximize the "efficiency" of their land—in a positive light. These photos traveled in exhibitions that depicted the resettlement projects in a "determinedly upbeat, determinedly safe" manner.[169] Note that the chosen activities for this deceptively sunny photograph are braiding and sewing, activities that signify "respectable" and appropriately gendered work; the rag rug here functions within a wider representational strategy to visibly evidence the skills and productivity of black women. While Hammond employs the braided rag rug as a threshold object that pivots from high art to lower registers of making, the Lakeview students are depicted as if on the reverse path, using the rug as a device of upward mobility. Such a photograph serves as a reminder that textiles are always contingently situated in race, gender, and labor histories of material.

Within nineteenth-century literary works, rag rugs were understood as symbolizing, nostalgically, "a great and enduring simplicity of working-class life."[170] However, over the course of the twentieth century they also began to be associated with middle-class whiteness. A photograph from circa 1964–69 of a community education class at Elgin Community College in Illinois shows four primly dressed white women in the process of learning and making braided rugs.[171] In front of a cabinet labeled "triangles" and "t-squares" and perforated hardboard on which hang various wooden shapes (such tools align their class with a technical workshop rather than the quasi-domestic scene common to many "home economics" classrooms), the oldest, who might be the instructor, holds a narrow roll of fabric in her hands as her pupils are busy braiding with their hands. The roll indicates that they are not using cast-off rags but rather purchased uniform strips. With their rugs-in-process laid out on the table in front of them, the photograph presents an image of white suburban learning in a pedagogical setting and emphasizes that not all who came to rug making in this decade did so using kits.

Hammond did not grow up with such rugs in her Illinois house, not so far from the braided rug class in Elgin, and does not recall them being underfoot in her childhood. Instead, she taught herself braiding techniques from books as she immersed herself in research about basket making and women's weaving (her "weave drawings" of the early 1970s were based on this research). Such books might have included Helen Howard Feeley's *The Complete Book*

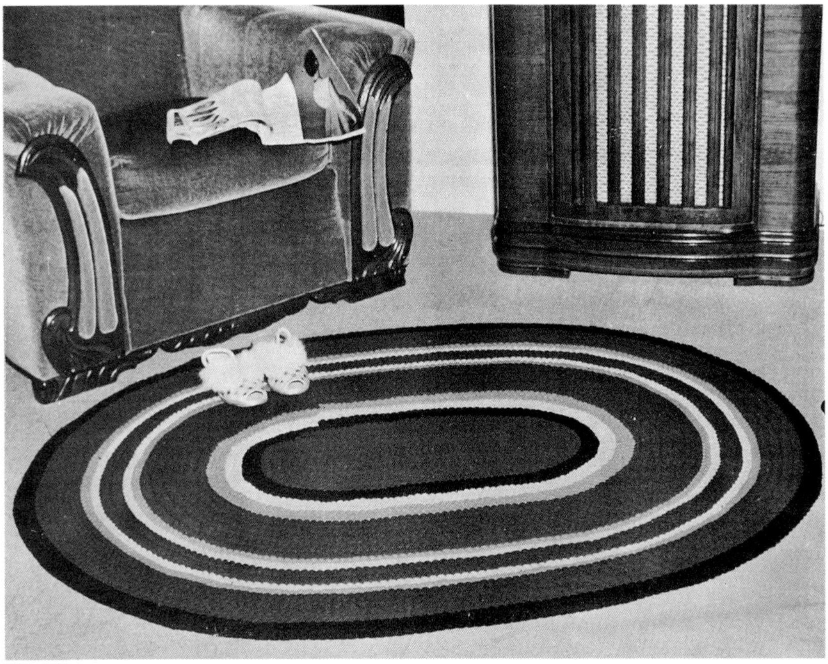

Fig. 1.35. "The Plymouth" rug design, from *How to Braid a Rug in One Day*, Nu-Flex Company, 1949. Collection of the author.

of Rug Braiding, from 1957, whose dust jacket shows a classic example next to a spinning wheel, as if to suggest an entire sensibility of frugality and textile homemaking in which the entire chain of production, from yarn to completed object, might be contained within a single room of the house. There are many such instruction guides for handmade rag rugs, including pamphlets dating back to the early twentieth century that showcased a variety of techniques (hooking was particularly popular).[172]

For many women in the postwar era of overconsumption in the United States, craft projects such as braided rugs offered a measure of hands-on control that was lacking in their jobs and were seen as a positive creative outlet. The instructional manual *How to Braid a Rug in One Day*, published by the Nu-Flex Company in 1949, describes braiding rugs as the "work of women" and "a happy work." It features photographs of some of the most popular designs in situ, including "The Plymouth," a name indelibly associated with US colonial histories (fig. 1.35). Here the rug is placed in an interior scene, demarcating a cozy area of domestic relaxation. A welcoming easy chair is set in the corner next to a wood-paneled radio. The (presumably female) spectator is beckoned into this scene of comfortable bourgeois leisure—distinct from its earlier evocation of nonwhite and/or working-class scrappiness—with a magazine left open to an image of a fashion model, and a pair of house slippers waiting on the edge of the rug. The rug's contrasting rings of light and dark pick up the wooden detailing of both the chair and the radio, and its design bears a strong formal resemblance to the photodocumentation of Hammond's *Floorpiece VI* as it skews from round to oval.

Comparing her art with this photo reminds us of the distance between her museum-sited works with their applications of paint and the space of the home. Yet the similarities between Hammond's piece and this handmade rug also demonstrate that she was in dialogue with white middle-class hobby culture as well as indebted to the traditional "high" crafts such as Delaunay's tapestries (not to mention her debts to fine arts textile-based abstraction such as the unpainted cotton duck of a Helen Frankenthaler canvas, the *thangka* paintings of Faith Ringgold, or the soft, drooping grids of Howardena Pindell). As has been suggested, other histories of the rag rug situate the *Floorpieces* in an oblique, unresolved conversation with Native basketmaking, sweatshop factory work, and working-class African American textiles. In addition, they participated in a wider interest in rugs produced with all types of techniques at that moment. A seminal show dedicated to US rug traditions, *Hooked Rugs in the Folk Art Tradition*, was mounted at New York's Museum of American Folk Art in 1974—the same year Hammond's braided "rugs" were on display at the Nancy Hoffman Gallery—further indicating that fine arts and folk visibilities often mirror each other or coemerge.[173]

Hammond does not recall how long it took to make a given rug—"braiding doesn't take all that long"—but emphasizes that the entire coil, once complete, was stitched onto a fabric backing and then painted.[174] The *Floorpieces* carry within them the traces not only of industrial fabrication and mass waste but also of the labors of women's craft—the remnants, debris, and fragments of these histories that cannot be unraveled. The *Floorpieces*' reference to folk floor coverings, which starts quite literally with braiding rags, is thus not an ironic citation of the "low" but an earnest appreciation of this form of making in all its classed and raced cultural iterations. This leads us back to understanding Hammond's rugs as a sort of camp, for, according to Sontag, camp is the "genuine reveling in the base or the low," viewing bad objects with "a mode of enjoyment, of appreciation," and transforming them with something like love.[175]

The claim that Hammond's work implicitly refers to lesbian sexuality is open to debate, but there is no question that she experienced handmaking as a means of physical gratification that was motored by bodily desires and pleasures. It is a desire that, due to its falling out of favor within some circles of postwar art that eschewed such overt hands-on making, has been repressed. As analogous "illegitimate" passions in the 1970s, textile craft resonates yet again with queerness. The *Floorpieces* align handmaking with queer worldmaking to propose art as a disruptive and libidinal terrain and lay the ground for alternative identities within both domestic and institutional contexts.

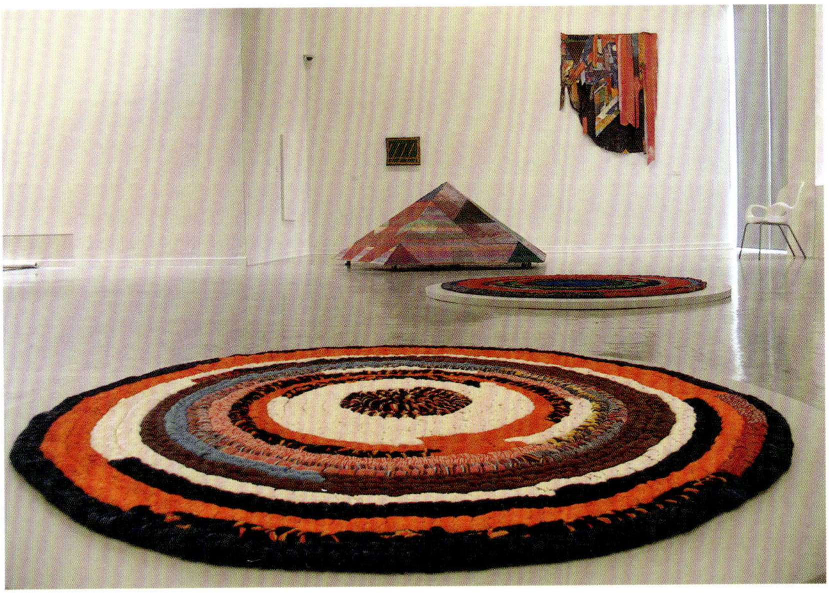

Fig. 1.36. Installation of Harmony Hammond's *Floorpieces*, *High Times, Hard Times*, Museo Tamayo Arte Contemporáneo, 2007. Independent Curators International. Art © Harmony Hammond / Licensed by VAGA, New York, NY.

In their ideal installation, Hammond envisions all five of the completed *Floorpieces* (not including the early transitional piece) together in one space with nothing on the walls. With this geometric configuration, they would move distinctly away from having domestic associations and instead would become a site-specific installation that holds the ground with its multiple spirals that activate negative space between the sculptures. If viewed together on the same plane, they would become relational, each spiral a distinct personage that might also refer to the leveling of difference within same-sex relationships or evoke a collective conversation vitally occupying the ground. Unfortunately, she has never been given the opportunity to display them this way. (As of this writing in 2016, she still owns all of these works.) Instead they are usually exhibited singly, in isolation from the rest of the series, or placed near wall-based works. Because of this, although they were originally exhibited directly on the floor, she now shows them on top of low, inch-and-a-half-high round platforms, preferably painted to match the gallery floor, so people do not accidentally trample on them as they back up to see the nearby wall work; this is how they were displayed in *High Times, Hard Times* (fig. 1.36).

Desiring Craft

After the catalyzing process of creating the *Floorpieces*, Hammond began making the geometric, abstract sculptures for which she is best known, such as *Duo* from 1980 (fig. 1.37). These ladderlike structures refer back to braids (there is a type of braid called a ladder braid), and their visceral bodily shapes also suggest interdependency, leaning in, and mutual support. (They also recall *The Ladder*, the magazine for the pre-Stonewall lesbian organization Daughters of Bilitis.) Two similar objects set side by side have come to obliquely signify homosexuality—from Jasper Johns's *Ale Cans* (1964) to Félix González-Torres's wall clocks in *Perfect Lovers* (1991)—and *Duo* echoes this abstract same-sex dynamic.[176] With their biomorphic skeletal armatures covered in soft cloth in an interplay between strong black and ruffled, frilly pink, *Duo*'s forms also allude to a butch–femme dynamic. Hammond undergoes a tactile, full-body process when making such sculptures (many of them are larger than life size), and there is a muscular eroticism to works like *Duo* with their swollen forms, ligatures, and obsessive bandaging. These are reminiscent of bodies described by Wittig, as in these forms Hammond seems to "build something out of itself, with its insides visible on the outside."[177]

In this work and others, Hammond continues to draw inspiration from textile craft techniques, but none of her other works have flaunted their crafty origins as flagrantly as the *Floorpieces*. Those were unique in her oeuvre, singularly unembarrassed about their debt to craft as well as their allusions to female bodily processes such as menstruation and lesbian sex that are often the source of shame and pleasure. Given this, they are also about vulnerability; they are paintings that could, after all, get stepped on. Within the *Floorpieces*, pleasure and desire, vulnerability, and a measure of shame about "inferior" status complexly bind queerness to textile craft.

Among artists and art historians alike, textile craft has been unfairly opposed to conceptual practices; in some scholarly circles it has been cast as a bad object choice, unworthy of serious contemplation. Despite cyclical embraces of craft within the art world, there is often a lingering taint of embarrassment about it as "low," a formation that is articulated through class and race as well as gender. The drive to get distance from craft is demonstrated in the decisions, in the 2000s, to excise the word from the names of the California College of Arts and Crafts (now the California College of the Arts) and the American Craft Museum (now the Museum of Arts and Design). (In a 2005 guerrilla installation, queer artist LJ Roberts placed a hand-knitted sign reading "& CRAFT" at the college's San Francisco campus as a defiant assertion of the ongoing importance of craft.) Yet many artists and art historians are recognizing that conceptually oriented art need not be separated from craft-based practices and that to utilize traditional handiwork techniques is not necessarily to nostalgically fetishize the touch of the artist's hand. Many younger queer artists have been influenced by Hammond's use of textile craft (as have some straight male artists like Mike Kelley, who used appropriated braided rugs extensively in his work). For instance, Fritz Haeg's

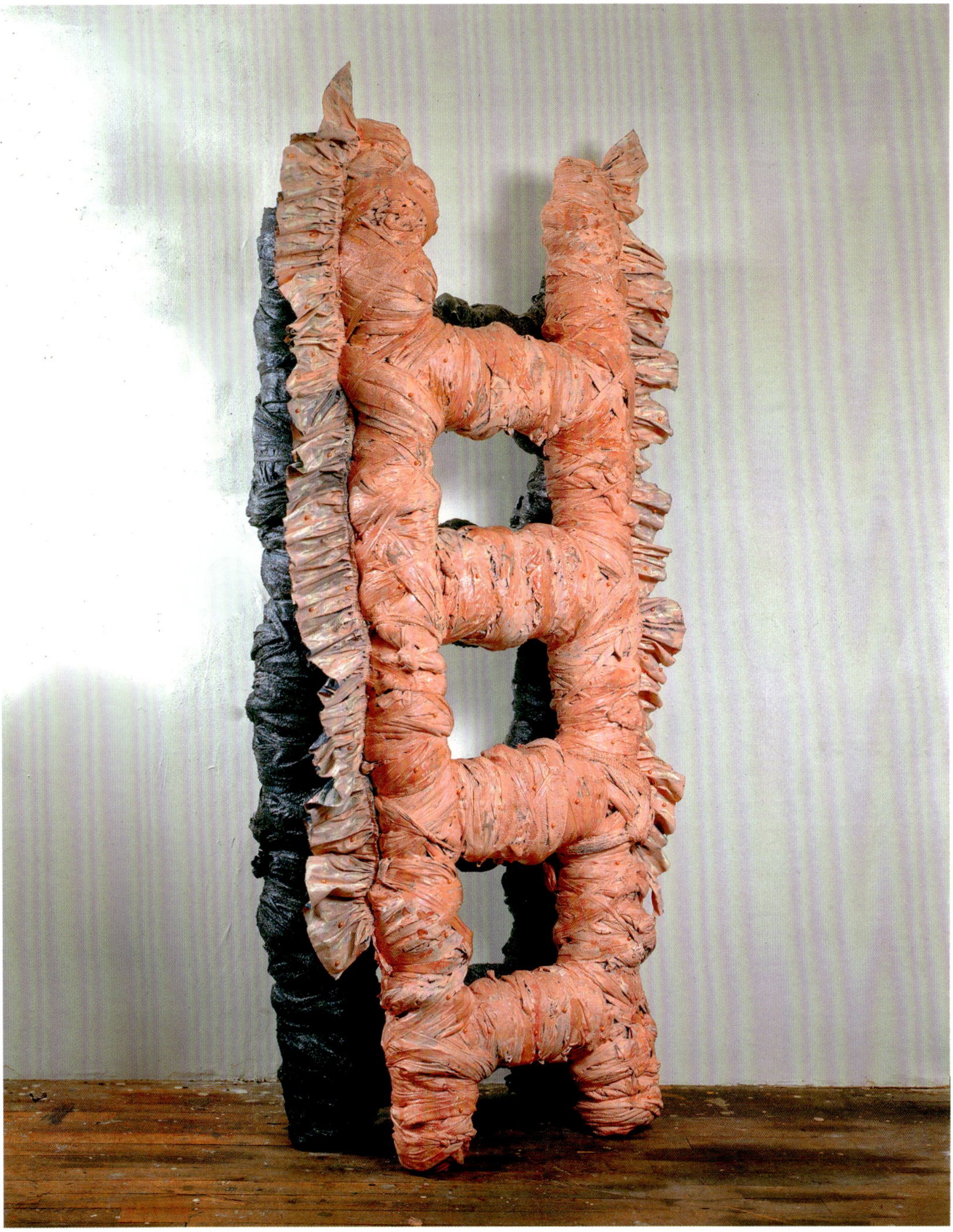

Fig. 1.37. Harmony Hammond, *Duo*, 1980, wood, cloth, gesso, acrylic, rhoplex, beads, and glitter, two units, 84 × 45″ each. Collection of the New Mexico Museum of Art. Gift of Judith Danziger, 2006. Art © Harmony Hammond / Licensed by VAGA, New York, NY.

monumentally sized, ever-growing, and participatory rag-rug project *Domestic Integrities* (2012–ongoing) incorporates rags from the locations to which it travels, and when it is displayed, viewers are invited to sit upon it as a way to create a sense of common ground or a shared social space.

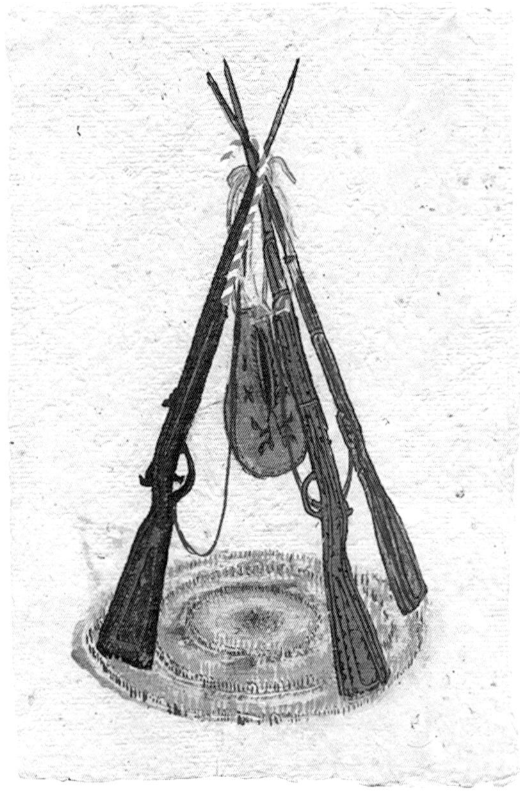

Fig. 1.38. Allison Smith, *Stack-Arms,* gouache and colored pencil on handmade recycled paper, 8.5″ × 5.5″, 2004, illustration of installation featuring coiled rug, handmade wood and aluminum guns, and a cloth bandanna. Courtesy of the artist and Haines Gallery, San Francisco.

To cite another example, a work by Allison Smith called *Stack-Arms* from 2004 features as its centerpiece a circular rag rug (seen in a drawing made of the installation: fig. 1.38). Smith's work refers to Civil War reenactments, among other interests; here, in a conscious homage to Hammond's *Floorpieces*, the rug becomes the foundation for a stack-arms formation of handmade guns, a configuration that indicates readiness for battle. Draped over the guns is a small handmade pouch. Based on the small pouches women carried before clothes had pockets, this historical object was distinctly queered by Smith as she made it out of a paisley bandanna. The bandanna refers to gay male flagging through the hanky code, the practice of men signaling their particular sexual desires by placing handkerchiefs of different colors in their back pockets, thereby rendering those desires visible in spaces of cruising but illegible to those unfamiliar with these codes. Its queerness also involves specifically lesbian associations: Smith calls the pouch an "erotic pocket" and a "pussy pocket," noting that the paisley pattern has vaginal connotations.[178]

Smith utilizes handiwork and conventional modes of making as conceptual methods to investigate historical artifacts and their interpretation. Her installations are rich with allusion: the rag rug is Smith's way to honor Hammond's queer craft and bring it into the present. For Smith, Hammond's painted floor-bound sculptures offer up a profoundly flirtatious encounter. Hammond's important activism in lesbian arts, as well as her use of textiles, paved the way for queer feminist artists interested in handmaking, and in *Stack-Arms* her work becomes a literal support. With this piece Smith also activates the sexual euphemisms embedded within the *Floorpieces* (though, with its reference to the hanky code, they still remain on some level encoded).

Hammond's objects themselves articulate a kind of queer theory, a theory that resists being limited to her biography and exceeds attempts to tether

her art securely to her "essential" identity. Cottingham states that "an examination of Hammond's work from the 1970s does not immediately reveal the lesbian identity of its maker; nor does it indicate—through any abrupt alteration in content, color, style, or form—at what point she underwent this transition from straight to lesbian."[179] However, Hammond's going down to the floor does indicate a queer shift in her own methods of production and her formal means (regardless of her "lesbian identity"). While Hammond never conceived of the *Floorpieces* as explicitly lesbian statements, I argue that an unruly queer desire was embedded in, latent in, and complexly constitutive of the process of making these works. Revisiting them with a queer lens produces a lesbian art history that polemically does *not* rely on intention but is motivated by productive misreadings, metaphoric leaps, and imaginative provocations. (Since the original publication of my thoughts on this work in 2009, many have asked me what Hammond thinks of my reading. The answer is that she has embraced it and has assigned my essay to students during guest-lecturing visits at art schools. Rather than understand this as a mark of her full endorsement of its argument, I see it as part of her long-standing commitment to critical generosity.)

My queering is less a forensic hunt for hidden codes that might magically unlock the "real" meaning of the art, as if such things are ever totally knowable, stable, or unified, than an intentionally open-ended engagement with the work, with its potential to mean in many different registers through time as they are continually resignified for new audiences—queer and not. This does not involve the "unmasking" of hidden symbols but instead posits that some readings attach themselves, belatedly, to art in ways that their maker might not have foreseen. In fact, the *Floorpieces*, with their unmoored multiple meanings, challenge the spectator to reconcile painterly abstraction with ordinary floor coverings. In a similar vein, lesbian filmmaker Barbara Hammer argues that "radical content deserves radical form," and she defines that radicality as both queer and nonrepresentational.[180]

In recent years Hammond's *Floorpieces* have been positioned as readymade sculpture, seen as formal examples of the expansion of painting, or recuperated as examples of feminist craft. But they are none of those things—or, rather, they are *all* of them. Beyond their braided and painted materials, the sculptures interweave somewhat disparate conceptual strands—sexuality, abstract painting, and hobbyist textile craft culture. They exist in a liminal, queer in-between space that also conjoins lesbian handiwork with feminist labor. Indeed Hammond stages an encounter between class, camp, and the handmade. She has never been interested in a simple inversion of craft and art. As she explained about the boundaries of what is included in the white Western male art tradition: "Women are out. However, many of us are questioning if we even want in. Getting 'crafts' into the 'fine art' museum is not the answer."[181] As exemplified by Hammond's braided rugs, textile craft objects, like queer desires, can be multiple, crossing beyond the high–low divide: they are props, they are surrogates, they are functional, they are decorative, they are frivolous, and they are usable. Mostly they refuse to be any one thing. Gregg Bordowitz writes: "Queer things don't yield easily to comprehension. They refuse to recognize, or to be recognized. They work from, or occupy a place of shame or embarrassment."[182] Hammond's textile-based works exemplify this generative definition.

In 1982 a roundtable related to the exhibit *Extended Sensibilities: Homosexual Presence in Contemporary Art* was convened at the New School to discuss the question: "Is there a homosexual aesthetic?" Hammond was there, as was gay art critic John Perreault, who said:

> On a deep level, we are male or female or both. We're examples of bothness rather than either/or-ness. Art work is not form *or* content. It is both. Craft is craft *and* art at the same time. We must apply insight to other artificial binary models. The gay aesthetic should yield good art, be against the dull, the drab, and against the pretentious. It should be biographical, personal, universal, embarrassing; it should celebrate the arbitrary nature of gender, be against "good taste." If we are outsiders, act like it.[183]

Perreault's statement has the ring of a manifesto; Hammond's *Floorpieces* go as far as any artworks do to enact his exhortations. With their insistence on the slipperiness of categories, their blurring of binary identity, their embrace of the embarrassing and the shameless, their investment in pleasure, their transgressive reveling in lowness, they demonstrate how craft and queerness might be braided together. The "places" activated by *Floorpieces* are also multiple: the works insist on the place for textiles within contemporary art, the place of class within formations of gender and sexuality, and the place of lesbian desire within feminist art history. These histories have not always been openly stated but now refuse to be swept under the rug.

Coda: Heterodox Handmade

This chapter has examined how queer makers in the early 1970s turned to hybrid forms of textile politics to define themselves in relation to new genders and new forms of feminist lesbian art. In the costumes of the Cockettes and the *Floorpieces* of Hammond, debris, scraps, rags, and fragments have been repurposed into something more vivid and colorful. The techniques examined have been decidedly heterodox within the rubric of craft—gluing, safety-pinning, painting, set alongside sewing, stitching, and braiding. In both cases I emphasize how the textiles unevenly bring their histories along with them, their pasts as conventional tablecloths from the 1940s or machine-knit remnants from New York's then thriving garment industry.

The concept of "heterodoxy" relates, too, to queer conceptions that complicate notions of singular identification. The internal multiplicity of the Cockettes and of Hammond's practices implies a productive fracturing of authorial identity, as what was previously taken to be stable is exaggerated, encoded with double entendres, and textured by material significance. The Cockettes and Angels, along with Hammond, were dumpster-diving, rag-picking, and transforming their foraged finds into unforeseen constructions, yet leaving traces of their former lives as intact doilies or unpainted industrial fabric waste. Each of these objects is in the fray of debates about the intersections between sexuality, class, and race; indeed they cannot be seen apart from the frictions that continue to inhabit these intersections. That is to say, these textiles hover in an in-between space between the economics of mass production and the imperfections of handmaking as they gesture to the privileges of consumerism. The skin of paint applied over one of Hammond's rugs does not fully cancel out its softness, its connection to labor, or its familiarity, and the Cockettes' agglomeration of feathers and trinkets does not diminish the tender and distinct bodies underneath.

THREADS OF PROTEST

2

El perro para la ropa sujeta la revolución, revolución dentro la revolución.
(The clothespin fastens the revolution, revolution within the revolution.)[1]
Cecilia Vicuña, June 1973

Just days after the death of democratically elected socialist leader Salvador Allende in Santiago, Chile, on September 11, 1973, the lead editorial for the London paper *The Economist* concluded with a scandalous, if overused, fabric-based metaphor: "The military-technocratic government that is apparently emerging will try to knit together the social fabric that the Allende government tore apart."[2] Placing blame at the feet of Allende rather than the bloody US-backed coup of General Augusto Pinochet, who would go on to rule Chile as a repressive dictator until 1990, the free-trade champions of the *Economist* claim that Pinochet's strong-arm tactics will "knit together the social fabric" rent asunder in the previous years. This statement, which precedes an endorsement of the death of democracy as a necessary evil, exemplifies a politically conservative evocation of textile politics—knitting as brute force, executed in a "military-technocratic" style, something that binds regardless of the desires of those being bound.

In this chapter I explore how this "social fabric" was contested, turning to textiles as a resource in Chile since the early 1970s by considering two case studies: the fiber-based work of Chilean artist and poet Cecilia Vicuña and select *arpilleras*, small burlap-backed cloth wall hangings made by women known as *arpilleristas* that graphically depict tortures and other human rights violations of the Pinochet era. Both put textiles to use to resist and make visible, in the broadest possible sense, the loss of democracy and the shattered dream of Allende's socialism—and other ruptures within the "social fabric"—in Chile. As Macarena Gómez-Barris writes in *Where Memory Dwells: Culture and State Violence in Chile*, "Culture . . . not only offers a view into the past but is constitutive of that very past in ways that thread together and pull apart social worlds."[3] To transition from the exuberant, campy use of textiles within the incipient liberation movements of US gay rights to the unraveling yarn and worn fabric swatches used by Vicuña and the arpilleristas during the dictatorial regime of Pinochet is to acknowledge the distance between these spaces and the wholly different historical situations unfolding in the early 1970s. Indeed, it is a dissonant juxtaposition, intentionally so. Though these examples overlap chronologically, I am interested in how textiles—as a flexible rubric weighted with local histories and as a vexed method of production—come to mean in different national and political scenes. To flesh out this context, I will briefly describe one aspect of textile production and the economy in Chile in the early 1970s: the socialization of the Yarur mill. Throughout, I consider the temporality of textiles, especially their ability to hold history and to figure contemporaneity.

This chapter will first investigate the work of Vicuña from the late 1960s through the 2000s, with an emphasis on the work she made in the 1970s and 1980s in exile during the Pinochet regime, homing in on her consistent exploration of fiber as a kind of line that mutates into a form of writing, as well as her understanding of breaking points, the snapping of thread, and the limitations of language. I end my discussion of her practice by placing her in dialogue with Daniela Rivera, a younger Chilean artist whose art from the 2000s deploys textiles as she, too, works through the legacies of the Pinochet era. I argue for an "expanded field" of fiber-based practice, examining not only work that uses conventional handicraft methods but also that which relies on deconstructed or what I call "preconstructed" fibers such as unspun wool and thread. Here I refer to Rosalind Krauss's essay on the "expanded field" of sculpture to argue that in Vicuña's work, craft as a formerly discrete set of skilled practices has broadened from its traditional significations of handmade functionality to include raw materials in their incipient stages, not yet fully transformed into usable or aesthetic things.[4] Krauss's essay proposes that sculpture in the 1960s and 1970s operates between terms—architecture and not/architecture, landscape and not/landscape—and her diagram helps signal the in-betweeness of textiles as they shuttle between the functional and the not-functional, for example, or the handmade and the manufactured. In addition, Vicuña's work relates to architecture, and to landscape, and to the nonsites of these terms.

The second part of the chapter takes up the origins and circulations of the arpilleras, in particular how they have been marshaled repeatedly as a celebratory example of dissident amateur handmaking. As in chapter 1, however, I am concerned with how such craft is hybridized, subject to marketing, and complicated by the procedures of mass making. And once again I stitch side by side two different registers of textiles: one practice that was originally directed to a fine arts audience and made by someone who considers herself an artist, and one that was not, or was not *necessarily*, but was carried out by women who did not identify themselves as artists in any systematic way and whose work was meant for the broadest possible audience. Again, I do this not in order to maintain a specious high–low binary but to reveal the instabilities of these categories by suggesting that they are insistently and sometimes surprisingly interlaced.

Cecilia Vicuña's Concepts and Quipus

In 1966 Cecilia Vicuña, originally from northern Chile and then not yet twenty years old, created one of her first art pieces, titled *A Quipu That Remembers Nothing*. I reproduce no object because none was created, and I describe no photograph because none was taken. The piece consisted of her act of thinking about a quipu—the knotted-cord method of communication used by Andean peoples beginning around 3000 BCE.[5] Composed of a single horizontal string from which other, knotted, strings hang, a quipu might be made of cotton yarn or plied fiber from the wool of alpacas, llamas, or vicuñas (given Vicuña's family name, note the felicity of the name of this Andean animal, whose coat makes an exceptionally fine, highly prized wool; fig. 2.01). Used for administrative accountings, the quipu might also have had more narrative or storytelling functions. Varying in length and color—the strings were often dyed—the cords can contain attachments and adornments, bits of matter such as stones or shells, embedded in the knots.

There are no preparatory sketches, no material remains, of Vicuña's imagined quipu, aside from her recounting her thought to others and writing about it as a little note after the fact.[6] This "mental thread" stretches from her mouth to this page like an oral history, told first to herself and then retold by others, reknotted as it is rearticulated over time.[7] It was, she says, "a thought that was a perfect complete concept."[8] The work exists as a feat of ideation and nothing else: an act of thinking, naming, and dating. In this sense it exists just as much in your own mind, as you read these words, as it did in Vicuña's: it is as pure a work of conceptual art as one could conjure. As a linguistic proposition, it is not unique, as within the annals of global conceptualism there are many such thought pieces, but Vicuña's persistent evocation of and return to fiber-based materials within the larger rubric of conceptualism is strikingly distinctive.

The so-called dematerialized art of the 1960s was rarely actually so but rather generated material residues in the form of postcards, contracts, pho-

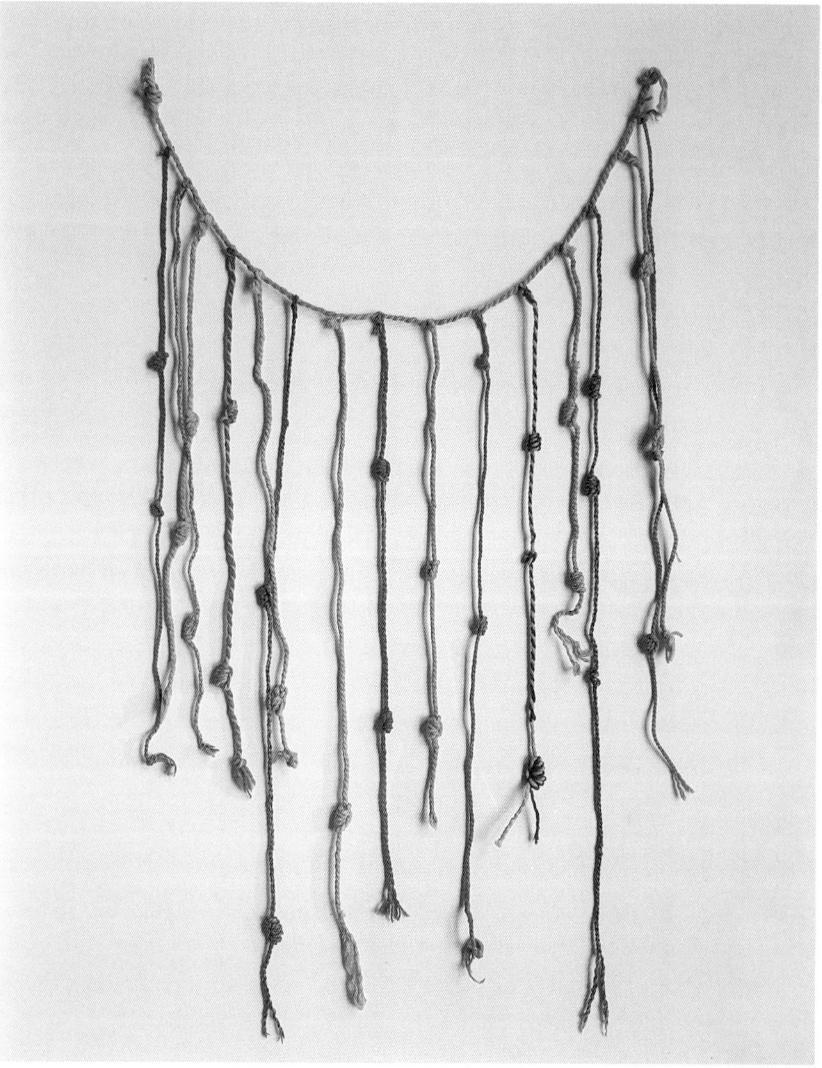

Fig. 2.01.
Archaeological Inca quipu, ca. 1500 CE, northern Chile. Collection of Cecilia Vicuña. Photograph by the author.

tographic documentation, and the like, stuff of undisputed concrete materiality that nonetheless was widely understood at the time to be somewhat resistant to the market's lust for commodity-objects.[9] In Vicuña's conceptual evocation of the quipu, this truly dematerialized artwork exists, paradoxically, as a thought about *material*—a connective thread punctuated by an indeterminate number of moments, all dedicated to the marking, and erasure, of memory. All the more significant is the fact that quipus, or "talking knots," were used as an embodied mnemonic device for recordkeeping, as touching the cords triggered the recall of information in a somatic or tactile form of reading, a literal pivot between text and textile.

A Quipu That Remembers Nothing is uncommon within Vicuña's work, approaching a zero degree of authorship where it dissolves into generalized philosophical speculation. Yet it raises questions not only about the methodological problem of the unstable or disappearing archive that resides in the shifting memories of a living artist, but also about the capacity of her work to bring together two seemingly disparate strands of postwar practice—namely, textile handicraft and conceptualism. Vicuña's art exists at the intersection of word, thread, and gesture as she plunges into the fray of politics. Her practice not only speaks to traditional craft techniques but also opens into a metaphoric realm of signification regarding line, communication, and the body using ever-evolving forms and means.

Vicuña became interested in quipus when she was a teenager in the mid-1960s, at a time when it was unusual for a Chilean student to learn about them; as indigenous artifacts they were not well integrated into systems of Chilean national knowledge such as school curricula.[10] The quipu immediately gripped her imagination, because she had learned to knit at a young age from her mother and was drawn to stories and myths about fiber, including precolonial Andean legends about knitting, weaving, and sewing. As a poet who also practices spoken word, Vicuña grasped the quipu as a mediating object that spanned textile form, bodily performance, linguistic structure, and the Native cultures of the Andes. In the years when Vicuña started to learn about the quipu, which is also spelled *khipu* (Cusco Quechua for "knot"), relatively little was known about them. Some Spanish accounts described the cord-based quipu of Incan peoples during the time of the conquest strictly as a method of quantitative administration, or bureaucratic accounting; others from the eighteenth century describe more romantic notions of the quipu as an enchanted type of noble diary or literature.[11] In some positivist scholarly circles in the 1960s and 1970s, quipus were looked to as proto-computer modes of coding, and some drew parallels between ancient systems and developing technologies.[12] (Though Vicuña attended a cybernetics summer course in 1964 at the Universidad Federico Santa María, she did not learn about these associations then; she has since become interested in the computational aspects of quipus.)[13] Most importantly, she understood the quipu as a form of embodied language that takes shape like chords of music or visual poetry, with every colored string, knot, or shell a semantic unit to be read, heard, and interpreted in dialogue with the other knotted strings.

Regardless of the wider academic understanding of its functions at the time, the quipu for Vicuña is a powerful visual manifestation of the ways that fiber-based creations hold and organize information, as well as a tactile, spatial way to transmit memory. Her title suggests that indigenous knowledge systems might be fragile threads that have been severed by colonial regimes and cannot easily remember their own histories. The quipu is a complicated subject, open to multiple interpretations, cultural mistranslations, and colonial speculation, and it has been a source of fascination for archaeologists eager to unlock its secrets for centuries. As such, the quipu is a transitional object of communication that thematizes rewriting and erasure. As one scholar has noted about the quipu, "What we do not have are direct, native translations of their contents unmediated by Spanish hands or voices."[14] More recently, continuities have been found between older string-based data and recordkeeping systems and current ritual practices among indigenous Andean communities in modern-day Peru.[15]

These continuities between past and present are of great significance for Vicuña, who has long immersed herself in indigenous craft procedures and has throughout her life been compelled by Andean lore. She has repeatedly discussed these procedures as part of a broader anticolonial and anti-imperial politics; in a BBC news program from 1973 featuring Vicuña's life in London, she says, "I have always felt very much on the side of the Indians."[16] Indeed, after her 1972 move to London she was marked as "brown" and was widely treated as racially other. Sociologist Patricia Richards in her study of racism in Chile asserts that the vast majority of Chileans have some indigenous ancestry, yet identifications of being mixed race or *mestizo* are more often acknowledged by those who have been raised in Native communities than by those who were not; the latter Chileans tend to deny the real possibility of any such mixing and proclaim their roots to be purely white and European.[17]

Though I assert that Vicuña has always also been fundamentally grounded in conceptualism, her connections to folkloric, craft-based, and indigenous cultural formations have been distasteful to many art historians, placing her critically at odds with accounts of Chilean contemporary art which suggest that her work operates at a vast remove from conceptually oriented art under the Pinochet regime. While she has not been widely understood as part of the progressive narrative of Chilean practice, her feminist, fabric-based assertion that "the clothespin fastens the revolution" tenuously inserts women's textile work into the realm of political art.

The Problem of Thread

Along with *A Quipu That Remembers Nothing*—nothing, that is, except itself—Vicuña's earliest pieces, made before Allende was elected in 1970, were performance based. Vicuña was interested in what she calls *arte precario*, precarious temporary objects assembled out of everyday materials or rubbish, small constructions often held together by yarn, rope, or thread set up outdoors, that might be blown away by the wind or carried away by currents. Her first

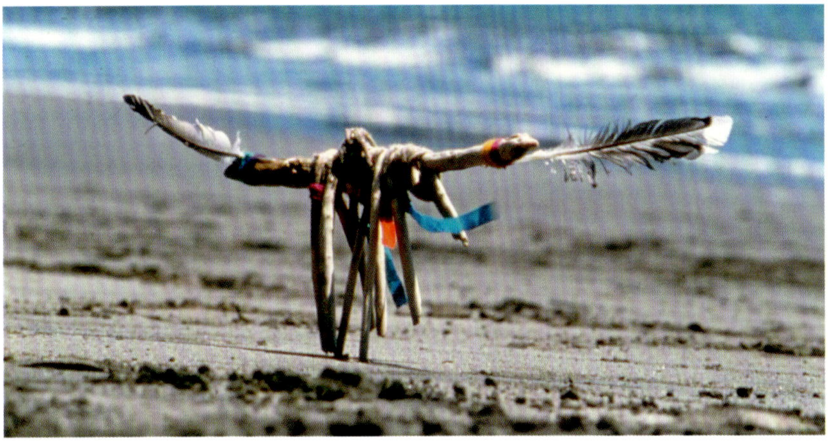

Fig. 2.02.
Cecilia Vicunã, *Guardian, precario* of found objects installed by the ocean, Chile, 1967. Courtesy of Cecilia Vicuña and England & Co. Gallery.

precario, accumulated from things collected at the beach, was a spiral shape reminiscent of what is called, in Chilean Spanish, "the ass of the basket" (the innermost curl that initiates the process of basket weaving), set on a stick like a ritual implement. She made fleeting installations at the lip of the sea that were documented and then abandoned, left to be swept into the ocean tide. In these early works, feathers, sticks, trash, stones, and lines in the sand evoke rites of drawing and collection, while her use of ephemeral or discarded materials relates to her feelings of affinity with marginal peoples in the wake of colonization as well as suggests the mutability of the ocean, and indeed all matter. In such pieces, yarn or thread serves a vital connective function; it holds things together or binds but is also fragile, with the potential to be easily broken (fig. 2.02). Vicuña has talked about this method of construction—in which sticks are nestled straight up in the sand, with a piece of driftwood placed at the top to form a T-shaped figure and bound by yarn and colored scraps of fabric—as an abstracted form of weaving, which is to say the organizing of horizontal and vertical elements in space. It looks like a relic from an unknown ceremony, and for Vicuña the washing away of these things is not the work's destruction but its culminating final stage, its completion.

Vicuña's artistic work, with its transitory filaments, summoning of ancient epistemologies, and tattered cloth, has not yet been widely institutionalized; she is better known as a poet.[18] It is through her poetry that she provides a critical terminology for her textile practice, and I often use her own words, including her poetry, as a kind of heuristic for thinking about her visual work; these realms are closely interrelated. If Vicuña's work has not been widely collected in major museums (though as of this writing those conversations have started to happen, and a group of precarios are now in the Tate's collection), this is a byproduct of its usually evanescent duration:

most of her art no longer exists, if it ever existed at all in tangible form. In the early years of her practice, she was not vigilant about documenting her work with statements or photographs, the commonly recuperated byproducts of other transitory conceptualisms. Impermanence, dissolution, and change have been at the heart of her work since its inception; these are not qualities prized by the art market or museum, and her witchy, womanly slant has meant that her precarios have sometimes been dismissed as strange charms rather than serious sculptures. So while one of the art-historical and archival "problems of thread" is its delicacy, this preservation problem of thread lies alongside the *theoretical* problem it poses, by which I mean that her work offers a proposition about fiber that might have a variety of possible solutions and multiple matrices of engagement.

For Vicuña weaving, spinning, crocheting, and sewing are inextricably feminized and intimate forms of corporeal labor; as M. Catherine de Zegher writes in the one major monograph about the artist, "Being perishable, the textiles themselves at best only provide fragmentary evidence about women's lives, but materials and metaphors of weaving do inform, since they permeate both childbearing and food."[19] Across Chile, many (but not all) Native textile traditions have been the exclusive purview of women, including weaving cloth and making objects for ritual uses.[20] (However, it is impossible to generalize about all textiles across Latin America as strictly or uniformly women's work, since in some places men also spin or weave. This is largely a result of colonization, as the Spanish conscripted Native men to weave at the treadle loom in oppressive sweatshop conditions.)[21] Such textile work has also played a significant role in gender socialization; skills like sewing and weaving were passed down through generations from grandmother to mother to daughter.[22] Vicuña has pursued specifically South American traditions and idioms related to the fiber-based crafts, and riffs on the idea that in Chilean slang to say "I have no wool" means "I have no money." As a poet, she is concerned with such textures and layers of language, and writes that "they say in the Andes, 'The spindle is the axis of the world' and 'To weave is to think.'"[23] Constantly building on connections between weaving and writing, it is significant to her that in Quechua (spoken by Native peoples in Peru as well as northern Chile and parts of Bolivia), the word for language also means "thread."

Originally performed when she was still in high school in 1966 and recreated in 1994 for the purposes of her 1997 monograph because no good images of its first iterations were available, *The Glove* masses together red and orange yarn that tether two hands to the railing of a city bus (fig. 2.03). As this piece indicates, Vicuña was experimenting with various interfaces between the human body, space, gender, and fiber, writing in a poem that

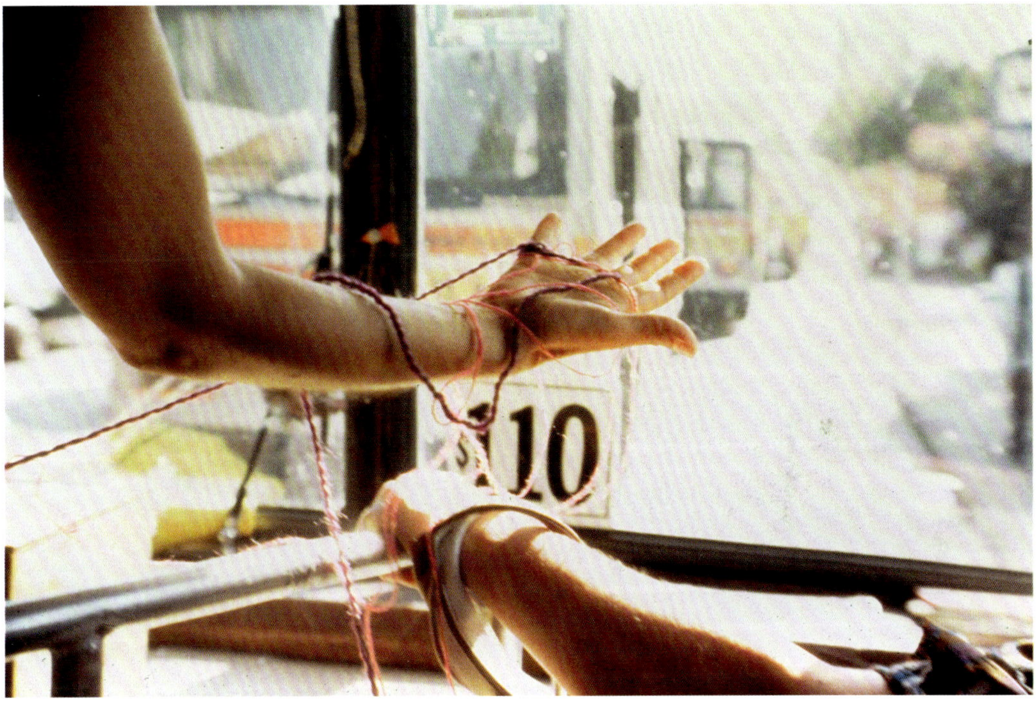

Fig. 2.03.
Cecilia Vicuña, *The Glove*, first performed in Chile, 1966, re-created 1994. Courtesy of Cecilia Vicuña and England & Co. Gallery.

accompanies a performance, "When a girl is born, her mother puts a spider in her hand/to teach her to weave."[24] Meant as a sharp swerve away from the normative protocols of bus riding, in which typically one rides in close proximity with other bodies that are barely acknowledged or engaged with, she describes the "ridiculousness" of riding the bus attached to this tangle of yarn and explains that here she was conceptually weaving in space, as the crisscrossed gazes of the people on the bus formed an intangible weft and warp. The weaving of gazes: discussing the textile aspect of Vicuña's work is complicated by the extreme dematerialization of her work and her often insistent refusal to coalesce her materials into actual objects, preferring to use materials in various states of becoming or incipience. These conceptual projects are part of an expanded field of textiles she helped conceive and make possible.

From very early in her oeuvre, Vicuña utilized a range of craft techniques, including crochet, as in the 1969 *Sweater of Holes* or *Chalequito*, a little vest that she wears over a dark shirt when posing for a photograph, standing in front of French doors whose gridded right angles provide a formal contrast to the organic netting of the vest and her frank, unsmiling face (fig. 2.04). Composed using a crochet stitch so open that the vest is more holes than fiber, and clasped together across the breastbone, the vest paid homage to the importance of negative space in Andean cosmologies. Vicuña saw af-

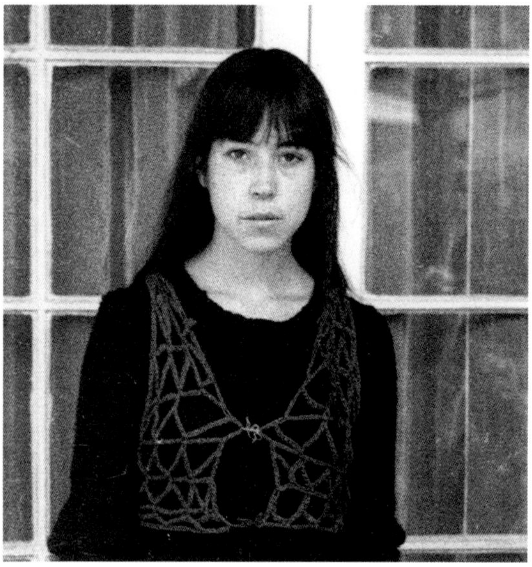

Fig. 2.04. Cecilia Vicuña wearing *Sweater of Holes* or *Chalequito*, 1969. Courtesy of Cecilia Vicuña and England & Co. Gallery.

finities between the vectored webbing of constellations and the mesh of crochet. By wearing her handmade vest, she nods to the extensive gender, economic, and status codes embedded in garments, not least the importance of regional craft in Andean clothing that can, rather than disappear, become more entrenched as a response to industrial fabrication. For instance, as Blenda Femenías writes about local dress in the Colca Valley of Peru, "the availability of more modern technology and materials has encouraged residents to accentuate the distinctive appearance of their costume, and it has changed their social relationships, both internal and external."[25]

Into the 1970s, Vicuña interrogated the generative nature of strings and yarns but also their potential to constrain or strangle, as in "Head Net": "Life and death are knotted in a thread / the hanged man's rope, and the umbilical cord."[26] In an accompanying performance, fibers press into the face's flesh, forming a geometric mask that binds the eyes shut in a moment of eroticism and intimate play. The photo in figure 2.05 is dramatically lit, with light entering from an open window to illuminate the side of the face, masked by a gridded veil that presses its features into an indecipherable blur. This was an instance of Vicuña utilizing mass-produced materials, the webbed bags that hold fruits, available in any grocery store, as a kind of readymade. In this, again, she practices her own version of conceptual art that is as concerned with nominating everyday objects as with delving into the tensile properties of fiber—its ability to withstand stress. These tensions manifest themselves in multiple directions; for instance, she has said that she appreciates the "beautiful opposition" of putting hand-worked thread in conjunction with industrial materials.[27]

From these corporeal experiments, she extended out further from the body, moving from fitting a garment around the structure of her own ribcage or face to an intervention into architecture, making installations that touched on the same conceptions of negative space—for example stringing up blue threads in her bedroom in the seaside town of Con Con to create *Hilo azul* or *Blue Thread* (fig. 2.06). Barely visible at some moments of the day, at other times bristling and invasive, the threads of this "spatial weaving" were blue not because that color was freighted with meanings or associations but because it was the only thread carried in the village's little store. Vicuña

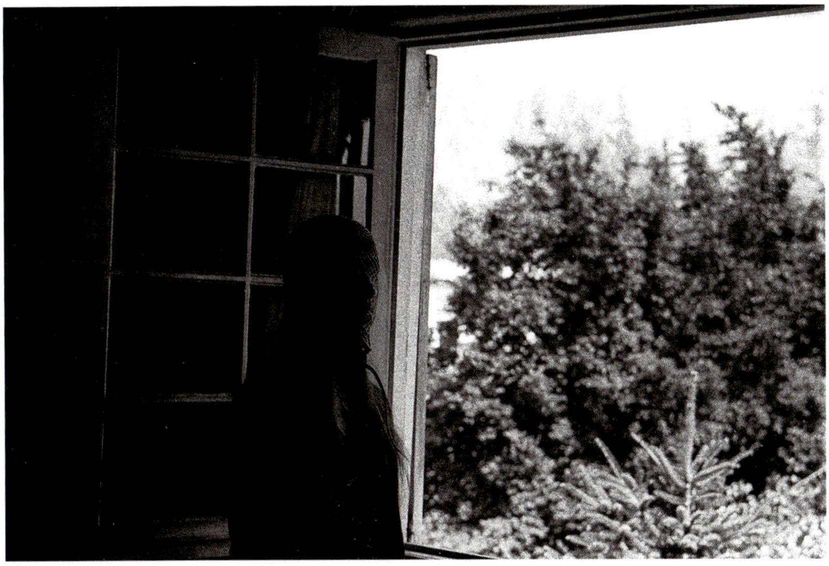

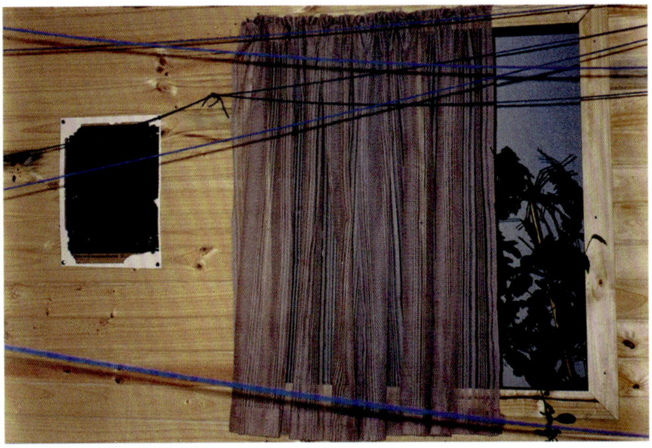

Fig. 2.05.
(*Top*) Cecilia Vicuña, *Head Net* or *Tied Face,* performance with net bag, Chile, 1970. Courtesy of Cecilia Vicuña and England & Co. Gallery.

Fig. 2.06.
(*Bottom*) Cecilia Vicuña, *Blue Thread* (*Hilo azul*), room-based installation with thread, 1972, re-created 2000. Courtesy of Cecilia Vicuña and England & Co. Gallery.

has frequently integrated industrial or commercial materials in her work, relishing these oppositions and making do with materials on hand, found, scavenged, and cheaply purchased.

Though Vicuña did not yet know about Marcel Duchamp and his readymades, nor about movements like Fluxus and Arte Povera, nor the simultaneous explorations of manipulable objects in space by the Brazilian neoconcrete artists, nor the geometric nets in space made by Venezuelan artist Gego, she was aware of the sculptures of Pablo Picasso and Kurt Schwitters that used scraps of metal and wood.[28] She was even more inspired by so-called "primitive" cultures, whose artifacts were shown in the anthropology exhibits of the Museo Nacional de Historia Natural but that felt alive to her, coexisting in the present, made vibrant in the handmade usable objects all around her.[29] Vicuña's serious study of indigenous women's craft traditions is somewhat distinct from the inspiration proclaimed by other twentieth-century artists, including Bauhaus weaver Anni Albers (who also had great respect for South American textiles), because Vicuña perceived indigenous women's craft as belonging not to a nostalgic or "ancient" past from which modernism can learn aesthetic lessons, but as equal to and continuous with contemporary forms.[30] For her, Native textiles were not only part of writing and cosmology, as with the quipu, but also existed within larger networks of communication and adornment, conjoining social life, memory making, and signifying practices that might be legible within a locality and illegible outside of it.[31]

Spinning a Yarn

Vicuña was in London studying on a fellowship at the Slade School of Fine Art when Pinochet seized power, and she decided not to go back to Chile but to live the life of an exile. She stayed in England until 1975, at which time she moved to Bogotá, Colombia, where she lived until 1980. She has since relocated to New York and now splits her time between Chile and the United States. Her oeuvre has deep connections to London; some of her first major shows were launched there, at the Institute of Contemporary Arts, and she was involved with a larger political scene related to Latin American struggles unfolding in England. In 1973, a few years into Allende's rocky presidential tenure, when rumblings of a potential right-wing takeover were growing louder, Vicuña began a series called *A Journal of Objects (for the Chilean Resistance)*, which grew to four hundred small assemblages made out of found debris. Like Harmony Hammond in chapter 1, she picked scraps from the garbage bags of textile factories near her flat, for instance using remnants of velvet to cover small metal spirals found in the street. Created over the course of about a year, her visual chronicle was meant to symbolically support Allende's progressive government as it was shaken by forces internally and abroad that were threatened by his reforms.[32]

As she wrote about these minute but in her view potent gestures or "little prayers," bundles of sticks and feathers secured with yarn, or matchsticks placed in a loose grid, she was "trying to kill three birds with one stone. Politically, they stand for socialism, magically they help the liberation struggle, and esthetically they are as beautiful as they can be to recomfort the soul and give strength"[33] (fig. 2.07). For her, these pieces of cloth, shell, litter, stone, and wood tell stories as they become totems to ward off despair. They also bespeak an uncertainty about how an artist struggling to pay rent in London,

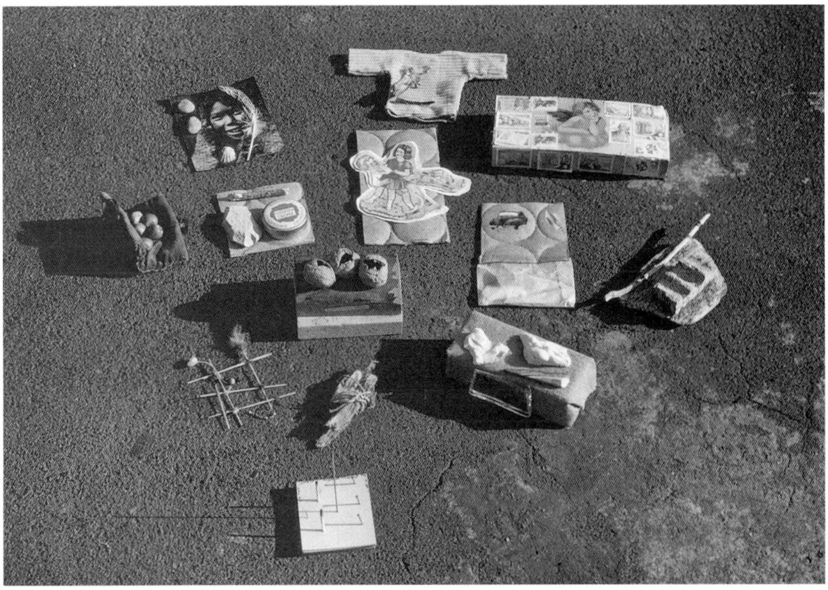

Fig. 2.07. Cecilia Vicuña, selection from the series *Journal of Objects (for the Chilean Resistance)*, *precario* sculptures, 1973–74. Courtesy of Cecilia Vicuña and England & Co. Gallery.

far from Chile, might express support in some way (however "magically" or symbolically) for Allende's cause. On the face of it, these small sculptures of quotidian stuff could seem absurdly inadequate to the task she has charged them with, but in her reckoning, their modest size and ordinary or deskilled methods of construction (tying, bundling, cutting, pasting) were part of their socialism. This deskilling is also fundamental to their conceptualism, as eschewing specialized training in favor of tasklike activities was inherent to what many felt was the democratizing promise of conceptual art: art made from anything, by anyone.

The *Journal of Objects* with their desperate prayers speak to a branch of conceptualism that has existed since its inception, namely its mysticism. Recall Sol LeWitt's early proclamation that "conceptual artists are mystics rather than rationalists. They leap to conclusions that logic cannot reach."[34] The risks Vicuña takes with these objects' ephemerality, as they are continually in danger of disintegration, speak to her almost obsessive need to create. One could speculate that her continual making was therapeutic, as she relied on the soothing and stabilizing function of using one's hands to reshape materials. But their very proliferation seems also fueled by an anxiety about the futility of such making.

These constructions take sometimes recognizable form, as when she repurposes a tiny sweater for an unknown doll, a photo of the face of a child adorned at its side with a glued-on feather and some small shells, and a box covered with stamps, but many are more enigmatic. She rearranges popular culture found images, for instance juxtaposing cut-out decals of a red-dressed girl and a blond boy perpendicularly against each other. In *Saborami*, this combination is described as revolutionary feminism giving way to a new relationship of interdependency between male and female, but these statements of political yearning are more evocative than programmatic.[35] Others are less representational: A fabric pouch holds a few seeds, like a compulsive hoarder's special stash. A painted bit of wood is combined with a feather and a trailing piece of net. In another work, a needle and thread are perched on a small cardboard station, but are they at the ready, just about to be put to use to sew something, resting midstitch? Or are they done, used up, finished? Such precarios speak in different tenses, existing simultaneously in a multiplicity of temporal states, oscillating between the not-yet made, the making do, and the unmaking. Using bits of garbage or found scraps in her *basuritas* was of great significance for Vicuña as a female Latin American artist, for as she commented, "We are made of throwaways and we will be thrown away."[36] (In fact, fewer than fifty of the original four hundred objects still exist.)

In one work, *Bandage* (*Venda*), made in 1974, a bright orange-red cloth hangs from a stick like flowing blood, tethered to a tool-like object with a few loops of thread (fig. 2.08). The rough-edged pieces of wood are lashed together by twine, and when seen flat against the white wall, the entire assemblage takes on the graphic configuration of a letter of an alphabet. How might this crude implement—or partial utterance—be used, and to what effect? Still existing in the realm of poetic association, Vicuña's postcoup precarios speak to the Chilean situation in an oblique manner. She wore this piece of red silk as an armband after encountering Vietnamese guerrilla fighters in person and deciding to signal her allegiance to their cause; the silk remained on her left arm for at least a year, and when it finally fell apart she made another artwork using wood as a surrogate limb. Such a piece—in which a piece of fabric transitions from a sign of resistance visibly worn on the body to a sculptural configuration made to be exhibited—raises unanswerable questions about Vicuña's understanding of protest as an inward relation or private communication (of the self to remind the self) versus protest as an outward and legible communication between the self and more public audiences. Knotted around her wrist and hanging down like a string of a quipu to be read, the silk strip also recruited her own body as a text to be interpreted. (Later she made a series of ponchos that refer to the ability of textiles to function both as clothing and as shelter.)

After the coup against Allende, her works pivoted to more squarely confront the Chilean context; she became more interested in the social registration of her precarios in a wider field of interpretation, moving from quite cryptic to arguably more legible signs of dissent. In one very small book made of found material, bits of tissue paper, and collaged elements, a dark page

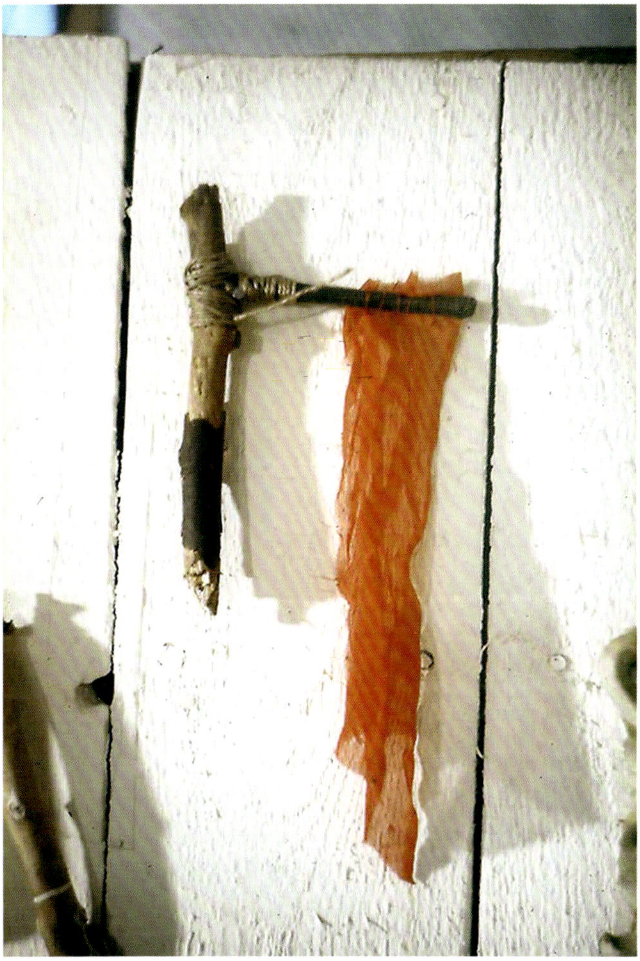

Fig. 2.08.
Cecilia Vicuña, *Bandage* (*Venda*), stick, thread, fabric, from the series *Journal of Objects (for the Chilean Resistance)*, 1974. Courtesy of Cecilia Vicuña and England & Co. Gallery.

with a faded hand-drawn Chilean flag—flags, after all, are the prototype of political textiles—is split down the middle with a bright red tiny quipu, riven by this knotted thread that divides, bleeds, and promises to remember. The opposing page has a delicate paper cutout (from the edge of a decorative doily) washed with pastel colors; this lacy form contrasts with the geometry of the flag, whose jagged shape is pinned to the page by its red cord. When I held this book, it felt slight—not only little but light—yet the act of turning the pages generated a distinct nonnarrative force. Vicuña's careful attention to the scale of the hand means that every detail reads as significant. A small blotch of discoloration has turned the brown tissue paper red, as if the color were seeping out across the book. Historically, in preconquest cultures across Latin America, including in the Andean regions, crimson dye made from cochineal was a hugely important commodity and carried significant metaphoric weight. The red thread interrupts the surface of the flag, which

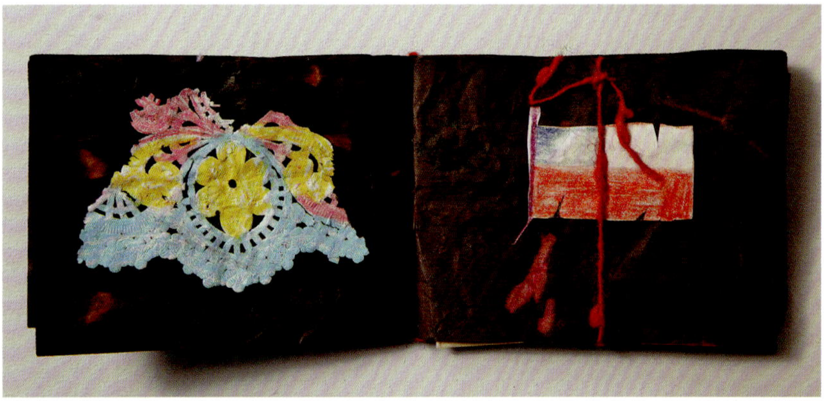

Fig. 2.09. Cecilia Vicuña, artist's book, detail, from the series *Journal of Objects (for the Chilean Resistance)*, London, 1973. Courtesy of Cecilia Vicuña and England & Co. Gallery. Collection of Tate Modern.

is, as Vicuña wrote in June 1973, "a fetishistic object" that holds symbolic and affective meaning far beyond its material existence[37] (fig. 2.09).

In another piece, minute square bundles of paper tied with string and sealed in a package become "mental newspapers" that have the potential to speak the truth rather than the falsities spread by Chile's tightly controlled news venues that trumpeted Pinochet's progress and echoed what she called, in a related poem, "the CIA's lies."[38] Vicuña's understanding of the *Journal of Objects* as an alternate archive, however imaginary, to combat the regime's propaganda relates to another Chilean artist, Catalina Parra, who in 1975 created her *Diary of Life* by stacking *El Mercurio* newspapers, sewing their edges together with gray thread, and encasing them in Plexiglas that was bolted tightly to produce a rigid, unreadable mass: a sculptural gesture of refusal regarding the censorship of the print media in Chile under Pinochet.[39] Drawing on an Araucanian myth of a creature, the *imbunche*, with all its orifices sewn shut, Parra embarked on a different series in which she cut out and restitched pages from the newspaper using red thread, interspersing Chilean stories with English-language ads, indicating gaps, seams, or inconsistencies in the narrative, as well as a tactile interruption of its purported authority.[40] In this, stitching is related as well to the wound—it sutures over what has been cut (fig. 2.10).

Importantly, Vicuña understood her precarios of the early 1970s as a collection of objects destined for a gallery space, ideally displayed together as a discrete installation, not private artifacts to be kept secret or contained within the domestic sphere; she first showed them at the Arts Meeting Place, London, in 1974. In an installation photo with some of the *Journal of Objects* hung against the vertical wooden slats of the gallery (fig. 2.11), one can see the miniature sweaterlike garment on the lower left, pinned at either arm; a few quipulike constructions and grids of small sticks; and an image of Pinochet in dark glasses. At the upper right, a length of flexible telephone wire spells

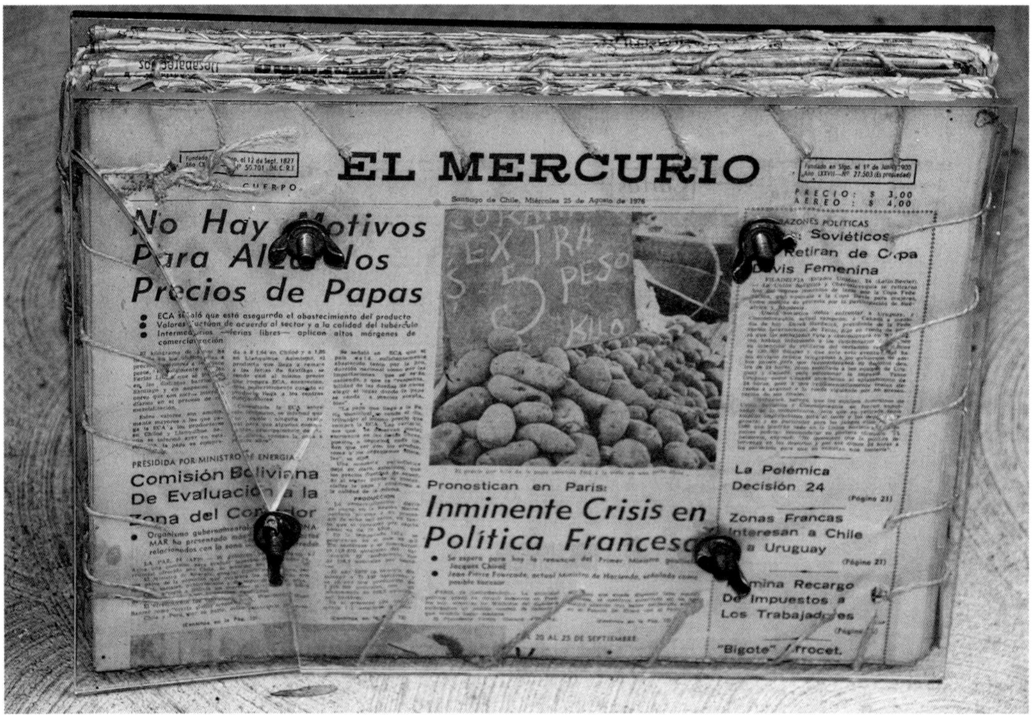

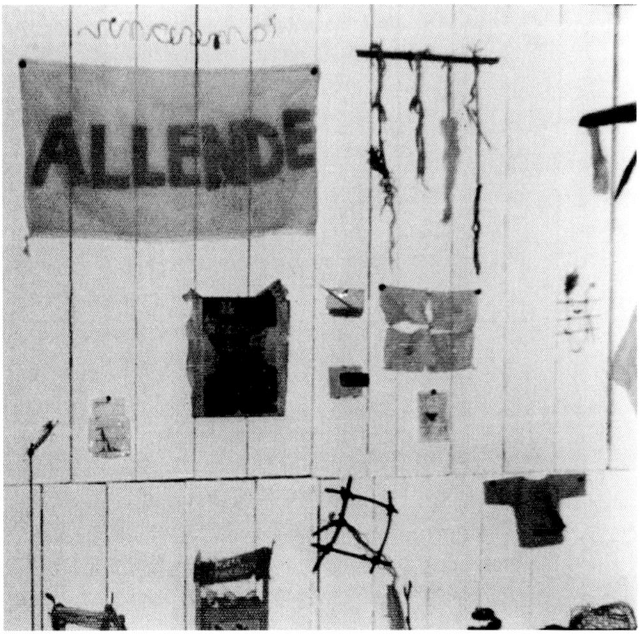

Fig. 2.10.
(*Top*) Catalina Parra, *Diary of Life* (*Diario de vida*), 1975. Newspapers, thread, Plexiglas, bolts. Photograph by Isabel Soler Parra. © Catalina Parra and Isabel Soler Parra.

Fig. 2.11.
(*Bottom*) Installation of Cecilia Vicuña, *Journal of Objects (for the Chilean Resistance)*, featuring her *precarios*, Arts Meeting Place, London, 1974. Courtesy of Cecilia Vicuña and England & Co. Gallery.

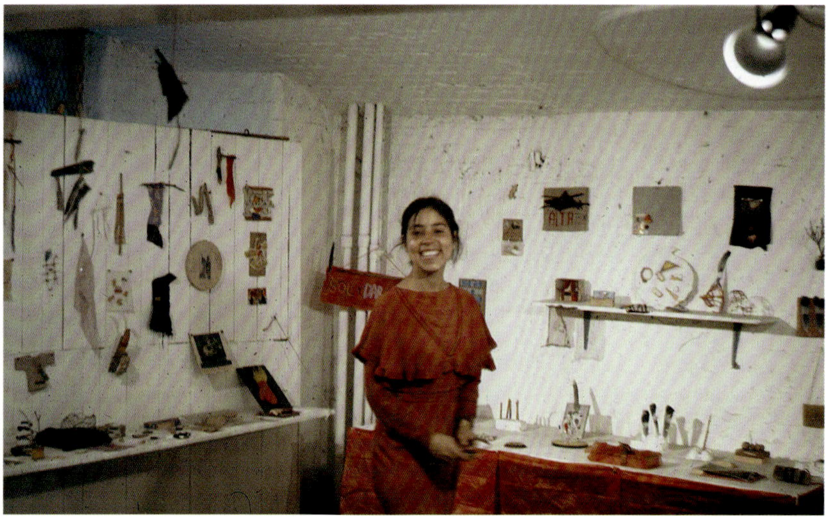

Fig. 2.12. Cecilia Vicuña at the opening of her show, Arts Meeting Place, London, 1974. Courtesy of Cecilia Vicuña and England & Co. Gallery.

out *venceremos* in cursive ("we will win," which was used as the title of Allende's rallying campaign song). The word hangs just above a fragile shroud made of two sewn-together layers of thin transparent fabric, between which are suspended cut-out cardboard letters that spell ALLENDE, mingling her own invented alphabet of signs with legible text-based works.

With the objects arrayed somewhat haphazardly on walls, narrow shelves, and low tables, some of them propped up or clustered together in one corner of the gallery, they take on an impressive formal strength in their very improvisatory aesthetic. When isolated, the objects have their own power, evoking the involuntary sculpture photographs of Brassaï, but the installation as a whole takes on the homespun look of a jeweler's booth at a craft fair. I do not mean this disparagingly, for she recruited the visual rhetoric of the handmade pointedly and polemically. Yet Vicuña's resistance to the formalism and conventions of the white cube, as well as the fact that these works were often slight signals that speak their politics only allusively, meant that her objects dropped below a threshold of critical visibility within this group show. In fact, in a positive review of the Arts Meeting Place show in the London *Times* in 1974, critic Guy Brett does not mention her works or even list Vicuña as a participant.[41] She speculates that her art was often not taken seriously because of its association with textile handicraft and because of her status as a Latin American woman; throughout her time in London, though they knew each other well, Brett (a prominent critic of Latin American art) never once reviewed her work; he had, as she has said, "a blind eye" for her art.[42]

In another installation photograph with the artist posing in front of her corner, *Bandage* with its orange-red cloth is visible on the right hand side at the top of the divider; this installation demonstrates that some of her pieces can be oriented in several directions (fig. 2.12). Vicuña stands in the middle of the space wearing a red dress with softly ruffled draping around the shoulders; the fabric that sets off her smiling face echoes the red cloth with frayed edges she typed for the exhibit's wall text. In an extended version of text written for this exhibit, she describes the objects: "As I am a woman with no nation, they have to be very small in order to travel with me. Their poverty is their socialist character (they can be done by anyone). They are very precarious, they can't endure, they fall apart by themselves, I stick them together with glue or little nails."[43]

In one of these works, a small faceless figure, about the size of a human hand, is made of medical bandages with noose-like twine around its neck (fig. 2.13). Its torso has been stitched together with black Xes of thread, and on its chest is a small typed label: *momio*, or male mummy, which is a tweak of the Chilean slang for the wealthy reactionaries who conspired against Allende. (The word for mummy in Spanish is *momia*, so this is a conscious change in genders that alludes to masculinist power.)[44] Like a version of exorcism that depends upon an apotropaic charm, she has created a mummy in order to miniaturize, defuse, and possibly control it and all it stands for. In some respects this piece is crudely made: odd proportions, rectangular torso, awkwardly placed limbs, undifferentiated features. Yet this also imparts a sense of urgency—its wrapped bandages imply coiled energies that might be unleashed, but they also seem on the verge of coming undone. Like her small books, the figure solicits an intimacy with the viewer, and raises questions about proper methods of display. Leaning against a corner? Laid flat on a shelf? Pinned to a wall? Or tucked under a pillow?

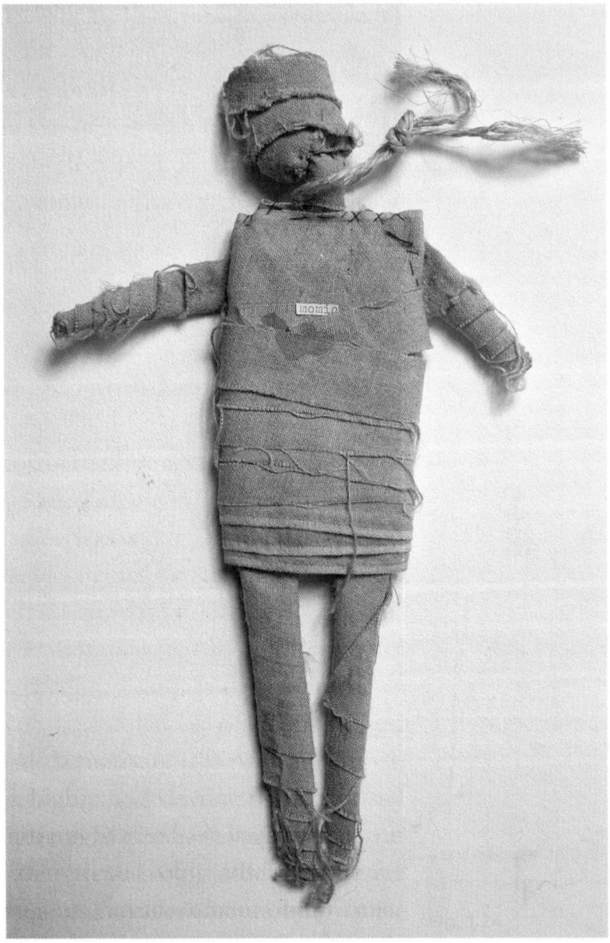

Fig. 2.13. Cecilia Vicuña, *Momio*, from the series *Journal of Objects (for the Chilean Resistance)*, London, 1973. Courtesy of Cecilia Vicuña and England & Co. Gallery.

London was the site of some of Vicuña's more frankly political textile pieces, as she made work that was directed toward specifically Chilean concerns (even if it could not be seen or known there), using the freedoms afforded to her by exilic circuits of dissemination and reception. If there was supposed to be actual magic in these objects, it was ultimately futile, failed: Allende died. Pinochet ruled for seventeen years. But Vicuña never meant her precario objects to be literal spells but rather material workings-through, or affective outlets, of first her hope and later her grief.

Textile Labors

Just as Vicuña was exploring threads, sewing, and crocheting in the early 1970s, the politics around textile making within Chile were visible as never before. After Allende won the election with his sweeping promises to socialize the country's industries, workers at the Yarur cotton mill did not wait for a top-down governmental intervention but seized their factory and forcibly socialized it in April 1971.[45] The Yarur mill—the nation's largest, and the first to modernize and adapt the principles of F. W. Taylor's "scientific management"—spun and wove cotton fabrics of all kinds, including sacks for flour and cloth for inexpensive garments. This sort of industrial mill did not comport with idealized visions of artisan textile making far from capitalism and a strict division of labor. As Peter Winn informatively writes about the Yarur plant, "On the factory floor, the workers were controlled by the Taylor System in which every movement was regulated and each moment monitored, converting them into optimally efficient extensions of the machines they tended."[46] This text is accompanied by a photograph of a worker laboring to tend to a massive mechanical bobbin, recalling images by Lewis Hine of textile factories from the early part of the century meant to shock the US public with their depiction of industrial abuses and worker isolation.

Though the Yarur textile empire had been built in the early twentieth century on the backs of mostly teenage girls, who were paid less than men and were viewed as more docile, this shifted after the 1960s brought pay equity and maternity leave to Chile, and by 1968 the mill gave hiring preference to men under twenty-five.[47] The work was physically taxing and the workplace was very noisy. In 1971 a mix of unskilled and skilled spinners, weavers, and managers (both men and women, older and younger) forged an unprecedented alliance by combining forces: blue-collar manual laborers, or *obreros*, together with white-collar *empleados*, clerks and office employees. They organized not just for better wages or working conditions but to rule the factory themselves, to collectivize its governance in accordance with Allende's promises.

Without waiting for Allende's official intervention, the workers effected a *toma* (takeover or seizure); once it was accomplished, they strung at the mill's entrance a white banner made from the cloth produced by the factory itself, dyed red and blue (Chile's national colors), that read "Yarur: Territory Free of Exploitation," announcing to all that the newly socialized factory was meant to fulfill communist ideals of work without the alienation endemic to capitalism; the name of the factory was also amended, even more emphatically, to read Ex-Yarur (fig. 2.14). Yet in a 1971 photograph of another worker tending a mechanical bobbin (fig. 2.15), it is unclear from the image itself if we are pre- or post-*toma* (it differs in no visible way from pictures taken before the takeover). The same basic work must go on, requiring bodies to perform identical motions, even if the economic and managerial circumstances have been radically altered.

This *toma* was the culmination of several years of increasing militancy and political activity within Yarur. Later, in the politically unstable days leading up to the coup, when Chile was in a state of virtual class warfare, women workers of Ex-Yarur marched holding up factory-produced fabric and a banner that read "Here Is the Work of the Workers," a public reminder of the bodies and wages behind textile politics, and its tangible products (fig. 2.16). The worker-controlled factory did not last long. After Pinochet's coup, the workers' socialization "from below" was undone and plants were reprivatized under his neoliberal regime.[48] Further, his aggressive free-trade policies swamped the country with low-cost goods from abroad. Chile's textile industry was basically destroyed, leading to drastically rising rates of unemployment after 1973 for the working poor and mass layoffs at Yarur and elsewhere.[49]

Vicuña knew about the short-lived victories at the textile plant; her cousin spearheaded performances there as part of El Teatro Nuevo Popular.[50] In a lecture delivered at the Institute of Contemporary Arts in London in 1973, she read a paragraph about the theater troupe rehearsing in front of the nationalizing textile mills and asking workers to participate in the play as a means of seizing cultural as well as economic means. El Teatro Nuevo Popular had been formed in the early 1970s as part of a larger pedagogic and cultural program of the Central Única de Trabajadores, and one play, by Gloria Cordero, was written after extensive consultation with the textile workers who had seized their factory (though this utopian cross-class collaboration was not without its controversies).[51] Though Vicuña's reading of this text in London has been taken as evidence of her long-standing interest in oral performance, it additionally points to her knowledge of the struggles for worker-controlled textile plants during the Allende years.

What is more, it indicates Vicuña's heightened awareness in the early 1970s of the stakes of making textile-based objects, for textile work *as work*

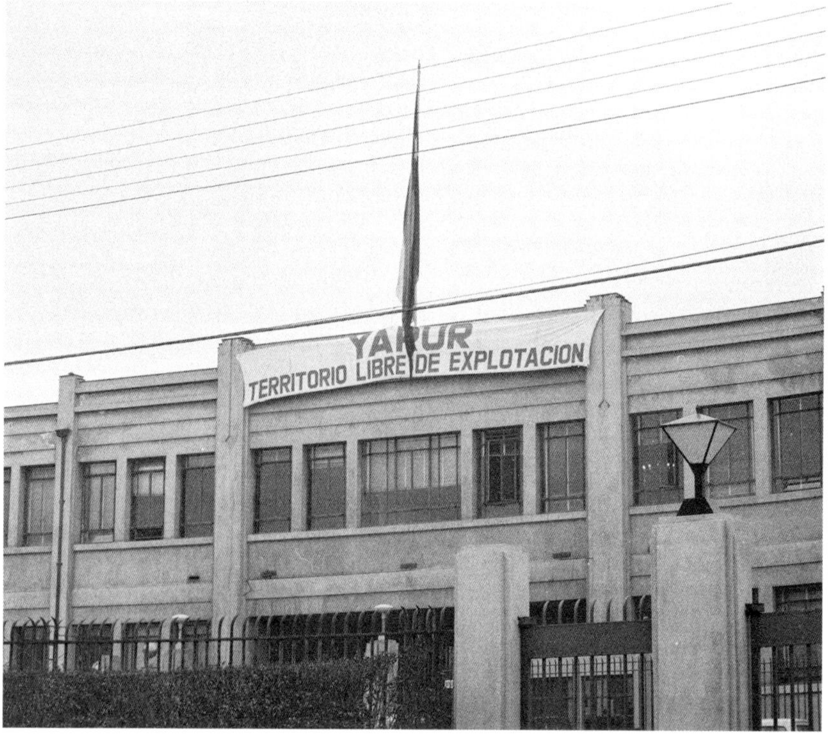
YARUR
TERRITORIO LIBRE DE EXPLOTACION

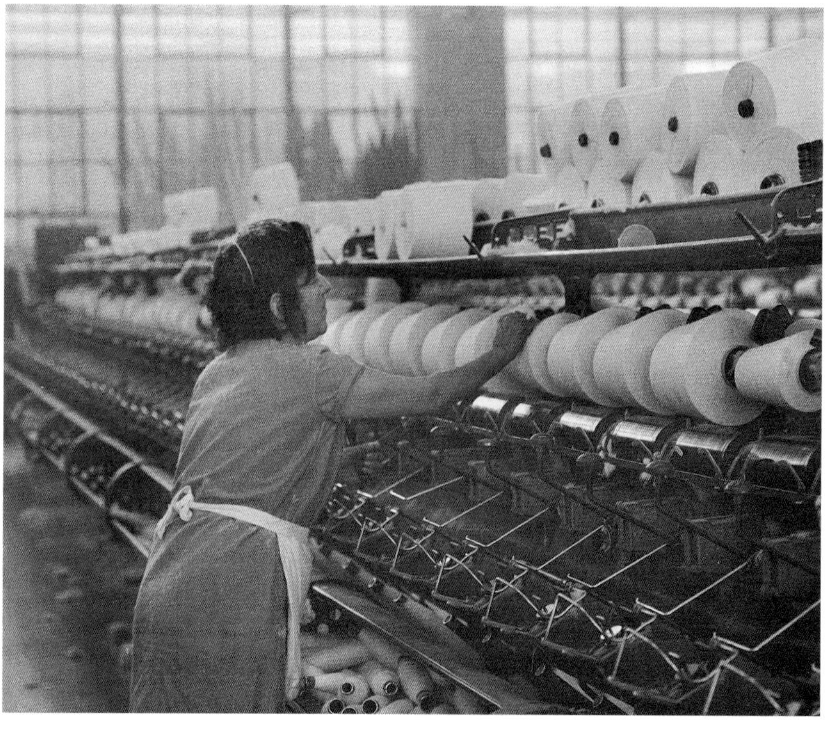

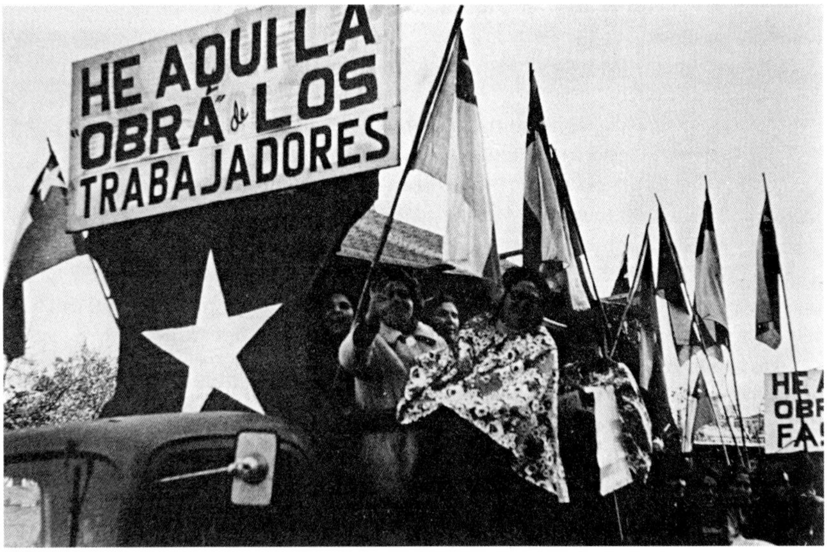

Fig. 2.14. (*Facing, top*) *Yarur: Territory Free of Exploitation*, banner installed at entrance of textile mill, Santiago, Chile, 1971. Photograph by Armindo Cardoso. Collection of the Biblioteca Nacional de Chile.

Fig. 2.15. (*Facing, bottom*) Textile worker at the Ex-Yarur mill, Santiago, Chile, threading bobbins, 1971. Photograph by Armindo Cardoso. Collection of the Biblioteca Nacional de Chile.

Fig. 2.16. *Here Is the Work of the Workers*, banner on truck carrying women workers adorned with fabrics designed and manufactured at Ex-Yarur, Santiago, Chile, October 1972. Photograph by Peter Winn. Courtesy of Peter Winn.

was a significant site of contestation about laboring bodies, at once romanticized and alienated. That her own fiber-based objects with their evident, visible stitches were so tenuous, so barely held together, unraveling, incomplete, and partial, suggests that textile making, for her as well as for the Ex-Yarur mill workers, needed to be announced in public as in crisis, unresolved. Her investment in unformed textile materials means that her works only gesture toward completion, perhaps by factory processes that are entirely uncertain or unknown. Under what conditions will these materials be picked up and turned into salable commodities? In a time when these procedures were under great scrutiny, Vicuña refused to turn her materials into finished, functional textile products. (That resistance continues today. When I asked her if she had ever woven a piece of cloth from start to finish, she said, "Never, and that's why the weavers detest me."[52] Hence, while she has not been integrated into histories of conceptual art, she also has yet to be fully embraced by the studio craft world.)

In London, while Vicuña was making her small amuletlike sculptures with bandages, trash, and feathers, she was also busy becoming an activist, and she saw these actions (art making and political organizing) as cut from the same cloth. In 1974 Vicuña helped found a coalition of artists, curators, and writers called Artists for Democracy that included John Dugger, David Medalla, and critic Brett; they agitated against Pinochet and advocated for the rights of peoples around the world. Together they organized the Arts Festival for Democracy in Chile in 1974. A monumental strip banner made by Dugger, in the tradition of the trade union banners of the United Kingdom, dramatically set the stage for a demonstration for Chile that unfolded in Trafalgar Square. It read "Chile Vencerá" (Chile will win), and the use of the future tense signaled the movement's broader anticipatory politics. The banner was drawn from an oral history provided by Vicuña; in a series of production notes, Dugger writes that the "first drawing-study" was completed "at Cecilia Vicuña's house based on discussion with her."[53] It was a pioneering example of the strip banner as "a new, large-scale form for the pictorial image, which could function outside the art gallery and the museum, in the fast-moving world of political agitation and protest."[54] A much smaller version of the banner, held by Vicuña, is shown in figure 2.17. Its schematic style of simplified cut-out silhouettes representing a spectrum of workers, from copper miners to cultural laborers, made it seem "modern in comparison to the more Victorian style of the British trade union banners among the crowd."[55]

Occupying one full side of the base of Nelson's Column, the banner, which was appliquéd and embroidered, was sewn with an industrial thread for stability and cut in strips so it could be easily transported. The cloth alone (minus the rigging ropes) weighed more than fifty pounds.[56] This type of banner, with its strips of cloth hanging down from an organizing horizontal element, also formally echoes the quipu, and Vicuña returned to the format in 1977 for a banner that said "Chile Salutes Vietnam!"

Dugger went on to be an important figure in the history of political banners, seeing them as mobile monuments. During his time working with the Artists for Democracy, he also executed a work designed by Vicuña, an appliqué fabric piece titled *Arte emancipación / Arte participación*, from 1975, in which the wordplay of "emancipation" and "participation" stream out from "art," diverge, and then are woven back together for their final syllables (fig. 2.18). Gesturing hands signal as they radiate out from the central amorphous shape, implying many arms, many causes (the top letters, "man," which are exaggerated, imply *mano*, or hand, while "parti" might signify departure or division). The orange and pink of the letters vibrate against the neutral cotton backing, with the letters in a cursive dark brown and visible threads dangling to emphasize a lack of finish.

Vicuña continued to work with fabric, including abstract textiles on burlap, while living in Colombia; those she ultimately discarded because few people were interested in them.[57] This is a painful reminder that though the current art world is keen to recuperate and collect textile work, this was not always the case in recent decades. One of the perils of women artists' work with textile handicrafts in the 1970s was the accusation of essentialism, a charge that Vicuña, no less than Hammond, faced. I will return to burlap in part two of this chapter, because it is significant that Vicuña knew about burlap-backed arpilleras—indeed, she owned one, though it was eventually lost in one of her many transnational moves.[58]

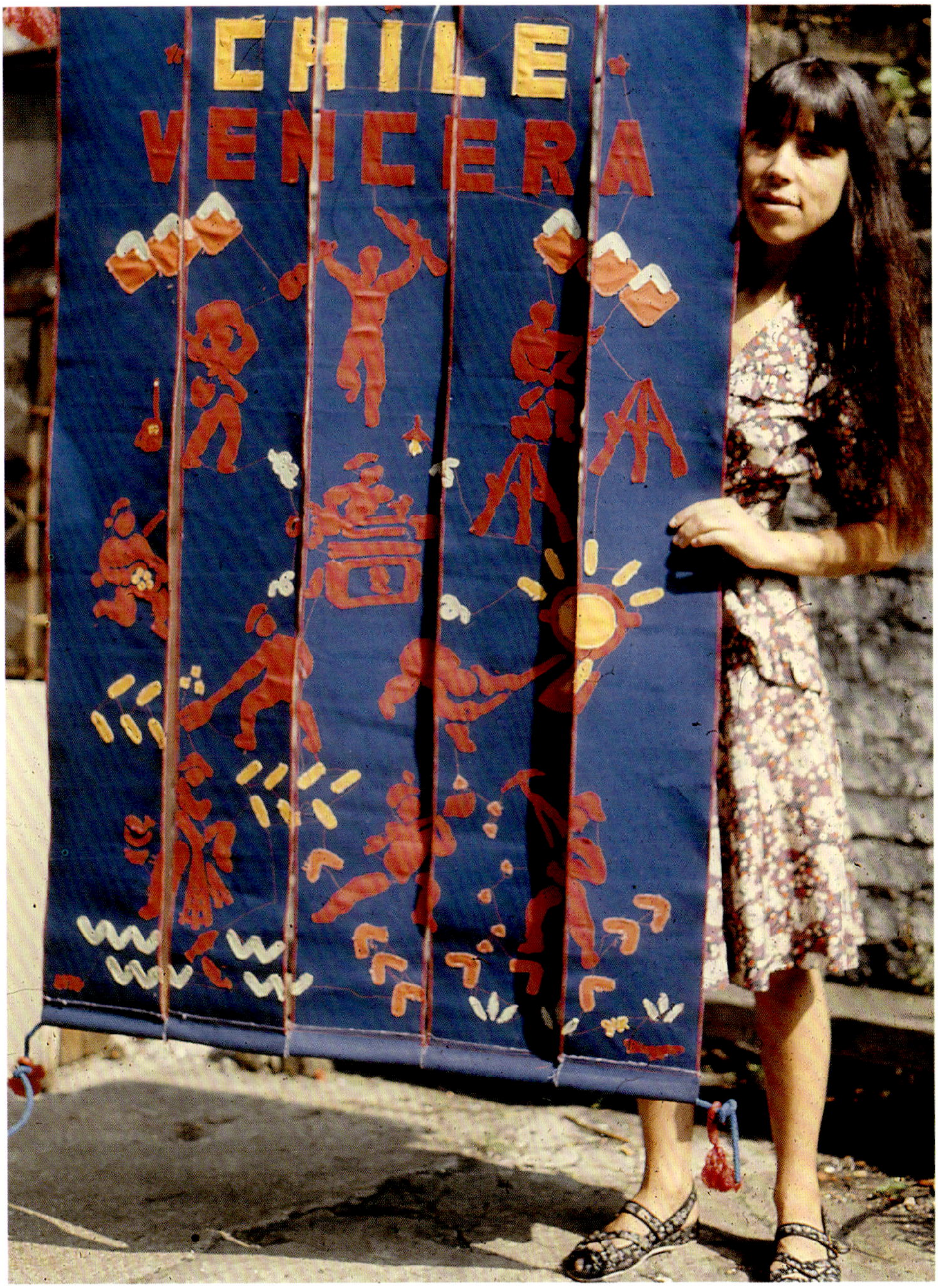

Fig. 2.17. Cecilia Vicuña holding a small model of John Dugger, *Chile vencerá*, banner, inspired by oral narrative by Vicuña, London, 1974. Courtesy of Cecilia Vicuña and England & Co. Gallery.

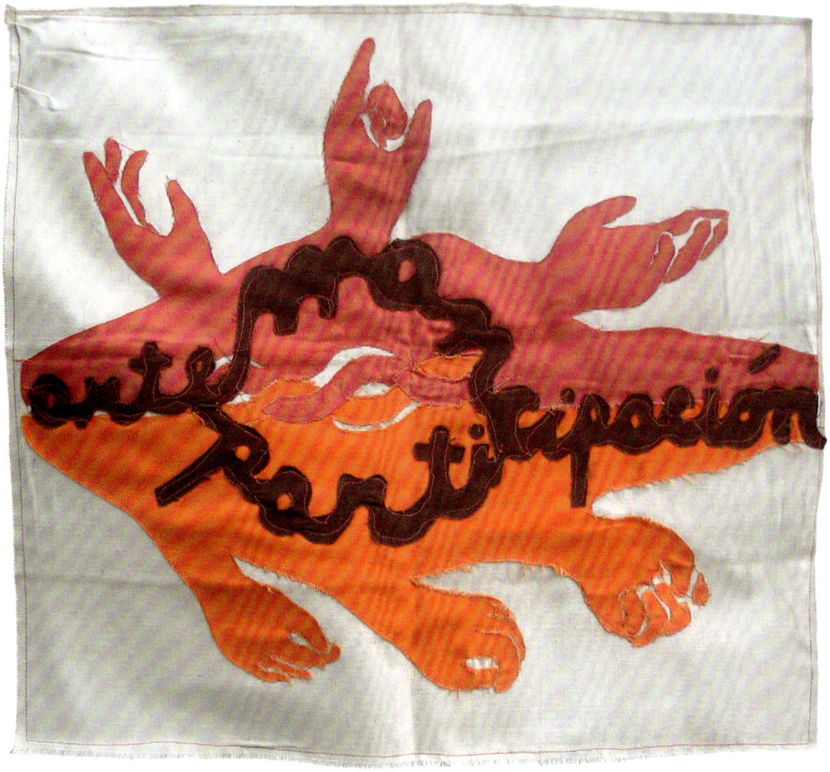

Fig. 2.18.
Cecilia Vicuña, *Art Emancipation / Art Participation (Arte emancipación / Arte participación)*, appliqué fabric sewn by John Dugger, 1975. Courtesy of Cecilia Vicuña and England & Co. Gallery.

Street Weavings

Vicuña increasingly became interested in going back to her site-specific roots and her outdoor work. In 1979, while living in Bogotá, she created her piece *A Glass of Milk*, in which she spilled a glass of milk on the street by tugging at a red thread made of vicuña wool tied around the upper portion of the vessel (figs. 2.19 and 2.20). The work had multiple origins: it was created after an invitation was issued by the Chilean group CADA (Colectivo Acciones de Arte), *Para no morir de hambre en el arte* (*So as not to die of hunger in art*) in which, among other elements, they distributed half-liter packets of powdered milk in La Granja, a largely impoverished area of Santiago.[59] Vicuña recalls that when she was invited to do a collaborative work in solidarity with CADA as part of a series of actions that would unfold simultaneously in Chile, Colombia, and Toronto, she "accepted immediately."[60] Mindful of her local context, she took the opportunity to create a work using the symbolics of milk as nurturance and sustenance, drawing attention to the scandal of poisonous milk being distributed at the time in Colombia, what was known

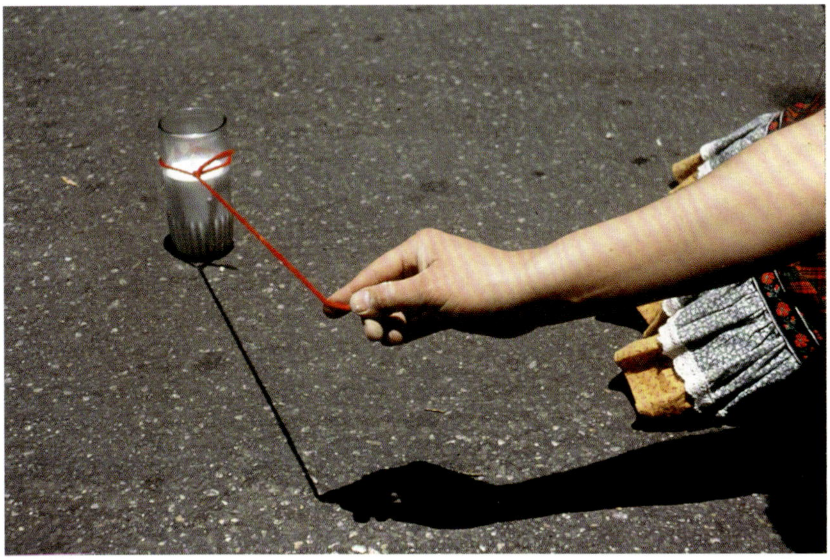

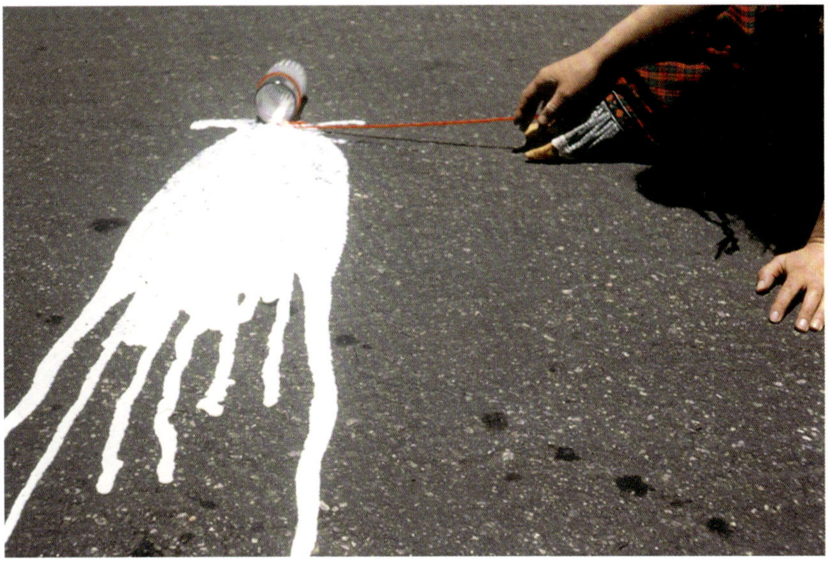

Fig. 2.19. Cecilia Vicuña, *A Glass of Milk* (*Un vaso de leche*), photograph of performance, Bogotá, 1979. Courtesy of Cecilia Vicuña and England & Co. Gallery.

Fig. 2.20 Cecilia Vicuña, *A Glass of Milk* (*Un vaso de leche*), photograph of performance, Bogotá, 1979. Courtesy of Cecilia Vicuña and England & Co. Gallery.

as the "milk crime," in which almost two thousand children died from drinking contaminated milk.[61] She announced the performance, executed in Plaza Simón Bolívar, by putting up posters made "in a recognizable style, using the format that announces bullfights, a bloody popular spectacle in which the bull always dies."[62] The poster states that the piece was made under the rubric of CADA and does not mention Vicuña by name.

In addition to the single glass being spilled in front of her small audience of about a dozen, she scrawled a poem on the sidewalk: "the cow is / the continent / whose milk / (blood) / is being / spilled. / What are we doing / with life?"[63] In contrast to her earliest works, for which no documentation exists, this piece was staged to be and now exists as a series of photographs, and as photos they present a certain kind of story—tightly cropped to capture a scrap of the border of Vicuña's colorful patchwork skirt and her extended arm and hand as she holds the red thread taut. The camera and its record were crucial to the material staging here, as the glass was filled not with cow's milk but with Colbón glue, whose opacity photographs better than milk and whose slow-pouring fluid mechanics are more controllable. In another photograph from the series, we see another hand braced against the pavement. As viewers we are positioned just above, the camera angled down to record the dark grain and grit of the asphalt as it contrasts with the rivulets of white "milk." We are brought in quite close, no doubt because this was a way to center and make visible this modest action as it threatened to be overwhelmed by its surroundings, but it dislocates us spatially, as we have no horizon, no sky, no sense of the urban environment. Indeed, in many of the photographic documents of her installations or textile-based performances, such as *The Glove*, there is a sense of a narrowing of vision, a framing that renders the pieces specifically in their local textures (skin against pitch, thread drenched in milk) while making them somewhat siteless.

CADA's turn to milk, and Vicuña's use of it, refers to the politicization around milk, poverty, and nourishment in Chile as it harks back to a widely known campaign promise made by Allende in 1970: that under his socialist principles, every child in Chile would receive a free liter of milk every day from the government. A poster, now hanging in the Fundación Salvador Allende in Santiago, shows a child raising a glass of milk as if to drink, with the slogan "Milk every day for the children of Chile with Allende" (fig. 2.21). Though Vicuña's performance was directly related to CADA's, it is not mentioned in the main account of the *avanzada*, the term given by critic Nelly Richard to those artists who stayed within Chile during the dictatorship and had to work around censorship by using sophisticated visual and conceptual codes, producing their own forms of meaning. Richard writes: "The *avanzada* artists dared to gamble on a form of creativity able to disrupt the order imposed on language by the figures of authority and their grammar of power."[64] She argues that through nonaggressive and often fugitive sign systems under heavy censorship, these artists invented a new language of dissent; she does not include Vicuña even though her work also interrogates systems of language and illegibly. As an exile, Vicuña did not face the same sorts of institutional silencing as those who stayed in Pinochet's Chile. Though she had connections with the artists of CADA and her actions were explicitly performed as part of their international network, she has not been fully written into its history.

Throughout the 1980s, Vicuña continued to investigate extrainstitutional and guerrilla public projects, in particular when she was still in exile but began to travel occasionally back to Chile. She performed a number of fiber-based street interventions; for instance, she used string to weave together sides of a road, literally preventing traffic. This was a visual metaphor for bridging divides but also for disruptions to speech and thwarted gestures of communication during the dictatorship. Looping string around rocks in a river as one part of a temporary installation that joined the two banks, Vicuña used thread like a syntactic unit, one that speaks to a rupture in the public sphere, as well as an imaginative attempt at repair. Recalling the work of the Peruvian artist Jorge Eielson with his quipu-inspired artworks, but moving the knotted fibers beyond both the frame of the canvas and the gallery space, this work used thread to demarcate spatial arenas, bringing together Vicuña's investment in the hand with a gesture of extension out from the body to the realm of visibility in the social space of the street.

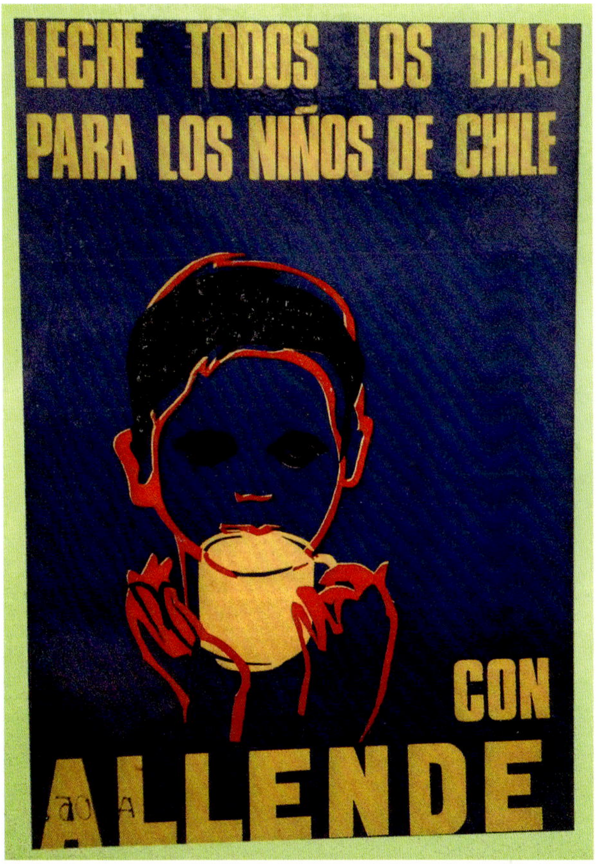

Fig. 2.21. "Milk Every Day for the Children of Chile with Allende," Salvador Allende campaign poster, 1970. Fundación Salvador Allende. Photograph by the author.

Vicuña's street weavings intervene in public space to somewhat double-edged purpose: as embellishments of streets, construction sites, gutters, and staircases, they create a dynamic tension between the malleability of fibers and the rigidity of their surroundings. *Quipu in the Gutter*, a street installation, returns to the form of the quipu, but rather than serve as a system of accounting or information, strands of yarn unfurl down from the rough gray pavement into a murky puddle of water in the road—debased, fallen, abandoned, perhaps, but also embroidering and thereby enlivening public space with its vibrant red, pink, and orange strands (fig. 2.22). Some seem like accidental placements, remnants mislaid from a garment factory floor, as in the length of white fiber in figure 2.23, placed on a stoop and anchored at both ends with stones to keep it from drifting away. What sort of labor is invoked here? By leaving her materials somewhat unworked, such as wool fleece and unspun

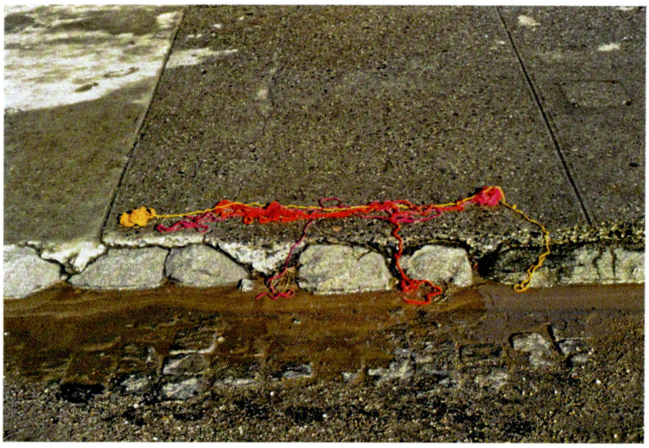

Fig. 2.22.
Cecilia Vicuña, *Quipu in the Gutter*, New York, 1989. Courtesy of Cecilia Vicuña and England & Co. Gallery.

wool roving, Vicuña goes back to the initial stages of textile creation, using what I term preconstruction to recall histories of shearing and gathering as well as to gesture toward these materials' futurities and afterlives as they propose themselves as the incipient materials of production, ready to be spun and woven. Deliberately unfinished, or even, in the case of *Quipu in the Gutter*, drawing attention to procedures of unraveling and unweaving, they refuse to be fully transformed into polished commodities. They ignite thought about what is to come, asking what sorts of factories and what sorts of working conditions might be put to use in the service of their reanimation, suggesting the nascent, the about to happen, the almost, the gearing up. As she writes about her attraction to unspun wool, "It's no thing / it's pure potential."[65] Such materials also imply a halting of a process, the arresting of some future instrumentalization, as when stones weigh down a length of white wool, making it inert and unusable for any functional purpose—harking back to work stoppages, strikes, and, as with the Yarur mill, reclamation.

As these examples illuminate, throughout her practice Vicuña has returned to her originary encounter with the quipu. Over the years she has made many versions of quipus, including ones that continue to link her long-standing interests in language, fiber, and feminist form as they speak their own semantic systems, sometimes referencing bodily anatomies with blood-colored curling tentacles suggesting veins, ovaries, or entrails. (She also began to title works in Quechua, a continuation of her commitment to indigenous systems of knowledge that are threatened with expurgation.) Vicuña expanded on the quipu in her work *El quipu menstrual*, which has been repeated in three different configurations. It was first performed to mark the occasion of the election of Chile's first woman president, Michelle Bachelet, and to underscore Chile's ecological fragility. On January 15, 2006, the day of the runoff election that secured Bachelet's first presidency, Vicuña laid long

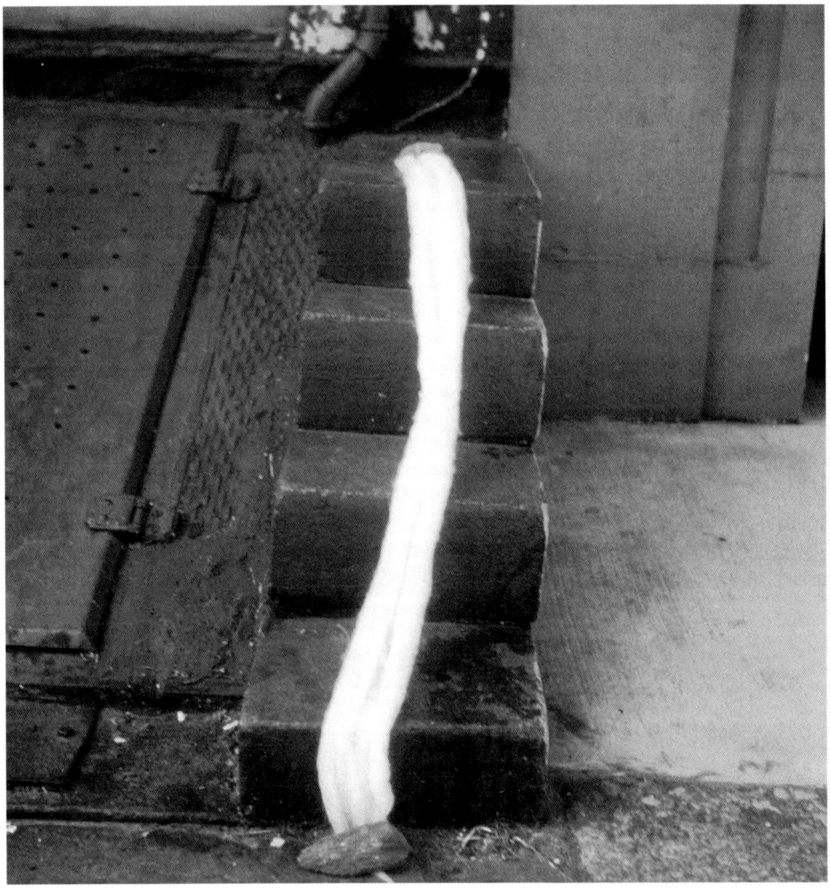

Fig. 2.23.
Cecilia Vicuña, *White Hair on White Street,* New York, 1994. Courtesy of Cecilia Vicuña and England & Co. Gallery.

knotted red woolen lines at the foot of El Plomo's glacier in a symbolic casting of her vote, a celebration of the sustaining female body that is at the same time one capable of political power[66] (fig. 2.24). Menstruation, which was a key theme of 1970s feminist art globally, has fallen out of favor as a motif in more recent decades; yet Vicuña embraces these female processes in her abstract evocations. (An earlier painting titled *The Angel of Menstruation*—Vicuña has a robust practice as a painter—depicts it openly.)

The performance of *El quipu menstrual* was semi-private, conducted in near isolation in this rural landscape, with the Andes in the background; unlike the documentation of *A Glass of Milk*, in which the viewer does not see Plaza Bolívar in Bogotá, for these photos there is a sense of vastness and the dwarfing of Vicuña's intervention by its surroundings. However, the red textiles were also gashes; this earthwork protested mining in the glaciers in the Andes and was meant to call out to Bachelet to halt environmental despoliation. It was accompanied by a strongly worded letter to Bachelet, sent in May, about preserving the natural resources of Chile, saying "You have the

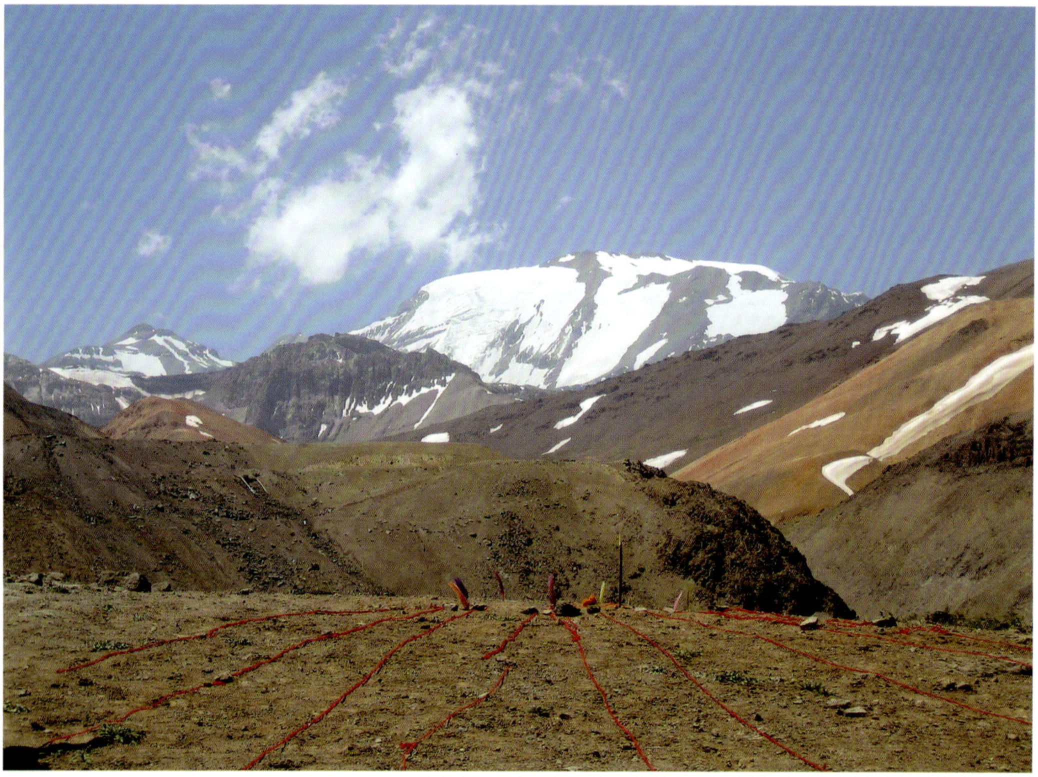

Fig. 2.24. Cecilia Vicuna, *El quipu menstrual*, El Plomo glacier, Chile, 2006. Courtesy of Cecilia Vicuña and England & Co. Gallery.

chance to reconnect water and blood."[67] Flowing down the face of the land, the fibers also become tears, connected to the milk / blood / bodily fluids that Vicuña has long put into conversation.

Later that year, Vicuña installed a related, greatly expanded work in the newly opened Cultural Center La Moneda—the governmental palace that had been bombed in the coup and had become Pinochet's heavily armed headquarters during the dictatorship—as part of a show on contemporary Chilean women artists, *Del otro lado*.[68] For this installation, *El quipu*'s horizontal lines, which were like a scribbled drawing on the dirt terrain of the mountain, were made multiple and vertical as Vicuña hung twenty-eight streams of blood-colored fleece from floor to ceiling, in reference to women's powers of regeneration and fertility and to the number of days in an average menstrual cycle. A monitor next to the fiber installation showed footage of the El Plomo installation. As the strands of fiber pool and clot on the floor, they evoke a seeping down of blood from above; the Cultural Center is in the basement of La Moneda, that is, underneath the site of Allende's death.

When some other artists in the exhibit protested that Vicuña's work took up too much space and made it difficult to view the other pieces (though she insisted she used only as much square footage as she was given), she thinned

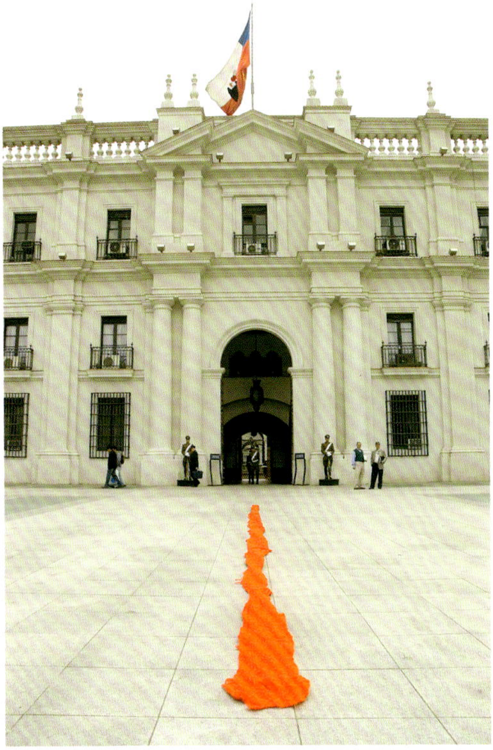

Fig. 2.25.
Cecilia Vicuña, *Blood of the Glaciers / El quipu menstrual*, La Moneda, Santiago, Chile, 2006. Courtesy of Cecilia Vicuña and England & Co. Gallery.

the piece down and used the removed fleece in a performance outside La Moneda, retitling it *Blood of the Glaciers* in her continued protests against the possibility that large chunks of Chile's land would be sold for profit (fig. 2.25). Unspooled by Vicuña onto the ground, the wool was raised aloft by a line of women, and as the performers held the textile in silence, it became a collaborative performance prop, fusing the gestures of the performing body with fiber-based materials. Directed at Bachelet and the selling of the glaciers, the work cannot but also recall the death of Allende, as the long red strand invokes blood flowing out of the mouth of the palace with armed guards stationed at the entrance and the Chilean flag flying above. Like the performance in the mountains, at La Moneda the camera backs up from its previously narrow focus on the fiber itself to show how it is situated in a wider landscape, a landscape both earthly and political.

Conceptual Craft

I have argued that Vicuña negotiates an unexplored overlap between dematerialization and materiality, or "conceptual textiles," a relation that has placed her at the margins of both conceptual art and handicraft. Though some critics have cast her work as regressive, feminine, and folksy (in large part *because of* her investment in textiles), since the early 2000s Vicuña has become hugely important for a new generation of artists in Chile, who have looked to her work with language and thread in her several exhibits and as her art has circulated in reproduction. Building on her practice, some younger Chilean women artists use fiber to work through the legacies of Pinochet's dictatorship and the fraying of memory, as well as to consider the national history of textile production. One such artist, Daniela Rivera, was born in Santiago in 1972 and came of age under Pinochet, living in Chile until 2000, when she relocated to the United States. In her 2012 work *Línea continua* (*Continuous Line*), which was part of a commission from the Rockefeller Center for Latin American Studies at Harvard, Rivera rolled a long woven line into the middle of the streets of Santiago (fig. 2.26).

Rivera's work could be seen simply as a direct reference to one of the best-known works of political conceptual art from the Pinochet era in Chile, Lotty Rosenfeld's *A Mile of Crosses on the Pavement* from 1979–84. In her piece, Rosenfeld (a founding member of CADA) made crosses, or *X*s, out of the dividing lines on streets using white tape, effectively negating the presumed direction of traffic while also creating an impromptu memorial for those disappeared by the regime[69] (fig. 2.27). Rosenfeld chose potent sites for this installation, not only in front of La Moneda but also in front of the US White House, to point to the financial and ideological support provided by the United States to Pinochet's regime. With these marks—a kind of cross-stitch onto the street—which she documented and circulated among the progressive Left, Rosenfeld produced a sign system that was not overt enough to openly threaten the regime but maintained a productive encodedness.[70]

In Rivera's homage, Rosenfeld's lines on the pavement have been triply displaced: First, spatially, they no longer function as potent *X*s of accusation or memorial crosses sited near the spaces of loss, grief, and responsibility. Second, they have been temporally dislocated; they exist at a historical remove of over thirty years from Rosenfeld's first incarnation. Third, and most critically, Rivera chose to redo the lines not with white tape but with woven wool, in a continuous rather than broken line. In this choice of textile material, Rivera's work thus references Vicuña's oeuvre as well as Rosenfeld's, and her placement of fiber in public streets is an elliptical acknowledgment of Vicuña's precedent.

In other words, Rivera's work insists upon a dual legacy: both the political conceptual work of CADA and its cohort and the textile craft of Vicuña. In influential writings by Richard, Vicuña has not been understood as a vital part of the trajectory of the Chilean *avanzada*; rather, Richard has upheld di-

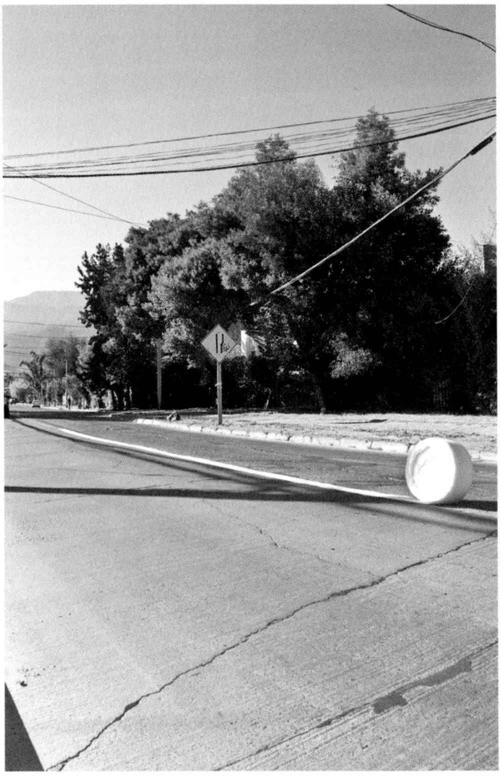

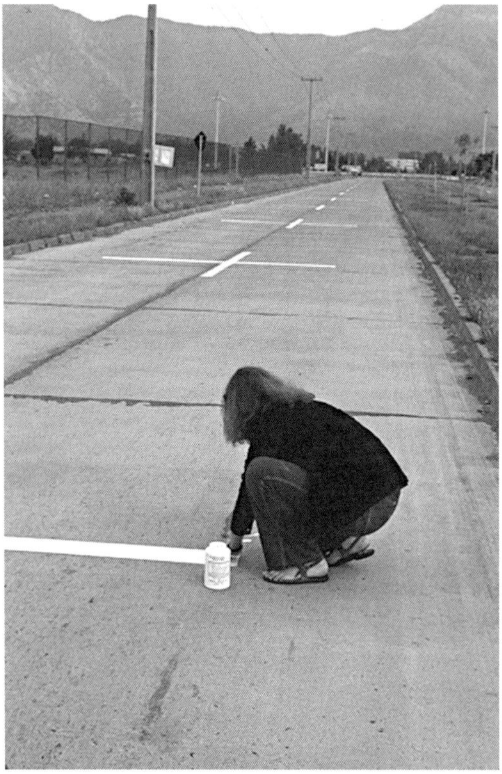

Fig. 2.26.
Daniela Rivera, *Continuous Line* (*Línea continua*), Santiago, Chile, and Cambridge, Massachusetts, 2012. Courtesy of Daniela Rivera.

Fig. 2.27.
Lotty Rosenfeld, *A Mile of Crosses on the Pavement* (*Una milla de cruces sobre el pavimento*), performance in Chile and Washington, DC, 1979–84. Courtesy of Lotty Rosenfeld.

chotomies of the conceptual, the semiotic, and the political versus the crafty and the expressive. (Though Vicuña made performances in the late 1960s that were known to Chilean artists at the time, Richard writes, "There is no significant record of any use of the body in Chilean art prior to 1973."[71] She also does not mention Vicuña in her chapter on poetry and writing and its intersection with Chilean visual arts.) But Vicuña, with her tactile, feminine, and mythic fibers, is at the same time political and semiotic, and Rivera rightly understands Rosenfeld and Vicuña not as opposites working with divergent mediums but as fellow interveners in public space using a stitchlike line, and thus as operating on similar frequencies.

However, Rivera, unlike Vicuña, emphasizes the transformation of raw materials of textile fabrication rather than using materials in preconstructed forms. It is important to Rivera that this is *woven* fabric, not unspun roving or a mass of threads. She is keen to emphasize the local traditions of pedal weaving on the Mantero loom in central Chile that, though prized for over a century, are understood today as endangered practices.[72] Mile-long lines of woven wool were produced in a collaborative effort involving a family (men and women) of weavers from La Ligua, known for its knitwear and woven goods. Though both females and males can be weavers, one scholar of con-

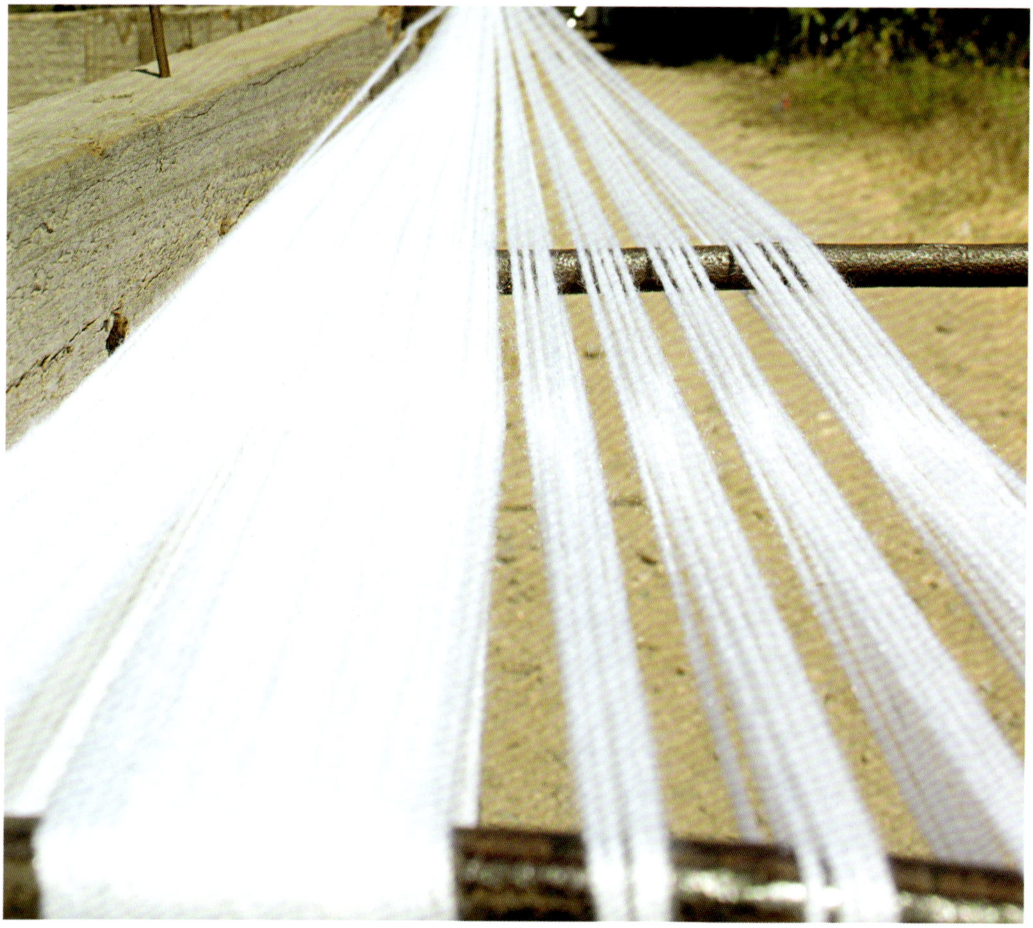

Fig. 2.28. Daniela Rivera, *Labored Landscape #2*, still from video, 2012. Courtesy of Daniela Rivera.

temporary Chilean textiles tells us that in many regions "horizontal loom weaving is the terrain of women, while the pedal loom, which was introduced in the colonial period, is done by men."[73]

In her 2012 video *Labored Landscape #2*, Rivera documents the two months it took to create the woven line in order to pay witness to the artisans who did the spinning and weaving. To record this video, she attached high-definition cameras to the weavers' bodies, showing the line's creation from their point of view and emphasizing the rhythms of work, the sounds, and the streaming strings as they are drawn out, impossibly long, across the screen's field of vision. Importantly, she does not show their faces, seeking not to efface the bodily labor but to spectatorially inhabit their position (fig. 2.28). Rivera has written of *Labored Landscape #2*, "My intention was to focus on the physical labor involved in the production of the line rather than on the narrative aspects of the activity."[74] In the video, the parallel lines begin to take on their own life, vibrating next to each other and stretching to seemingly endless lengths that move out of the space of the workshop down a path, with a barely visible terminus. These strands show, once again, how textiles might stretch between the working body and the sphere of the political.

IN THIS SECTION, I have argued that Vicuña's work acts as a model for thinking through the temporalities of textiles and that her use of fiber belongs as much to conceptual art terrain as it does to the disciplines of craft and industry. In her hands, textiles move across and between gendered bodies, labors, and histories, writing a text for others to read. For Vicuña, textiles exist within a contradictory temporal field of production, one that speaks to the accelerated time of capitalism as well as holds histories in their fibers, much as with the quipu. Vicuña's invocation of both indigenous textiles and industrial matter interrupts the flow of colonial, chronological time, stretching between a still living past and a ruptured present, marking time as she remakes memory. In the next section, I consider small tapestries made by Chilean women who by and large were not invested in the category of "art" but who were, like Vicuña, using cloth and thread as a form of making to tell urgent stories and to push at the boundaries of textile politics. Like Vicuña's fiber-based performances and installations, which are suspended between conceptualism and handmaking, arpilleras are caught in the fray. They are contested objects constantly pulled between dialectical oppositions and temporalities—between folk art and journalism, originality and duplication, nostalgia and currency, and decoration and testimony.

Arpilleras, "Tapestries of Defamation"

The hand-stitched tapestry shown in figure 2.29 is about the size of a pillowcase. Appliquéd onto a coarse piece of thin burlap (*osnaburgo*) material are eye-catching, vibrant fabrics that have been affixed with cross-stitches of matching thread. Three-dimensional cloth dolls, about two inches high, occupy a mountainous landscape under a solid dark blue sky, punctuated by an orange sun whose rays are formed by threads sewn in long straight lines. Aside from the sun, the composition is insistently symmetrical, with the two lime hills framing a peaked-roof building—a courthouse, according to the black writing on the facade—in the center of the scene, flanked by two tall green trees. Several printed fabrics are included in the cotton/polyester pieces, including a brown patch printed to resemble rough woven cloth, indicating earth, and a speckled print used for the mountain range. In a row in front of the arched doorway stand eight figures clad in bright colors with various hues of yarn bunched around their tightly stuffed heads to indicate gray, brown, or black hair. Their genders are not clear, as each has some version of the same schematic pale pink face, with two tiny horizontal black stitches for eyes and a third red one underneath (sometimes crooked, sometimes scrunched up near an eye), indicating a mouth. (In most arpilleras, pink, white, and very light beige are the default "skin tone" colors, choices that do not make visible a complex variety of identifications, hierarchies, and classifications around skin color and race in Chile.)[75]

With their basic cruciform torsos that indicate spread arms but lack hands, the dolls present a white banner upon which is sewn a question that, with no question marks to frame it, also reads as a demand, written in capital letters: "DONDE ESTAN LOS DETENIDOS DESAPARECIDOS" (WHERE ARE THE DETAINED DISAPPEARED).[76] This sober statement mitigates the overall cheerful visual effect of the tapestry. The words are addressed in part to the drivers of cars and pedestrians in the foreground, including one pedestrian who fully faces the courthouse—but also to me, as the spectator, and possessor, of this arpillera. *Arpillera*, which is Spanish for burlap, has become the broader term for such pieces made on a backing of sackcloth by Chilean women during the Pinochet era.[77] I purchased the one described from the gift store of Santiago's Museo de la Memoria y los Derechos Humanos (Museum of Memory and Human Rights) for 20,000 Chilean pesos in 2013—at the time, about US $40. Next to a rack of postcards, contemporary arpilleras of both horizontal and vertical orientations were available in the museum shop, prices pegged to size (fig. 2.30). (This gift store has since closed.) Visible among the postcards are contradictory fragments of memorabilia from the dictatorship—such as a photograph of Víctor Jara (assassinated in the days after the coup) jarringly displayed just above the pro-Pinochet slogan *SÍ*—indicating how the store traffics in nostalgia, ironic or not, across the political spectrum. I also saw arpilleras for sale at the Centro Cultural of La Moneda, sheathed in plastic sleeves and piled on a low table, and at other touristic artisanal shops in Santiago during trips I made in 2009 and 2013.

Like many such objects designed to read not as fine "art" but as popular folkloric "artifact" or vernacular souvenir, the arpilleras on display were unsigned and anonymously produced, and their style appeared to hew closely to a set of conventions. The handicrafts contain minute variations (slightly different color choices and rearrangements of figures within the landscape) that make each one feel distinct, special, and individual. Positioned at the very crux of one of the paradoxes of this type of "low" handmade object, these arpilleras are simultaneously culturally valued—indeed, culturally made visible—by virtue of being patterned on recognizable principles of construction, yet at the same time prized for their "one-off" nature: every

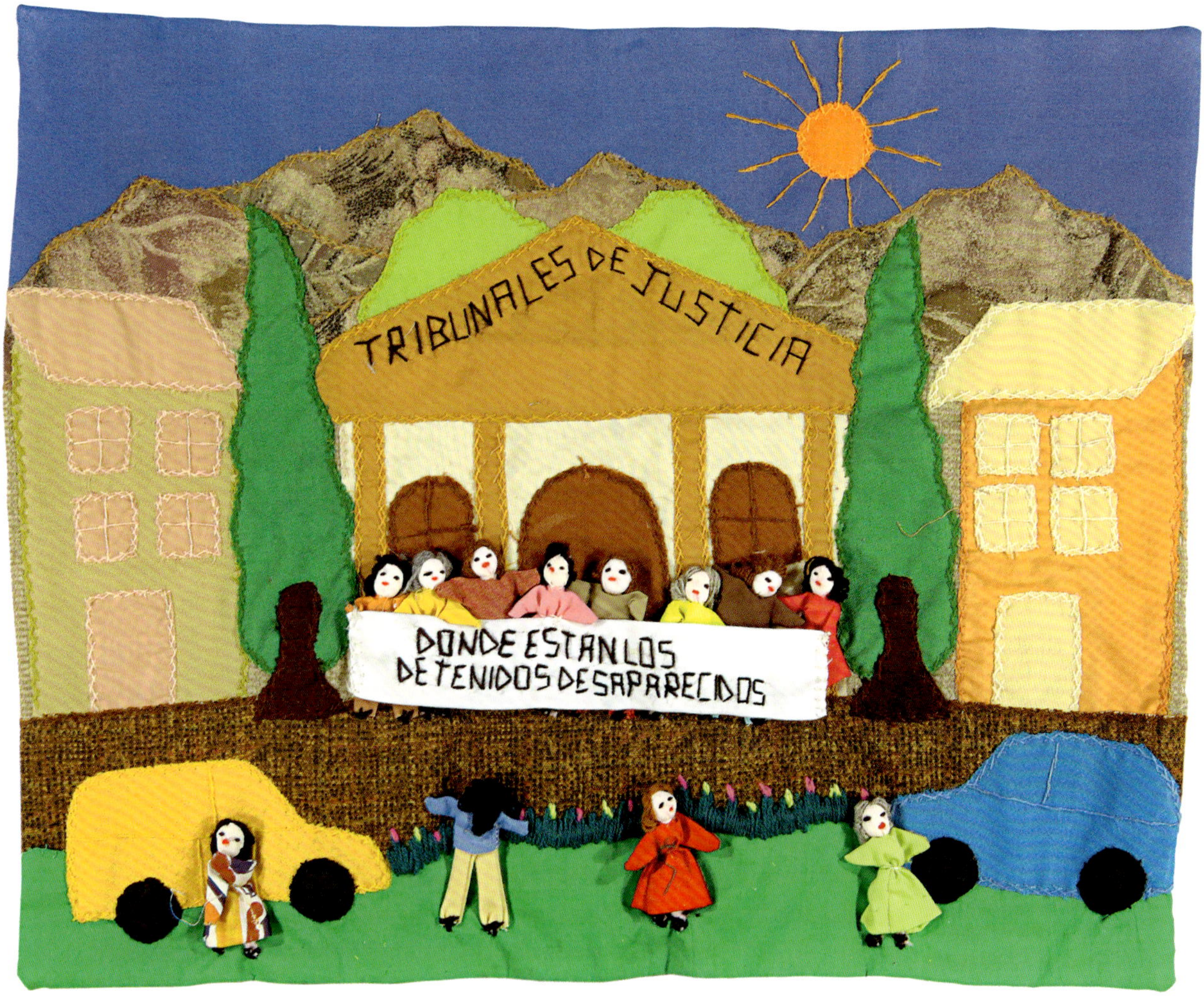

Fig. 2.29. "Donde están los detenidos desaparecidos (Where Are the Detained-Disappeared)," anonymous arpillera, 2013. Collection of the author.

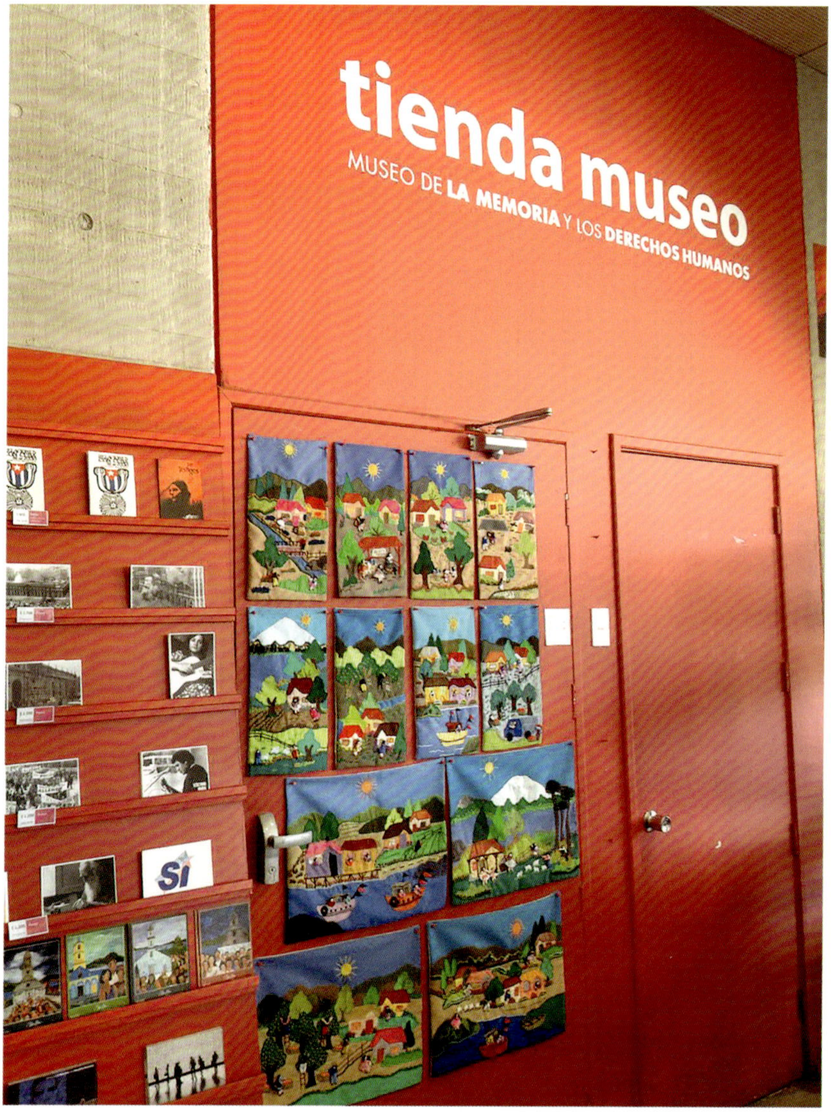

Fig. 2.30. Gift store of the Museo de la Memoria y los Derechos Humanos (Museum of Memory and Human Rights), with display of arpilleras for sale, Santiago, Chile, 2013. Photograph by the author.

purchaser feels satisfied by their choice, reassured by small details that the one they selected is theirs alone.

Henry Glassie writes about folk art, "It is only a rare folk artist who strives for innovation; his replication is an affirmation of a tradition. This does not mean that the folk artist is an exacting copyist or that there is no margin for variation within folk tradition."[78] More recent feminist and postcolonial scholars of traditional arts emphasize not repetition but individual variation within themes, newness, and constantly changing techniques.[79] It might be arguable whether these needlework tapestries belong in the category of folk art (as I will outline, some authors contest this), but certainly the con-

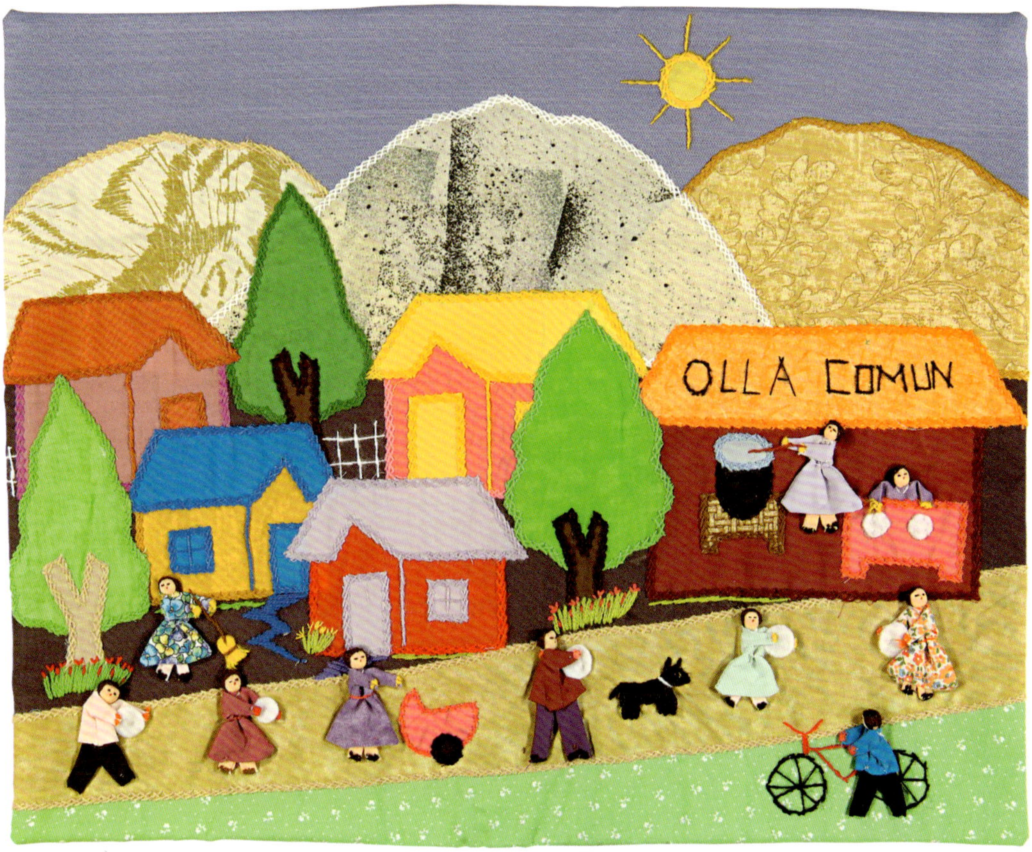

Fig. 2.31. "Olla común (Communal Kitchen)," anonymous arpillera, 2013. Collection of the author.

temporary arpilleras made for gift shop consumers stick to a few common themes, including postdictatorship courthouse gatherings and *ollas comunes*, the communal cooking pots / soup kitchens that proliferated during the dictatorship, in which poor women pooled resources to create nourishing meals, usually for neighborhood children (fig. 2.31). At first glance, the *olla común* textile has much in common with the one representing a protest regarding the disappeared: same ratio of sky to ground, similar little figures (called *monos* or, in the diminutive, *monitos*, acknowledging them as toylike, comiclike), but closer inspection reveals divergences. In the *olla común* arpillera, strict symmetry has been replaced with an asymmetrical progression, as the skewed lines of the lower third move the eye upward and rightward to the central visual incident: the woman who tends to the pot and the person seated at a table on the far right. Here the figures' faces are more finely stitched and in proportion with their bodies, and they have hands (a few simple stitches) and fabric rather than crocheted legs.

That said, all the contemporary arpilleras for sale are made with the same general techniques, riffing on a design template. All depict the same recognizably Andean mountain range, set high in the frame, that has come to signify Chilean topography. To point this out is not to diminish the arpilleras nor to discount their aesthetic pleasures—and their profound historical importance—but to note that this appliqué format, which in Chile in the mid-1970s was a wide-open field of possibility and whose compositions were sometimes wildly inventive, has congealed, at least for now, into one shared style. In addition, I do not think it disrespectful to note that not only is the pictorial imagery of the "tribunales" arpillera formulaic but its actual fabrication has been accomplished with somewhat variable skills, as the arpilleras surely gain strength as "authentic" souvenirs through their unpolished aesthetic. Some aspects of the sewing in the figure 2.29 arpillera look hastily assembled, as when threads dangle from the dress of the doll by the yellow car or when shoes are indicated with a rough jumble of black threads. Other portions are more finessed, demonstrating care and close attention to detail, including the flashes of pink and lime green flowers springing up from hand-embroidered thread stalks and the crocheted yarn legs that peek out from the red dress on the lower right. The wide arms of most of the figures, which could signal embrace, are more likely a quirk of the convenience of sewing little torsos in T-shapes (note the extra step taken to pin down the arms of the figure by the yellow car).

The form of the arpillera seems determined to speak a double language—visually, it is consistent with the grammar of the naive (using handsewn doll-sized figures), while its iconographic content, that is to say its demand for justice and accountability, speaks in a different tone. This hybridization is not unique to the arpilleras, of course, though little attention has been paid to the sometimes stark oppositions at play within these works, the friction between the quaintness of the dolls and the graphic, sometimes bloody, political messages. An early scholar and collector opined that "the bright color and easy attraction of the arpilleras may hide the truth of their message;" but what if we understood that "easy attraction" as complexly constitutive and fundamental, rather than as a diversion, distraction, or cloak?[80]

Néstor García Canclini, in his book *Hybrid Cultures: Strategies for Entering and Leaving Modernity*, has discussed the bifurcation of craft and high art with polemical words about the flattening effect produced by condescending art-historical attempts to claim creativity, originality, and innovation for artisanal methods. He writes:

> This recognition has given certain popular artisans and artists entrée into museums and galleries. But the difficulties in redefining what is specific to art and to crafts, and in interpreting the links between each one and the

other, are not arranged with goodwill openings onto what the neighbor is thinking. The way out of the deadlock in which this question is caught is a new type of research that reconceptualizes the global changes in the symbolic market by taking into account not only the intrinsic development of the popular and the cultured, but also its crossings and convergences. With the artistic and the artisanal being included in mass processes of message circulation, their sources of appropriation of images and forms and their channels of distribution and audiences tend to coincide.[81]

Following Canclini, it is vital that the arpilleras, once made by a threatened underground network of women, have been incorporated into official spaces of memory and commerce as a source of national pride. To what tense does the arpillera with the banner belong? Was it meant to speak to the present, to ongoing pleas for justice for the disappeared since Pinochet was never tried or legally held accountable for the crimes of his regime? Or is it embedded in the past, as if made during the era of the flourishing of the critical and political arpillera, when bits of cloth and hand-stitched words were among the few articulations of pointed dissent? Such an object holds in its threads a measure of melancholy—as a reminder of recent crimes that might appeal broadly to a foreign visitor (like me) eager to hold a scrap of the "real" Chile, and as a sentimental souvenir of a time when the sewing needle had a sting.

Stitching the Story

During the first few years of Pinochet's rule, under the auspices of the Comité Pro-Paz (Pro-Peace Committee) and then the Vicaría de la Solidaridad (Vicarate of Solidarity), a human rights agency affiliated with the Catholic Archdiocese of Santiago, women across Chile began to make clandestine textiles on burlap grain bags, sewing together in church basements and shantytown homes.[82] Using their own unraveled sweaters, cast-off fabrics, and donated clothing, they produced appliquéd scenes that became some of the most potent and lasting depictions of poverty, human rights violations, and resistance in Chile during the 1970s and 1980s. Some arpilleristas were the mothers, sisters, and wives of the disappeared from various class backgrounds who came together to process shared grief and strategize about how to agitate on behalf of their missing loved ones. They cut up the worn garments of missing children and husbands to embed into the arpilleras their smells and the tactile associations of the bodies that they clothed.

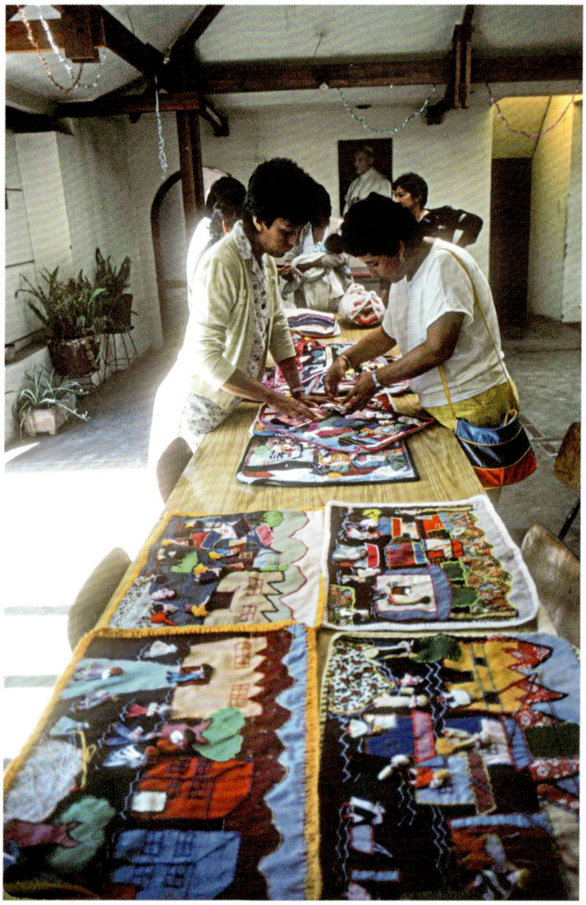

Fig. 2.32. Arpillera workshop, Santiago, Chile, 1983. Photograph by Marcelo Montecino.

Others came to the Vicaría workshops out of a sense of solidarity and wanted to offer their assistance by participating in a common humanitarian project. Most, however, were women from impoverished neighborhoods who came for economic reasons, because making arpilleras eventually promised a steady and reliable source of income. Many of the arpilleristas were already skilled seamstresses and embroiderers when they began to participate in the workshops, while others had only rudimentary sewing skills; the cut-out appliqué and stuffed-doll techniques were flexible enough to accommodate a range of abilities (fig. 2.32). They could be made by a single arpillerista who conceived and sewed a piece from its inception, or produced collectively by a workshop that practiced a division of labor.

Appliqué is often considered one of the more luxurious domestic textile practices, since it places fabric on top of fabric and hence requires a reserve of excess cloth, but many arpilleras were first made of scrounged, donated, and used materials. The textile works were primarily made to be exported and were smuggled out of Chile, sold in gift stores in Canada, Europe, and the United States, understood by such consumers primarily as craft testimonies that partook in traditions of folk cultural production while also telling necessary stories about a country in crisis. They circulated to transnational communities through networks of Chilean exiles, feminists, humanitarian aid organizations, progressive church groups, NGOs, global trade gift stores, and the like. From the outset, the contradictions inherent in making marketable objects about tough subjects such as torture or hunger incited interesting tensions between form and content. As Winnie Lira, former director of the Fundación Solidaridad, the organization that was central to the exporting of arpilleras, puts it, "We knew they would decorate children's bedrooms, and so they needed to be colorful, but the scenes themselves were dark."[83]

Part of the strategic canniness of these textiles was the fact that they were durable and portable: they could be rolled up, crammed in suitcases, and slid between layers of clothing as they passed through national borders largely undetectable by a regime that heavily censored any oppositional or critical voices. Shipments of arpilleras leaving the country (labeled with false return addresses) were discovered and publicized by police on a few occasions, however, generating negative press about "tapestries of defamation," antigovernmental "propaganda," and "subversion"—bringing fear of retribution to the arpilleristas, who were referred to in sarcastic scare quotes as "artisans."[84] One gallery whose owner dared to show the works, Galería de Arte Paulina Waugh, was bombed and destroyed in 1977.[85] Since they were meant to raise money and awareness outside the country—and were forbidden to be displayed within it—the arpilleras were not widely collected within Chile itself in the 1970s and 1980s; however, there are now calls for cultural repatriation and pleas for collectors abroad to send them back to their country of origin.[86] Though the original workshops no longer exist, arpilleras have become a widely visible cultural form. Historical arpilleras—those made from about 1974 to 1989—are increasingly institutionalized within Chilean museum contexts, prominently displayed in places like the Museum of Memory and Human Rights (less frequently in art museums), with contemporary examples, like the ones pictured previously, for sale in gift stores.[87]

Early literature on arpilleras from the 1980s, such as the pamphlet *Arpilleras: Otra forma de denuncia*, focused on the dissenting depictions of torture and suffering by the relatives of the disappeared.[88] Several foundational publications have had more comprehensive narrations of the arpilleras, including two books by Chilean-born writer and poet Marjorie Agosín and two books by the Chilean American sociologist Jacqueline Adams.[89] Arpilleras from Chile and elsewhere have been featured in many international exhibitions both monographic and thematic, some of which have produced helpful catalogues, such as *Arpilleras de la resistencia política chilena*.[90] They have also figured in American and British books on protest art and populist mediums, including Guy Brett's *Through Our Own Eyes: Popular Art and Modern History* and Lucy Lippard's *Get the Message? A Decade of Art for Social Change*.[91] I am greatly indebted to these works, while I approach from a slightly different angle—that is, I undertake a formal exploration of the scenes depicted in the arpilleras and describe the techniques used from an art-historical perspective. I think through the visual text of the textile in order to delve into the uncertainties of artisanal making that the arpilleras raise, looking closely at shifting discourses of professionalization, amateurism, and the fluctuating status of "art."

I first encountered arpilleras in 1994, when I spent a college semester living in Santiago, Chile, and made the acquaintance of a woman who had sewed briefly in a local workshop before finding a job as a housekeeper. She kept some arpilleras hidden in a trunk near her bed, fearful that they might be discovered (though Pinochet was no longer ruling as president, he was still commander-in-chief of the military). I remember only one of them in any detail; it depicted a tanklike military vehicle next to an array of small figures covered in a tangle of red thread, all set against a patterned mountain range. The nubby texture of the burlap used for the background contrasted with the smooth printed fabrics of the landscape, and the sewn-on figures reminded me of worry dolls. The arpillera raised more questions—who were these people? what was this bloodshed?—than it could answer. Did it refer to a single incident, or to a series of quashed protests, or more generally to a pervasive atmosphere of fear? Was it meant to be fingered and tactilely explored, framed behind glass, or kept out of sight? Intimate in scale yet oddly schematic in its approach to violence, it was one of the strangest and most powerful textiles I had ever seen.

There were thousands of arpilleras created during the dictatorship, and though far fewer are now made, their production continues. At the height of their export during the 1980s, it is estimated that between eight hundred and two thousand arpilleristas were at work sewing at the rate of about one completed textile a week. It is an overwhelming archive. Though I have personally handled and photographed over six hundred historical arpilleras and have seen reproductions of hundreds more, these are but a drop in the bucket.[92] Understandably, given how rich each piece is and how variable their designs have been over time, many writings about the arpilleras tend to include as many illustrations as possible in their pages while doing very little to address them individually, relying on brief explanatory captions, or attempting a quasi-taxonomic sorting in which they are placed within overarching categories. While it is tempting to try to illustrate all the examples I found most captivating, I will take the opposite tack, focusing on a very limited number of arpilleras in order to spend time with them in their details. My examples include ostensible "outliers" in both form and content (i.e., those that seem outstanding or unusual due to their compositional boldness or more esoteric iconography) as well as those that conform to the purportedly "typical" or "generic" norms.

Picturing the Workshops

The arpillera in figure 2.33, from the small southern town of Villa O'Higgins, thematizes its own making in a workshop: it is an arpillera about sewing arpilleras, and it thus functions as a visual meta-comment about its own creation. On the left-hand side, we see a table as if from above with six women gathered around it (fig. 2.33). Each has a small red square of fabric in front of her, and coiled bunches of thread and a pair of green scissors—the tools of their trade—sit on the checked surface (fig. 2.34). On the right, two women pull strands from balls of yarn while others face their fabric patches. More balls of red and purple are piled between them. One figure is placed near the top of the textile and assumes a compositional dominance as her work straddles the two sides: she sits on the right but her fabric rectangle is on the left, facing the table as if she is also overseeing the work of the others. As viewers we seem to be positioned in an interior, as two windows, barred by thin lengths of black gridded thread, punctuate each half.

Yet there is little else to give us an indication of what sort of room this might be, and the entire scene is marked by spatial dislocation. The table legs, for instance, splay awkwardly out from the lower edge, underlined by the black stitches under most figures on the left side that suggest shadows. On the right side, the shadows are light gray, and they could indicate that this side exists in a different time. It is common in arpilleras to bring together two distinct temporalities to indicate the passage of time, sometimes indicated by different-colored backgrounds, as is done here. Written in unevenly sized letters across the top of the cloth is the name of the workshop, Taller Arpilleras Villa O'Higgins, which has a titling effect for the textile itself, though it could also be written on the roof of the building, as the edges of the fabric become surrogate walls for the architectural space the figures occupy.

Emphasizing the communal nature of making and the steps in the process, the figures are clearly engaged in collective work, pooling resources, and sharing equipment. Three smaller figures—children?—stand under the table; it is hard to interpret what they are doing. One holds a pink square, edged on only three sides, as if it is a purse or satchel, with the word LANDY, perhaps a name of the girl in the arpillera, or the maker herself. This could signify a contraction, L'Andy or La Andy—the addition of *la* in front of a female name is very common in Chile as an endearment. The *Ls* in "taller" are much more angular than this initial line, which means it could also be a curlicue continuation of the *A*. It could also read CANDY, which would be unusual, as arpilleras rarely use English words, but of course this is not impossible. The *D* might also be an *O*, in which case it might be the name Lanoy; as with much about the arpilleras, deciphering these various elements is not straightforward.

For this textile, the figures' bodies are rendered in appliqué, and their patterned scraps of dresses are attached to the cloth background using contrasting threads. Their faces are indicated with a series of embroidered stitches, as skin tones range from off-white to light orange. Some have articulated hair

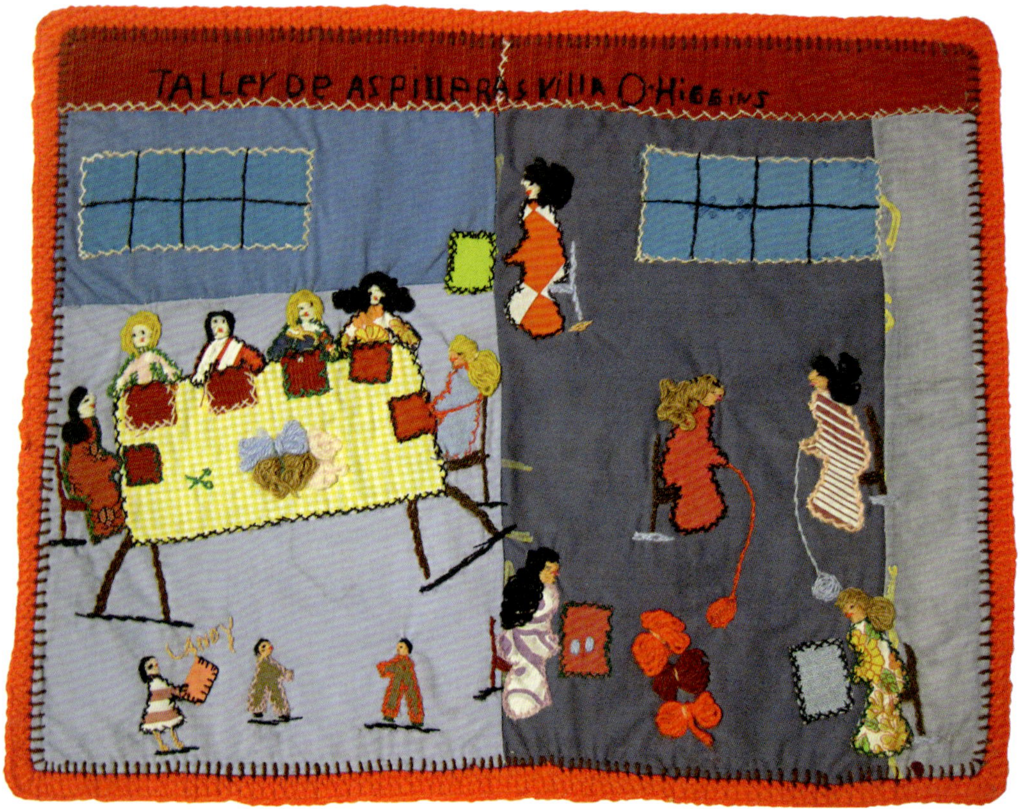

Fig. 2.33. Taller O'Higgins workshop, anonymous arpillera, date unknown. Genevieve Jacques Fund. Collection of the Museo de la Memoria y los Derechos Humanos. Photograph by the author.

that becomes almost animated, as when great curling masses of black yarn hair bunch around a face or spill down a back. When used on the edges of some torsos, the cross-stitch has a certain effect, as it seems to bite into the bodies and can register as injuring rather than affixing. The stitching also produces a different sense of the compositional integration of the figures into the scene than do the three-dimensional stuffed dolls, which rise up from the surface of the textile. Ringing the entire arpillera is a red woolen crocheted edging, an extra insertion of textile handicraft that is present on nearly all the historical arpilleras but absent in current versions. The yarn is the same color used in the balls being wound, and again the arpillera is self-aware of its materiality, taking pains to illuminate and integrate the materials of its own making. As viewers, we have full visual access as we witness this performance of craft, which unfolds as if on a theatrical stage. This sense of the transparency of the scene—as if we are glimpsing some truth of the object's own making—is compromised by the simplified, abstracted nature of the figures and the space itself, as it does not conform to the usual laws of gravity or perspective. In other words, we do not view the workshop as much as we imaginatively inhabit it.

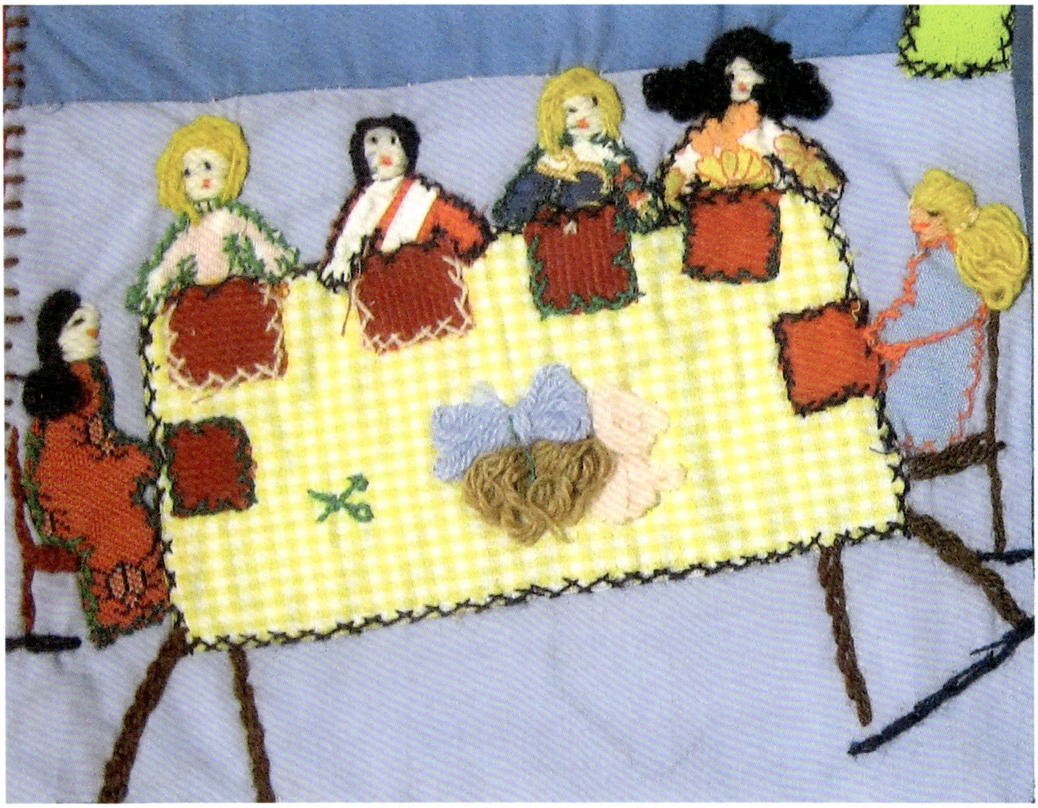

The arpillera is created from many folk needlecraft traditions—crochet, embroidery, cross-stitch. Yet exact origin stories and speculative lineages vary. Even the date on which the arpillera workshops first began is contested, as "contradictory accounts" of their beginnings have flourished.[93] In terms of format, possible precedents include the yarn-based tapestries (also called arpilleras) of Chilean artist and singer Violeta Parra, who was dedicated to reviving folk traditions across media; the patchwork aesthetic embraced by hippie fashion in the United States in the 1970s, discussed in the previous chapter; scenic woolen embroideries made by women known as the *bordadoras* in Isla Negra; decorative embroidered work from the neighborhood of Macul; woven ponchos of the Mapuche; and the elaborate *molas* of Panama.[94] In fact, the style of appliqué found in the arpillera is not unique, as examples can be found in other Latin American countries like Colombia and Peru, but using this textile format to explicitly criticize a political regime was specifically developed in the 1970s workshops in Santiago.[95] At the same time, not all proffered a legible critique against the dictatorship; some, like the one in figure 2.33, showed scenes of making or work, while others depict moments of play or leisure, such as children flying kites.

Fig. 2.34. Detail of Taller O'Higgins workshop, anonymous arpillera, date unknown. Genevieve Jacques Fund. Collection of the Museo de la Memoria y los Derechos Humanos. Photograph by the author.

Textures of Cloth

Not all arpilleras build upon the activities of everyday life; some were more openly symbolic or oneiric (fig. 2.35). In this arpillera the burlap itself takes center stage, as there is no colorful cloth backdrop to provide a setting for a narrative. Instead, the tapestry is constructed around contrasting textures, bodily fragmentation, and spatial confusion. Behind prison bars, two crying eyes, ambiguously gendered female by their long lashes, drip tears into two open hands, fingers cupped to receive the silvery-gray drops. The hands, made of yellow fabric and embroidered around the edges with brown thread, demonstrate technical knowledge of foreshortening. Two other hands, chained together by gray handcuffs, float along the outer edges of the textile, fingernails and knuckles carefully rendered in brown thread.

There are two or three bodies suggested here, but part of the strength of the composition is that we cannot know how these disembodied parts belong together. Notice how much thought and preplanning went into this design: the maker had to plot each element in relation to the others and know what to stitch first, so that the vertical gray prison bars were embroidered over the eyes, one tear just hitting the lower black border as if about to dissolve it. Barely visible red lines on the fingers, and brown lines evident on the burlap under the hands, indicate guidelines before the yellow fabric was cut and stitched. Though they are not contained by the bars that make up a surrogate face encaging the eyes, the hands are restricted by the chain that binds them and by the crocheted edging—in many arpilleras a vivid contrasting color, but here a muted brown that matches the burlap fabric. Its chain stitch echoes the chain of the handcuffs, becoming another enclosure around the boundary of the square cloth. The rough texture of the backing is charged with meaning; its coarse grid registers as confinement. In this way, like the arpillera that depicts its own making in the workshop, the textile references and metaphorizes its own materials.

Many arpilleras display a similarly keen attention to the specific properties of fabrics and fibers and their powers to suggest multiple meanings. In the figure 2.36 dictatorship-era arpillera of an *olla común*, the light blue sky is a narrow band at the very top of the textile, as the serrated mountains crowd out any room for a sun. One frequently recounted story about the workshops is the perpetual shortage of blue cloth: because so many arpilleras depicted a wide expanse of sky, and arpilleristas were loath to piece the sky together as a patchwork of different hues, blue was one of the most in-demand colors.[96] Here houses with patterned roofs are arranged around a central black cooking pot, and female figures gather around it, many of them bearing actual

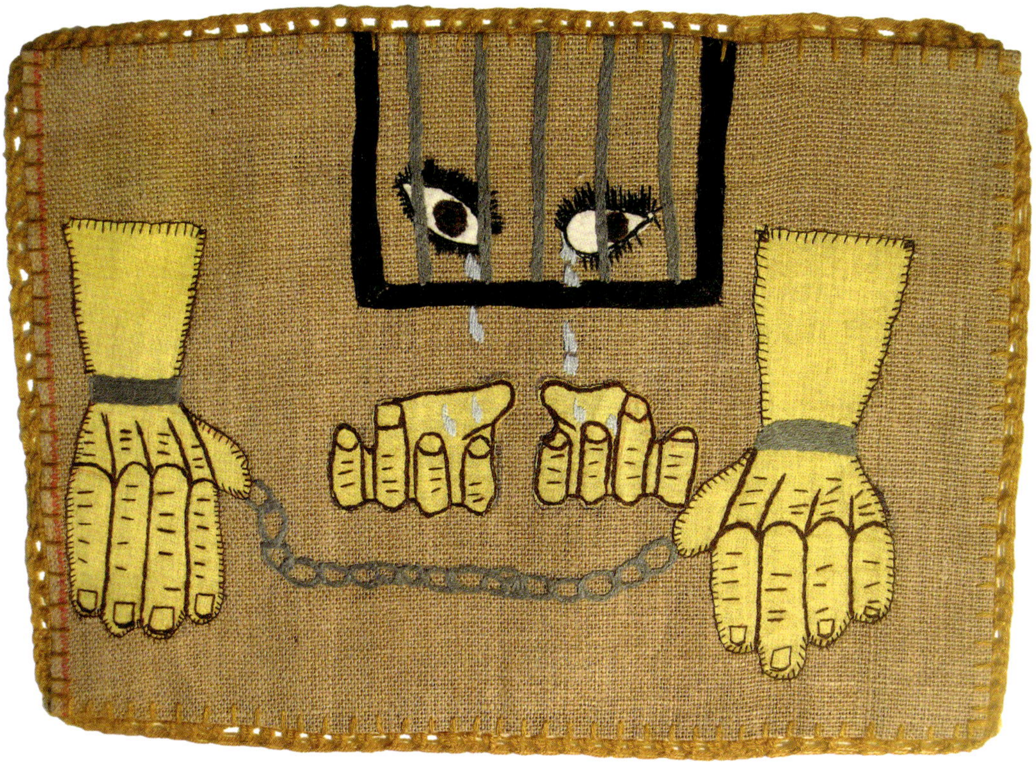

ingredients for the food—grains of rice, thin broken vermicelli noodles (fig. 2.37). Some of these foods are cradled in the plastic protective cups, both oblong and round, cut out of drugstore pill packages. The steaming pot sits on a vigorous fire, its flames fed by real wooden sticks sewn onto the dark green cloth. As this detail indicates, a range of found objects are often embedded within the textiles, such as seeds or grains piled in bowls, wooden matchsticks that become broom handles, cardboard squares transformed into book covers, aluminum shaped into cooking utensils, wires that twist into bicycle frames, toy plastic tires set on fire with bright red and orange thread, scraps of newspapers bundled together with bits of twine.

Fig. 2.35. Anonymous arpillera, date unknown. Collection of the Museo de la Solidaridad Salvador Allende. Photograph by the author.

If some of the materials on this list sound familiar—seeds, sticks, cardboard, thread, and newspaper—it is because they closely mirror the scavenged bits used by Vicuña in the precarios she made as part of her *Journal of Objects*. As a Chilean in exile traveling widely, Vicuña would have been *more* likely to know about arpilleras than had she stayed in the country, where they did not freely circulate; as mentioned previously, she owned one, though she is not sure when exactly she acquired it. (It is possible that she owned one of the cheery embroideries from Isla Negra, rather than one of the arpilleras produced under the auspices of the Vicaría workshop.)[97] Regardless of exact

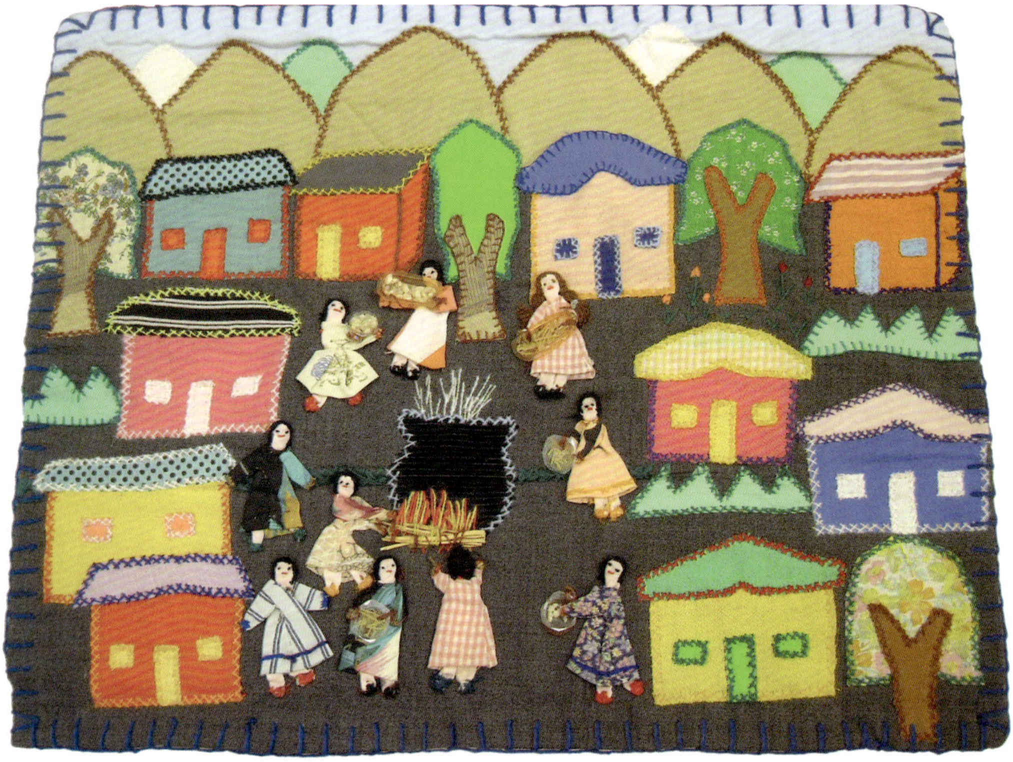

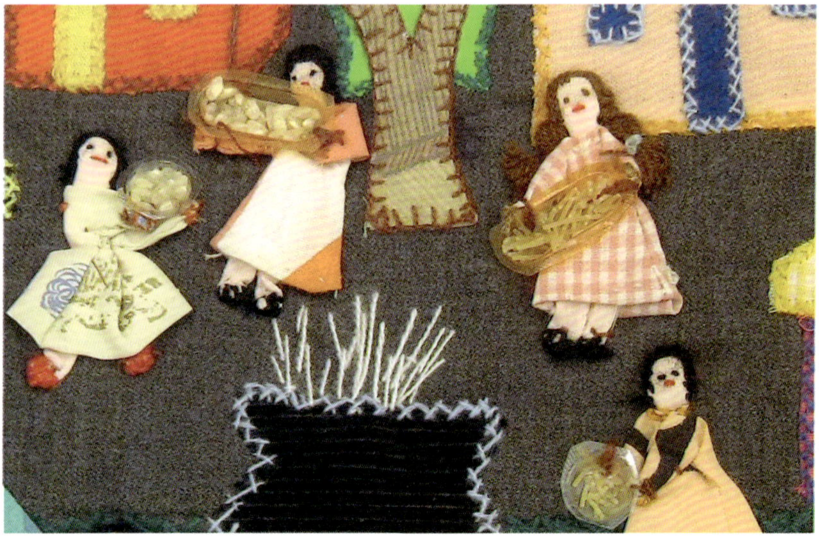

Fig. 2.36. (*Top*) Anonymous arpillera, date unknown.
Collection of the Fundación Salvador Allende. Photograph by the author.

Fig. 2.37. (*Bottom*) Detail of anonymous arpillera, date unknown.
Collection of the Fundación Salvador Allende. Photograph by the author.

vectors of influence or knowledge, several aspects of her work in the 1970s resonate with the arpilleras, including how her miniature sweater resembles the garments that make up the torsos of the figures. Though obviously taking different form (from allusive assemblages meant to be understood as a kind of visual poetry to representational incidents), both Vicuña and the arpilleristas use found objects as a way to embed the stuff of daily life into their work.

As I discuss below, many arpilleras have also been considered "diaristic" in nature, though the treatment of the tapestries as personal inscriptions has been disputed. These talismanic objects convey a dollhouse verisimilitude that is at once precious and uncanny—so like life, so recognizably of our world, but rendered in miniature. In the *olla común* textile, the dollhouse effect is both cute and chilling; the colorful fabrics, embroidered flowers, and smiling faces belie the fact that what is being represented is at once an image of resourcefulness and one of malnutrition, privation, and Pinochet's devastating neoliberal economic policies that exacerbated income disparities.

Paint, Thread, and Blood

Nowhere are the disjunctive aspects of the political arpilleras more apparent than in the ones that depict militarization and violence. In one, police vehicles and army-green clad figures with guns occupy the lower band of the textile, offset by a background of bright red (fig. 2.38). Two people who had been apparently in the act of painting graffiti on the street—"PARO N," or the beginnings of "paro nacional" (national strike)—have been caught, and perhaps shot, as they lie horizontally on the pink pavement. Within the visual vocabulary of the arpillera, because they wear pants and not dresses or skirts, they are likely gendered male, but this is by no means conclusive. Between the two painters is a can overflowing with red, matching the blood-red stitching used for the letters as they trail off. The heads of the brushes, loaded with red paint, are so chaotically stitched that they resemble embroidered flames. The figure on the right has two thin threads of red emerging from its torso and leg, but his crocheted pink arm still grips the brush that is suspended, aloft, defiantly continuing its stroke. Some of the most innovative uses of everyday materials are found in police scenes like this one, as the transparent plastic pill casings used for bowls in the *olla común* arpillera are repurposed into helmets, or, as here, bent around faces to make protective shields. Adding a sinister edge of hardness that contrasts the softness of the fabric, these plastics also show the arpilleristas' heterodox embrace of all kinds of materials, not only the fiber-based matter typically associated with appliqué (fig. 2.39).

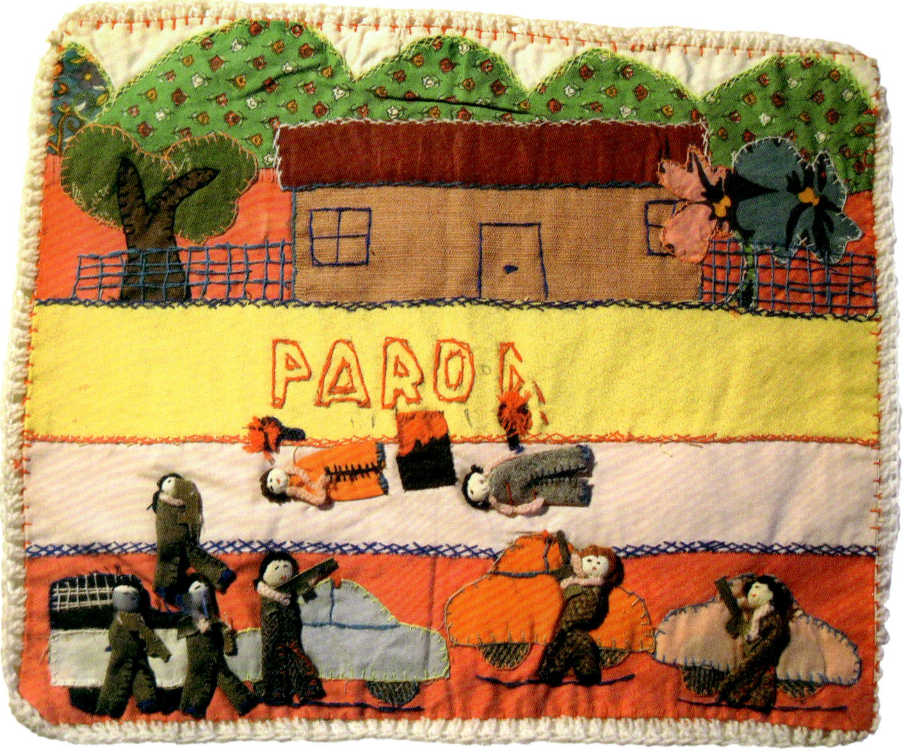

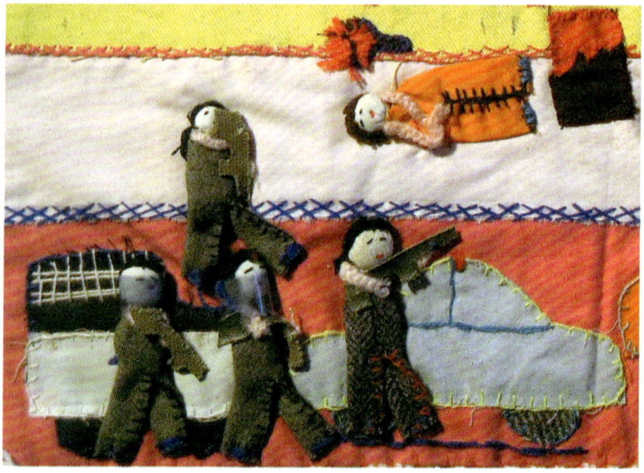

Fig. 2.38. (*Top*) Anonymous arpillera, date unknown.
Collection of the Museo de la Solidaridad Salvador Allende. Photograph by the author.

Fig. 2.39. (*Bottom*) Detail of anonymous arpillera, date unknown.
Collection of the Museo de la Solidaridad Salvador Allende. Photograph by the author.

It is tempting to try to correlate the street painting and the apparent shooting with actual incidents of violence—many arpilleras do refer to events of their time. Some arpilleras have small pockets and pouches sewn on their backs into which paper notes are folded, containing handwritten explanatory words or messages about missing loved ones. And some are inscribed with dates, as if to pin down the events to specific days and months. More often, however, the scenes float free of certain signification and might refer to many events collapsed temporally into one, or are invocations of things that could happen or are in the realm of possibility. There can be no seamless translation of "facts," particularly those about resistance efforts that were only partially circulated and haltingly transmitted due to widespread censorship, to the often opaque schematizations of the appliqué format.

At the same time, the PARO N arpillera might remind us that in July 1986 there was a national general strike against the Pinochet regime in which two young protesters (one male and one female) demonstrating in Los Nogales were sprayed with gas and burned by a military patrol in what came to be known as the "el caso Quemados" (the case of the Burned Ones).[98] Rodrigo Rojas, who was nineteen years old, died of his injuries. Some claimed the teenagers were set on fire by their own Molotov cocktails rather than by the police. But a secure referent remains somewhat elusive, as the arpillera's indecipherability between the red paint and the flames strategically opens onto multiple interpretations. The burned protesters were participating in a busy street barricade, yet the arpillera's composition carefully isolates the two figures, with no other figures in the frame besides the military police bristling in the lower portion of the textile.

Instead of trying to tie such an arpillera to a certain incident, it might be more productive to consider how this envisioned episode (which, even if it had some actual precedent, is heavily interpreted) proclaims its affinity with other forms of protest. In this textile, the arpillerista herself becomes a kind of graffiti artist as she letters the word PARO. Like a wall, a piece of fabric, as a scrap of space, is a contested public arena. The visual languages for murals and for appliqué are clearly distinct, but both forms can vocalize dissent. Like arpilleras made in neighborhoods such as Los Nogales, murals and street art were deployed to reclaim territory.[99]

Looking more closely at this PARO arpillera, we can observe how peculiar its depiction of public space is. For one thing, the two halves of the arpillera are startlingly dissonant. The top half of the arpillera resembles a fairly standard iteration of most of the outdoor scenes, with an emphasis on the flowered pattern of the rounded green mountains that jut up against the edge of the textile, and two large printed hibiscus-type plants that have been cut out from a different fabric and sewn individually. The low, long brown building—an institution? a home?—is framed on either side by a blue fence, and much attention has gone into getting the geometry of the fence right, even as the showy pink flower on the right bursts forth and over its boundaries. The white crocheted edging matches the white sky, though it has been attached with the same red thread used in the graffiti letters. Yet the static symmetry of the upper portion background becomes animated by the six police *monitos* and their vehicles. Unlike the horizontal painters with their inert little bodies, the police are on the go, their legs are crossed or actively cocked at angles to signify movement as they hold small floppy guns pointed in many directions. The building with its closed windows is a facade of indifference, and the fence on each side adds to the sense that the painters are trapped, hemmed in. As viewers, we become the only eyewitnesses to this crime.

These arpilleras are hard-hitting, and during the Pinochet era such works were considered subversive and illegal forms of speech. As noted earlier, they were frequently confiscated when intercepted leaving the country, leading to sensationalist newspaper reports about counterpropaganda being exported to international audiences.[100] The workshops were granted some special protections by virtue of being affiliated with the Catholic Church. Still, those who smuggled the arpilleras out of Chile faced serious repercussions, and the Vicaría was infiltrated, surveilled, and subject to ongoing harassment by the police.[101] At various times the Vicaría was forced to deny "sponsoring politicized craftworks."[102] (Lira recalls having to notarize paperwork declaring that her shipments contained nothing but "artisanal objects," as if such objects were necessarily harmless.)[103] Following the paradoxical logic of censorship, in which the act of censoring brings even more attention to the disputed image, photographs of the contested arpilleras sometimes accompanied the newspaper reports, granting them far wider exposure within Chile than they would have had otherwise.

Dividing Lines

The form and the content of the more political arpilleras are insistently contradictory: police dolls that shoot and torture, oppressive poverty that unfolds within sunny mountainous landscapes. Since they began to be shown and discussed within and beyond Chile, these contradictions have only sharpened, as they have been subject to divisive interpretations. Apparently basic facts are frequently contested, such as how many arpilleristas were active during the dictatorship and when precisely the workshops began.[104] Much of the literature discussing arpilleras has understood them to be more or less transparent glimpses into the daily lives of their makers, akin to reportage or journalism. Brett claims that "from these thousands of images a complete and detailed chronicle could be made of the experiences of the Chilean working class since the brutal military coup of 1973."[105]

Unlike Vicuña's symbolic "journal" of objects, arpilleras have been widely viewed as direct, literal inscriptions of women's lives. Arpilleristas do use frequently the language of the "diary" to discuss their designs. For example, María Teresa Madariaga does so in her statement for a Chilean documentary, but she also talks about how she "translates" her life into fabric, emphasizing at once its relevance to the everyday and the heavy filtering enacted by her hand. In the same documentary, Cecilia Sánchez emphasizes that her arpilleras capture a "feeling" or a "sentiment," drawing attention to their generation of affective meanings rather than their "realistic" portrayals.[106]

Agosín writes that certain arpilleras "might be classified as chronicles detailing the crimes of the dictatorship. They can be 'read' as easily as one reads a daily newspaper, so closely are they connected with daily events."[107] She also refers to them, in their quickness to absorb and represent the realities of everyday life, as being "like a newspaper sketch."[108] Adams, though more skeptical of these claims, states that "although mediated, they do represent shantytown women's 'truth': the arpilleras were their photographs of sorts."[109] The notion that the arpilleras are akin to documentary photographs—and that they reveal even more information than a photograph can—is widespread; Emma Sepúlveda says in her introduction to a book of testimonies of arpilleristas, "All the arpilleras are true photographs because they tell a history that goes beyond what we could understand in a single glance."[110] Arpilleras are figured as more penetrating and more insightful than a photograph, because they are imbued with affect and laden with emotion that is understood as truth-telling and "authentic." This reading ignores the significant editing and decision making on the part of the makers, as well as the interpretive uncertainty of the audience viewing these works.

In addition, there are major ideological conflicts in the literature regarding agency, creative control, and expressive choice. This debate can be encapsulated by summarizing the differing language used by Agosín and Adams. Agosín has been the primary literary ambassador of arpilleras, as she was one of the first to write comprehensively about them for the audiences who were buying them abroad, namely American, Canadian, and European leftists. In 1987, while Pinochet was still in power, she published an article about arpilleras in the US feminist publication *Heresies*, and her work was translated into German.[111] Agosín writes movingly of her first experience talking to arpilleristas and visiting arpillera workshops during the height of their production under Pinochet, and focuses, as the words *hope* and *love* in her *Tapestries of*

Hope, Threads of Love title indicate, on the healing aspects of making as well as the women's forging cross-class affiliations and creating a new feminist version of political power.

She writes: "With their big round suns and the peaks of the Andes framing the background, these simple cloth pictures assembled by women, some illiterate, some from the upper levels of society, travel to the far corners of the earth speaking for those who have no voice."[112] Agosín has also situated the arpilleras within the bumpy history of women's rights within Chile, drawing on Elsa Chaney's *Supermadre* (Supermother) to argue that women have been constrained and silenced by dominant gendered divisions of labor.[113] Agosín, like many whom she has influenced, writes that the arpilleristas turned those constraints on their heads by placing dissent squarely within the realm of the typically feminine domestic handicrafts. For Agosín, the arpilleras are at the same time diaristic accounts and artistic invocations of memory, experiential truth, loss, and expression.

By contrast, Adams writes from a social sciences perspective, gleaning from arpilleras "evidence" about life during the coup from the women makers and emphasizing that the visual images are "an excellent source of data."[114] Unlike Agosín, she is quick to downplay creative choice within the arpilleras, instead focusing on the standardization imposed by the Vicaría and by the international marketplace where they were bought and sold. In Adams's account, the arpilleristas were told what color combinations to use, how many figures should be placed on an arpillera, what subjects to represent, et cetera. Those not adhering to such expectations about quality or the strict rules about content were rejected. She argues, "The arpilleras, then, were not the 'free' expressions of their makers. The arpilleristas worked within constraints and controls imposed by the Vicaría through quality control; orders for particular content and form; the banning of certain depictions; and instructions regarding colors, type of cloth, and elements within the arpilleras."[115]

Agosín and Adams both root their analyses on interviews with the arpilleristas and firsthand trips to Chile, yet they come to opposing conclusions about agency and choice. The two authors also diverge when discussing the impact of selling the textiles. "They never became objects of marketing, were never meant for mass production or sale," states Agosín.[116] Adams, however, traces how they became increasingly commercial, and as a result more generic, as they were exported and sold abroad as part of what she calls the "solidarity art system."[117] (Her emphasis on standardization and routinization of design seems to belie her use of the term *art*, which she does not explicate in any detail.) Adams claims that "rather than the raw expression of women's thinking . . . they are mediated by buyers and sellers abroad and by the Vicaría. . . . Even when the Vicaría did not make explicit orders, the women knew the kind of subject-matter it wanted, and censored themselves accordingly. Individuals selling the arpilleras abroad were another influence, since they told the Vicaría that their buyers wanted more arpilleras on certain subjects and fewer on others."[118]

Artists, Artisans, Workers

So what about the category of art? Some insist that the arpilleras were largely a collective project, with no sense of individual ownership, while others emphasize that the arpilleristas were artists who through the workshops came into a growing sense of their own authorial voices. In some cases, no one is more surprised than the makers themselves that these cast-off scraps are valued now as artistic objects. Aprillerista Adriana Rojas told Agosín, "It was first our handkerchief and now it is an art."[119] Note that she does not say that she herself is an artist but rather is commenting about the material as a product. Putting themselves more firmly in the realm of active dissidents or knowledge producers, some arpilleristas referred to themselves as "'pamphleteers' and 'journalists.'"[120] As one scholar, Hernán Vera, writes, "The women who create arpilleras do not consider themselves artists: many of them do not even know how to draw, and many of them learned how to sew and embroider only to produce arpilleras for money to help them cope with their immediate survival needs, not to follow any expressive or decorative inclinations."[121] Very rarely do arpilleristas discuss the artistic nature of their craft, as when Victoria Díaz Caro, whose father was disappeared in 1976, states, "I believe that I am one of the few women of the group that was interested in the artistic value of the arpillera."[122] At times, the variable understandings of artistry generated tensions within the workshops, as some arpilleristas felt socially elevated by virtue of their crafting beautiful objects, while others felt compromised selling their skills.[123]

Carla Miranda, curator at the Museo de la Solidaridad Salvador Allende, insists that the arpilleristas had no concept of themselves as artists. "For these women, handicraft was a chore. Crocheting was not a way of making art but more like mopping."[124] She argues that in recent years, with more state investment in ideas of cultural patrimony, the originally anonymous popular work of the arpilleristas has been recuperated and absorbed into a capitalist notion of individual art making. Miranda is not alone when she sees this as part of a broader conservative thrust within Chilean culture to promote handicrafts as part of a solidified national identity, a push that began under Pinochet when his wife, Lucía Hiriart, took over the Centro de Madres de Chile (CEMA Chile) and promoted traditional domestic making as a way to keep women in their place as mothers and wives—quiet, apolitical, and preoccupied with tending house.[125] Normative gender roles, then, were upheld by the patriarchal military regime in the service of discipline, order, and patriotism. The restriction of women to the private space of the home, consigned to sewing and other tasks, participated in a "cult of docile femininity and domesticity—both now reinforced by military control of government, institutions, and ideology."[126] These policies were bound together in Chile's neoliberal push: the embrace of free-market economies occurred in parallel with the strategic emphasis on women as wives and mothers, which "restored a vision and feeling of normalcy in Chilean life."[127] The sewing workshops, which could be understood as small-scale entrepreneurialism as well as an affirmation of women's traditional work, fit loosely into this schema.

Along with contested notions about their artistic value and their role in the new economy, there is no easy or set answer to the question of how arpilleras function as protest—much less as *feminist* protest. Arpilleras offered a platform for women to tell alternative histories, particularly within the context of what Chilean feminists call "the silencing of women" and historical difficulties around the political place of women, including lack of access to divorce and abortion.[128] Though the arpilleristas did forge a common sense of purpose in the workshops, Adams argues that they were largely following an established set of rules to make money rather than intending to critique the dictatorship. Others, like Camila Fernanda Sastre Díaz, discuss the workshops as routes to the arpilleristas' broader politicization *as women*, regardless of the content of the textiles. In her view, this hinges on class; poor women began to identify themselves as more than wives, mothers, and sisters, using the textiles to break official silences about issues like poverty from a domesticated space of feminized craft that both continued to interpellate them as women and was nonetheless potent.[129]

Given these differing viewpoints, virtually no space for agreement emerges: Did the form of appliqué emerge spontaneously and collectively, or did one crucial volunteer at the Vicaría introduce the idea? Were the textiles made in an assembly-line factory, wherein different women were tasked with stuffing the human figures or cutting out the houses, or was each of them one woman's vision from start to finish? Both practices happened. Generalizations are impossible to make, as workshop practices varied from region to region across the country. We do know that communal making was not unusual—if one woman in a workshop got sick, others would pitch in to finish her arpillera so she would still be paid her salary for the week.

In part, the ideological fault lines that break over the meaning and categorization of the arpilleras are based on the fact that, as stated, they were made by two purportedly distinct populations—the mothers, wives, and sisters

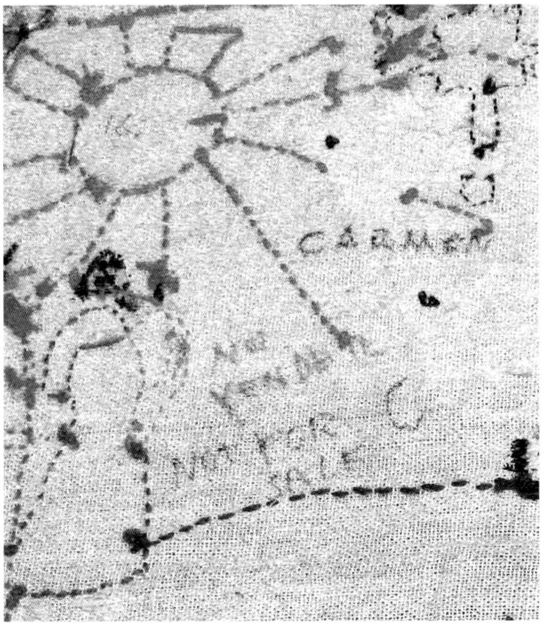

Fig. 2.40.
Back of arpillera stating "not for sale," made by Carmen, 1973–74. Carmen Waugh Fund. Collection of the Museo de la Memoria y los Derechos Humanos. Photograph by the author.

of the disappeared sewing with scraps from the very clothing of their missing loved ones on the one hand, and poor women churning out formulaic textiles for an income on the other. Which reading one chooses depends in part on which archive, and which makers, one prioritizes. Yet to binarize these groups so neatly is to assume that one might be able to easily ascertain which textile belongs to which camp: not so. Poor women also made works about torture, just as mothers of detainees made generic landscapes. What is more, some arpilleras were never intended for sale, as in figure 2.40, which is marked on its back in both Spanish and English, along with the year and the first name of its maker, Carmen, "no vender / not for sale." Rich with visual interest, the underside of the arpillera reveals its process of making, with stitches radiating out from the sun and dense clots of thread for hair.

There are so many contested stories, so many wavering memories and disputed facts, so many partial names and missing dates, that in some crucial sense the only thing we know for sure about the arpilleras is what they look like. They do not belong only to the realms of artistic making and folk practices. Though they may be handmade, as I argue throughout this book, textile handicraft is never just itself, for it always defines itself in opposition to some other category—the realm of industry, say, or work. And in some cases of the arpilleras, the standardization came not from arbitrary top-down rule making but because of availability of materials—they were mostly around 37×45 cm because that was the size of a dry-goods sack. Even when the workshops stopped using found bags for the backing and relied on purchased burlap, the entire exporting system had calibrated itself to these measurements (smaller and larger sizes were also produced but were not common).

To insist upon overarching similarities across the arpilleras is to miss the textured range of responses evident in their making. One does not need recourse to the defended category of "art" to be aware of extreme inventions on display here. In the scene shown in figure 2.41, arpilleristas demonstrate extraordinary sensitivity to the properties of textiles, in particular their haptic, bodily charge. This work contains two related vignettes occurring under a brown mountainscape. In one a lone female protester holds a sign that calls for the end of the Central Nacional de Informaciones (CNI) and its policies of torture.[130] She functions as a surrogate for the arpillerista herself, with her arpillera-shaped banner that has visibly hand-stitched edging. A trail of broken blue stitches could track her path from under the palm tree on the right-hand side. Meanwhile, inside a dark building something else is happening, hidden under a flap of white cloth. The viewer is invited to engage with the cloth via touch, lifting the small square, in an interactive moment that calls on the natural curiosity fostered by a pop-up book or Advent calendar.

But what lies under the bandagelike flap of fabric is hardly child's play (fig. 2.42). A naked doll—her crocheted pale torso and pink limbs tender and exposed—has been secured to a *parrilla* (metal frame), and a masked figure wields a red wire that snakes from the wall to its hand. Light pen marks make electrical zigzags above the wire, and the same instrument has been used to make tears staining the face of the tortured doll, whose spread legs suggest that the wire is destined for her genitals (a form of torture widely used during the dictatorship).[131] One survivor of such torture recounts, "They looked for breasts to hit you, or the vagina to put an electrode; they looked for the most sensitive and prurient parts of your body, it was done specifically to torment you. For them it was routine."[132]As we too uncover the body here, do we become complicit in this scene?

In a different scene of torture (fig. 2.43), issues of concealment and visibility are again thematized through an inventive use of fabric. Unified by the oranges and reds that appear in the checked fabric of the mountain range, the background, and some of the stitching that tacks down the tree branches and holds the crocheted edging to the main tapestry, this grim scene announces itself with the words "aquí se tortura" (here they torture, or torture is done here). The phrase emphasizes the place—*here*—more than the identity of the perpetrators. No matter, as the rest of the tapestry points fingers, clearly attributing the torture to the CNI, whose initials are lettered on the building as well as the cars parked outside. The walls and roof of the building are demarcated with thick black bands, inside which two dolls are sewn down between a pair of torturers. Yet what is unfolding there is not entirely accessible to

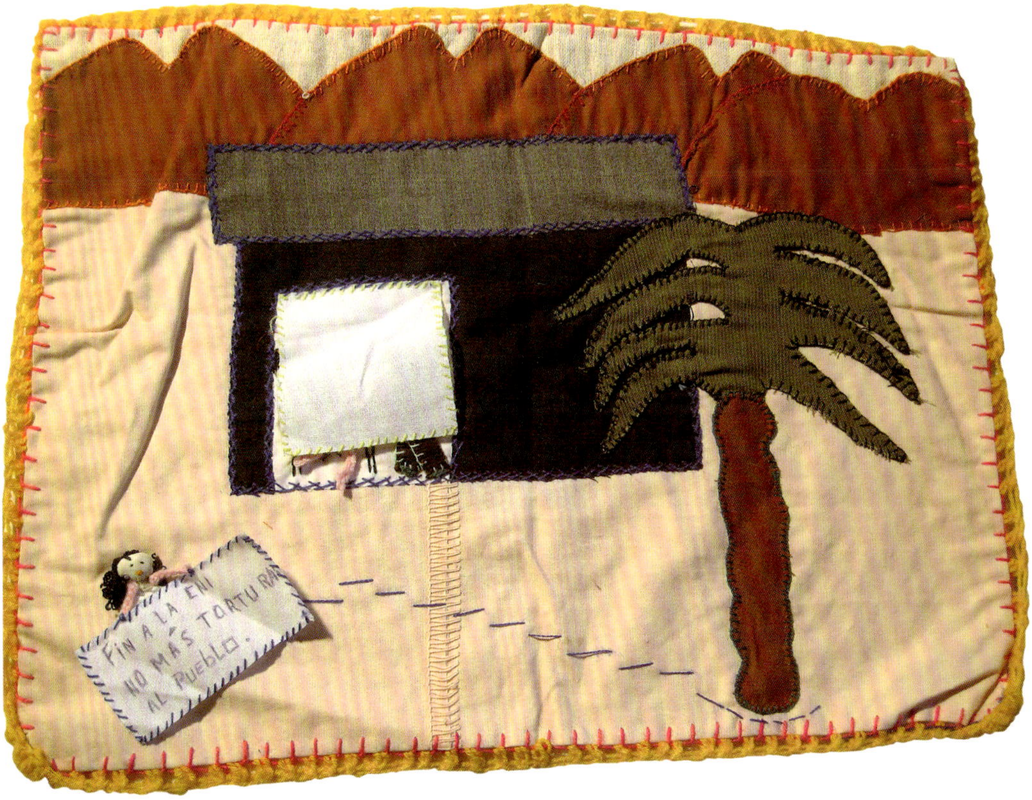

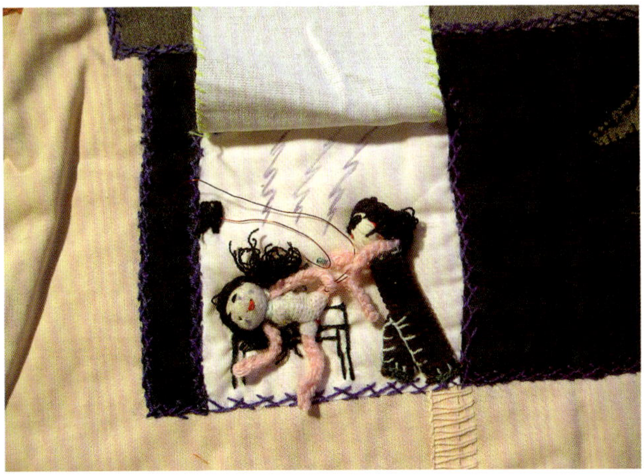

Fig. 2.41.
(*Top*) "No más tortura (No More Torture)," anonymous arpillera. Collection of the Museo de la Solidaridad Salvador Allende. Photograph by the author.

Fig. 2.42.
(*Bottom*) Detail of "No más tortura (No More Torture)," anonymous arpillera. Collection of the Museo de la Solidaridad Salvador Allende. Photograph by the author.

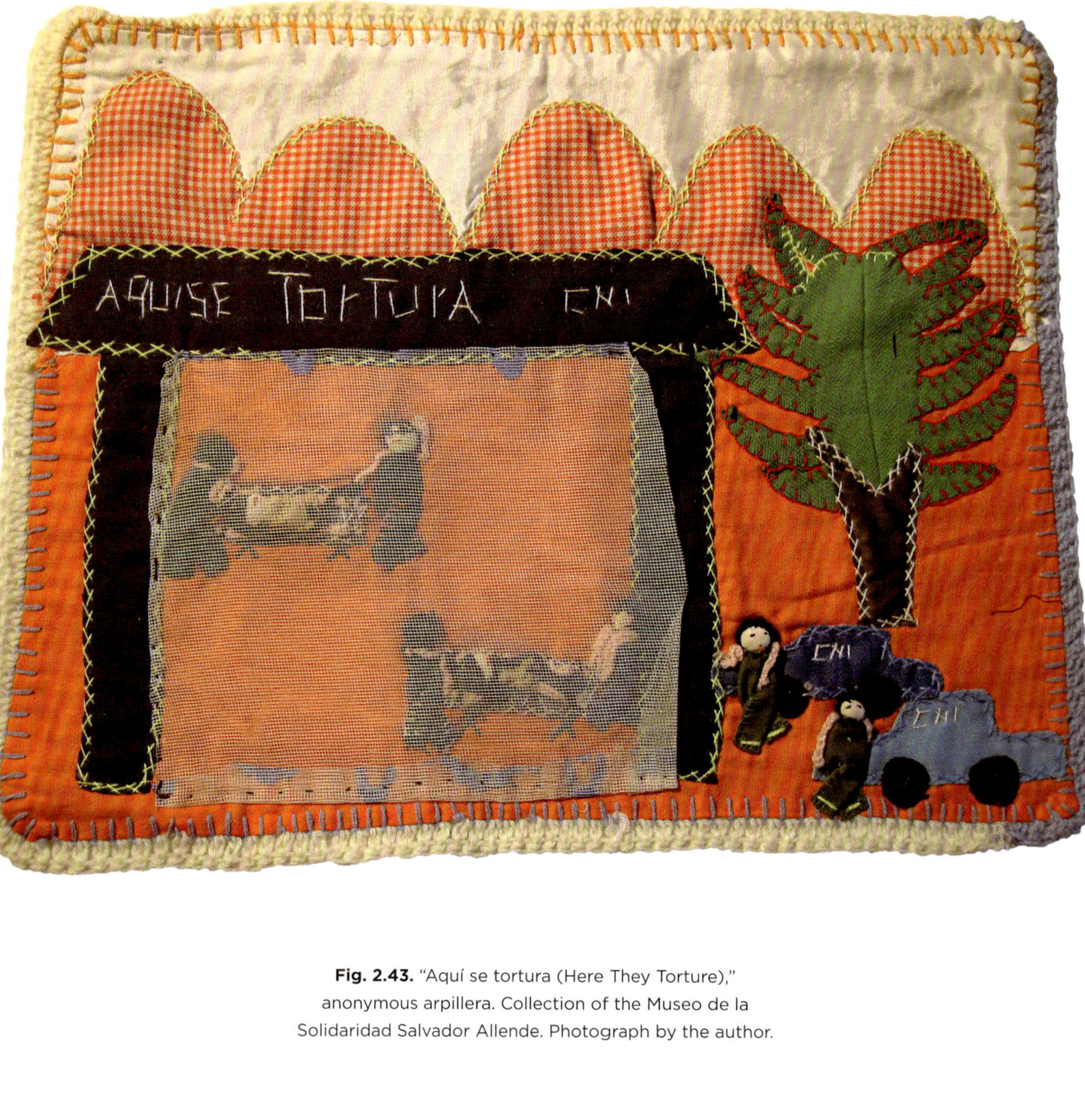

Fig. 2.43. "Aquí se tortura (Here They Torture),"
anonymous arpillera. Collection of the Museo de la
Solidaridad Salvador Allende. Photograph by the author.

us, as a piece of mesh has been sewn over the scene, obscuring it from our gaze. As with the previous, interactive arpillera, one is tempted to try to lift this veil, but it is tacked down with stitches on all sides. Is this an attempt to preserve some dignity for those being tortured? A recognition that we do not and may never have unimpeded access to what goes on in such spaces? A practical compositional choice made to hold down the many messy threads? Or, finally, is it a reckoning with the fact that this depiction of torture was destined for a marketplace where representations of human rights violations were valued because of their recognizably Chilean origins, but could be too explicit or disturbing to be salable?

Humanitarian Consumerism

The arpilleras are in many respects structured by the frictions between making and selling, oscillating between cheerful decorative souvenir and gruesome testimonial. When they first began to be sold abroad in the mid-1970s, arpilleras cost about seven US dollars each.[133] The Vicaría pooled profits in a communal fund and distributed monies (accounted for by designated treasurers in each workshop) so that every arpillerista received an equivalent salary. About a decade later, when the *New York Times* wrote about arpilleras in 1984, the article concluded by saying that arpilleras were available for purchase directly from the Vicaría for the price of twenty dollars.[134] According to Lira, the explicitly violent ones raised a bit of a dilemma for some vendors, and buyers abroad began to specify ratios of neutral versus "strong" or political textiles, as when a group in Switzerland requested a shipment containing "80 percent pretty pictures and 20 percent poverty and human rights."[135]

Figure 2.44, a photo of people browsing objects made in the solidarity workshops, offers a glimpse into a moment of their display and marketing for a Chilean audience. Customers crowd around a table laden with jewelry and textiles, while hanging on the walls in the background are arpilleras, though they are not in focus enough to decipher aside from vague mountain ranges. What are the politics of such a purchase? Does it fall within the realm of a humanitarian consumerism that reassures the consumer that she is an agential force doing the "right thing," but ultimately is devoid of activist content and "lacking any reference to the exercise of power," as one critic of such consumer-based movements puts it?[136] Or does it make broadly visible and productively instantiate struggles for justice within people's homes? By the mid-1980s, arpilleristas openly wondered about these issues; as Agosín states, "Now the women worry about the commercialization of their arpilleras, about overproduction, and a decline in the number of buyers."[137] There

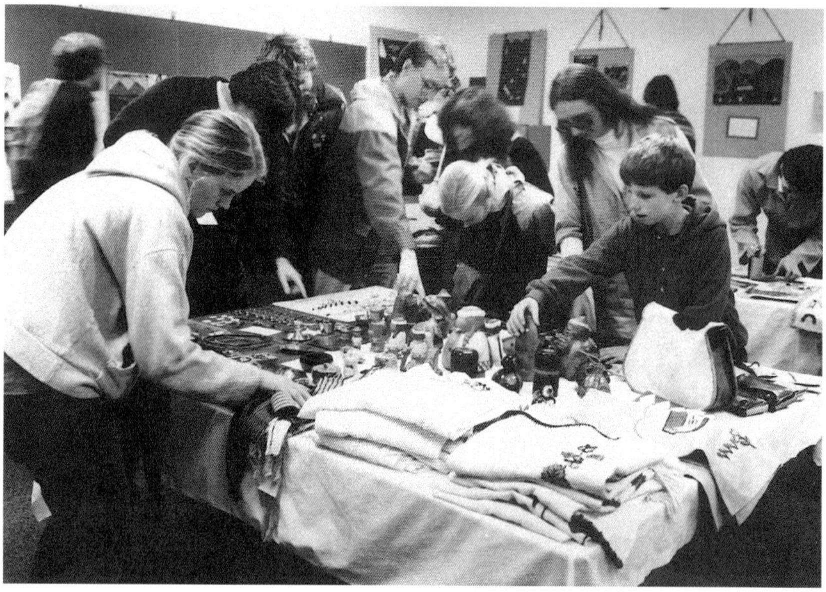

Fig. 2.44. Sale of artisanal crafts made in solidarity workshops, ca. 1990. Marijke Oudgeest Fund. Collection of the Archive of the Museo de la Memoria y los Derechos Humanos.

is no question that commercialization had a material impact on the lives of the arpilleristas, who began to make a real wage from the textiles. Ironically, this income was in large measure *dependent* upon the dictatorship, for just a few years after Pinochet was voted out of office, in 1992, the Vicaría that coordinated the exporting of the arpilleras was dissolved. There are still arpilleristas at work, as the contemporary tapestries in gift stores demonstrate, but they are not made via the same network of linked workshops nor sent in large numbers overseas, where they carried an implicit sense that one was resisting Pinochet with one's pocketbook. Though "commodification" has come to be demonized by contemporary art scholars, it was exactly their commodity status as affordable artisan products that motored the arpilleras' international circulation. In the case of textile production, commercial success is often an extension of the maker's autonomy, not a compromise of it.

Other, more performance-based cultural forms arose from the arpillera workshops alongside the textiles themselves. Some arpilleristas affiliated with the Association of Families of the Detained and Disappeared formed folklore and performance groups and became central to the emergence of the *cueca sola*—a haunting modification of Chile's official national dance, the *cueca*, which is usually performed by partners.[138] In the *cueca sola*, women dance by themselves, waving white handkerchiefs, sometimes with photos of their missing husbands, sons, or fathers pinned to their shirts, summoning the absent presences of the disappeared. The use of the identification photo within Latin American campaigns to raise awareness of the disappeared is widespread; the personal incorporation of the pictures on the cloth outfits

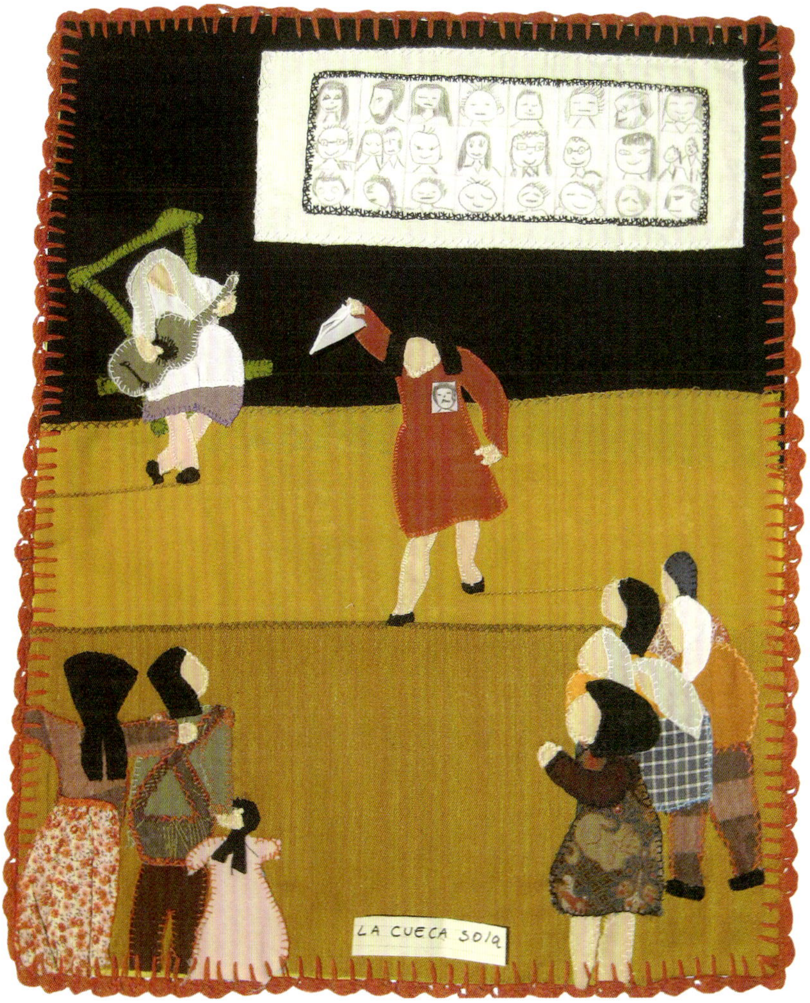

Fig. 2.45.
"La cueca sola," anonymous arpillera, date unknown. Collection of the Museo de la Memoria y los Derechos Humanos. Photograph by the author.

of these dancing women relies upon the corporeal properties of textiles as forms of signifying text. Little has been written on the connections between the dance and the tapestries—besides noting that some women participated in both arenas—even though it is striking how both rely upon fabric (including the white handkerchief) as a kind of testimony. The *cueca sola* became the iconic dance of resistance during the dictatorship and was a highly visible form of protest in public space.[139] Many arpilleristas took part in other demonstrations and protests, including hunger striking, illicitly painting walls, and chaining themselves to governmental offices; some of these scenes made their ways into the arpilleras, including the *cueca sola* with its white handkerchiefs and identification photos (fig. 2.45).

In addition to the dance, a play about the making of arpilleras, produced by the Santiago-based Taller de Investigación Teatral (Investigative Theater

Workshop) titled *Tres Marías y una Rosa*, written by David Benavente in 1979, explored the dynamics of the workshop as the women in the play sew and talk within an entirely feminized space—no men appear on stage. María de la Luz Hurtado claims that such plays "constituted one possibility of reviving memory and remaining committed to a stand against [the dictatorship's] reality" and that *Tres Marías*, with its focus on relationships between poor women and their lives, fulfills a "sociopolitical function of cultural resistance."[140] At the same time, the narrative of the play touches on the tension between individual expression and standardization that shadows the arpilleras, as the so-called Central Office repeatedly rejects one woman's designs. Seasoned arpillerista María Ester instructs the newcomer, Rosa: "The first thing you do is sew on the mountain range . . . the Andes, not the coastal mountains. Because we're in Chile. It's so foreigners can tell. . . . To save time, you can make a bunch of mountain ranges first, then stick them on one after another."[141] As Alice A. Nelson argues, within the logic of the play, "if the arpillera sells, one's own history is validated by the public—that is, by the international market. The international market indirectly becomes the target audience and broker of personal histories."[142]

Behind, Advanced, Again

Much emphasis has been given to the recycled scraps and used clothing found in the arpilleras. In the early days, arpilleristas used their own garments (in some cases the precious garments of the disappeared). Later, however, demand outstripped their meager supplies and they needed fresh and frequent infusions of material. Donations were solicited from the general public and coordinated by the Vicaría; presumably most of the bags of clothing they received were from people cleaning out their closets. Where were such fabrics made? Given the aggressive free-trade policies pushed by Pinochet's neoliberal Chile, it was increasingly likely that used clothes sold in Chile were not made in local textile mills such as Yarur but made elsewhere, including the United States, which was flooding the market with cheap goods and dampening local production.

The art collective mentioned in the first section of this chapter, CADA, did a project utilizing used clothes in 1983, titled *Residuos americanos*, in which secondhand clothes from the United States sold in Chile are returned to the United States (for an art show in Washington, DC), strewn around the gallery space as they slump out of a wooden crate.[143] With a text on the wall that poetically connected "clothes and misery / mind and merchandise / sickness and symptoms of sickness," CADA employed used clothes not only as a bodily substitute for their wearers but as a gesture of global commerce, the imbalance of markets, and the "residue" of circuits of exchange (fig. 2.46). It is instructive to imagine contemporary arpilleras, too, not only as "products of Chile" (as they are currently marketed) but as embedded with cloth from elsewhere that returns that cloth to its international origin, remade and refashioned to tell a local story.

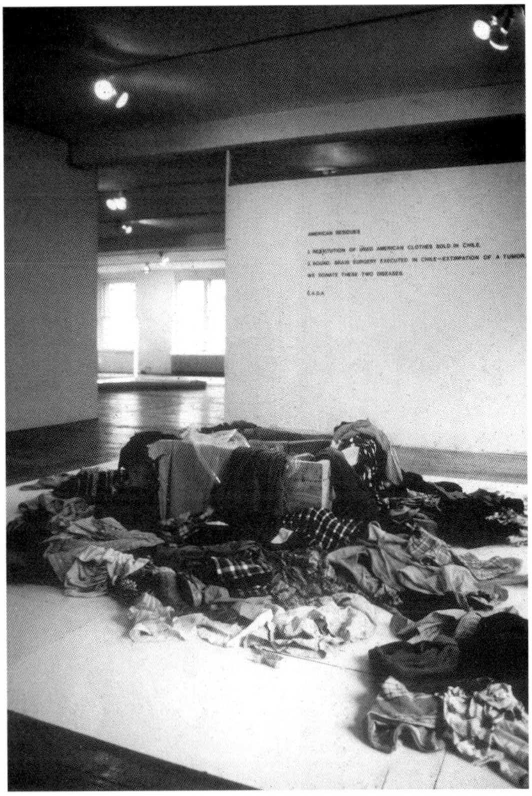

Fig. 2.46. Colectivo Acciones de Arte (CADA), *Residuos americanos (American Residues)*, installation with used clothes, wooden crate, Washington, DC, 1983. Courtesy of Lotty Rosenfeld.

Unlike the works of CADA, arpilleras are not considered "advanced" art; however, their status as folk, as low, or as "naive" is often difficult to secure. Their makers were paid for their work, for instance, which muddies their status as amateur. Furthermore, the fact that most are not signed with first and last names was partly a reflection of the dangers that known authorship would bring—the anonymity was a consequence of heavy censorship rather than the facelessness characteristic to some folk making. In addition, feelings of solidarity led many women to decide not to sign their works individually, as they felt that each was a collective product of the whole, no matter whose hands literally sewed the textiles.[144] What unites their making as "low," then, is their connection with *textile craft* and *gender*—every arpillera was made by hand by a woman, regardless of class, regardless of connections to the disappeared, regardless of other self-identifications as artist or as artisan or as activist.

The arpilleras have been hailed as many things—photographic, journalistic, and diaristic "self-narration."[145] They have been understood as therapeutic objects healing a traumatized country and have been called a "pedagogic tool for popular education and political dialogue."[146] In some cases, the arpilleras surely function in such ways. But in my analysis they are, at heart, scenes of imagination, of desire, of fantasies both sunny and nightmarish, scenes that were generated not only by the makers but also by the buyers, as reports of what sells and what does not filtered back to the workshops. They are not, however, mechanistic products of market forces, as their variations are infused with meanings that are not always legible. Again, keeping in mind Canclini's call for a hybrid method that takes into account crossings and blurrings, it is not important to me to fully recuperate arpilleras as art; rather, I argue that as textile objects they are "in the fray"—unsettled and unstable in attempts to pin them down. Their instability can be part of what made them effective, as their slippage between categories allowed them to circulate during the dictatorship. If folk art can be about repetition and representing continuity with the past, while newspaper reports "break" stories by marking the current moment, arpilleras confuse these categories with their attention to contemporary events that are then made and remade in conventionalized formats.

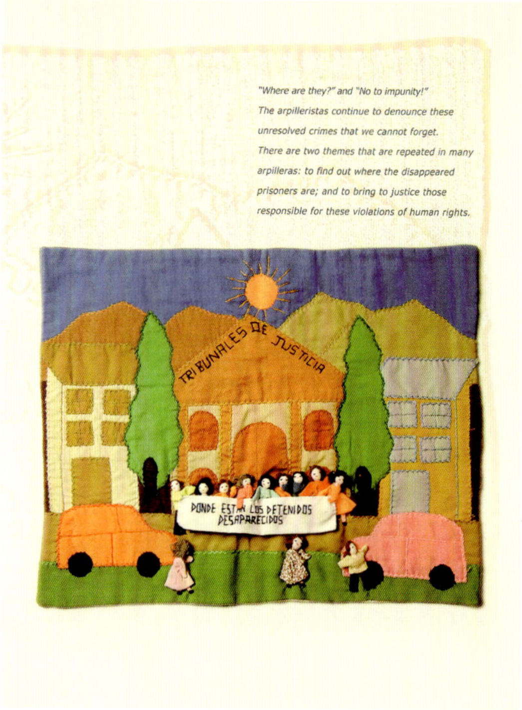

Fig. 2.47. Page from *Dignidad hecha a mano / 30 años: Handmade Dignity / 30 Years: 1975–2005*, Fundación Solidaridad, 2005.

I do not want to diminish the aspects of repetition in order to insist on some phantom notion of artistic originality; indeed, the repetitions are of interest, as they point to certain narratives crucial enough to warrant returning to them, again and again. Recall the gift-store arpillera from 2013 asking "WHERE ARE THE DETAINED-DISAPPEARED"—similar works have been made for over two decades now, long past the dictatorship and long past the era in which such protests occurred with any frequency. Consider an arpillera described in 1989, in a review of a show at the University of Connecticut: "One particularly poignant arpillera shows women dressed in all colors of the rainbow standing in front of the Tribunals of Justice; an X on the door denotes it is closed. The women are holding up a large banner that asks '¿Donde Están?'—'Where are They?'"[147] And in a book put out by the Fundación Solidaridad in 2005, a remarkably similar—in fact, nearly identical—arpillera appears, with a text caption floating above it to explain the banner[148] (fig. 2.47). Surely such a scene has been replicated again and again because it sells, of course, but also because it captures something at once picturesque and potent: collective protest by women.

Coda: Craft Contradictions

To conclude, recall the arpillera that I purchased in 2013, that of an *olla común*, one of many such tapestries that repeat this motif. It summons, as has been described, a progressive narrative of ingenuity in the face of Pinochet-era poverty, and one can see why it might be a popular and long-lasting theme. On display at the museum gift store were others with precisely this scene that did not include the clarifying text, and for a foreign audience that might not be familiar with the phenomenon of the collective cooking pot, the action represented could be read another way—namely, as a reference to the high-profile *cacerolazo* protests against food shortages under Allende by well-off women in the early 1970s, known in English as the March of the Pots and Pans, which became a visible manifestation of right-wing women's political power.[149] The little figures appear to be carrying plates, but their schematization is so extreme and the detailing so basic that they also resemble empty pots and pans, and as they walk toward the pot they appear to be parading through the street. Markers of class and race that might distinguish the right-wing women of the *cacerolazo* demonstrations from the poor women of the *olla común* are obscured and indecipherable due to the rudimentary means of their fabric scraps and stuffed heads. The pots-and-pans marches were another moment of women coming together in public space to demand change—though ideologically they are opposed to the human rights and anti-Pinochet messages of the arpilleras.

I am not suggesting a hidden agenda on the part of these makers, who no doubt mean to create scenes of an *olla común*; rather, I am saying that the arpilleras are subject to different readings contingent upon context, as all texts are. I want to keep open the possibility of multiple temporalities colliding to produce a more textured visual field, one that might have several levels of reference. The tactile dimensions of the textile, with all the instability that its form promotes, produce readings that exceed its label as only and certainly an *olla común*. Many contemporary arpilleras depict scenes from the Pinochet era as if such activities continue in a perpetual present, reflecting a kind of nostalgia for the dictatorship's privations and resistances. Yet the contemporary viewer in a museum gift store might attach to this scene of plates and pots a narrative that steps outside of those temporal confines. Though arpilleras have been understood as straightforward "evidence" or "data," as visual forms they are filled with uncertainties and contradictions. These multiple interpretive possibilities signal the connections between frayed craft and frayed political imputation.

THIS CHAPTER HAS considered two very different cases of textile making from Chile from the late 1960s to the present day. Looking at the ambivalent politics of textile production under Pinochet through an artist in exile who is drawn to the ancient form of the quipu—Vicuña—and arpilleristas embedded within the dictatorship who used appliqué to depict contemporary conditions, I have brought together unlikely forms of handmaking that stretch between the past and the present. These textiles have proliferating temporalities, including uncanny returns, echoes, and reiterations, whether of the knotted threads of the quipu or of stylized appliqués. In such objects this temporal elasticity correlates with an interpretive pliability, whereby a woman in a workshop might have a very different understanding of her scene than might a foreign consumer, for example. Together, these textiles continue to ask questions about how fibers and cloth are charged with the complex task of memory keeping, even as, like fabric, memories fade, wear through with too much use, and go threadbare.

REMAINS OF THE AIDS QUILT

3

The photograph is unbearable to look at and impossible to forget: a gaunt man lies in a bed, his body swallowed by the swirls of his black-and-white shirt. Though diminished physically, his arresting presence, which appears suspended between life and death, is undeniable as his open eyes gaze out beyond the camera's lens. This is AA Bronson's *Felix Partz, June 5, 1994*, taken a few hours after the titular subject, Bronson's partner in love and in work (both were part of the Canadian art collective General Idea), died of complications due to HIV/AIDS[1] (fig. 3.01). The bed is a study in textures and designs: solid-colored pillowcases next to multihued dotted sheets next to plaid and striped blankets. Bronson describes Felix's last few weeks: "As he became more ill, he became more and more vibrantly colored and surrounded with pattern. More full of life in a way."[2] Thus, while this is surely a memorial image in dialogue with a long history of postmortem photographs, it is also a picture about textiles, about the properties of fabric as they cloak us, warm us, and help us make meaning. The photograph signals, among other things, how cloth, human life, and loss are interwoven.

This chapter considers the textile politics of one colossal project conceived in response to the HIV crisis: the NAMES Project Memorial AIDS Quilt (hereafter called simply the AIDS Quilt, or the Quilt). The AIDS Quilt, which was a polarizing object in the 1980s and early 1990s, continues to be vexed by logistical issues and ideological conflicts over its legacy and its ongoing purpose. My previous chapters approached distinctly different case studies in their stitched-together halves, split around the contentious high–low fault line; here I extend (and also refuse) that structure to provide a detailed look at both amateur modes of making and fine arts responses to the Quilt. Rather than neatly bifurcated into two clean parts, in this chapter my organizational logic itself frays, following the Quilt's very unruliness. In the first half, I trace the beginnings of the Quilt and its evolution into the major visual platform for national conversations about AIDS in the United States. In the second half I stay with the Quilt, first considering its reception in the

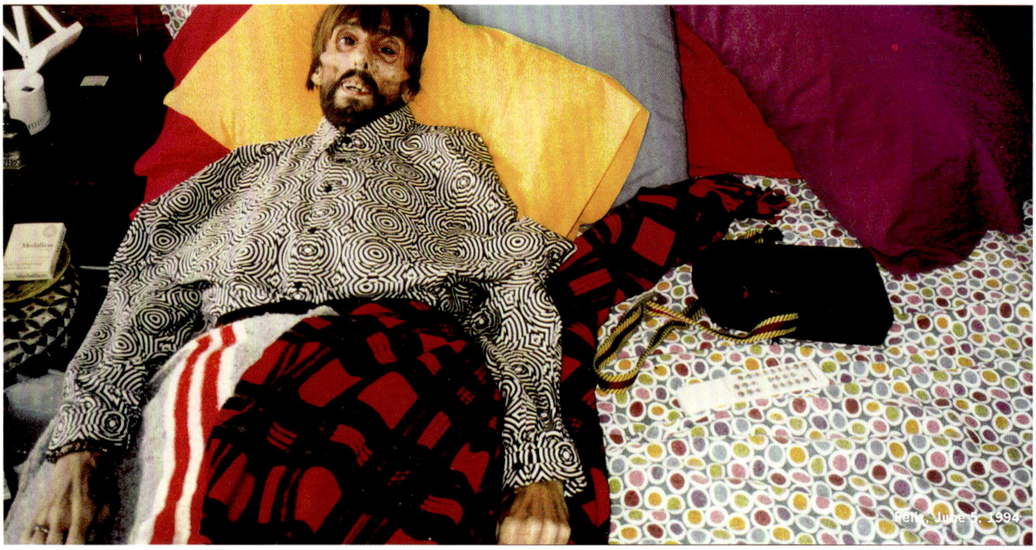

Fig. 3.01. AA Bronson, *Felix Partz, June 5, 1994*, digital inkjet of lacquer on vinyl, 120 × 240", 1994/1999. Courtesy of the artist and Maureen Paley, London.

crucial year of 1992, then mapping more recent reiterations and mediations, putting it in constellation with other contemporary artists' quilts as I grapple with its current state of disrepair.

I have seen many sections of the Quilt in person, beginning in 1990 when a large chunk of it traveled to Houston, Texas. I was an unfolder for its display at my high school and was part of an organization that made a panel for former students and teachers. I saw it again in Washington, DC, in 1992, when during college I took a trip to view it installed in its entirety. My memories of these experiences of mass mourning are vivid, in particular witnessing people weep openly and feeling, piercingly, the losses in my own life (including my best friend's father and several classmates). For the purposes of research for this book, I documented sections of the Quilt around the San Francisco Bay Area in various installations from 2010 to 2015; in its full display in Washington, DC, in 2012; and at its current headquarters in 2010 and again in 2015.

As with the thousands of Chilean arpilleras made during the Pinochet era, the amount of material that makes up the AIDS Quilt—panels, names, fabric—is dauntingly enormous. As with the small sample of arpilleras I examined in detail in the previous chapter, I delve into a handful of examples from among the Quilt, not to inventory its full scope but to take seriously some of its formal propositions. Examining the Quilt both in its enormity and in its specificity, I spend time with some of its panels, as opposed to glossing over their individual character by creating generalizations and abstracting from the whole. In many cases I draw from parts of the Quilt I have seen in person, for, as with the arpilleras, much of their dimensionality is flattened in reproduction; this approach helps focus attention on the process of making. In my view, every Quilt panel, like every arpillera, is revelatory in its own way—whether precisely because it is archetypal or because it is exceptional.

Bronson's photograph of Felix Partz fuses the bed and the body together as one picture plane and thus sews together the independent fabrics into a singular surface. He arguably creates a quilt of sorts, one in indirect dialogue with the NAMES Project. But one major difference stubbornly separates the photo from the Quilt—namely, their textures. The smooth surface of the photographic print is quite unlike the variably tactile surfaces of the textile, which is laden with objects that protrude from its cloth backing. Texture is a unique quality, Eve Sedgwick argues, as "textual perception always explores [the questions] How did it get that way? and What could I do with it?"[3] Texture thus invites two distinct temporal imaginings, as the viewer both considers the object's origin (looking back to its process of conception and the whole sweep of its physical existence) and projects forward to a future moment of speculative touch, fondling, and interaction. In her figuration, Sedgwick emphasizes how the historicity of nonglossy things is animated through, after Renu Bora, *texxture*, "the kind of texture that is dense with offered information about how, substantively, historically, materially, it came into being."[4] As will be examined, the texture of the Quilt is often painfully on offer, providing glimpses of past lives through its materiality while its possibilities of varied physical encounters in the present are generative for affectively estranged, varied, and complex futures.

In 1994, when Bronson took his photograph, the AIDS Quilt was beloved by some and bitterly despised by others. In some respects, beginning with a picture of Felix makes central what so many of the critics of the Quilt felt was absent in its representations of the crisis—namely, a distinctly queer male body. As I demonstrate, the Quilt did linger on faces, and queerness, and flesh, again and again, but because it did so in the ambivalent language of (feminized) textile handicraft, its politics were understood by many to be treasonously muted. Attending carefully to the origins of the Quilt, analyzing its material aspects, and focusing on its present state brings into focus the contradictions that accompany its depiction of masses, of crises, and of sometimes strained solidarities.

Piecing the Names, 1985–1992

Figure 3.02 is a photograph of the US National Mall, a site made recognizable by the distinctive obelisk of the Washington Monument thrusting into a blue sky lightly streaked with clouds. The lower half of this postcard-perfect vista

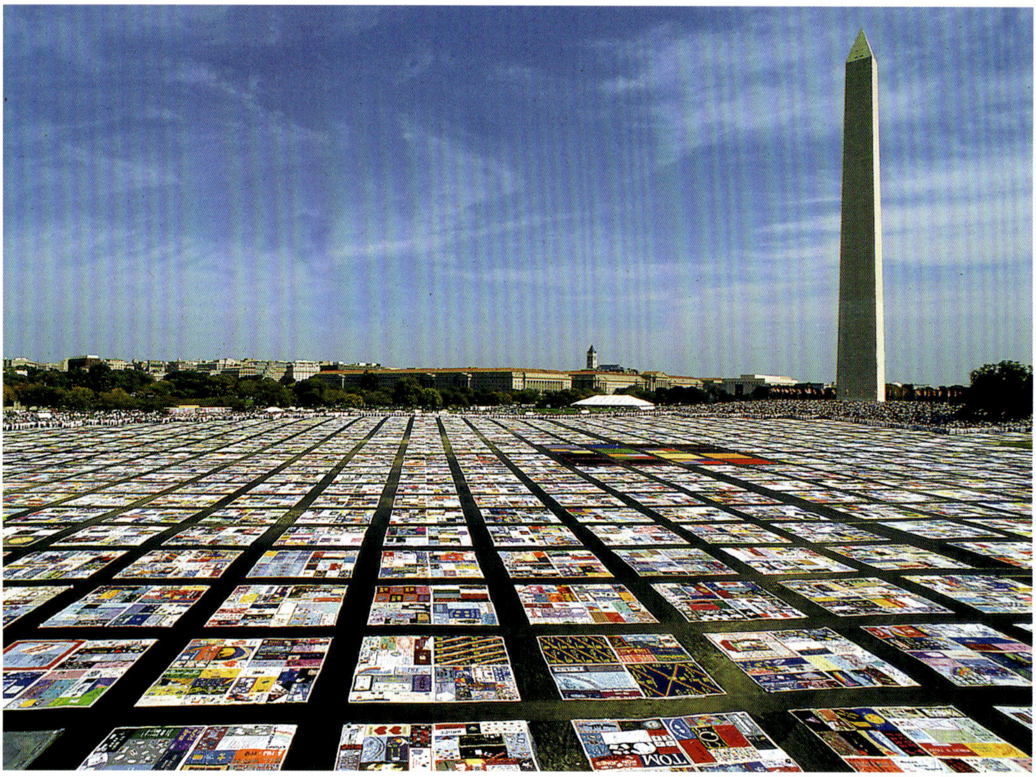

Fig. 3.02. NAMES Project AIDS Memorial Quilt, aerial view, Washington, DC, 1996. Courtesy of the NAMES Project.

is dominated by a massive quilt, a series of colorful squares laid out in neat rows whose converging lines recede into the horizon. Clustered at the far edges are spectators waiting to wander the aisles of grass that lie between the squares. Taken from an elevated perspective, the picture, and the geometry of the textile, transform the Mall into an almost pastoral plain, echoing tilled farmland under a brilliant sky. What blankets the nation's capital is a massive display of the AIDS Quilt, which was founded in 1987 and continues to operate to this day. The Quilt consists of over forty-nine thousand individual panels that are laid out like a cemetery to commemorate lives lost to the HIV/AIDS epidemic; almost one hundred thousand of those who have died of AIDS are named. Covering over one million square feet, it weighs fifty-four tons and has been seen since its creation by some eighteen million visitors. It is, by any reckoning (from the number of participants to actual acreage), the largest ongoing community arts project in the world.[5]

Yet here is a sentence that sums up many current academic assessments of this work: "As a text visually representing the magnitude of the global AIDS crisis, the AIDS Quilt fails miserably."[6] This provocative assertion comes from a 2007 special issue of the journal *Rhetoric and Public Affairs* dedicated entirely to the Quilt. This statement was revised and rewritten to soften its harsh tone in the subsequent book version of the special issue, *Remembering the* AIDS *Quilt*: there the authors argue that the "representative failure" of the project ultimately lies with viewers and is not inherent to the Quilt itself.[7] In this chapter I move beyond questions of failure or success to consider how textile textures make evident contested notions of memorialization in uniquely material ways. I examine the Quilt to assert that it is not only a text, as the quote above states, but a *textile* and that one must take into account questions of cloth and craft to do justice to its complex visual field and to account for what have been seen not only as its insufficiencies but also as its plenitudes.

The Quilt was conceived in 1985 by San Francisco–based activist Cleve Jones at an annual candlelight vigil in the Castro to mourn the death of Harvey Milk; Milk, the city's first openly gay member of the board of supervisors, had been murdered, along with mayor George Moscone, in 1978.[8] (Jones had spearheaded the first such vigil, organized on the anniversary of Milk's death.) Given the increasing numbers of gay men dying of AIDS in the Castro in 1985, this march for Milk felt to Jones especially meaningful, so he and his friend Joseph Durant handed out posterboard and markers so that participants might carry placards inscribed with the names of friends or lovers who had died of the disease. At the conclusion of the vigil, marchers placed these squares with block lettering on the walls of the federal building, which housed the West Coast offices of the US Department of Health and Human Services, covering its surfaces with a patchwork of names (fig. 3.03). Jones recalls an epiphany in front of the wall of names in San Francisco: "Standing in the drizzle, watching as the posters absorbed the rain and fluttered down to the pavement, I said to myself, *It looks like a quilt.* As I said the word *quilt*, I was flooded with memories of home and family and the warmth of a quilt when it was cold on a winter night."[9]

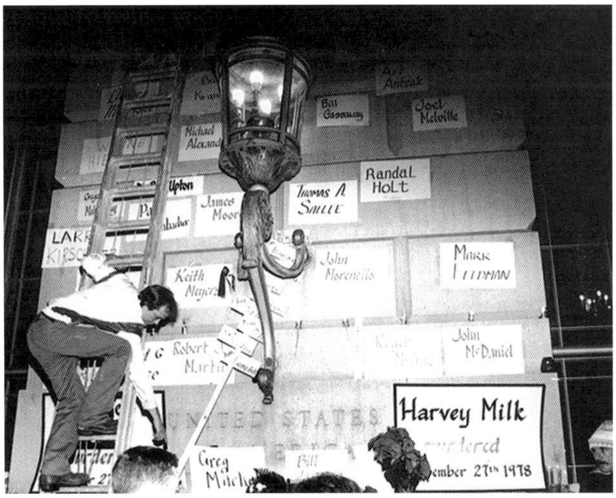

Fig. 3.03. Vigil for Harvey Milk, federal building, San Francisco, 1985. Courtesy of the NAMES Project.

It is a romanticized origin story, of course, and Jones alludes to a cozy and nostalgic associative chain that was triggered by the word *quilt*—memories, home, family, warmth—that is starkly unlike the posterboard squares where first and last names, in a defiant act of publicizing, were affixed to an architectural support on a rainy evening. From the outset, and as its full title in-

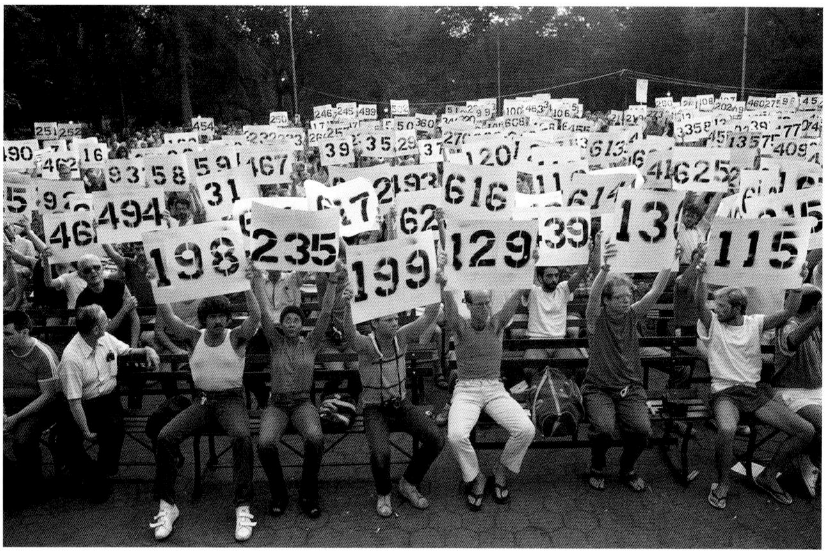

Fig. 3.04. Candlelight vigil for AIDS deaths, Central Park, New York, 1983. Photograph by Robert Maass. © Robert Maass / Corbis.

dicates, the NAMES Project AIDS Memorial Quilt was intent on countering any shaming imperative to keep the dead anonymous and thereby untainted by an association with the disease. Jones envisioned creating a quilt of personal names, not numbers, a laying out of the dead that would be devastating and colorful and serious and soothing and overwhelming, all at once.

The somewhat spontaneous matrix of names on the federal building recalls but substantially differs from an earlier AIDS memorial service that occurred in 1983 in New York, in which people held up numbers that corresponded to patient numbers (as indexed by the Centers for Disease Control), in a graphic tally of the growing ranks of the dead (fig. 3.04). There the use of stenciled black numbers on white placards created a unified and bureaucratic aesthetic. Each number was held aloft by a living body; together they receded into the distance as a swarm of numbers and arms and hands and faces, suggesting a close connection between the holder of the sign and the death the number represented. However detached or anonymous the numbers may read now, they were not to those who took part in the memorial. "The stigma around AIDS may have forced the numbers to stand in for the names, but for the people who carried the signs the correspondence between the number and the name was known," writes David Román. "For the community assembled the numbers were clearly identifiable with the people who had died."[10]

The year 1985 was a flashpoint in AIDS awareness in the United States; it was the year that celebrity icon Rock Hudson died, bringing new attention to a disease that had already killed thousands of people in the United States, and the year that President Ronald Reagan finally began to develop governmental responses to AIDS.[11] As Richard Meyer argues, Hudson's death had implications for understanding both queer bodies and the body politic within a national rhetoric gripped by fear of contagion.[12] The conjunction of (long-delayed) state attention to the epidemic and the death of a major star meant that conversations about AIDS were taking shape in the public sphere in new ways beyond queer communities; Jones saw an opportunity to capitalize on this growing attention and marshal it for memorial purposes. Integral to Jones's vision was exactly this sort of broad national visibility, and he decided he wanted the Quilt to be displayed on the National Mall. As he has said, "By providing a glimpse of the lives behind the statistics, it will create an extraordinary, dramatic illustration of the magnitude of this epidemic—to the president, to Congress, and to the country."[13] Thus from the very beginning, the Quilt was intended to be a visual address to politicians and to the US citizenry, one that would be made unmissable by its high-profile spot in the nation's capital.

Panels and Blocks

It took Jones a few years to begin to realize his vision. Figure 3.05 pictures his first panel, made for Jones's best friend of fourteen years, Marvin Feldman, who died in 1986. Like all the panels to follow, it measures three feet by six feet, the standard size of a human grave. Note that this is not a quilted panel but was made with spray paint on a cloth backing; at the time Jones did not know how to sew.[14] In this panel, geometric shapes emerge out of a smudgy gray background, and the sharp edges of the stenciled name blur a bit around the edges, a product of the spray paint's diffusion. Overlapping blue and pink triangles form a Star of David, gesturing to Feldman's gay and Jewish identities as these symbols float up to the surface in a decorative pattern. Not only did this panel set the dimensions for those made subsequently, but it was designed by Jones at the same time that the iconic logo "SILENCE=DEATH," which also employed the pink triangle, emerged as the signature graphic of ACT UP.[15] Douglas Crimp and Adam Rolston comment that its significance "depends on foreknowledge of the use of the pink triangle as the marker of gay men in Nazi concentration camps, its appropriation by the gay movement to remember a suppressed history of our oppression."[16]

As ACT UP member Avram Finkelstein states, in the hunt for a unifying visual element, "we decided to tweak the familiar symbol but leave it enough intact to invigorate its codes. Changing its color from pale pink to vivid fuchsia seemed an acceptable reinvention that reflected graphic trends and suited the aggressive tone of the poster. Turning the triangle upside down was another gesture of reinvention that skewed its connection to the death camps,

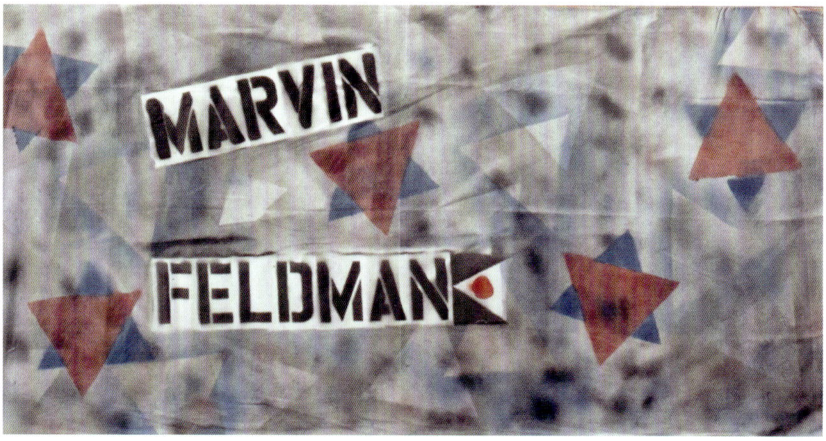

Fig. 3.05.
Cleve Jones, AIDS Quilt panel for Marvin Feldman, 1987. Courtesy of the NAMES Project.

at least in our minds, and signaled a disavowal of the victim matrix."[17] It is possible that Jones knew of the ACT UP logo and was working, after its example, to resignify the pink triangle. It is also possible that he came to this design, which innovates in many ways, not least its Star of David element, with no awareness of the ACT UP graphic. In Feldman's panel the pink triangle is multiplied, reoriented, spun around, and paired with a blue triangle as it is converted away from its origins as a brand of disgrace to one of ethnic and queer pride. Feldman's panel signals that from the Quilt's early days there was a mirroring between some of its formal strategies and those of ACT UP, despite persistent claims—discussed below—that these two responses to the AIDS crisis were at odds with each other or even on opposing ends of the political spectrum.

Figure 3.06 shows what Feldman's panel looks like when it is integrated into what are called, drawing from the language of quilting, "blocks": compilations of panels grouped, or bundled, and sewn together to form twelve-by-twelve-foot squares. After the panels are stitched together, each block is rimmed with off-white canvas and fitted with sixteen brass grommets, spaced evenly along the edges, so that they can be lashed together with cable ties. Normally a block contains eight panels, as this one does, though occasionally people make panels that are larger, or smaller, than the normal three-by-six foot size, so there are sometimes variations. With two vertically oriented panels on the left and right sides and six horizontal panels, this block comes together in a rough approximation—at greatly outsized scale—of a variation of a traditional log-cabin design that is made by fitting rectangular elements together orthogonally to create a square.

Feldman's panel, in the lower left corner, is the only one with a stenciled name, as the others, including Scooby Bowman and José Ramírez, are spray-painted in freehand with abstract backgrounds. Rick Claflin's panel includes

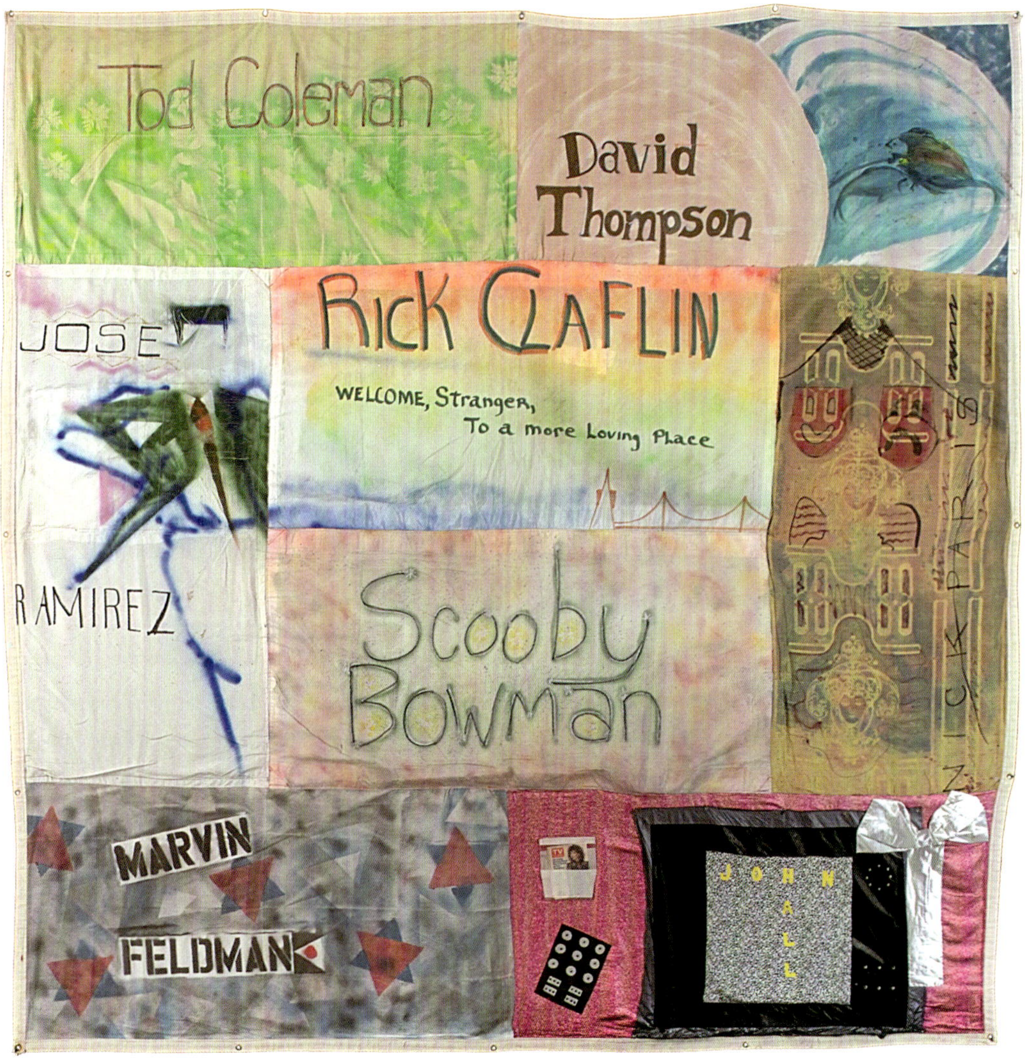

Fig. 3.06. AIDS Quilt block 0006, with Marvin Feldman panel sewn at bottom left, 1987. Courtesy of the NAMES Project.

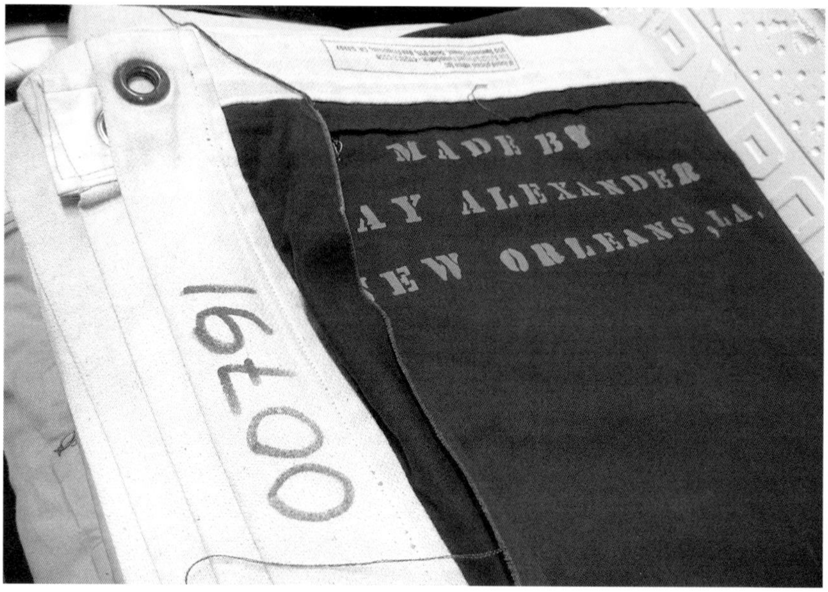

Fig. 3.07. Back of AIDS Quilt block 00791, with hand-stenciled attribution "MADE BY JAY ALEXANDER, NEW ORLEANS, LA." Courtesy of the NAMES Project. Photograph by the author.

a phrase written over the skyline of San Francisco, as indicated with minimal means by a single recognizable building (the Transamerica Pyramid) and the Golden Gate Bridge. The blocks, while still very large, break the Quilt into more manageable and mobile units that are easily rearranged and transported. Such a patchwork assembly is integral to its aesthetic: panels are rarely displayed independent of these blocks, generating a relationality among the names by which to apprehend one is necessarily to hold in one's line of sight several other panels. The effect is to see each name—each life—not as isolated but as ensconced in a visual dialogue; the sewn-together interdependency of the blocks is vital to the way the Quilt operates formally.

One perhaps surprising aspect of the Quilt is that, as the back of a panel shows in figure 3.07, it does not have an insulating padded layer of batting, or a backing. Hence while the AIDS Quilt mobilizes metaphoric associations with warmth and comfort, it is not technically a quilt, which by definition has two or more layers of fabric fastened together, but consists of one layer of pieced-together fabric that does not have the characteristic multilayered sandwiching nor the overall unified stitching (known as "quilting") that binds the layers and gives the textiles their name.[18] Quilts, which like braided rag rugs have been considered one of the oldest and most typically American crafts, a homespun activity rooted in survival, "actually date from a postcolonial, industrialized period": their construction was made possible by shifts in manufacturing and an abundance of cotton cloth.[19] For Jones, however, quilts were importantly associated with a distinctly national heritage; he understood quilting as "a particularly American folk art."[20]

Quilting has long been associated with domestic women's work, labors that have too often not been recognized or appreciated; one of the major achievements of the reclamation of crafts during the feminist movement of the late 1960s and early 1970s (discussed in the introduction) was insisting that quilts have not been anonymous slog work but refined products of skilled and creative women. Within much modernist twentieth-century art history, textiles have stayed firmly in the domain of the living room or the bedroom, understood as artifacts of material culture that are only occasionally—in fact, exceptionally—admitted into the realm of the art museum. It was precisely this denigration that feminist artists sought to challenge when they turned to fiber-based work in the late 1960s and early 1970s. Decisively making the case for the legitimacy of craft techniques such as knitting and sewing, feminist artists and critics in the 1970s did not just assert that quilts could be "as good as" paintings but, even more radically, looked to textiles as a way to produce an alternative to masculinist ideas about "quality." These artists were less interested in producing "fine art" versions of quilts than in demolishing distinctions between low and high.

These reevaluations of quilts put their making at the center of American artistic practice—not just as folkloric artifacts but also vying for the status of "art." Patricia Mainardi summed it up with her groundbreaking feminist article from 1973, "Quilts: The Great American Art."[21] Mainardi's essay was catalyzing for many textile historians and feminists, and a long bibliography of writing on the centrality of quilting for women followed in her wake.[22] Jones absorbed these lessons and felt that associations with female work helped make the AIDS crisis more universal: "That it was women who did the sewing was an important element."[23] During the 1970s, women artists, including Miriam Schapiro and Faith Ringgold, increasingly turned to quilted or quiltlike pieced fabric-based forms. (Ringgold's quilts are touched on later in this chapter.) Schapiro pioneered what she called *femmage* by layering fabric swatches and painting to create a lively optical effect, writing in 1977 that *femmage* is "a word invented by us to include . . . activities as they were practiced by women using traditional women's techniques to achieve their art—sewing, piecing, hooking, cutting, appliquéing, cooking and the like—activities also engaged in by men but assigned in history to women."[24] Schapiro's theorization makes clear that this embrace of textiles by female artists in the 1970s was not a neutral formal choice; it was part of a broader feminist reevaluation of women's overlooked histories, the meanings of everyday materials, and gendered associations of craft techniques.

By the 1980s, quilts had been spottily integrated into mainstream art museums, with more recognition of the overlap between the ostensibly discrete categories of art and craft (particularly on the West Coast), including, in 1986, a traveling exhibit that originated at the Los Angeles Municipal Art Gallery titled *The Art Quilt*.[25] The inclusion of two male quilters within this curated exhibition no doubt helped shift quilts away from their stereotypically essentialized connections to women's work; as one reviewer wrote, the show "takes the lowly coverlet a long way from the ladies room."[26] The AIDS Quilt emerged at a time of greater acceptance of quilts within multiple arenas (from hobby craft to fine arts) and as an activity performed across the gender spectrum. Unlike some of the pieces shown in *The Art Quilt*, the Quilt was meant to function not as a usable quilt—that is, to warm a body—but as a showpiece (quilters themselves use these categories, with show quilts or presentation quilts distinguished from lap or bed quilts).

Adding any sort of backing would have been tremendously expensive and time consuming, and would have contributed to the blocks' already hefty weight. Backing the panels would also have hidden the many personal messages, notes, signatures, and special instructions written on their undersides. Sometimes treated as a space for attribution where the maker declares his or her own name and location—"made by Jay Alexander, New Orleans, LA"—the reverse side of the Quilt not only includes assertions of authorship but is treated as a semi-private arena, a site for intimate communications that will not typically be viewed by the public. Some messages read as if they are written directly to the person depicted on the recto, as makers are aware that the underside will not face up to the living but will press down into the earth, addressing the dead. This indicates that creators of panels are often keenly conscious of the specialized conditions of spectatorship allowed for by the Quilt. Rather than elaborate windows that give transparent access to those lost, the panels propose a highly mediated, textured encounter between maker, spectator, and name.

A Community of Makers

In 1987 the first forty panels (many of them made by Jones himself and vigil collaborator Durant) were displayed at the San Francisco gay and lesbian parade, strung from the balcony of the mayor's office at city hall in order to drum up support for its eventual display that October on the National Mall[27] (fig. 3.08). Even in this preliminary formation, the panels have been sewn into blocks, and they hang from the railing over a banner that reads "America Responds to AIDS · OCTOBER 8 & 9 · WASHINGTON DC." Flying in the center of the display is the rainbow gay pride flag, designed in 1978 by Jones's friend Gilbert Baker in another instance of a San Francisco–based queer textile.[28] Though in this early display the panels are suspended high in the air,

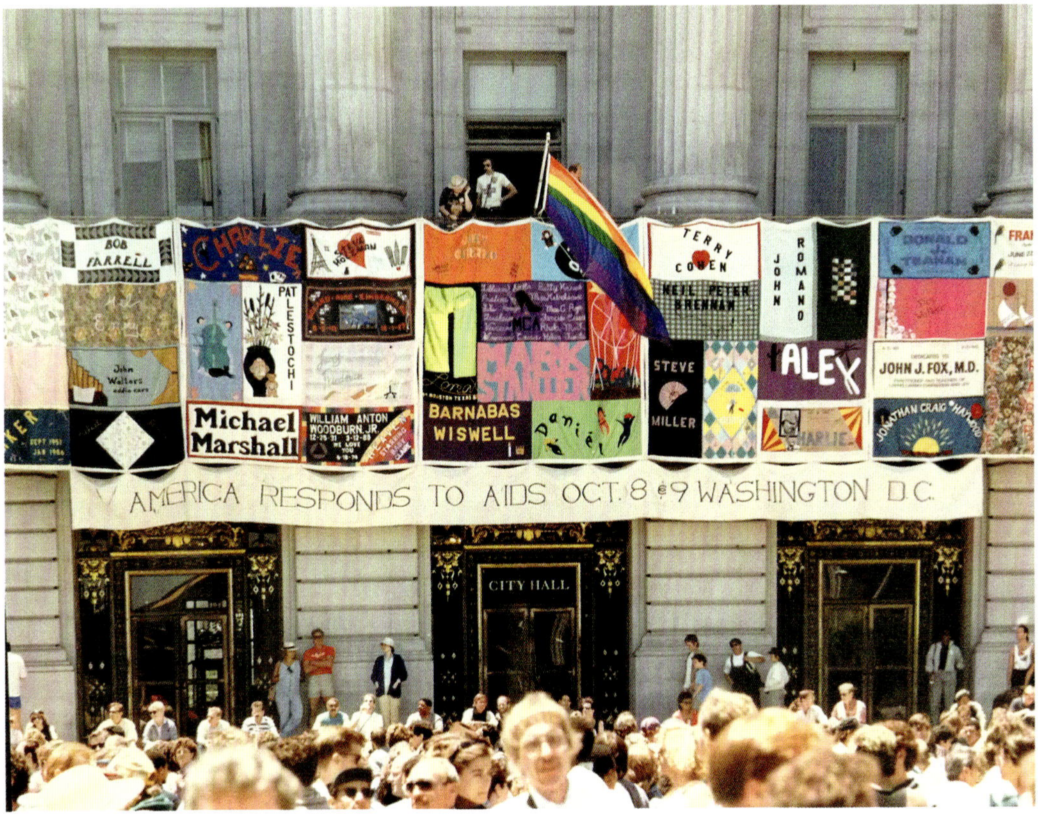

Fig. 3.08. First public display of NAMES Project AIDS Quilt, San Francisco city hall, 1987. Courtesy of the NAMES Project.

Jones always intended for the Quilt to be shown on the ground. He was quite adamant on this specification, to the point of losing the support of Durant, his close collaborator, who argued that it would more respectful and honoring to hang the panels from flagpoles or other supports such as specially rigged scaffolding.[29] Jones, however, wanted people to kneel down, to touch the fabric, to have a personal bodily interaction with the individual names that he felt could be fostered only when the Quilt was placed, like Hammond's braided *Floorpieces* in chapter 1, horizontally, down low. After this initial showing at city hall, the second display of the AIDS Quilt was in the windows of the Union Square Neiman Marcus. Jones writes, "We now had chic!"[30] This display in a high-end retail establishment indicates a rapid commercialization of the Quilt that would prove, like so many other aspects, controversial.

From the making of the first panels, the project quickly gathered steam, as community meetings encouraged wide participation and hosted gatherings at places like the San Francisco Women's Building. A flyer on bright yellow paper from February 1987 declares the intention of the Quilt to be "a National AIDS Memorial," stating: "We are constructing a memorial com-

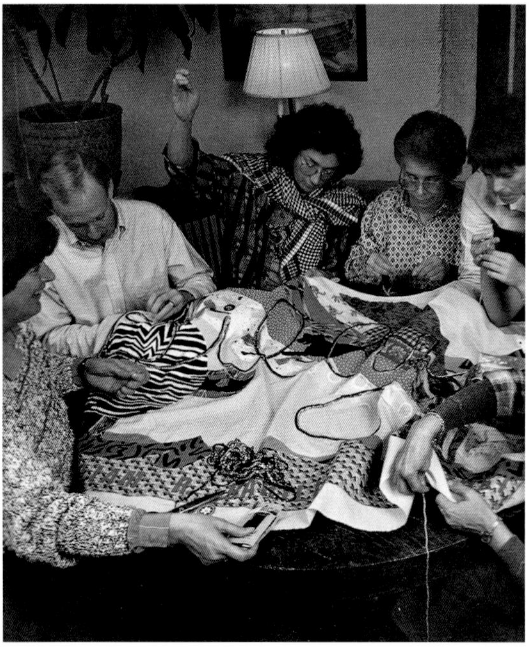

Fig. 3.09.
Sewing panels for the AIDS Quilt, ca. 1988. Courtesy of the NAMES Project.

posed of thousands of individual fabric panels, each bearing the name of a single person lost to AIDS . . . Find out how you can participate in this project by attending this meeting."[31] In addition to holding informational meetings, the Quilt organized collective panel-making workshops, once the organizers realized how many people did not know the most fundamental facts about sewing and did not have access to equipment. Tapping into communal crafting conventions, families and friends were encouraged to make AIDS Quilt panels together, and there are reports of how people sewed and remembered the lives commemorated on the Quilt, connecting it to centuries-long traditions of women's quilting bees. There were workshops where people of all ages, genders, and sexualities could drop in; in the promotional photograph shown in figure 3.09, such gender and age diversity, and the use of sewing as an act that literally fastens material together, is underscored by the circular formation of sewers seated tightly next to another, shoulder to shoulder, stitching simultaneously. The brightly colored patterns of their shirts and scarves visually incorporate them into the eye-catching piecework panel that they are hand-sewing, emphasizing their bodily connection with its fabric—and, by extension, the person represented. As founder Jones saw it, making panels was "a way for survivors to work through their grief in a positive, creative way."[32] The early years of publicity about the Quilt underscored how the act of crafting itself might transform or alleviate the pain of loss for the living.

Not everyone felt the Quilt was an available outlet for them as they grieved; in the second part of this chapter, I delve further into its occlusions specifically around race. Access to the Quilt was also structured along class lines: there are panels that were not made and will never be made for intensely isolated folks or for those whose families and friends did not have material or economic access to fabric (not to mention the time to make a panel). There were further significant psychological blocks around confronting losses and making them concrete that kept some from participating. I recently asked my friend Cara O'Connor, whose dad Patrick O'Connor died of AIDS-related causes in 1991, if she ever thought to make a panel for him. She wrote: "No, I never considered participating. Or maybe it's more accurate to say that I didn't let myself think about it? I liked the idea of the Quilt, but it seemed like a distant thing and not really accessible to some kid in Houston (though it probably was). I also associated it with loss, naturally. I think I believed that medicine or technology was on my dad's side . . . and the Quilt was about people who really were dying or dead."[33] She knew about the Quilt—as mentioned, it made a special appearance at our high school—but that knowledge alone did not compel her to participate (nor did her own strong abilities as an artist). To make a panel for her father would have been to finalize his death, to lay him to rest too definitively.

Despite these barriers, in its first year alone, the Quilt underwent exponential growth, which led to a burgeoning, and increasingly bureaucratic, support system, including renting a storefront at 2362 Market Street in the Castro, incorporating as a nonprofit foundation, and producing an informational newsletter sent to volunteers, those who contributed panels, and AIDS activist groups. The first issue of the newsletter, called the *NAMES-Letter*, was published in December 1987 and includes reports about the Mall display, instructions for making a panel, and advertisements for some of the Quilt-related merchandise that sprang up around it, including posters and buttons.[34] Such salable objects served several purposes: profits helped raise money for costs like the canvas for edging, transportation for its public displays, and sewing machines for workshops. They also allowed people to keep tokens of the Quilt for themselves: if making the panels might be a profound act of memorializing, incorporating a panel into the Quilt means letting go of it, an act that proved difficult for many makers, who had sewn onto their panels treasured mementos like favorite T-shirts or stuffed animals. These were precisely the kinds of objects one might hold close during a time of mourning.[35]

At one height of production before the Quilt was taken on a four-month national tour in 1988, there were over fifty full-time staff and volunteers working to attach panels together, edge the blocks with canvas, and insert grommets. The headquarters was awash in fabrics of every sort; panels were made, sewn into blocks, and hung from the walls in a rotating display; in one view, the pink-and-yellow panel for Rafael Pinto hangs prominently over many bodies bending over work tables (fig. 3.10). Lovers and siblings made panels for each other; mothers and fathers made them for children; children made them for fathers and mothers and uncles and brothers. Ranging outside the bounds of the conventional family, friends, coworkers, and neighbors made them to honor those they knew both closely and casually. Sometimes organizations made panels that included large swaths of their membership; hence rather than naming an individual, these panels commemorate groups of social workers, or "unknown federal employees," for instance. Beyond

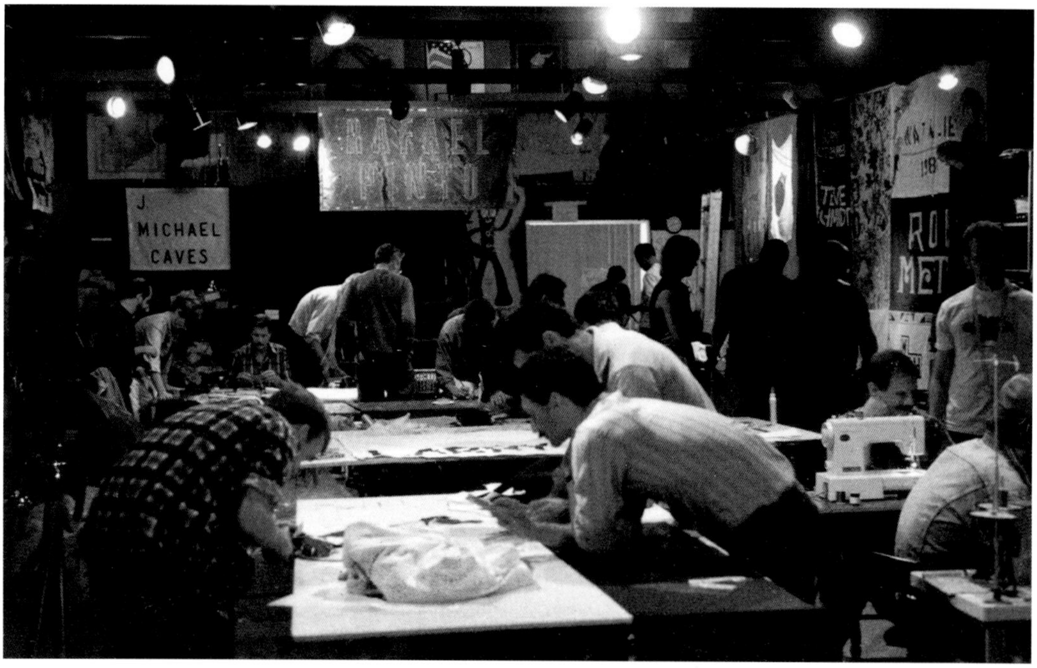

Fig. 3.10. AIDS Quilt Headquarters, Market Street, San Francisco, 1988. Courtesy of the NAMES Project.

occupational affiliations, people made panels to highlight other populations that might not be legible otherwise (e.g., deaf people with AIDS).

While the majority of people represented on the Quilt are gay men, reflecting the demographics of the initial years of the epidemic in the United States, it also includes heterosexual men, women, and children. In fact, one of the most frequently occurring names on the Quilt is that of Ryan White, the young hemophiliac teenager from Indiana who became a well-known face of the disease, as well as of the phobias that surrounded it. Fears about his potential to infect others led to his being barred from middle school in 1985, which prompted public support for greater HIV education and awareness. For many involved in AIDS activism in the late 1980s, White became a problematic figure: he was used to draw distinctions between "innocent victims," who were by and large heterosexual, and presumably "guilty" gay men, who were being punished for their sinful transgressions (even as White himself resisted this reading).[36]

The Quilt block in figure 3.11 shows a panel for White on the lower left, his name on red cloth in black-and-white houndstooth fabric floating over a schematic, idealized schoolhouse scene with a flowering tree (perhaps in reference to White's being banned from school). The panel is sprinkled with neatly scissored houndstooth flowers, alongside other names, such as Tom Ryan, identified as a Vietnam veteran whose panel proudly bears a US flag; the first-name-only Steve; a large central square panel dedicated to students and alums of Columbia University; and Luis Ortiz—the text tells us that "he loved designer clothes" and is embellished with a row of buttons. The panel above White's, for Edward Kennedy Quast, features clowns, theater masks, and a shamrock, all symbols that were used again and again in the Quilt to render, in shorthand, a person's attachments, complexities, and multiple identifications. One strength of the additive approach of the Quilt is that it inserts a figure like White into the context of a diverse spectrum of AIDS lives and deaths, including fashion-forward Latinos and Vietnam War veterans. To see White's panel is to see him proximally to these men, and with the suggestion of some affinity with them. We are encouraged to read the panels together, I suggest, in a dialogue of contiguity within each block, for while the panels are independent units, many blocks also have a kind of parataxic syntax in which no one is subordinated to the other and yet together they form a conversation. (There are also multiple panels made by fans for many celebrities, such as Rock Hudson, former Cockette Sylvester, and British rocker Freddie Mercury—Mercury, in my calculation, is, along with White, one of the most heavily represented figures on the entire Quilt, which suggests that Jones's emphasis on the "national" US aspect of the Quilt was never taken as a hard-and-fast mandate.)

The AIDS Quilt resembles folk traditions of group or community quilts, in which members of a town or neighborhood contribute individual squares to make up a larger whole, often created as a collaborative gift.[37] Because they incorporate many squares designed by different hands, they are emphatically eclectic, with techniques ranging from sophisticated uses of embroidery to hot-glued creations. In the initial news reports on the Quilt, its raw, amateur, and "crafty" nature was emphasized; as a 1987 *New York Times* article stated: "Some apologized for a crude first attempt at sewing. 'A rather ghastly job of stitching, not to mention the cutting,' wrote a man from Oregon."[38] (It is estimated by the current executive director of the NAMES Project Foundation, Julie Rhoad, that 80 percent or more of the panels are made by people with no previous sewing experience.)[39] "Bad" craft, "low" craft—all was admissible in the inclusive project of the Quilt, which turned no panel away, even ones that did not conform to the standard three-by-six-foot format. (Smaller panels, called "little people," are grouped together and sewed onto backings, while every attempt is made to accommodate larger ones.)

Community or group quilts are often mentioned in relation to the AIDS Quilt, which has come to stand in for progressive crafting in the 1980s, obscuring another relevant precedent: the textile Ribbon International for nuclear disarmament that circled the Pentagon. Begun in 1982 by retired Denver schoolteacher and poet Justine Merritt, the Ribbon, like the Quilt, was composed of fabric panels made by individuals across the nation. It culminated

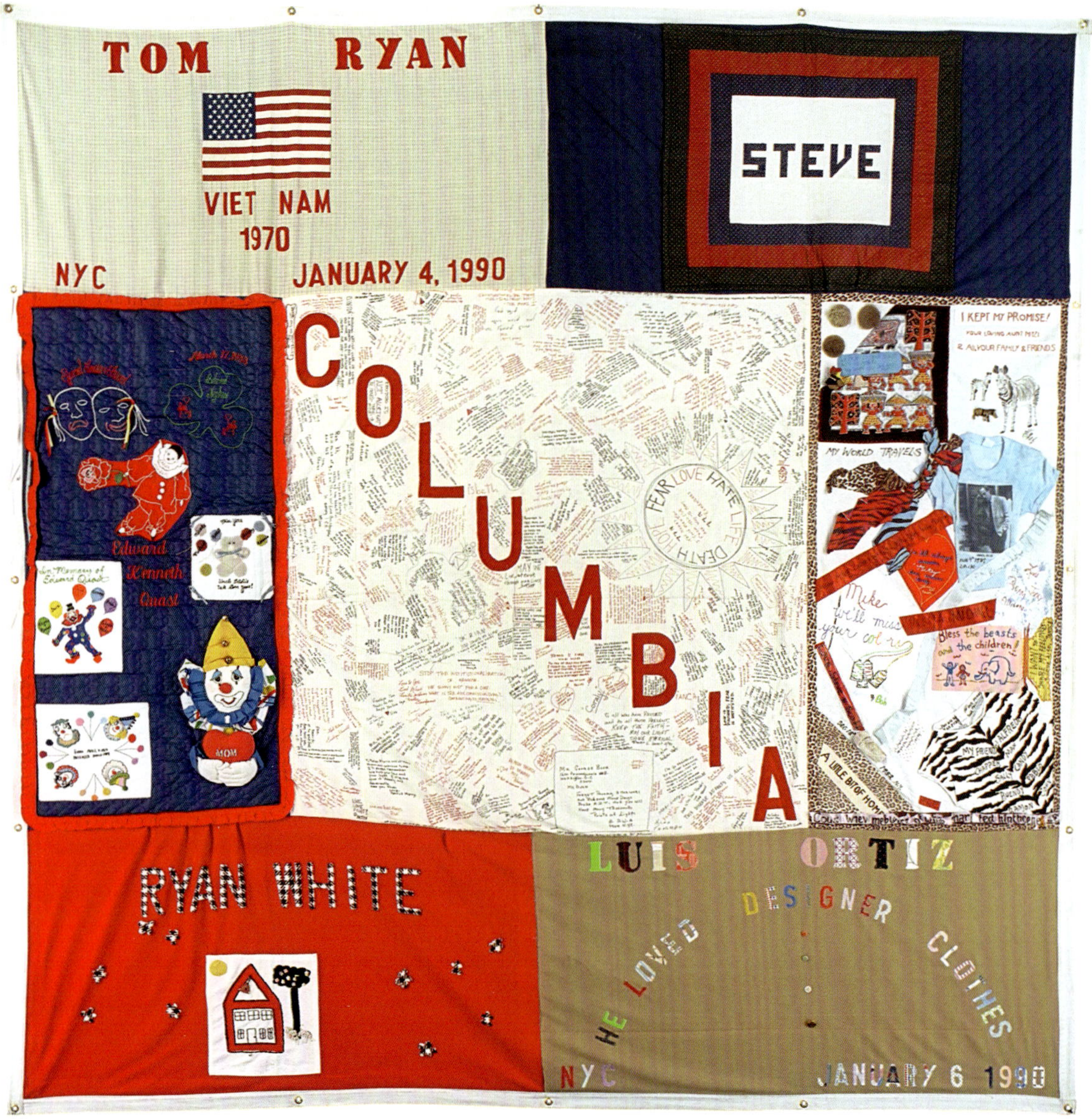

Fig. 3.11. AIDS Quilt block 1540, with Ryan White panel sewn at bottom left. Courtesy of the NAMES Project.

in 1985—the year Jones "spontaneously" had a vision for his Quilt—in a dramatic assembly of twenty-seven thousand panels that stretched over fifteen miles long, in part wrapped around governmental buildings and monuments in DC (fig. 3.12).[40] The Ribbon was heralded in its time as "the largest collaborative craft event in American history." Parallels between the two projects are striking, including word-of-mouth participation, grassroots organizing, and using needlework for political ends.[41]

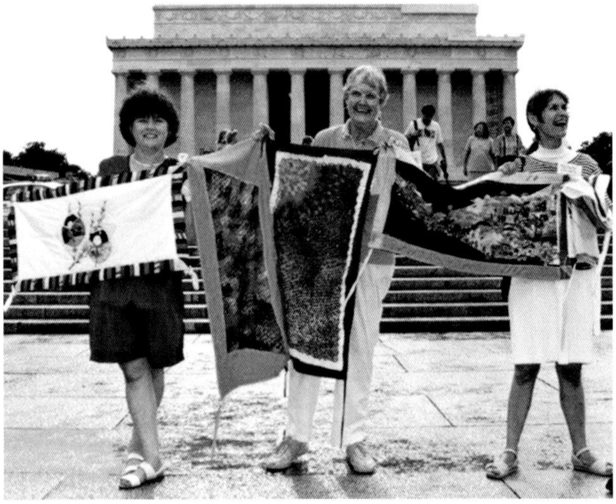

Fig. 3.12. Monica Willard, Justine Merritt, and Michele Peppers holding panels from the Ribbon International, tenth anniversary of the ribbon circling the Pentagon, Washington, DC, 1995.

The fact that the Ribbon International—so successful in the mid-1980s for galvanizing handmade protest from across the country but "predominantly a women's effort"[42]—is erased within the Quilt literature does not go unnoticed by some feminist scholars, who see the Quilt as a stark instance of gender appropriation:

> Also capitalizing on a comforting image of quilts and of "woman" in an effort to redeem AIDS and its mostly male victims of their association with (homo)sexuality, the NAMES Project has effectively staged a spectacle of mostly male suffering which the national "body" has recognized, embraced, and successfully incorporated. . . . Unlike the Ribbon, about which most Americans have never learned because of the negligible media coverage, panels from the NAMES Project have occupied center stage on the White House lawn and achieved a degree of legitimizing visibility that the other projects have failed to garner. There seems no little irony in the fact that the organizers of the NAMES Project appropriated an art tradition invented and perpetuated by American women.[43]

Far from an accepted iteration of activist craft that was indebted to female labor, the Quilt was viewed by some feminists as erasing previous efforts by women in order to eclipse—yet again—histories of female making. By contrast, some women came to the Quilt *because of* its connection with women's work. According to an article in an Austin, Texas paper, "Jo Anne Melody, a 49-year-old medical editor from Redwood City, Calif., said she donated a panel because it is in keeping with the spirit of traditional quilting bees."[44]

Quilt Aesthetics

In the rhetoric of the NAMES Project, as its promotional literature and its statement of core values testify, it sets "apart a sacred space where people heal, hope and remember"—an almost religious reliquary with tangible evidence of those who have passed.[45] But how do you summarize a life on a piece of cloth? The answer for many panel makers is to make recourse to material objects, possessions, the things we treasure and hoard, and many panels include a profusion of stuff. The list of objects found on panels is long and heterogeneous, including pantyhose, flowers, jewelry, Barbie dolls, photographs, feather boas, stuffed animals (there are armies of teddy bears), records and cassette tapes, baby clothes, human hair, medical scrubs, coupons for donuts, mementos like magnets and figurines, matchbooks, napkins from restaurants, ribbons and badges, military medals, shoes, jockstraps, bathing suits, shards of glass, postcards, news clippings, seashells, paper notes, buttons, patches, and a Walkman that plays music. This accumulation of stuff indicates how the Quilt became an opportunity for makers not only to publicize and mourn the names of those lost but to vivify and honor their lives. Along with these metonymic invocations, there are indexical registrations of the dead, including photographs. (The only items ever removed from panels are light bulbs and hypodermic needles, because they are deemed potentially dangerous for those who handle the Quilt.)[46] These objects may contribute to what some perceive as its banal or kitschy quality, but they also animate it, infusing it with the smells, stains, and textures of everyday objects used and held close. A handful of panels, including those for Alec Cunningham and Thomas Coolbaugh, integrate the actual cremation ashes of those they name, with the remains secured in pockets or pouches.

Textiles often mediate the threshold between life and death, and quilts have long been used to commemorate those who have passed, including memory quilts made from a loved one's possessions or funeral quilts composed of the ribbons from floral displays on caskets.[47] Following the tradition of "passage quilts," panels from the AIDS Quilt contain bereavement objects; yet unlike many passage quilts, they will not line coffins or enshroud bodies for burial.[48] Like the arpilleristas, many makers use clothes of the dead as surrogate bodies. Because of its larger scale, the pieces of clothing on the Quilt are able to evoke the bodies that wore them in a different, more literal manner than did the small scraps on the arpilleras: Quilt panels are big enough that makers can utilize entire outfits, such as sports jerseys arranged with arms outstretched to catch a phantom ball, jeans sewed on with legs splayed as if arrested in the midst of a dance move, or shirts intertwined in a ghostly embrace. Some of the outfits are shredded, bringing to mind the Jewish custom of rending garments in grief.

A vast diversity of styles is apparent across the Quilt; some panels were painted, others used marker, pen, thread, glitter paint, embroidery, or appliqué. If the Quilt is extraordinary in its memorial language and literal incorporation of those who have passed, it is simultaneously a profound document of the ordinary—and the lives on the panels are often commemorated by the most everyday, even clichéd, symbols: rainbows, balloons, hearts, flags, teddy bears. Panels frequently list dates of birth and death, enumerate favorite vacation destinations, are emblazoned with witty catchphrases, and declare hometowns or reference places of origin, with stitched-on Puerto Rican flags or Celtic designs. Many panels made for Texans with AIDS include the state's outline or its flag; it is the most frequently depicted state-related motif, and its reoccurrence throughout the Quilt illustrates the specific brand of regional pride cultivated within Texas, as well as signals how the large gay populations in cities like Houston were hit hard by the epidemic. In 1989 a report stated, "Since 1986, AIDS has been the leading cause of death for men 25–44 years of age in Houston, with Houston having more AIDS cases than 45 states."[49]

Erika Doss argues that teddy bears, pinwheels, and plastic flowers of the sort available at any drugstore have become the common memorial language of the United States, part of a wider "kitschification" of memory in which the dead—and the living—are infantilized.[50] Yet the teddy bears and T-shirts of the AIDS Quilt seem to me to not try to render the names "innocent" as much as they reflect a wish to embed the textile with artifacts of a deeply personal nature. The Quilt, like so much material culture, provides ample evidence of what new materialist Jane Bennett calls the "vibrancy" of matter. Bennett writes about "the ability of things to make things happen, to produce effects."[51] Part of the potency of textile politics—realized by quilters and the makers of the panels long before the development of new materialist theory—is how stuff is able to assert itself, how things have affective, and productive, agency.

But the very specificity of its materials, the object-heavy quality of the Quilt—the tangibility that makes it so personal—is more complicated than an embrace of its "vibrancy" can suggest. Crucially, the thingness of the Quilt—that is to say, its textured textile-ness as well as its glut of personalized items such as stuffed animals—has also weighed it down, tying it, inexorably, to the realm of the regressive, the romanticized, and the ineffectual. Far from vibrant, its thingness, for some audiences, threatens to suture it to the past, an infantilizing or nostalgic backward-looking and fetishizing of personal detail, rather than enlivening other futures and envisioning new collectivities. The material stuff of the panels takes on a reliquary status and

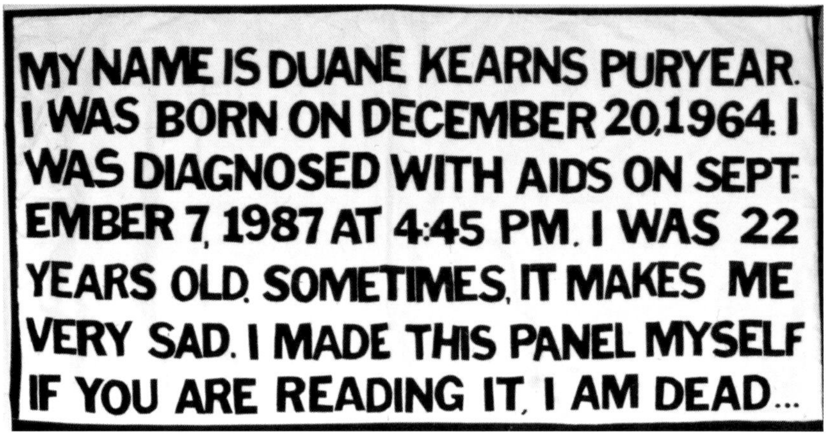

Fig. 3.13. AIDS Quilt panel for Duane Kearns Puryear. Courtesy of the NAMES Project.

ossifies the Quilt as a reminder of many histories, death by death, rather than as a progressive agent that agitates for broad structural change.

But it is not so easy to summarize the Quilt's overall temporality or its relationship to the past and future. For a few panels were created, in a grim act of anticipation, by those whose names are on the Quilt themselves: "My name is Duane Kearns Puryear. I was born on December 20, 1964. I was diagnosed with AIDS on September 7, 1987 at 4:45 pm. I was 22 years old. Sometimes, it makes me very sad. I made this panel myself. If you are reading it, I am dead . . ." (fig. 3.13). The panel, made to commemorate a life not yet lost, scrambles temporality as it presses past, present, and future together. Did sewing these words provide succor, or was it agonizing? Puryear's panel stands out formally, as the graphic starkness of black letters crowding a white background harks back to the simplicity of the stenciled numbers at the vigil in Central Park. With its dark border, it recalls death notices that are similarly framed by a black edging. The panel shares the pared-down and almost bureaucratic clarity of the aesthetic of conceptual art, and this kind of text-heavy panel leaps out of a block with a forceful clarity as opposed to panels that scatter objects as if arrayed for sale on a blanket. Puryear was not alone in taking the design of his panel upon himself; it was remarked in 1988 that "increasingly, people with AIDS are designing their own panels, and the quilting bee has become almost a ritual at wakes as friends gather after funerals to celebrate the life of the loved one they've lost."[52] What an expectant and resigned gesture: sketching out your own panel, choosing fabrics, maybe gathering the objects you want embedded in it, and hoping those who are left once you are gone will execute it as you desire.

To take the Quilt on its own terms is to acknowledge that it is a hybrid work that promiscuously draws from folk and fine art alike. Within its mixture of craft and noncraft techniques, the Quilt resembles a range of modern-

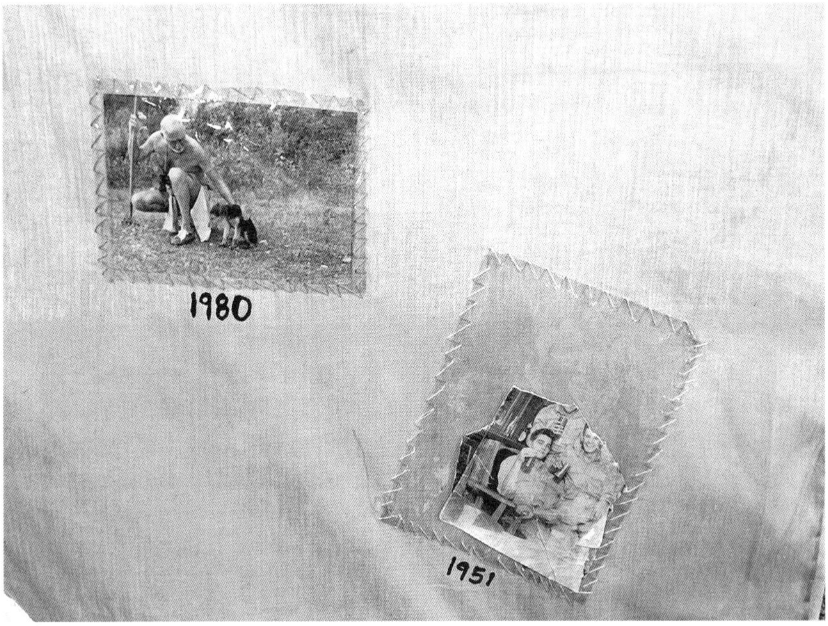

Fig. 3.14. Detail of AIDS Quilt panel for Bruce Allen Brazo, with plastic pockets holding photographs. Courtesy of the NAMES Project. Photograph by Mel Y. Chen.

day phenomena that cobble together objects imbued with meaning, from homegrown altarpieces to scrapbooks, not least because of its frequent integration of photographs. On the panel for Bruce Allen Brazo, photographs from throughout Brazo's life have been scattered across the surface, placed behind protective plastic, and sewn with large stitches. One, black and white and dated 1951, of three men drinking with jovial smiles, is torn at the top, but one cannot discern if this is due to the frailty of the old print or an intentional redaction of the figure within it. If the image of Felix Partz on his deathbed speaks one story about AIDS and mortality, the Quilt contains its own photographic work, ranging from handsome studio portraits to more informal snapshots. With the increased availability of fabric transfer paper, widely sold at hobby craft stores in both iron-on and printer-compatible versions, more and more panels have included pictures of the dead not as actual photographs in pouches, like Brazo's panel, but transferred directly onto cloth. Panels with such photos resemble gravestones etched with faces next to names, but unlike a stone marker with its unmoving elements, the drape of the Quilt causes the faces in its fabric to buckle unpredictably, warping, folding, distorting, constantly reminding us of the insistently textile nature of this memorial, as does the panel for Danny Quinton (fig. 3.15). In some cases the photos have cracked and the unstable ink has worn down due to multiple exposures to sunlight. So while transfer technologies allow panel makers to embed pictures into panels without relinquishing ownership of precious photographs, they also reveal the fragility of the Quilt.

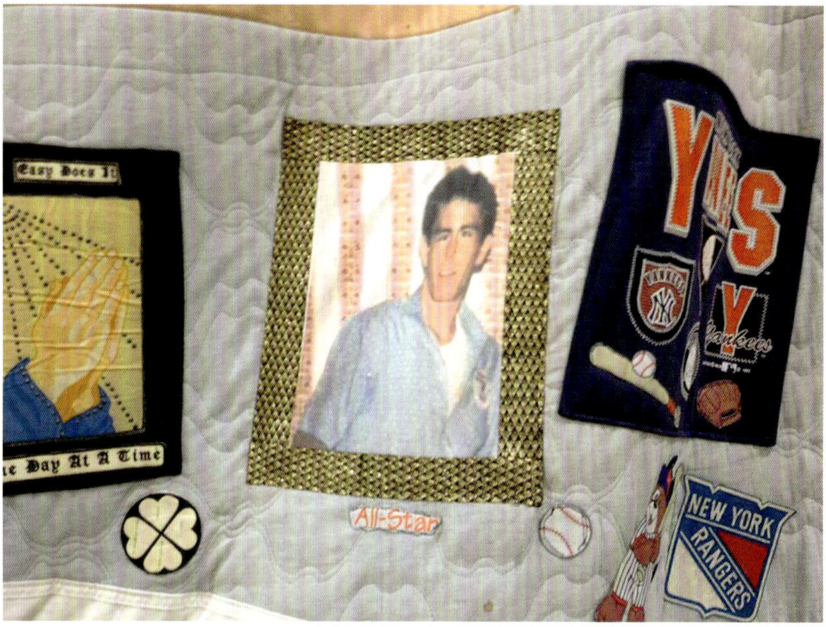

Fig. 3.15.
Detail of AIDS Quilt panel for Danny Quinton. Courtesy of the NAMES Project. Photograph by the author.

Designing and Performing the Quilt

Many blocks have been consciously designed; that is, the panels were clustered together by theme or color, organized with a keen eye for detail by the head seamstress Gert McMullin, who has been with the Quilt since its beginning (she has lost over three hundred friends and acquaintances to the disease). I want to emphasize the almost curatorial role of McMullin, who is not often discussed or acknowledged as a major figure but is largely responsible for how a block, and hence how the Quilt itself, is put together (fig. 3.16). McMullin, who had no formal training in sewing but was a self-taught seamstress—by the time she was in her teens she was making and selling handmade suits—organizes the blocks with an eye toward not only aesthetics but also functionality, such as putting heavier panels at the bottom (in case they are hung for display, this strains the fabric less) or placing panels with big lettering at the top because people can still read those from the ground. She also thinks about how panels look in relation to each other; the block in figure 3.17, for instance, has an overarching BDSM/fetish/denim look, featuring many metal rivets, and includes one of the heaviest panels on the Quilt, made entirely of leather for University of California–Berkeley alumnus Mark Metcalf. The block is also interspersed with more standard objects, like the ubiquitous teddy bear, buttons, a Texan flag made of sequins, a unicorn, and musical notes. McMullin made early and crucial decisions

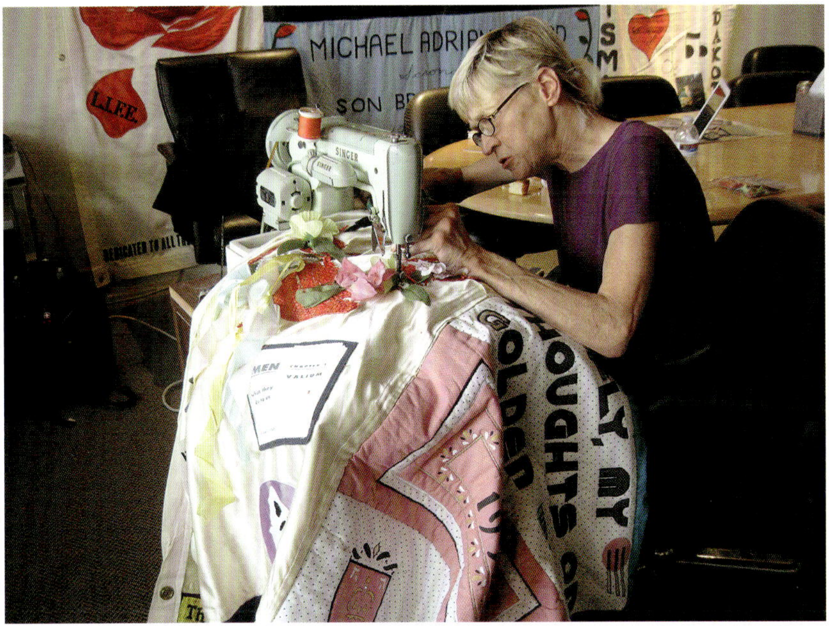

Fig. 3.16. Gert McMullin repairing the AIDS Quilt, 2010. Courtesy of the NAMES Project. Photograph by the author.

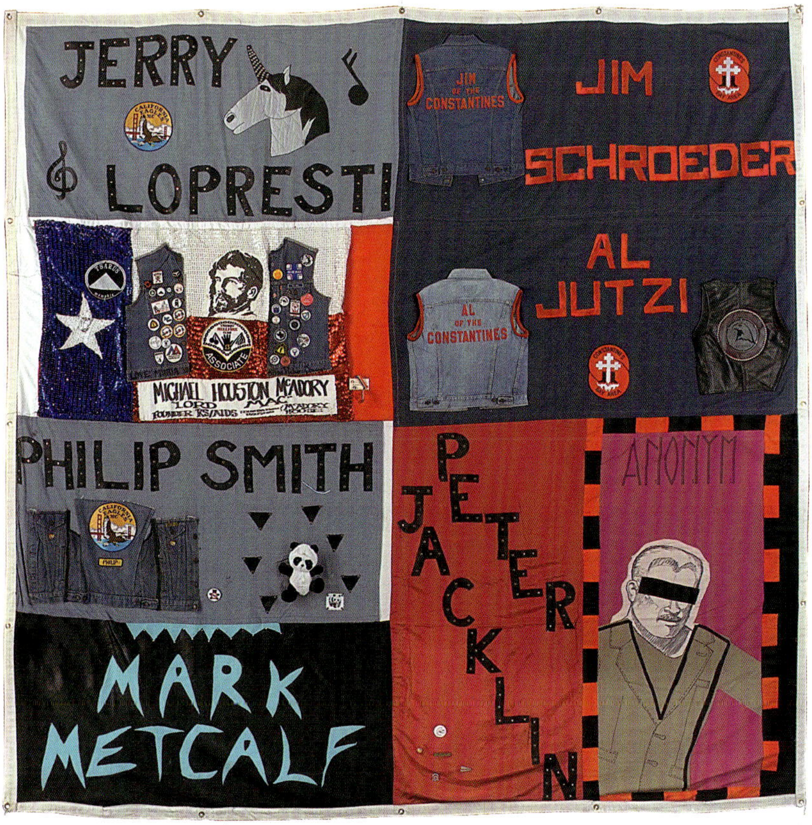

Fig. 3.17. AIDS Quilt block 0226. Courtesy of the NAMES Project.

about how the blocks would be assembled, and respected the makers' requests that often accompanied panels—for example, that they be sewn next to other ones to suggest partnership. In the figure 3.17 block, two lovers, Jim Schroeder and Al Jutzi, are placed together, one above the other, rhyming visually with their matching denim vests and red letters. Another panel, for "anonymous," shows the figure of a man, his eyes blocked out by a swatch of fabric; it is hard to know if this face, which is quite detailed, is a portrait, a composite, or a generic take on the many men who have died of AIDS whose names we will never know.

Because of the stigma of the disease, many of the original panels list such "anonymous" figures or include only first names—like the two panels on the right in figure 3.18, for David, and for Brendon, 1953–1987. Others have last names obscured, as in the panel on the upper right, where the last name of Glenn is covered with a piece of cloth that reads CENSORED, made, as the panel states, by his father and other family members. Viewed up close, it is evident that the makers took the effort to sew his surname onto the panel and then to efface it. In the panel for David (whose last name was Dulong), one of David's shirts has been tenderly tucked alongside a shirt owned by his lover, their arms interlocking and sewn alongside army insignias and a little Speedo. The maker of this panel, Mike (Mac) McNamara, was drawn to the NAMES Project in the late 1980s in Boston as a skilled quilt maker and a gay man whose friends were dying of AIDS.[53] He estimates that he has made upwards of twenty panels; his are often elaborate, skillfully finished pieces with detailed embroidery or intricate beadwork, as in a panel for a friend, Bill Hiatt, who "was gorgeous in drag" (fig. 3.19). As a detail of the panel shows, the beads are richly encrusted and their dark blues and greens match the fabric backing, rendering the name almost illegible in its excess.

Panels like Hiatt's are three-dimensional, pushing out into the viewer's space with their thick ropes of beads. As a result such beads can be easily broken off, and panel-making brochures from the late 1980s urge people to "remember that the Quilt is folded and folded many times, so durability is crucial."[54] Some panels are less vulnerable to this constant shedding than others—such as ones that have no affixed mementos and show a lack of skill, or perhaps a disregard or a disinterest in careful craft. In the block shown in figure 3.20 it appears that a person simply wants to see a name on the Quilt, no matter how it is rendered, and that act of marking—spray-painting a full name onto a piece of cloth—potentially comes from a space of urgency, not naiveté. These simple spray-painted panels are some of the most powerful ones on the Quilt, for they capture the sense that time is short; one senses crisis or expediency, much like a political slogan sprayed on a wall. I asked McMullin, who serves as a kind of institutional memory for the Quilt, about

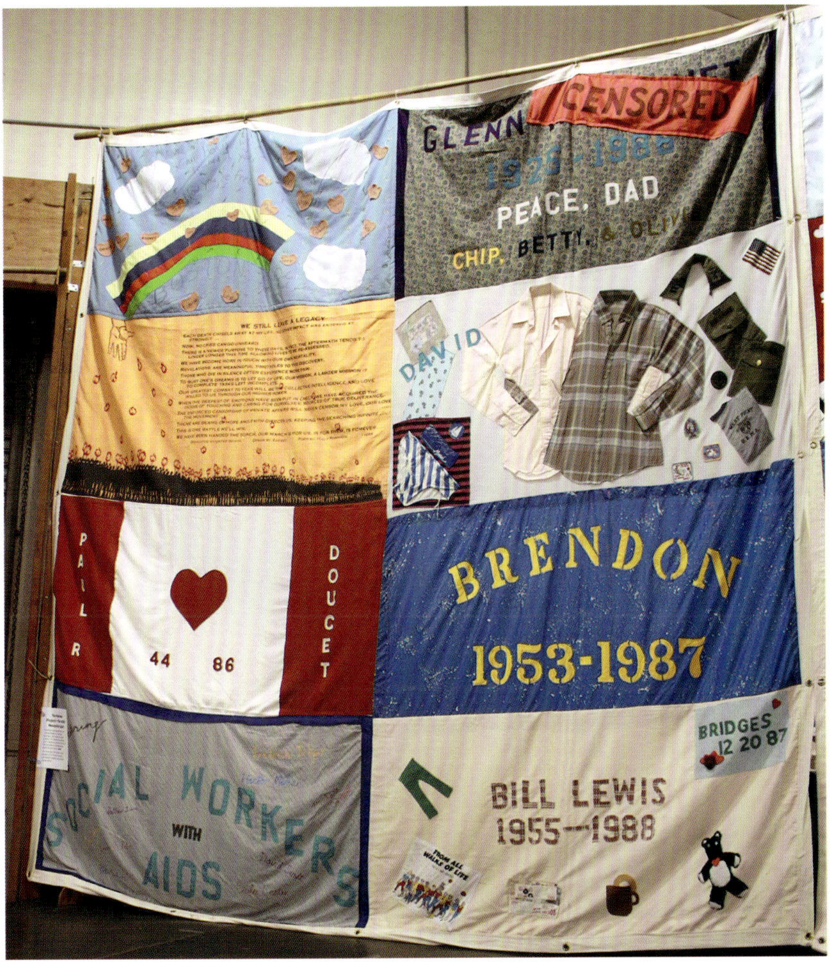

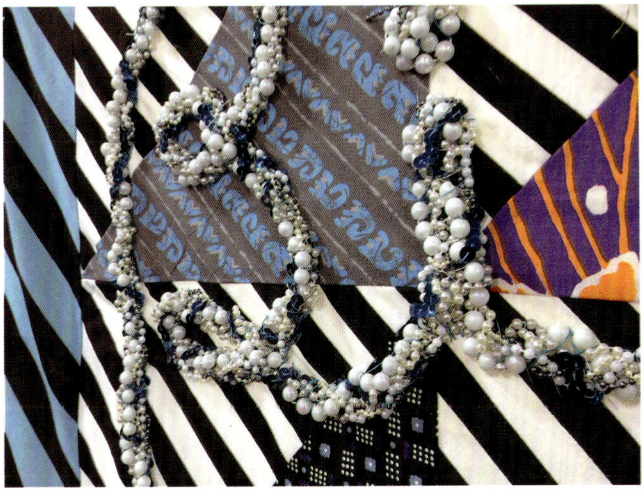

Fig. 3.18.
AIDS Quilt block at the Pajaro Valley Quilt Fair, Santa Cruz County Fairgrounds, 2015, featuring panel for David Dulong created by Mike (Mac) McNamara. Courtesy of the NAMES Project. Photograph by the author.

Fig. 3.19.
Detail of AIDS Quilt panel for Billy Hiatt, with beads, created by Mike (Mac) McNamara. Courtesy of the NAMES Project. Photograph by the author.

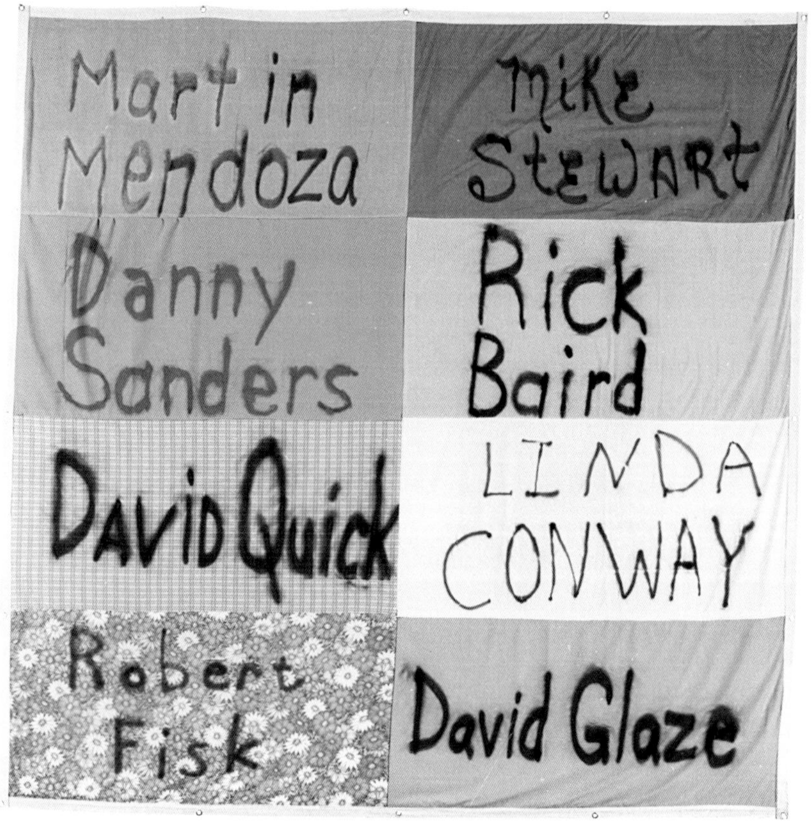

Fig. 3.20.
AIDS Quilt block 0349. Courtesy of the NAMES Project.

these panels, and she said these were from some of the earliest days, when the imperative was just to get a name on a piece of fabric, similar to the cardboard placards at the candlelight vigil.[55]

Some panels look like quilts and are in fact made from actual quilts, taken from family heirlooms. Chuck Morris (a journalist and the publisher of the gay newspaper *The Sentinel*) learned to sew after he was diagnosed with HIV in 1982 and worked for two years to create a quilt out of pink and purple fabrics. Though unlike Puryear he did not intend for this to be his panel, his partner realized when he died that it fit the exact dimensions—three by six feet—so after the addition of small red plastic flowers that spelled out his name, it became part of the Quilt[56] (fig. 3.21). This block was organized by McMullin into a visual theme of lavender quilting that becomes a kind of infinite regress: as small fabric pieces from actual quilts are added to make up the panel, panels are organized into larger 12'×12' blocks, and blocks are lashed together to make up even larger 24'×24' squares for display, with all the names facing out so visitors can read them in any direction.

In October 1987, almost two thousand Quilt panels were laid out on the Mall in its first ceremonial display. When displayed on the Mall, blocks are

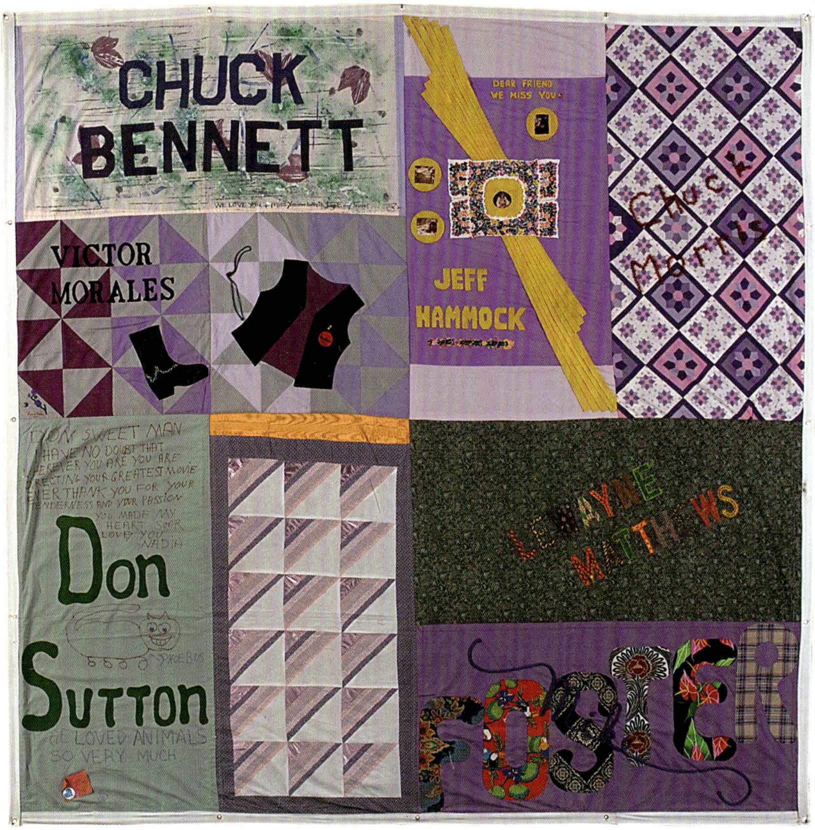

Fig. 3.21.
AIDS Quilt block 0206. Courtesy of the NAMES Project.

put down more or less randomly. This means that while each block should be understood as a visual unit, as a whole the Quilt is elastic in form, made of discrete particles that can be added to and recombined in endless variation. Photographs of this 1987 unveiling often locate it spatially by including the Capitol on one end or the Washington Monument on the other, mapping it in relation to US landmarks of power. In figure 3.22, the photographer so wanted to include the sunrise over the Capitol that the ostensible central action of the image—the unfolding ceremony—is abruptly cropped at the bottom. Here in its first full display, eight volunteers are preparing for the dawn unfurling of the Quilt, a performance loosely inspired by military flag-folding. They wear all white in a solemn theatrical display, while names of those lost to AIDS are read out by speakers at a podium. The Quilt is usually placed directly on the ground, with no protective layer of plastic between it and the earth, and temporary canvas walkways both shield the grass from foot traffic and unify the blocks into an overall design.

The ceremonial unfolding of the Quilt has been an important aspect of its display. Volunteers are instructed to enact a scripted ritual, starting by holding hands in a circle around each large 24'×24' square that has been

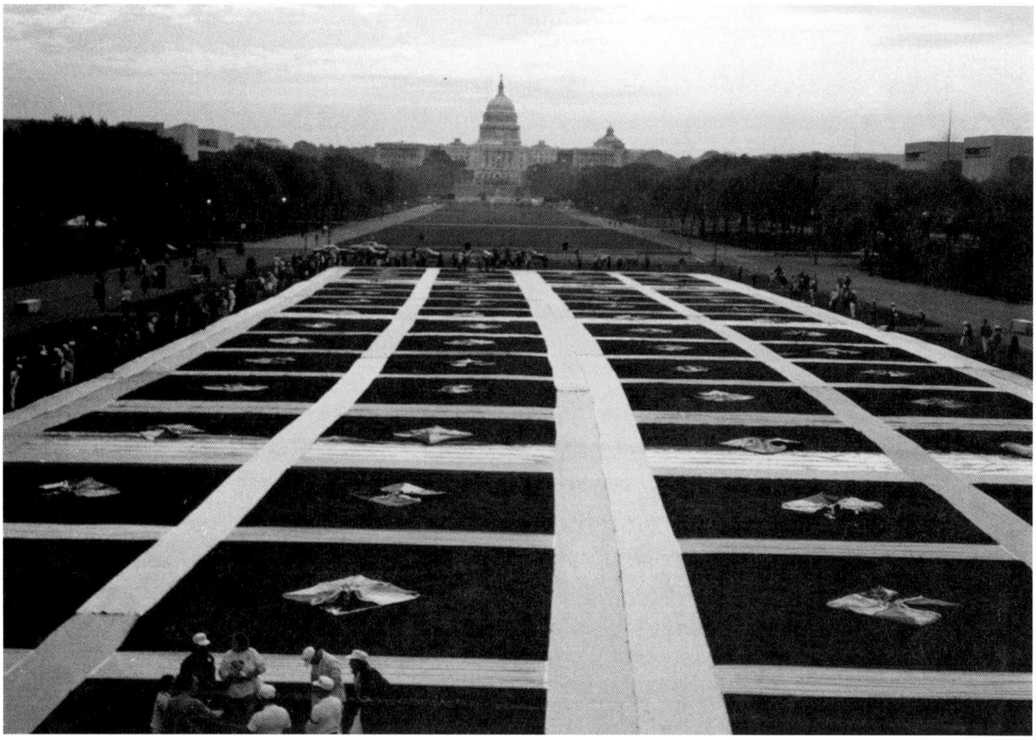

Fig. 3.22. Ceremonial unfolding of the AIDS Quilt at dawn by volunteers in white, with lotus-folded blocks on the ground and a grid of canvas pathways, Washington Mall, Washington, DC, 1987. Courtesy of the NAMES Project.

arranged in a "lotus fold," the brainchild of volunteer and tour director Jack Caster in 1987. The eight white-clad unfolders then walk in unison over the backside of the Quilt to grab each folded corner and open it in stages, spinning it around once it has been unfurled, and finally setting it down on the grass. Thus the Quilt is made and also *performed*, vitally connected to the choreographed bodies of the unfolders and the spoken names that resonate throughout its display. This balletic dance is highlighted in photography of the Quilt, as well as in the Academy Award–winning documentary *Common Threads: Stories from the Quilt*.[57]

Especially significant for the NAMES Project have been the readers who vocally enumerate the names; organizers aimed for a mix of steadfast volunteers, representatives from organizations such as PFLAG, and a sprinkling of high-profile celebrities to draw further press attention to the project. An early solicitation letter from September 1987, labeled "personalities/celebs letter," exhorted its recipients to join the "ceremonial reading of names" as handmade panels were "streaming in from all over the country, at the rate of 100 per day."[58] Included on an official roster of names of readers for the first display in 1987, which commenced with Jones at sunrise and concluded two hours later with César Chávez, are Whoopi Goldberg and Barney Frank, both of whom in the end, a handwritten addendum notes, were no-shows.[59]

In 1987, at its first unveiling in DC, the Quilt had 1,920 panels; by its second tour in 1988, it had grown to over 8,000. By 1992 there were over 20,000, and the installation required the donated labor of over five thousand volunteers, including a reading of names that took a full twenty-four hours. That year alone, it was seen by an estimated 400,000 visitors.[60] Along with these DC stagings, the Quilt toured the country, appearing at convention centers, schools, and other locations (rarely art museums) from Boston to Houston. The theatrical elements of the Quilt's display evolved over time, as regional Quilt chapters tailored the ceremonial unfolding performance to their communities. In 1990 in Hawaii, for instance, the opening ceremony is described like this: "With a stirring Hawaiian chant, a lone performer signaled the unfolding of the Quilt to the volunteers who were dressed all in white, except for the bright flower leis around their necks. . . . And then he began to dance, using a large black blanket with three faces on it. Sometimes the blanket covered him, sometimes he manipulated it with sticks. Slowly the dancer fell to the floor. Then he shed the blanket, coming out in a dance of celebration."[61] Dancing, reading names, volunteers scurrying to unfold the bundles, visitors strolling the canvas walkways: rather than passage quilts that wrap corpses in preparation for burial, live bodies surround and animate this textile. The Quilt also inspired performance, including *The AIDS Quilt Songbook*, a compilation or "patchwork" of songs composed about AIDS that premiered at Lincoln Center in 1992.[62]

"The Death Tarp"

Almost immediately after its initial display in DC, the AIDS Quilt provoked a storm of interest from the mainstream press (discussed in hundreds of articles in its first few years) and also a frenzy of controversy. As it grew in popularity, so too did criticisms. Some came, predictably, from conservative, homophobic quarters. Westboro Baptist Church leader Fred Phelps, well-known for wielding signs proclaiming "God hates fags," showed up in DC as well as at displays in Kansas waving placards that read "Guilt Not Quilt" and exhorting viewers to "burn the fag blanket."[63] Gary Bauer, assistant to Reagan and spokesperson for the administration's abstinence-based AIDS policy, wrote a piece titled "AIDS and the College Student" just after the Quilt's 1987 unveiling.[64] The article was accompanied by a cartoon in which a gay man, who is depicted whistling as an indication of his blithe disregard, and a junkie with the shakes are sewing panels together that read *Sodomy* and *IV Drugs*. The cartoonist has dislocated the Quilt from its factual closeness to both the Capitol and the Washington Monument and in a fantasy of removal renders these as minuscule, far off on the horizon. It forces an association between sewing needles and IV drug needles, in which those perceived as the most "dangerous" vectors of infection are depicted as quilters—a far cry from the Quilt's own literature depicting wholesome women, children, and families as the makers.

Other attacks on the Quilt focused on urban legends about the "perversity" of gay male sex practices, including a mocking "gerbil memorial quilt" that was created at the University of Iowa in 1991.[65] This vicious parody, displayed publicly alongside purportedly factual articles about "gerbiling," was in some respects startlingly faithful to the original Quilt, with individual panels listing dead rodent pets with names like "Fur Ball" and "Petey." Someone spent time studying the formal qualities of the AIDS Quilt in order to produce this homophobic version, evidencing a very attentive and laborious brand of hate. Not only did this disingenuous plea to "save the gerbils" diminish the catastrophic human losses caused by HIV/AIDs, but it also contributed to folklore that fed revulsion toward homosexual sex and stoked fears of the disease.[66]

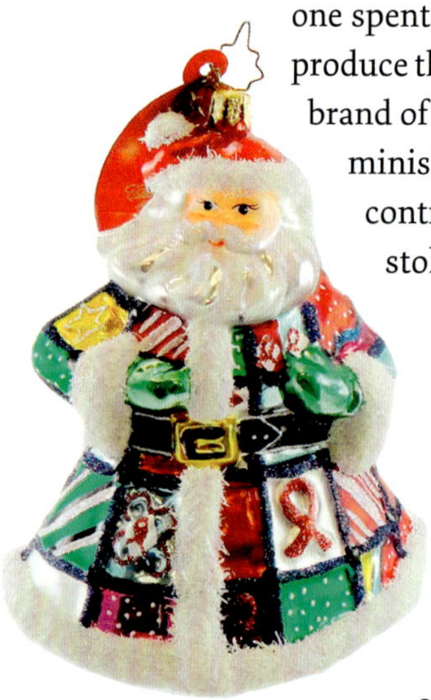

Fig. 3.23. Christopher Radko Quilt 'n Claus AIDS Awareness Charity Ornament. Hand-blown glass, made in Poland. Height 5.5", 2008. Courtesy of Christopher Radko.

But the most lasting and vociferous arguments against the Quilt came not from the homophobic Right but from those one might expect to be sympathetic parties—namely, the activist branch of HIV/AIDS organizers. Many lambasted it as contributing to a trivializing commercialization of the epidemic, especially as the Quilt generated branded merchandise far beyond calendars and posters, including coffee table books, hats, buttons and pins, T-shirts and jerseys, prepaid phone cards, the CD of the *Songbook*, a set of notecards and collector tins designed by sentimental greeting card doyenne and children's book illustrator Mary Engelbreit, and even (as recently as 2008) Christmas ornaments. See figure 3.23: rather than sporting his traditional red-and-white coat, this hand-blown glass Santa Claus ornament, produced in a limited edition as a charity fundraiser by the Christopher Radko Company, is wearing a Quilt-like robe that includes squares featuring the red ribbon for AIDS awareness, thus transforming the textile into a garment of holiday cheer.

At the height of the manufacturing of such desultory mementos, there was a large memorial gift store located in the Castro. "Making Kitsch from AIDS: A Disease with a Gift Shop of Its Own," read one skeptical headline.[67] During the Quilt's DC display in 1992, twelve merchandise booths ringed its perimeter, catering to those who wanted to purchase a souvenir commemorating their visit. These proliferating salable products fed accusations that the Quilt was not corporate in the sense of a collective body but *corporate*—a growth enterprise capitalizing on its visibility and centered on money.

Branded T-shirts, posters, and the gift store mentality seemed to monetize mourning and loss according to a neoliberal logic by which all affective relations become economic transactions. Beyond this commercialization, the Quilt's emphasis on personal names could be understood as partaking in the neoliberal impulse to atomize, individualize, and particularize. Throughout the 1990s, critics felt that the Quilt participated in the commodification not only of quiltmaking (understood as appropriated from its roots as a local activity by a marketing and publicity conglomeration) but indeed of the disease itself.[68]

Along with the Quilt, the symbolic red ribbon, featured in several of the souvenir objects though it was designed by a different HIV advocacy organization in 1991 (Visual AIDS), became for some a facile way to signal awareness of the disease while doing nothing else about it.[69] The red ribbon and the Quilt were seen as antithetical to the on-the-street protests of ACT UP members, who unleashed their anger at both, arguing, "You can't wear a red ribbon if you're dead." Another poster read, "We've turned our anger into a piece of quilt and red ribbons." A former member of ACT UP Philadelphia, one of the most vocal and militant branches, told me that the AIDS Quilt was referred to by some activists, dismissively, as the "Death Tarp."[70] ACT UP fought against the banalization of the disease that they felt the Quilt fostered, including the genericization of the deaths of gay men that the Quilt seemed to promote by virtue of its sheer numbers. As Jones recalls, "The loudest naysayers were the ACT-UP people. . . . It's not enough to make a quilt, they sneered; the Quilt is a passive thing."[71] Like Gilbert Baker's rainbow flag, the Quilt has been accused of being "assimiliationist" in its attempt to make gay lives palatable to the mainstream and to de-sex or deradicalize queer practices.[72]

Beyond condemnations due to its material and form, to the dismay of some activists, the Quilt was understood as taking a neutral stance in many AIDS fights. Jones, who takes up disproportionate space as founder and spokesperson in these debates, insisted, "We are, of course, absolutely nonpolitical."[73] He clarified: "We don't take stands on any of the political issues that surround the AIDS epidemic."[74] Yet the Quilt has never been Jones's alone, and many staff and volunteers also advocated for voters to educate themselves on candidate records about gay rights and HIV-related issues, urging them to ask that their elected representatives "make AIDS a federal priority."[75] Jones calls the Quilt "pure good,"[76] a phrase he wielded frequently until an ugly battle for ownership led him to step down as the head of the foundation in 2004. For many, his relentless insistence on the "goodness" or neutrality of the Quilt was its biggest problem. It was seen as a defanging, a depoliticization of the disease, muffling cries for direct action. The Quilt was lambasted as a sanitizing, de-queered failure that promoted tears and teddy bears instead of galvanizing action. Such an understanding has persisted among some academics. As Erin Rand writes in the special *Rhetoric and Public Affairs* issue on the Quilt, "I suggest that the commemoration of the Quilt conserves a limiting form of social recognition that severely constrains its potential as a site for activating social change."[77] Many feel that its focus on the Washington Mall too narrowly addresses a monolithic "public," as if there were such a singular entity, and as if it might be defined or delimited by a plot of land in the nation's capital.

The commemorative program for the Quilt's 1988 national tour states that the project builds a "powerful, positive, creative symbol of remembrance and hope."[78] One Quilt panel contains the message "Heal AIDS With Love." For many in ACT UP, this was exactly the sort of irresponsible, frivolous sentiment promulgated by the entire NAMES Project, as they carried out protests against the FDA and the politicians who dragged their feet regarding new treatments and policy changes. *Anger* and *change*, not *love*, *hope*, and *healing*, were their watchwords. To quote Douglas Crimp in his critical, nuanced article "The Spectacle of Mourning," "Does a visit to the quilt, or the media's approving attention to it . . . provide a form of catharsis, an easing of conscience, for those who have cared and done so little about this great tragedy?"[79] For Crimp, the ambivalence he feels about the Quilt—especially its address to a generalized audience rather than to the queer communities it commemorates—and its public "spectacle" reflects the ambivalent psychoanalytic structure of mourning itself. This is utterly persuasive, and I would go further to claim that a felt ambivalence about the Quilt is also tied to the uncertain, ambivalent status of textiles within contemporary art and culture, particularly a domestic craft form associated with low women's work. The tensile nature of textiles, which can be taken as a strength, can also be a hindrance: like ambivalence, fiber can pull simultaneously in opposite directions.

To push this thinking further: what politics does the AIDS Quilt have *as a textile*, and how can its textiles hold its politics? In part it is through its texture, that is, through its unevenly skilled material histories of gloppy glue and dazzling beadwork, and its implicit invitation to be touched. There is a tremendous investment in this object as a handmade thing, stitching work by amateurs and professionals together on the same level field. The Quilt was consciously chosen for its classically heterosexual family associations: Jones admitted that he and his staff "deliberately adopted a symbol and a vocabulary that would not be threatening to nongay people."[80] Jones has discussed being inspired by feminist works of craft reclamation such as Chicago's *The Dinner Party*, but the Quilt is as influenced by gay male aesthetics as it is by feminism.[81] Everywhere on the Quilt there are undeniable irruptions of queer life, from leather vests to men's shirts with linked sleeves to Judy Garland references. As Crimp notes, it is full of references both oblique and overt to gay sexual cultures (though while there are a lot of color-coded handkerchiefs and denim vests, there are fewer "cock rings, dildos, or Crisco labels").[82] To look in the Quilt for a comprehensive queer activist statement or a cohesive gay identity is to be frustrated, as instead it offers partial glances at lives interrupted, and the poignant ways in which such lives are gestured to, and incompletely captured, on a patch of fabric.

What the Quilt recalls are histories of textile making as a social and often strident act: as discussed in the introduction, needlework has a contentious past and continues to be a highly charged mode of making that has played a role in politics from the Right and the Left, as when women were exhorted to knit during wartime. Mainardi's article on quilts from 1973 not only made claims for women's handmaking as art but also speculated about the role of communal craft in fomenting American social movements, detailing how the quilting bee, where women could say "important things . . . best said out of earshot of men," could be considered a precursor to women's feminist consciousness-raising groups.[83] Within US history, quilts as carriers of social meaning have been understood both as normalizing busywork to keep women preoccupied and as active agents of opposition: consider the assertion that abstract quilt patterns were used among slaves to send coded messages along the Underground Railroad.[84] The ferocity that has attended these arguments makes clear that quilting is a charged site laden with ideological investments.

Quilting is recruited, one might say, in times of social and political turmoil, as it serves multiple, flexible functions, not least of which is to memorialize. Jones titled his autobiography *Stitching a Revolution*, despite his lack of sewing knowledge, and indeed the discourse of craft within the Quilt's rhetoric shifts between a set of specific processes with material histories and a free-floating metaphoric or symbolic trope assumed to be transparent, obvious, nonthreatening, or neutral. For textiles are often mobilized in the face of trauma, and not just to provide needed garments or coverings but also as a therapeutic means of comfort, a safe outlet for worried hands, a productive channel for the obsessive working through of loss—and it was precisely that ameliorating aspect that so many activists rebelled against. "We didn't want healing," the former ACT UP Philly member told me, "we wanted to open the wound further."[85] The polarization between ACT UP and the Quilt reached its most extreme articulation in 1992; in the next section I detail this clash and then discuss how the Quilt continues to function, and fray, across political lines.

Crafting Conflicts, 1992–Present

By the time of the 1992 Washington, DC, display that included twenty thousand panels, the AIDS Quilt had achieved unprecedented levels of visibility, eliciting both positive publicity and ever-more-negative scrutiny. The year 1992, I claim, was pivotal for the project. What made this year such a watershed moment for the Quilt? Once viewed by some in Reagan's hostile government as promoting IV drug use and risky gay sex, it now had broad acceptance from voices across the political spectrum. Such acceptance was heavily promoted by the NAMES Project. For instance, the following blurb, attributed to President George H. W. Bush, appears on the back of a book of Quilt panel contributors' letters *A Promise to Remember*, published in 1992: "These amazing quilts prove that no one is a statistic. Every life has its own fabric, its own colors, its own soul. No two are alike."[86] Though Bush elides the difference between the panels as separate "quilts" and the entirety of the project as a unified Quilt, there can be no doubt that this is a voice of approval, and one that heralds the Quilt's embrace by the highest office of US state power. The blurb sent shivers of revulsion up the spines of many activists, who understood Bush not as a respected figure to be asked for an endorsement but the very personification of government inaction and homophobia.

At the same time that it gained traction as the central vehicle for humanizing those who died of HIV-related causes (note Bush's emphasis on "souls," his celebration of individuality, and his omission of words such as *gay* and *AIDS*), criticisms about the Quilt as antithetical to radical activism were at their peak.[87] In October 1992, ACT UP New York organized the "Ashes Action," in which people threw cremation remains of loved ones onto the lawn of the White House—occupied by President Bush—as a "political funeral" to protest ongoing governmental neglect around AIDS. The Ashes Action was performed to coincide with the Quilt's unveiling on October 11, 1992, and members choreographed their protest as a direct confrontation with and visible retort to the Quilt. In the video made by AIDS Community Television documenting the Ashes Action, an organizer of the demonstration (and founding member of ACT UP New York), David Robinson, states that they chose the date because they "wanted there to be a counterpoint to the Quilt's approach to bringing home what's happening with AIDS."[88]

In the video, the camera pans over the Quilt being tended by white-clad volunteers as names are uttered over a loudspeaker. Text by Simon Watney scrolls across the screen: "The Quilt has become the acceptable face of AIDS death in the U.S. It provides a doubtless admirable and moving map of the epidemic. . . . But its focus is that of New Age religiosity rather than social or POLITICAL explication" (fig. 3.24). While the solemn "sacred" demeanor of the white-clad unfolders surely contributes to the sense that the Quilt partakes of "New Age religiosity," its status as handcrafted textile is implicated in this critique as well. Though one critic writes that this imputed "religiosity" implied "flights into transcendence" away from the corporeally devastating realities of the disease, the ritualistic aspect of the Quilt with its ceremonial unfolding, talk about the "sacred" quality of the panels, and solemn name-reading was also seen as an all-too-literally material response.[89]

The Quilt's tactile softness was linked to ideological pliability and political weakness, and the NAMES Project's evident hunger for public acceptance by the administration, such as Bush's blurb, was at odds with the accusatory demands of ACT UP. To cite two placards carried by protesters, Bush was viewed as a "murderer" and the "hate president." ACT UP members expressed sympathy for the Quilt while also decrying how it, in Robinson's words, makes "something beautiful out of the epidemic. . . . There's nothing beautiful about it. This is what I'm left with, a box of ashes and bone chips." Flinging ashes over the helmeted heads of police onto the White House lawn, accompanied by a cacophony of screams and chants and whistles and sobs, they declared: "This is what George Bush has done . . . [the administration has] turned our loved ones into corpses."

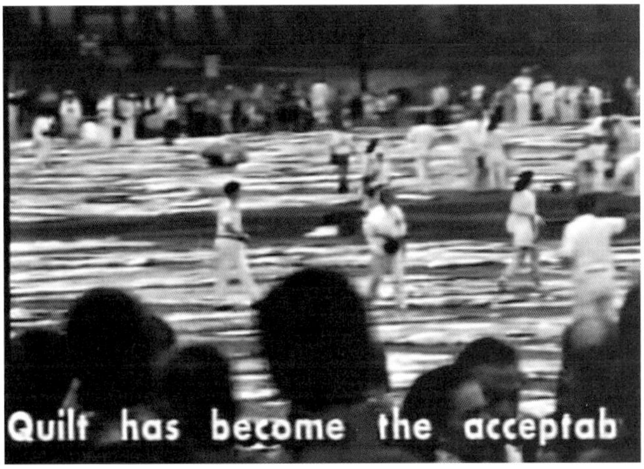

Fig. 3.24.
Still from James Wentzy, dir., *The Ashes Action*, video, 1995, 30 minutes.

According to Deborah Gould, with the Ashes Action ACT UP "implicitly drew a distinction between the Quilt's encouragement of grief and its own enactment of grief-inspired rage."[90] 1992 saw particularly ferocious contempt for the Quilt as a diversion, such as in an article published by ACT UP's Bob Rafsky, who declared a desire to find people who had made AIDS Quilt panels but now realized they were "inadequate" and to, with their permission, "piss on [them]."[91] If Reverend Fred Phelps wanted to burn the Quilt, so did some members of ACT UP. Avram Finkelstein (who helped design the SILENCE=DEATH graphic and participated in the Ashes Action) wrote in 1992 that he wished he could rip the panel he made for his lover, Don Yowell, out of its Quilt display and "heave it over the fence [of the White House], where it belonged"[92] (fig. 3.25).

Despite the continual positioning of the Quilt as antithetical to ACT UP,

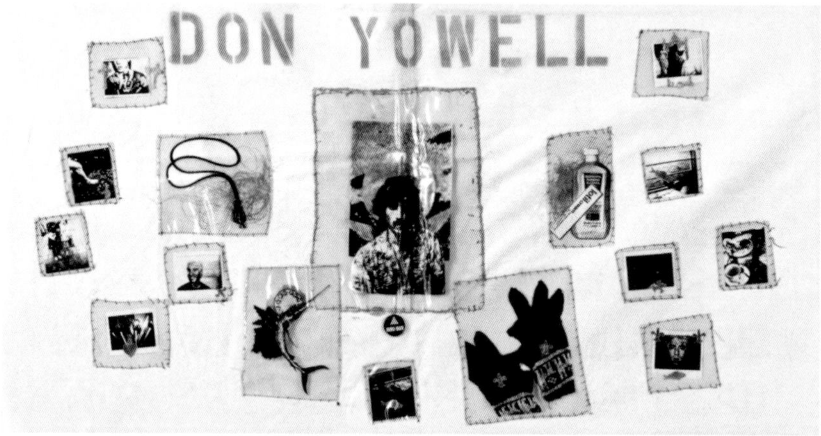

Fig. 3.25. AIDS Quilt panel for Don Yowell, made by Avram Finkelstein. Courtesy of the NAMES Project.

Finkelstein's quote points to moments of interconnection between these responses to AIDS—he might have later regretted it, but he did take the time to make a panel, and he clearly thought carefully about its construction as well as its composition. Finkelstein's panel for Yowell exemplifies both a conceptual and an object-oriented approach to panel making. Working with metallic paper die-cuts and textiles, he was influenced in its design by devotional prayer cards, with a central photo surrounded by actual objects as well as photocopies encased in vinyl plastic pouches and sewn onto canvas backing with black stitching that resembles medical sutures.[93] These include an image of a pair of gloves, because Yowell's fingers were always cold. Within its muted palette of black and white, the panel shows a sensitivity toward the affective registers of color by eschewing bright hues, drawing attention to the one exception on the panel: a SILENCE=DEATH button with its hot pink triangle (fig. 3.26). Its presence is unmistakable, and another ACT UP button is featured on the panel sewn above Yowell's. The constellation of objects included on this panel do not narrate a straightforward timeline of the full sweep of Yowell's life but provide glimpses of mediating objects that were meaningful within their relationship, including a thermometer and a bottle of alcohol from the fever-reducing baths Finkelstein gave Yowell toward the end of his life.

More recently, Finkelstein has acknowledged that there was more overlap between the strategies of the Ashes Action and that of the Quilt—which in fact had cremation ashes embedded in its fabric—than he had previously believed. He states,

> I was extremely surprised by how many people who were there for the Quilt spontaneously joined our action. We imagined many people at the Quilt would be offended by our action. But I think the imagined di-

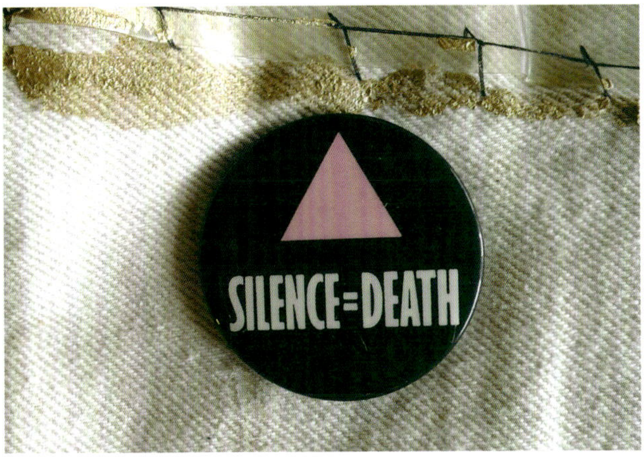

Fig. 3.26. Detail of AIDS Quilt panel for Don Yowell, with SILENCE=DEATH button. Photograph by the author.

> chotomy was a cultural perception exaggerated by a general framing of "activism" as intrinsically adversarial, a framework rendered moot by the onslaught of death we barely had time to process. Quilt and ashes were only oppositional in the abstract. Functionally, the lines were far blurrier.[94]

Finkelstein echoes Crimp's convincing argument that, no less than the mourning process itself, the structuring response to the Quilt is ambivalence. Though this ambivalence was felt acutely by many politically militant queers, I assert that there was a productive *mutuality* between activist groups like ACT UP and the Quilt: each needed the other as a foil, or ground, to throw its own stakes into relief. As Yowell's panel demonstrates, several members of ACT UP who contributed to the Quilt were also honored within it, such as on one stenciled panel that says, "STOP AIDS, FIGHT BACK, ACT UP" (fig. 3.27). Set next to another panel whose handwritten script reads, "To all the artists who died before their time," this panel explodes the notion that ACT UP, as some mythically unified entity, found the Quilt totally regressive and abhorred its very existence. Rather, ACT UP is registered as a visible presence within the fabric of the Quilt, in moments like the button on Yowell's panel and the posterlike panels that integrate ACT UP slogans directly into the Quilt.

Along with panels made by and for members of ACT UP, there are at least four panels dedicated to another figure who might be seen as unlikely to be memorialized in this "low" manner, French theorist Michel Foucault. One of these panels was made by Gerard Koskovich, a queer historian, graphic designer, and member of Queer Nation San Francisco who had interviewed Foucault and published an early account of his death to AIDS for a US audience. Like the ACT UP panel that reiterates an activist slogan, it was created with a stencil and spray paint to mimic the street graffiti of France[95] (fig. 3.28).

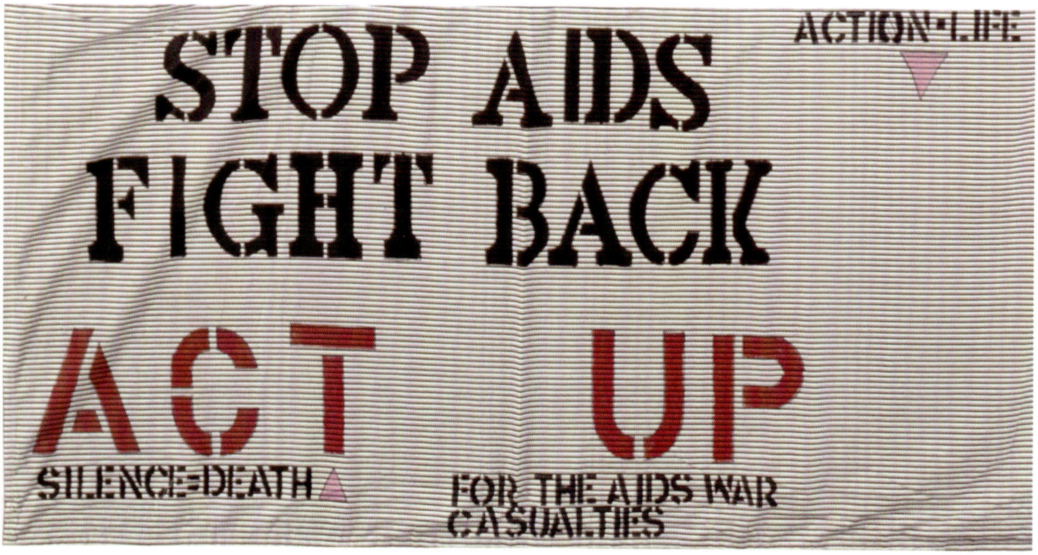

Fig. 3.27.
AIDS Quilt panel, Stop AIDS, Fight Back, ACT-UP. Courtesy of the NAMES Project.

Foucault's name and dates of birth/death are repeated, in gray and red, over the canvas-colored cloth, stuttering like the frames of a filmstrip. As with some of the earliest spray-painted panels that were made in the first months of the Quilt to mimic cardboard placards, Koskovich's choice of medium is inspired: not only does spray paint resonate with the political signage of graffiti and its qualities of diffusion (as when it "bleeds through" the strict lines of the stencil), but its variable intensity can make it appear somewhat ghostly, as on the left side of this panel, where the spray paint is unevenly applied and the name emerges from the neutral ground of the fabric. For Crimp, Foucault's presence in the Quilt was a central catalyst for his reflections on the Quilt's meaning:

> Seeing a panel bearing the name of Michel Foucault, who was an intellectual idol, whose writings I had depended on for much of my own work, and who had agreed to be a reader of my dissertation less than a year before he died—seeing that panel had less emotional impact on me than seeing, every now and then, a name I recognized as that of someone I'd only dimly known, or known about. . . . I had lost not just the center of my world but its periphery, too.[96]

Though his article makes no mention of the Quilt's crafted aspect, its textile flexibility, its closeness to the ground, or its gridded equivalence of names that keeps any given panel from being "central" or "peripheral," Crimp's account of being unmoored by the scope of loss represented on the Quilt (from intimates to those he knew only in passing) pivots crucially on its form: its

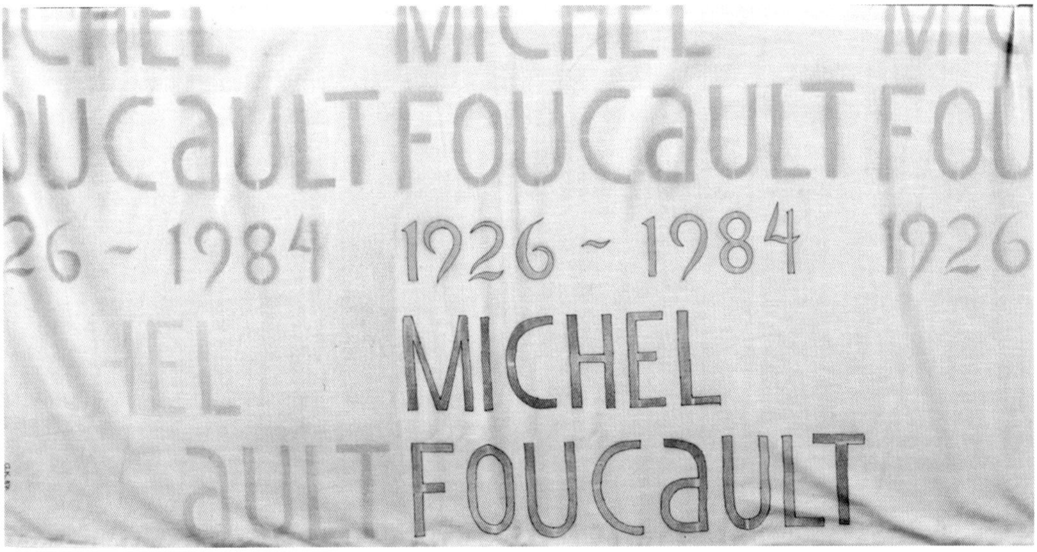

Fig. 3.28.
AIDS Quilt panel for Michel Foucault, made by Gerard Koskovich. Courtesy of the NAMES Project.

juxtaposition of strangers with unpredictable connectivity, and its "worlding" visualization of extraordinary numbers of deaths.

"A Colorless Amalgam"

When Bill Clinton became president of the United States in 1993, the NAMES Project was invited to take part in his official inaugural parade—this was understood as an indication of his administration's willingness to confront the AIDS crisis. Yet the chosen panels, isolated from their blocks and carried like banners, had the paradoxical effect of seeming somewhat triumphant—rather than mournful—as those who walked with them smiled and waved to passersby.[97] Volunteers and celebrities like the then-current Miss America and Ryan White's mother Jeanne carried individual panels along the parade route (fig. 3.29), including one for dancer Jeffrey Groff (on the left) and one for Max Robinson (on the right), who is identified with sewn-on black, green, red, and gold letters on a brown background as a "network TV anchorman." In fact, Robinson was the very first African American broadcast network news anchor, and his death in 1988 sparked conversations within black communities about the need for more AIDS prevention outreach and education specifically targeting people of color.[98] The panel carried through the streets of DC for Clinton's parade does not include a photo of Robinson, but the Pan-African color scheme of its text (black, red, green, gold) visually, if subtly, indicates his identification with African American heritage.[99]

Robinson is represented in two other Quilt locations: one all-red panel

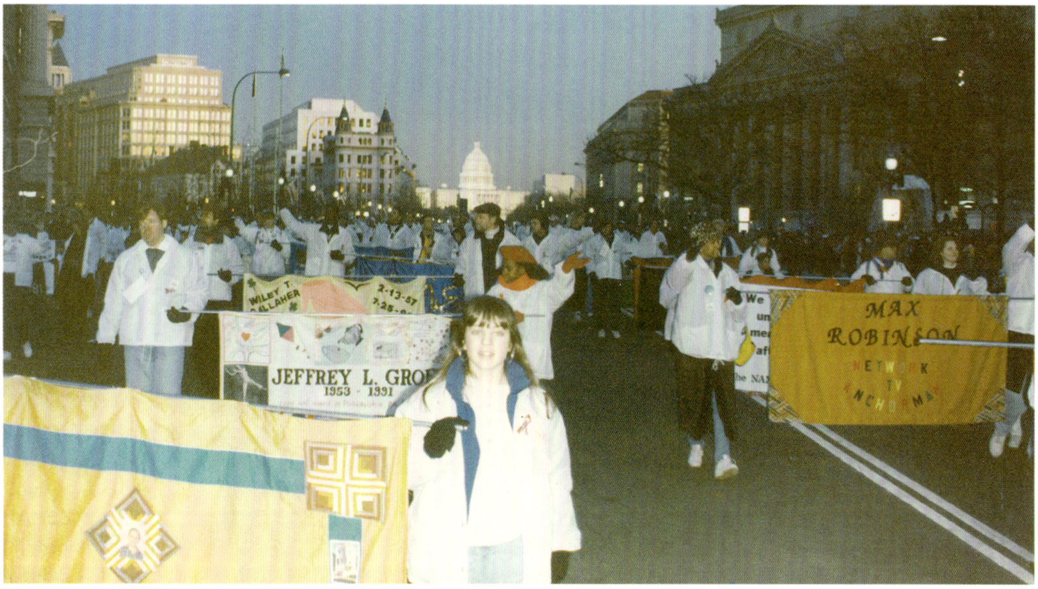

Fig. 3.29. AIDS Quilt panels carried in the inauguration parade for President Bill Clinton, including panel for Max Robinson (right), carried by Charlene and Brian Biggs, Washington, DC, 1993. Photographer unknown.

with his name spelled in beads that calls him simply a "newsman," and one entire block dedicated to African American entertainers, in which his panel is surrounded by some other black celebrities who have died of AIDS-related causes, including Sylvester, tennis player Arthur Ashe, and rapper Eazy-E, each of whom is represented with pictures of signature objects like a tennis racket and tennis balls, record albums, and, in the case of Robinson, drawings of television sets. Robinson's multiple panels crucially indicate how different facets of a person's life might be emphasized based on a panel's design as well as by its integration into a block that has been organized to accentuate commonalities: when his panel is sewn in close proximity to the likes of Sylvester or Ashe, Robinson's African American identity (and his star status) is highlighted. Once again, the block as an organizing unit for multiple panels works both aesthetically and politically to stitch together individual stories and lives.

Marita Sturken, writing in her important book *Tangled Memories*, contends that the Quilt "evokes a sense of Americana, yet it also represents those who have been symbolically excluded from America—drug users, blacks, Latinos, gay men."[100] However, if queerness is figured on the Quilt in a number of ways, both overt and encoded, so too is race. Sometimes the names on the panels themselves clearly point to racial identity (as do some Latino and Asian names), but the common use of first names only and the frequent lack of other information about a person has the potential to be deracinating. It was surely meant as a retort to the prevailing assumptions about the demographics of the AIDS crisis that an early panel commemorat-

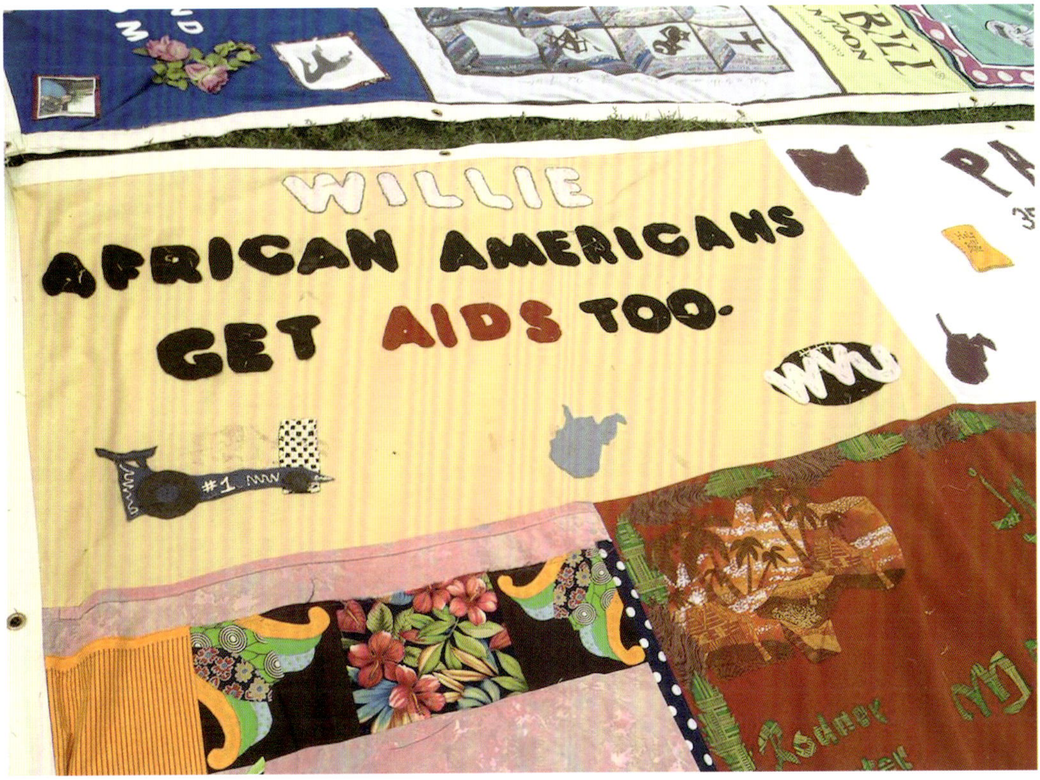

ing African American fashion designer Willi Smith baldly states, "AIDS is killing black America." A different panel for another Willie (first name only) states bluntly, "African Americans Get AIDS Too" (fig. 3.30). With its trio of pictorial details—a Formula One race car reaching the checkered cloth of the finish line, the outline of the state of West Virginia, and a football from West Virginia University—the panel presents a series of overlapping identifications via motifs of community belonging.

Fig. 3.30.
AIDS Quilt panel for Willie. Courtesy of the NAMES Project. Photograph by the author.

Indeed, since its founding the Quilt has faced accusations of bleaching the AIDS crisis. An anonymous letter written in the late 1980s contends that the corporatization of the NAMES Project has come at the cost of its ties to the true diversity of communities harmed by AIDS, including prostitutes, drug users, and people of color. Under the title "The NAMES Project Exposed," the letter states: "During preparations for the inaugural display of the Quilt in 1987, for example, the Project's leaders had to be begged, threatened, and cajoled into expanding their vision of the Quilt's constituency to include women, Blacks, Asians, Hispanics, and others."[101] In response to growing desires for the panels to more openly signify the range of losses from AIDS, volunteers advocated for panel designs that made some identities more immediately readable, openly inserting phrases like *drug user*. Though there are panels for occupational designations and other more amorphous groupings, such as social workers, actors, federal employees, and "those who have died hiding," for instance, there are none specifically for the categories of IV drug users, or hustlers, or the like—and recall that needles are one of the few objects that are removed from panels.

The letter goes on to detail "growing resentment regarding the 'dehomosexualization'" of the Quilt and argues that in the early days, leaders including Jones felt that "the AIDS epidemic primarily affects white gay men—so why put energy into other communities?" At the core of the critique is an argument about how race and other identities might be made more legible on the surface of the Quilt as it purports to take a fully inclusive approach.

> Inherent in the Project's corporate, middle-class style is a desire for "respectability." . . . As the Project relentlessly converts itself into a colorless amalgam, individual differences will simply become *invisible*. . . . The leadership of the NAMES Project has forgotten—if it ever knew—how much visibility means to people who have traditionally been invisible. As white, middle-class men, they have never really had to think about it. . . . [They] need to recognize that covering everyone with the same blanket doesn't include them, it obscures them.[102]

In this letter, some of the Quilt's detractors decry how the overarching concern with "corporate, middle-class . . . respectability" dilutes the power and perversion of queer politics. In this they prefigure debates about "respectability" that unfolded within queer theory in the late 1990s, in particular Michael Warner's critique of Andrew Sullivan's call to "normalize" queer subjects and queer practices (in 1995 Sullivan decreed gays and lesbians "virtually normal").[103] But the letter makes explicit not just the class politics but also the race politics of normalization, of pandering to corporate interests, and of respectability.

Looking beyond the rectangles of brightly patterned cloths that create an aesthetically diverse surface, the letter writer describes the Quilt as a "colorless amalgam" in light of its homogenizing leveling of names and its overwhelming whiteness. And in fact, the panels of the Quilt do not reflect the current face of AIDS in the United States, which now disproportionately affects African Americans—according to NAMES Project staff person Jada Harris, only about five hundred panels of the current forty-nine thousand are evidently for black men (and there are far fewer for black women).[104] It is a shocking statistic given that African Americans bear "the most severe burden of HIV of all racial/ethnic groups in the United States."[105] I say "evidently" because in most panels race is not easily decoded; names can eclipse

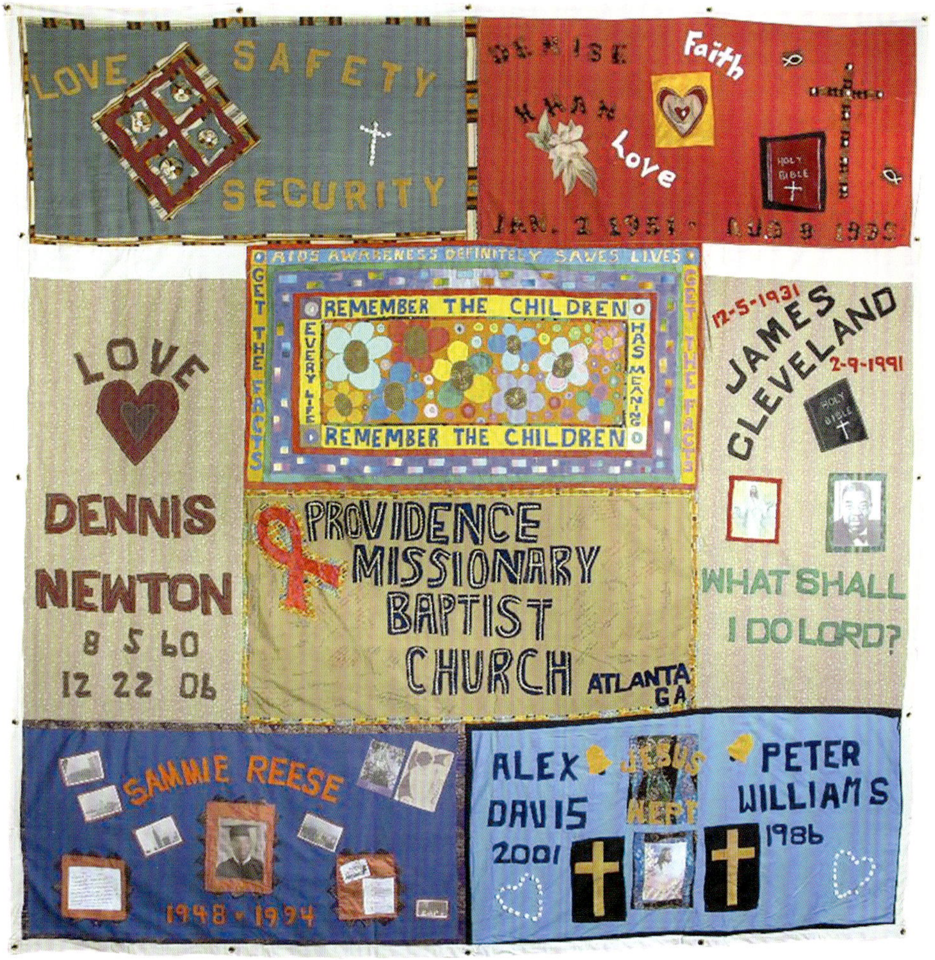

Fig. 3.31.
AIDS Quilt block 5789. Courtesy of the NAMES Project.

as much as they reveal, and some aspects of these lives lost are impossible to decipher given the format of the Quilt. (We might know a lot about Liberace when we see his name on a panel, but virtually nothing about Brendon in fig. 3.18 except his dates of birth and death.)

Harris's statistic about the paucity of black male panels was calculated using the forms that accompany panels, a form in which the panel maker/submitter ticks off boxes to indicate the race, gender, and age of the person memorialized. But only a small number of panels are sent in with filled out (self-reported) forms. As with the Robinson panel, there are other, visual methods for grasping the demographics of the Quilt. The figure 3.31 block, for instance, includes several panels featuring black men, including gospel legend James Cleveland. If read as a consciously organized block rather than as a series of disconnected single memorials, then one notes the unifying

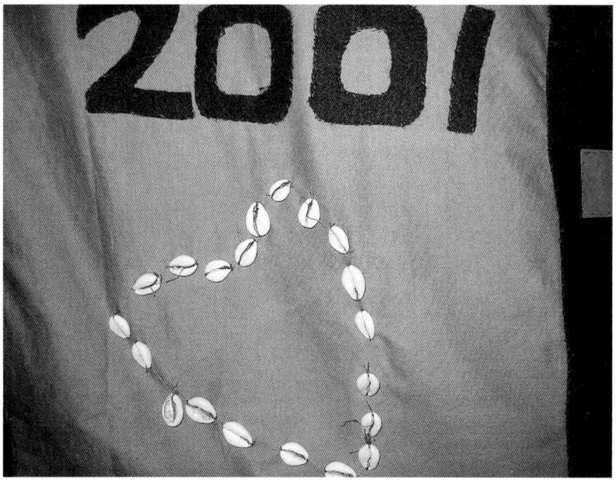

Fig. 3.32. Detail of AIDS Quilt block 5789. Courtesy of the NAMES Project. Photograph by the author.

incorporation of several distinctive elements associated with African American material culture, including cowry beads and kente cloth. The double panel for Alex Davis and Peter Williams (lovers? friends? relatives?), who share space with an image of Jesus and the phrase "Jesus wept," has been embellished with hearts made of cowry beads (fig. 3.32).

The emphasis on African American adornment and fabric throughout the block suggests that these panels might have been designed, perhaps by members of Atlanta's Providence Missionary Baptist Church—named in a central panel and framed by kente cloth—to register a distinctly black presence.[106] Instead of castigating the Quilt as a fully deracinating form, one might choose to read it as replete with culturally specific and meaningful fabrics, objects, and juxtapositions that can only hint at many kinds of (ultimately unknowable) lives. The Quilt, with all that it explicitly states, suggests, and also omits, is, like the arpilleras, an unstable space of constant projection on the part of the viewer. In some cases, its materials, such as fabrics, beads, and other crucial choices, reveal more about its narratives than do its names or other words; the textile elements of the Quilt's design and fabrication are the semantic units that become its text.

Within and Beyond the Nation

The lack of names of African American men speaks volumes about the occlusions and gaps in the AIDS Quilt as a troubled, incomplete library. In many respects the AIDS Quilt is a peculiar kind of archive, unjuried and accepting of all submissions, but still self-selecting in terms of who is encouraged, or feels invited, to participate. Whose family or friends or coworkers had the time, energy, emotional strength, knowledge, and resources to make a panel, and whose did not? The Quilt's potential to flatten the epidemic into a series of visual vignettes that includes some names, but not others, and then to amalgamate those names into the schema of an administered grid, gestures to the wider theoretical problematic, formulated by thinkers like Foucault and Allan Sekula, of the disciplinary effects of archives as sites of surveillance and regulation.[107] While it is not fair to dismiss the Quilt for its omissions as if the textile itself had some agency in this matter, the NAMES Project organization, at least in its initial years, did not sufficiently take multiple axes of difference into consideration. Yet it is also difficult to imagine how the Quilt, with its reliance on volunteer labor, might ever achieve any kind of comprehensive, encyclopedic status, with one panel corresponding to each person lost to AIDS.

The skewed statistics of the AIDS Quilt demonstrate that the United States is a country in which tears are not shed equally for all subjects. In addition, the organization's early outreach efforts and focus on gay white urban males, and maybe more fundamentally its emphasis on "naming," might have (intentionally or not) alienated some quarters and diminished participation from African American communities. This is especially lamentable when one considers the great importance of quilting to black cultures in the United States. Given the absence of official histories about everyday African American lives, folklorists have looked to quilts for "stories of individual and black collective experience."[108] Indeed, it was in the 1980s that Faith Ringgold turned to quilting in part to affirm its long history as a preeminent form not just of "great American art," as Mainardi would have it, but also as *African American* women's art.

Since her *thangka* paintings of 1972, mentioned in the introduction, Ringgold aimed to dismantle the craft–art binary and to integrate textile forms within her modernist art. Her turn to quilting in the early 1980s was what Freida High Wasikhongo Tesfagiorgis describes as an "afrofemcentric" affirmation of matrilineal knowledge and skill, in which her appliqué, piecing, and sewing paid homage to African American female labors.[109] Ringgold's "painted quilts," begun in 1980 in collaboration with her mother, were explorations into hybridized techniques, as she used painted and dyed fabric, text-heavy narrations, photoetching, patchwork, and stitching. This fusion of methods was an intentional recollection of hybrid quilting in the United States; as Lisa Farrington notes, "adopting the means of quilt fabrication from Euro-American traditions, women of color made quilt tops using their own African-derived designs."[110] In addition, given the deep connections between slavery and the cotton industry in the United States, African American women's use of cotton fabric, in particular, is a potent material decision.

Ringgold's story quilts can be seen as a crucial precedent for the AIDS Quilt in several regards, in that both her works and the Quilt use textiles to convey specific anecdotes and personal narratives, sometimes incorporating text, as well as to gesture to collective histories. Though often figurative, some are more abstract, relying on the effects of fabric to convey their meanings, as in Ringgold's *No More War Story Quilt* from 1985, which fea-

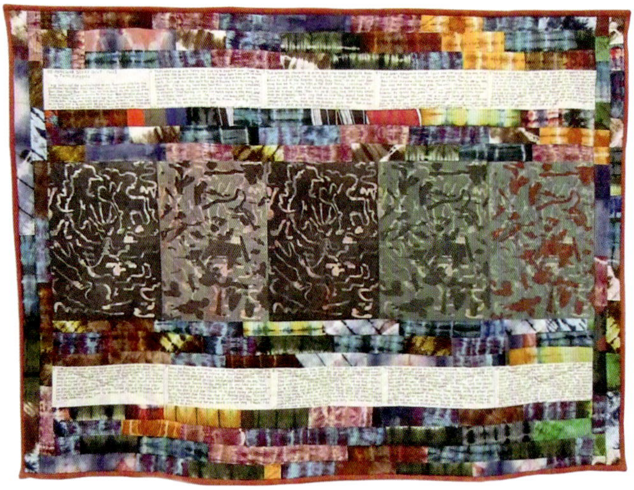

Fig. 3.33. Faith Ringgold, *No More War Story Quilt Part II*, intaglio printed, resist-dyed and pieced fabric, 1985. © Faith Ringgold 1985. Courtesy ACA Artists collection.

tures two bands of printed text (accounts of African American soldiers fighting in US wars in Asia) stitched above and below a sequence of five panels of camouflage fabric (fig. 3.33). Focusing on the (invoked but not depicted) figure of a black male, Ringgold's work uses coded cloth as a visual as well as discursive device in ways that would later be echoed in the panels of the AIDS Quilt, where a scrap of fabric—whether leather, camouflage, or lamé—might signal stylistic affiliations, professional groupings, or other sets of identifications.

There are striking connections—and disjunctures—between the greater visibility of black quilting and the emergence of the AIDS Quilt; just as Jones was conceiving of the Quilt around 1987 in San Francisco, an exhibition of African American quilts was on display at the San Francisco Craft and Folk Art Museum, *Who'd a Thought It: Improvisation in African American Quiltmaking* (it subsequently traveled widely).[111] Yet as Elaine Showalter has written, rather than embrace the racial and gendered implications of quilting as it gained ground in the late 1980s, the Quilt's rhetorical apparatus, as articulated in promotional literature that emphasized its massive scale above all, drew upon metaphors "of football, sales conventions, and cargo planes" to evoke "normative American masculinity" (and, I would add, normative whiteness).[112]

More recent efforts of the NAMES Project have acknowledged the racial lacunas within the Quilt, as well as the central place of quilting within African American memory-making, and have especially appealed to black churches in the southern United States to marshal their tremendous collective quilting energies and talents, with quilting workshops producing panels for those known and lost to AIDS through the churches' wider social networks. The NAMES Project's "Call My Name" outreach effort has received, according to Harris, "no resistance" from African American communities (fig. 3.34).[113] However, this initiative was somewhat slow to take off; it took over five years to reach the goal of adding one hundred new panels featuring black men to the Quilt.[114] Project staff found that in one-to-two day workshops, panels were started but not completed, and so as of 2015 the NAMES Project was focusing on finishing these panels in order to integrate them into viewable

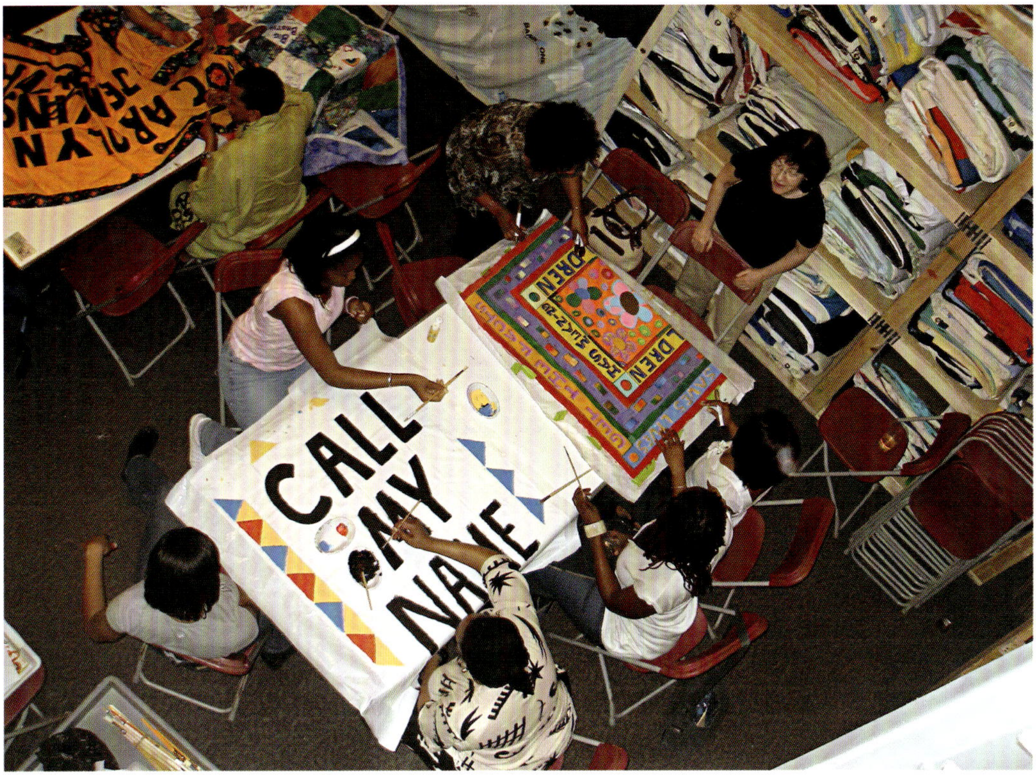

Fig. 3.34. Call My Name Workshop, Atlanta, Georgia, 2006. Courtesy of the NAMES Project.

blocks. The Call My Name workshops have generated new panels honoring Marlon Riggs and Essex Hemphill, among others.

At the same time that activists participating in the Ashes Action were condemning the Quilt for beautifying the epidemic, some queer theorists in the early 1990s were writing about the Quilt as an exceptionally moving example of national grieving. As Judith Butler wrote in 1993, "The NAMES Project Quilt is exemplary, ritualizing and repeating the name itself as a way of publicly avowing the limitless loss."[115] For Butler, the Quilt has effectively given voice to those she later called, in the context of torture enacted and war waged by the United States, "ungrievable," those whose lives are unmourned by the state and whose losses command little public mourning. She writes, "An ungrievable life is one that cannot be mourned because it has never lived, that is, it has never counted as a life at all."[116] In this respect, the Quilt's focus on uttering names and literally making space on the Washington Mall and elsewhere for the lives lost is a powerful rejoinder to a public culture gripped by homophobia that might otherwise erase these losses altogether.

Yet the Quilt's focus on the national stage as defined by the Mall, adjacent to the architectures of governance so antagonistic to radical queer politics, was always viewed as problematic, a part of what has been called "homonationalism," in which queerness is understood not as a disruption to the family or the nation but as a conventional, even strategic part of larger national ideologies of power. Jasbir Puar writes that homonationalism is "a brand of homosexuality [that] operates as a regulatory script not only of normative gayness, queerness, or homosexuality, but also of the racial and national norms that reinforce those sexual subjects."[117] Beyond accusations of "assimiliationist" gay agendas or normalizing queer practices, within the logic of homonationalism, queer subjects are made to function within and, crucially, *for* the state.

At the same time that the Quilt was accused of emphasizing how queer subjects were harmless (and dead) US citizens, around 1992, the NAMES Project was also turning its attention outside the boundaries of the nation. The Project began to more consciously internationalize and broaden out its focus, and the display that fall included over four hundred panels from eighteen countries, including Australia, Belgium, Brazil, Guatemala, Mexico, and Suriname.[118] The spreading of affiliated AIDS quilt projects around the globe brought significant logistical challenges, but even more significantly it revealed fractures around the Quilt's form and content. There are currently affiliate chapters in about forty countries, though the textiles produced in those countries are all far smaller than the US Quilt; for instance, only about three hundred panels exist in the UK AIDS Memorial Quilt, and fewer than one hundred exist in the German and Philippine versions. Beyond its relatively late introduction in other countries compared to the United States, why do the various international versions of AIDS quilts contain so few panels? For one thing, the project's insistence on individual names generated cross-cultural collisions around questions of disclosure. An article in the *NAMESLetter* from 1995 details how "intercultural differences . . . create barriers to panelmaking."[119] It states that, for instance, people in Scotland are hesitant about revealing full names on panels; other countries and cultures might share this cautious approach to naming.

In addition to resistances around issues of privacy, the medium of quilting was not widely embraced elsewhere. According to Carroll Jacobs, who is identified in the 1995 article as the international representative from the NAMES Project in Cape Town, "many South Africans feel that quilting is an American tradition, not an African art form." The article goes on to state: "To adapt panelmaking to the South African culture, Carroll is now teaching beadwork to Zulu women, and she has incorporated the art form into several panels created for friends."[120] (This statement glosses over the fact that American quilting is understood by many as a mixing of traditions, including African textile crafts, and also that Zulu women are famous for their beadwork; in this view, emissaries from the Quilt are portrayed as colonial ambassadors who teach the locals skills.) Since 1998 the International AIDS Memorial Quilt has been stewarded by the Global Quilt organization; as its website clearly states, it is "not affiliated with the NAMES Project Foundation." In fact there has been a proliferation of AIDS quilts that are "not affiliated with the NAMES Project" both within and beyond the United States, including among Native Americans, who have created a series of textiles regarding HIV/AIDS that integrate techniques and objects used in traditional healing practices.[121] According to scholar Max Carocci, though they are not technically quilts but rather sewn hide tapestries, they have been categorized as "memorial quilts" not only to acknowledge their associations with Native processes of patchwork, wrapping, and covering but also because this terminology names a desired resonance with the NAMES Project (even though these textiles are not destined for integration into the AIDS Quilt).

High Quilt / Low Quilt

In 1994 the International AIDS Memorial Quilt was displayed in Hyde Park, London; aerial photographs of its installation (fig. 3.35), with inner pathways thronged with visitors, reveal a much more modest installation than the displays on the National Mall. Hyde Park has historically been a famous site of political demonstration: its Speakers' Corner is a well-known arena for contentious speech and organizing. It is also the location of proliferating national memorials, including a Holocaust memorial, the Princess Diana memorial, and the 7 July bombings memorial.

The 1994 London display of the International AIDS Quilt included sixty-four specially designed panels that were created as the result of an initiative within the fashion industry. With its preponderance of gay men, fashion had been hit very hard by the AIDS crisis.[122] Begun in 1993 by Turkish-born, UK-based designer Rifat Özbek, in concert with a US effort spawned by the New York chapter of the NAMES Project, this initiative culminated in the integration of these high-profile panels at Hyde Park and the production of an illustrated volume, published in 1996, *Always Remember: A Selection of Panels Created by and for International Fashion Designers.*[123] Panels were made by fashion luminaries affiliated with design houses such as Isaac Mizrahi, Christian Lacroix, Vivienne Westwood, Gianni Versace, and Todd Oldham, and dedicated to models (Gia), muses (Tina Chow), and other designers (Halston, the aforementioned Willi Smith). Özbek gravitated to the Quilt in recognition of its affinity with his own textile-based profession: as the book's introduction puts it, "Rifat's years in fashion had left him no stranger to AIDS, and as a

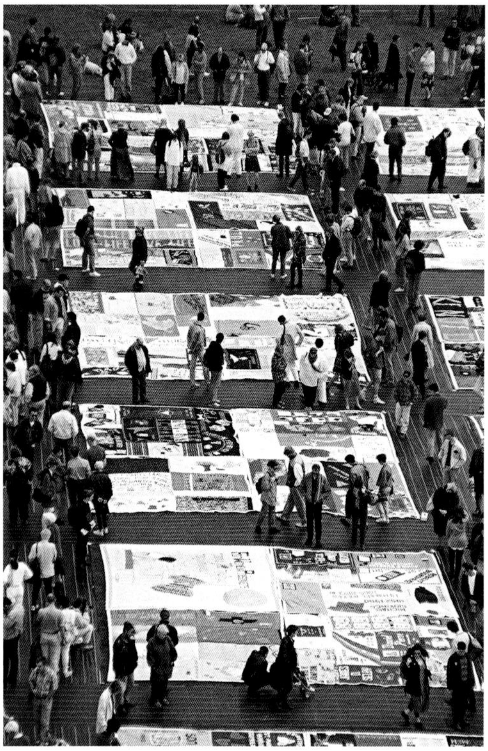

clothes designer, fabric was certainly a subject of considerable interest to him."[124]

The inclusion of so many actual items of clothing on the Quilt—from cruising handkerchiefs to underpants, from work uniforms to pajamas—underscores the capacity of textiles to suggest and invoke bodies. They movingly conjure the everyday lives of their wearers. Yet in the fashion-industry panels, the incorporation of brand-name clothes also speaks to the powerful impulses of corporate marketing and the rising economies of high-end designer goods during the 1980s. One panel, made by Angie Furlong on behalf of Guess? Inc., sews a pair of Guess? Jeans onto a red-and-white bandanna fabric; the jeans have been attached so the back pocket with its prominent triangle / question mark logo is visible. Even more crassly, a panel made by Donna Karan's company places *her* name—in brand-recognizable font—under the New York skyline (with a red ribbon at the top of a building), instead of listing anyone who has died of AIDS, inserting what is in effect an advertisement into a block that includes panels for Perry Ellis (made by Tommy Hilfiger) and Roberto Robledo (fig. 3.36). Did she (or whoever made it on her company's behalf) fail to understand the most basic function of the Quilt, memorializing the dead? When a company means to honor losses sustained within its organization, at times the corporate entity takes precedence over the individual names that were

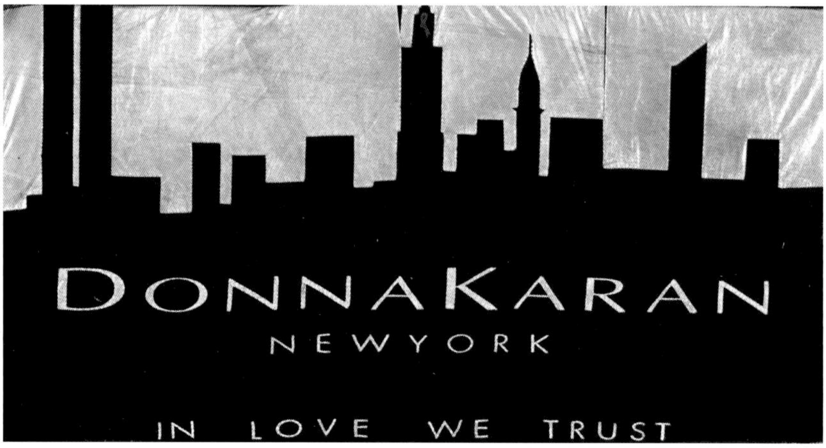

Fig. 3.35.
AIDS Quilt installed in Hyde Park, aerial view, London, 1994. © Marion Bull / Alamy Stock Photo

Fig. 3.36.
Donna Karan AIDS Quilt panel, 1994. Courtesy of the NAMES Project.

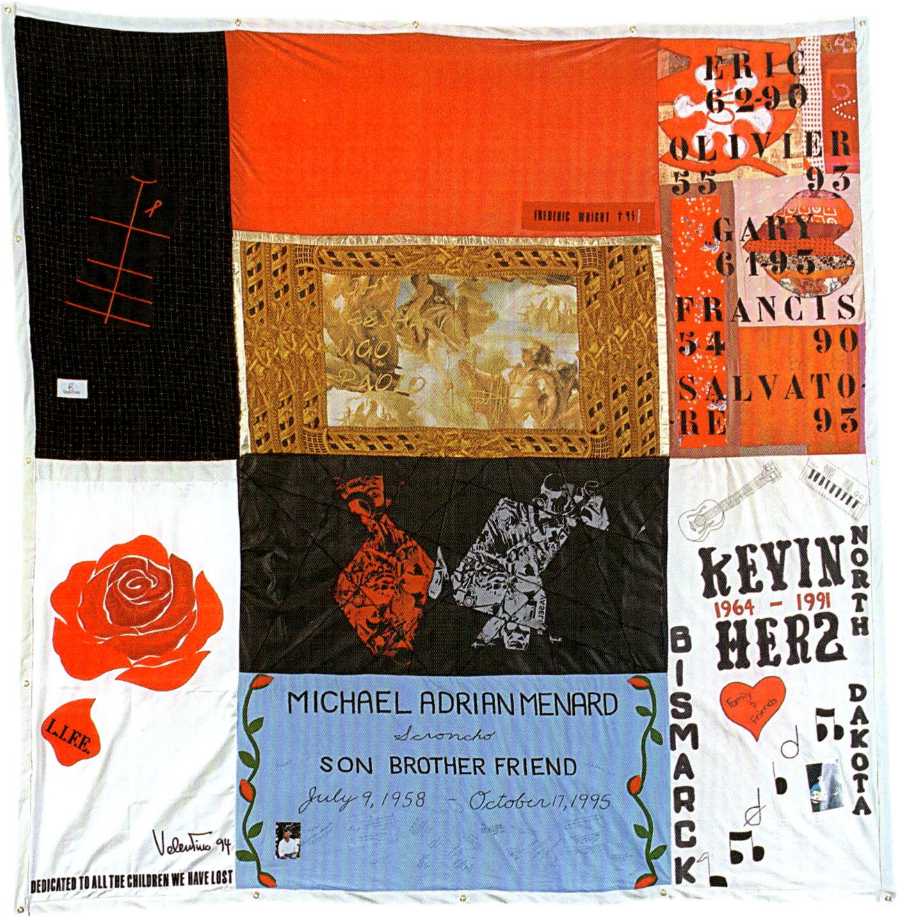

the basis for the Quilt's founding. In the case of Karan, because her personal name is the same as the company's, the mismatch is particularly egregious. (Donna Karan—either the person or the corporate entity—is not alone in this branding; a Quilt panel made to recognize employees of Alamo Rent-A-Car is also basically a glorified logo.) The drive to self-publicize was apparently irresistible for some of the designers, even those who grasped the Quilt's commemorative purpose; Valentino's panel, of a satin red rose appliquéd onto a white background, is signed flashily by him, with a date and the words "Dedicated to all the children we have lost."

Fig. 3.37. AIDS Quilt block 4514, with panels by Valentino (bottom left) and Helmut Lang (top center), 1994–95. Courtesy of the NAMES Project.

Others display more restraint, including panels whose aesthetic affinities with minimalism illuminate how that movement influenced fashion as well as sculpture: On the upper-middle portion of a block that gathers several panels generated from Özbek's campaign (including Valentino's) sits a panel in which a name, Frederic Wright, and a date, "94," appear very small in black letters against a plane of pure red fabric (fig. 3.37). In even smaller letters is

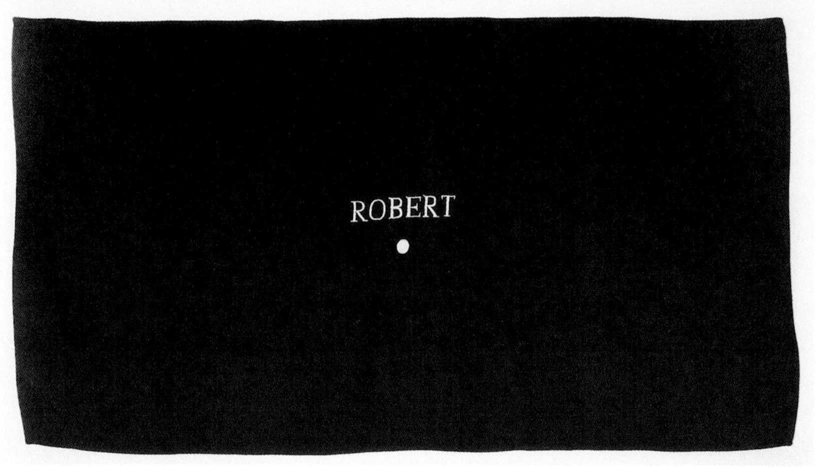

Fig. 3.38. Robert Mapplethorpe AIDS Quilt panel, made by Patrick Robyn / Ann Demeulemeester, 1994. Lost.

its attribution to Austrian minimalist designer Helmut Lang. Another panel, made by Belgian Jean Colonna, has an abstract black, white, and red scheme, recalling a Gilbert and George collage, but the stitch work emphasizes its material distinction from a photo-based work: thick seams crisscross this leather panel like scars or veins.

Thus, as much as the Quilt reflects a "low," or hobby/amateur sensibility, with its many glued-on toys and unskilled, unsewn, stapled-together panels, it also contains many panels that could easily be classified as "high." These panels, made by self-declared artists under the auspices of this fashion-industry initiative, include one for queer photographer Robert Mapplethorpe that was designed by Patrick Robyn, photographer and husband of avant-garde Belgian clothing designer Ann Demeulemeester (fig. 3.38). This panel, which echoes Mapplethorpe's own unrealized idea for a black business card "with a little hole in the middle," floats his first name over a small circle cutout in black fabric, reminiscent, perhaps, of a peep hole, glory hole, puncture wound, or the dark inside of a camera with a tiny window out into the world.[125] For me this is one of the most evocative panels of the AIDS Quilt—except, strangely, that it is not actually part of the Quilt, as it was never bundled with other panels in a block and is not part of either the International AIDS Quilt or the UK or US NAMES Project Quilt.[126] (Robyn has no idea what has happened to it and told me, "I don't know where it is or if it has ever been integrated into the bigger Quilt.")[127] Perhaps someone has kept the panel, perhaps it was lost in transit—but the fact that it was not merged into the overall Quilt means that it exists, now, forever as a photograph in isolation on page 30 of the *Always Remember* book, rather than sewn alongside other panels and available for viewing during occasional displays to a general audience.

Condition Report

Despite the protestations of some members of groups like ACT UP, who felt that the Quilt pacified, banalized, commodified, and sentimentalized the massive losses of the epidemic, it grew in size over the 1990s, and today the names on its panels represent about 7 percent of those who have died of AIDS in the United States. Sturken asked in 1997, "What if the Quilt continues to grow—how will it be housed? What if it becomes a burden?"[128] Her point is well taken, and indeed the Quilt has become an unmanageable size and has not been exhibited together in its entirety since it was laid over the Washington Mall in 1996 (it was displayed in many different sites scattered around DC when it returned in 2012). It is too costly to display and impossible to find a single site large enough to contain it.

So where is the Quilt today? It is stored in a warehouse in Atlanta, Georgia (fig. 3.39). The Quilt was moved from San Francisco in 2001 not only because the foundation needed more affordable rent for a warehouse space big enough for its bulky mass but also because the racial demographics of Atlanta (historically considered a "black mecca" and having one of the highest LGBTQ populations per capita in the US) more accurately reflect the contemporary AIDS crisis, with its disproportionate number of infections among African Americans.[129] Despite the lower rent, the foundation is plagued by ongoing financial difficulties. By policy there is no fee to submit a panel, and there exists no endowment, so the funds required for the significant work of edging, cleaning, bundling, blocking, shipping, and storing (not to mention supplies like canvas and metal grommets) must come from ever-shrinking sales of merchandise and fundraising.

Many kinds of daily attentions are required to keep the Quilt alive, such as mending panels whose objects were originally stuck on with glue or staples. A straw hat that has disintegrated over time must be repurchased and affixed. Fabric letters that were too loosely sewn on must be more securely reattached. Cracked or flaked puff paint needs fresh reapplication. The workroom in Atlanta is lined with sewing machines that have been retired after constant use. Originally, when AIDS was still largely figured as a gay white male "affluent disease," panels would come in with donations that averaged two hundred dollars for every name. After 1996, with the advent of expensive life-extending antiretroviral drugs, the relationship of class and race to AIDS-related deaths shifted dramatically, and the average donation dropped to around fifteen dollars.[130] The face of the crisis itself looks starkly different than it did at the Quilt's founding. The decay of the Quilt is telling: its fraying stitches and lost objects mirror a vanishing from sight in the West of the

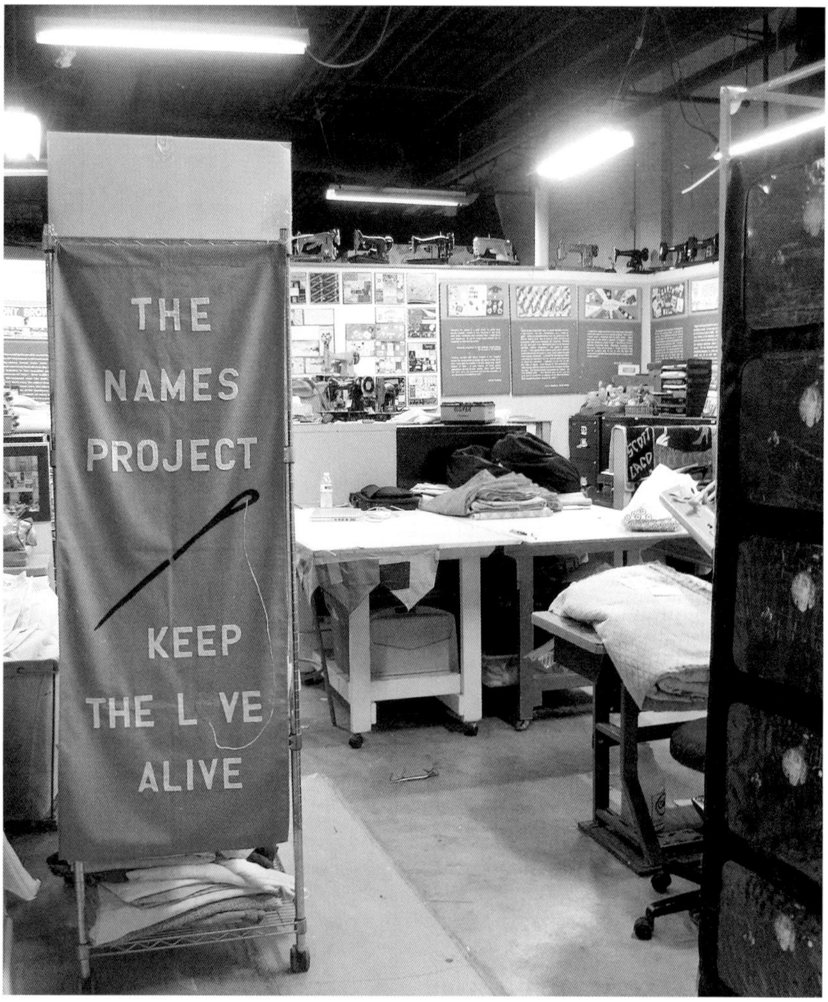

Fig. 3.39. NAMES Project Foundation headquarters repair room, Atlanta, Georgia, 2010. Photograph by the author.

ongoing pandemic, despite the spread of AIDS among the less privileged in the United States as well as globally. At one dire point around 2010, the Quilt's NAMES Project Foundation was half a million dollars in debt; that debt has decreased since the 2012 Smithsonian-sponsored display, which raised its visibility, but the entire operation is still underfunded.[131]

The Quilt's current unwieldiness raises the question of the value of an archive that is in many respects inaccessible: how or when will these panels be received, picked up, revitalized, or resignified? In addition to the material blocks that make up the massive Quilt, there are thousands of letters that accompanied the panels and keepsakes left at the Quilt during its display. Only a small selection of these are represented in the Bush-endorsed *A Promise to Remember*; most are stored in the Atlanta warehouse. Collectively they represent a huge range of responses by families, lovers, colleagues, friends, and

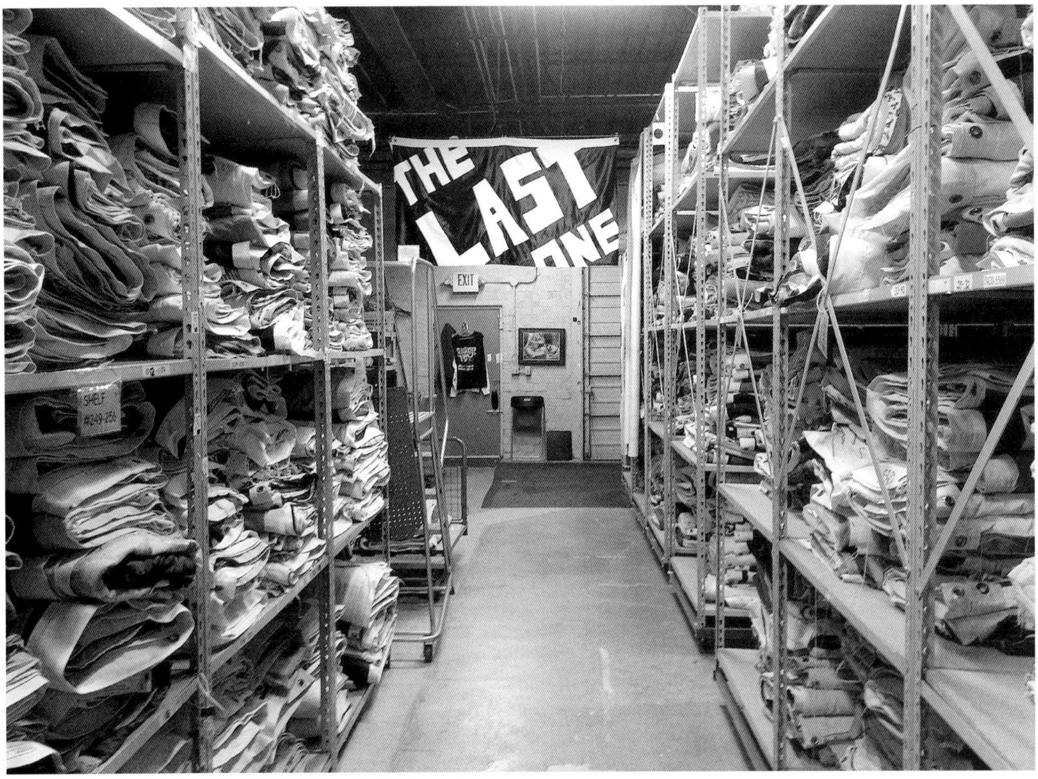

acquaintances, telling how the epidemic has touched their lives. Taken as a whole—a vast repository of names, stories, letters, and tangible mementos, an archive that exceeds its contents—the Quilt is now in a state of perpetual flux. To stand in the warehouse, with its shelves piled high with the folded Quilt blocks, is to feel powerfully surrounded by losses that are both evidenced and difficult to grasp, its urgent scream now muffled by virtue of its impossible enormity. The Quilt has been transformed in the past few decades from an active, highly visible memorial to a suspended monument to the fading of the HIV crisis from the public eye. Staffers have reserved one piece that they will not sew into a block until the crisis is over—a black-and-white text-based panel that reads "THE LAST ONE," hanging in the warehouse with its distant promise (fig. 3.40).

Fig. 3.40. Storage racks hold the folded AIDS Quilt, NAMES Project Foundation headquarters, Atlanta, Georgia, 2015, with panel for "THE LAST ONE" hanging from the ceiling. Photograph by the author.

As I have suggested, it might be more useful to understand the Quilt not as a registry or encyclopedia of names that aims to be a complete record of the losses from AIDS, but rather as what Ann Cvetkovich has described as "an archive of feelings," undergirded and made possible by an affectively rich set of community relations and shared histories, a repository of intimacies, love, trauma, loss, and tending.[132] Cvetkovich has argued that many of the organizing and activist responses to the traumas of the AIDS crisis were spearheaded by women, who significantly acted as "caretakers" but who have not always been made central to the story of HIV in the United States. This is certainly true in the case of the AIDS Quilt, which explicitly is meant to refer to women's work and has been held together at the seams by female staff. Gert McMullin works tirelessly to reattach letters whose stitching has broken, sewing on missing bits, reconstructing damaged parts, fixing edges, and replacing objects. And as Cvetkovich reminds us, "Attention has been given to the implications of the feminization of 'caretaking' and affective labor, but its 'lesbianization' also deserves analysis."[133]

One answer to the Quilt's perpetual decay is to photograph the panels and create a digital archive. By 1996 the textile's inherent fragility, along with its constant folding and unfolding for display, was seen as hastening an incipient crisis. In its early days some felt that the Quilt should be laid out over and over "until it falls apart," but that embrace of impermanence gave way to a sense of the urgency of archiving.[134] "With the wear and tear of the Quilt over time, there must be a permanent record," one donor was quoted as saying in the *NAMESLetter* after giving money for a matching grant by Levi Strauss and Co.[135] Since May 1995, the foundation has been photographing the 12'×12' Quilt blocks, though assembling this record has been a further costly endeavor.[136] Over time, the majority of blocks have been digitized and are now on the NAMES Project website, where one can search by block number and the name of the person or organization represented (though not by maker, region, or any other identifying factor, which makes the database extremely limiting).

As of this writing, about six thousand blocks make up the Quilt; to view each one in the digital archive for even thirty seconds (which is about the amount of minimum time needed to fully focus one's eyes on the individual panels in each block) would take fifty hours. I know this because—along with directly handling many panels over the years—I have looked at every single block on the AIDS Quilt website.[137] Even though I limited my viewing to a few hours at a time to avoid fatigue—and to try to give myself time to visually process all this material—clicking through them all on my computer screen took me several emotionally exhausting weeks. And this desktop browsing, however methodical, is not how the Quilt was meant to be viewed. The digitization of the Quilt opens up possibilities for individual viewership, making it available block by block—a great boon for those who are not able to physically travel to its infrequent displays. But seeing the Quilt through a mediated, screen-based interface is compromised. The photographic record tells only one part of the story and is unable to convey the importantly tangible aspect of the Quilt. For one thing, the photographs show only the front or face of the Quilt, ignoring the many signatures, pockets, and other embellishments found on its underside. In addition, at this point the public online photographic record of the Quilt is fairly low resolution and becomes grainy when one zooms in on its small flourishes. It is difficult to see details with any clarity—for example, the gloves put on by Finkelstein, not to mention the small, critical ACT UP button, are barely evident in the online image of Yowell's panel. Finally, this digital archive is insufficient because it does not capture the Quilt's full dimensionality of textures and materials that are so vital to its many meanings, from its careful beadwork to its tacked-on baby shoes to its different fabrics and stitch work.

At its triumphant height during the early 1990s, the Quilt was receiving thousands of panels a year and was staffed by chapters around the nation with more than twelve thousand volunteers. Since the waning of public attention to the HIV epidemic, that flood of interest has slowed to a trickle. Only about two hundred panels a year come to Atlanta, where a much-reduced staff of five works, most of them part time. The Quilt was last seen in its entirety in 2012 as part of the Smithsonian's Folklife Festival, under the name "Quilt in the Capital 2012"; this annual festival, begun in 1967, notably folded the Quilt back into the rubric of "folk art" (fig. 3.41). It filled the space of the Washington Mall to capacity, and the overflow was on view in diverse

Fig. 3.41. AIDS Quilt on the Washington Mall, Washington, DC, 2012. Photograph by the author.

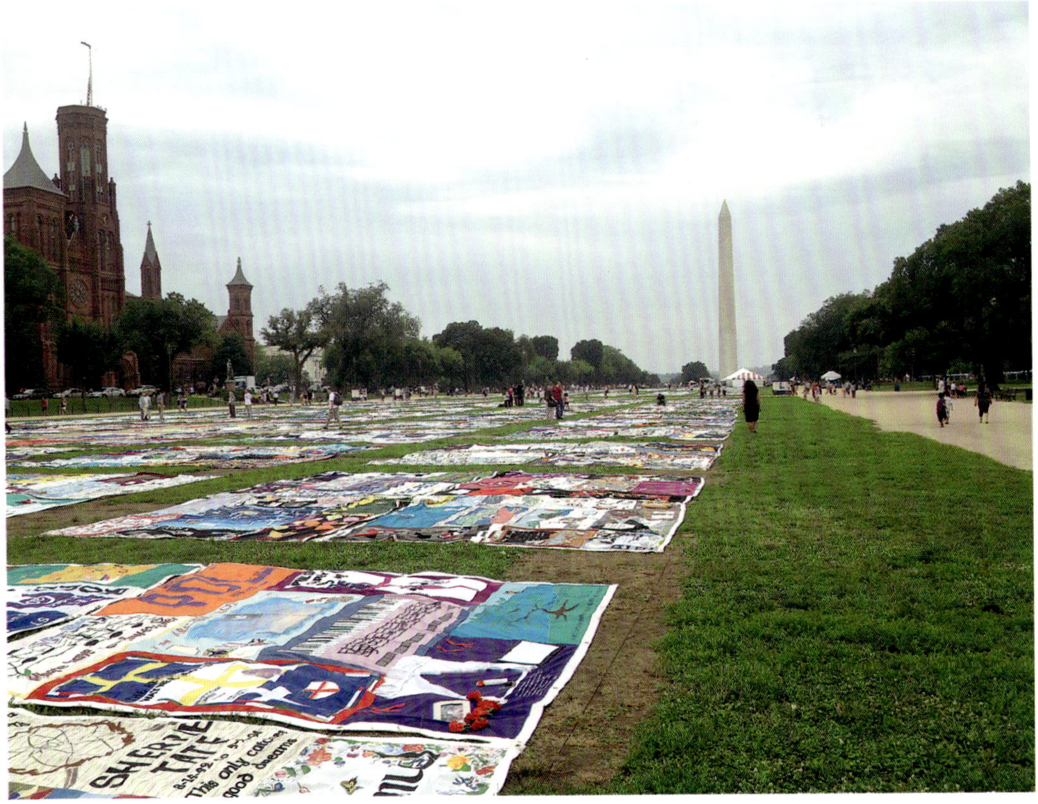

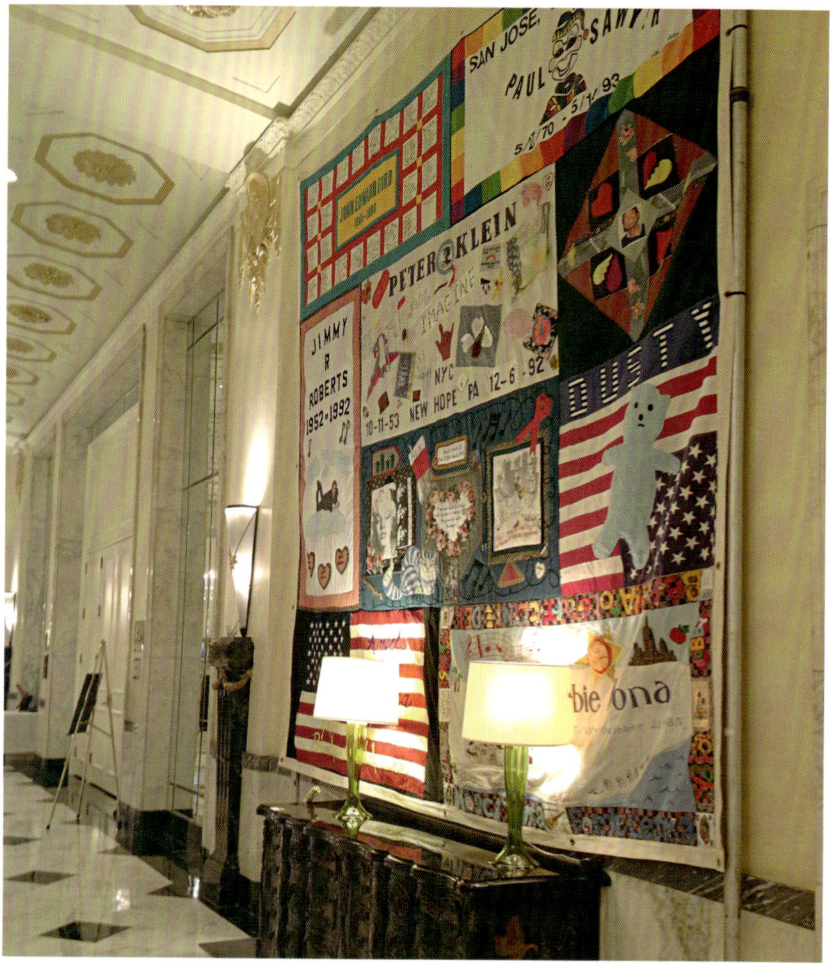

Fig. 3.42. AIDS Quilt on display in the Mayflower Renaissance Hotel hallway, Washington, DC, 2012. Photograph by the author.

and diffuse sites all over the city, including hanging in hallways in hotels like the Mayflower Renaissance, where lamps were precariously shoved up against its cloth surface. At the Mayflower no announcement identified what this object was, and the panel was an incongruous addition to the crystal chandeliers and marble floor of the ornate interior (fig. 3.42). Further displays were mounted at over forty locations, including the National Building Museum (where a large arrangement of blocks was laid out on the ground); the Textile Museum (a single block hung from the ceiling, illuminated by a spotlight); the Red Cross; and Bloomingdale's in Chevy Chase.[138]

At any given time throughout the year, and peaking on World AIDS Day, December 1, portions of the Quilt are shipped around the country for display in places like health clinics, NGO offices, and churches (there are between six hundred and eight hundred displays every year, with anywhere from one block to many on view).[139] Figure 3.43 shows a display in the library of the

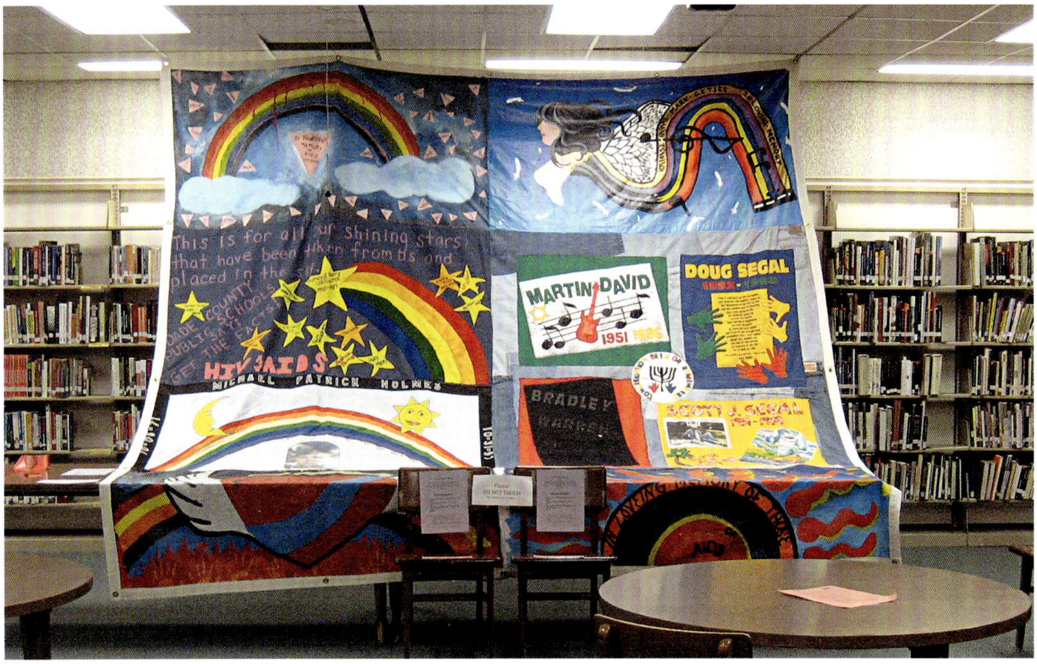

Fig. 3.43. AIDS Quilt on display in the library of the Ruth Asawa School for the Arts, San Francisco, World AIDS Day, December 2010. Photograph by the author.

Ruth Asawa School of the Arts in San Francisco, a block featuring numerous cheery rainbows. It is hung from the ceiling and slumps over a table with a small sign that reads DO NOT TOUCH. It is one of the explicit stipulations of the foundation, as enumerated in the official *Quilt Display Handbook*, that the Quilt not be put on the floor unless shown under the auspices of the NAMES Project—instead it must be hung. Since not everyone has twelve-foot-high ceilings to accommodate the dimensions of a block, the foundation does allow other creative ways of keeping it off the ground. Though the *Handbook* also specifies that "you must sell NAMES Project merchandise, and only NAMES Project merchandise, at your display," sales are not a possibility for smaller venues such as schools and community centers.[140] On World AIDS Day in 2015, I contacted several dozen of the places that had the Quilt on view and asked for pictures of their displays. Solutions to the problem of how to show the Quilt varied: some hung blocks directly in windows, where they absorbed harmful rays of the sun (Rhode Island School of Design library, West Hollywood city hall); from the ceiling and visible through a window of an empty, locked store (Coastal Grand Mall in Myrtle Beach, South Carolina); or from specially rigged display poles commonly used at quilt fairs (Central Tcxas Collcgc; Florida Dcpartmcnt of Hcalth).[141]

These ad hoc presentations at schools, malls, and governmental offices are far from the large-scale displays of decades past, and in these spaces the Quilt lacks any museum-style protection that might prevent damage from viewers who might be tempted to reach out and squeeze a teddy bear or stroke a lock of hair. In figure 3.43, no stanchions or ropes cordon off students from the library table where the Quilt is draped, and the posted sign seems insufficient to keep hands off it. Though it appears alarmingly naked to an art historian like me, accustomed to seeing precious artifacts in cases or behind glass, in conversation Rhoad dismissed my concern, exclaiming, "We want to minimize the sense that it is art. Let the eight-year-olds in cafeterias see it! The stains are a part of its life."[142] For her there is no question that as an additive grassroots campaign that lives and breathes, it must be viewed in the presence of a huge and potentially messy audience. Yet one consequence of its being shown in bright windows and school cafeterias as part of ongoing AIDS awareness campaigns is that it will more quickly degrade. With the foundation facing financial insecurity, the Quilt is seeking long-term institutional partners that might make it a viable continuing operation that stays in the public eye, creating long-term logistical difficulties that go beyond usual issues of textile storage and preservation. This openness toward flux and change (and the continual acceptance of new panels) is also why the Project has rejected ideas of closing the Quilt as an archive, deeming it "finished" so it might be fixed, stored, and preserved as a static object. Instead, Rhoad, McMullin, and other staff are insistent that it remain ongoing, waiting for the day that the disease has been eradicated, when the panel that reads "THE LAST ONE" can be added to the Quilt at last.

Legacies of the Quilt

Rhoad's decision to package the Quilt as a public health project, rather than as an art object, is strategic, for the Quilt has not been widely embraced in the art world. It has been seen far more in school libraries than in fine arts museums. Only rarely in the recent major retrospectives on art and activism in the 1980s—not to mention shows on fiber art—has the Quilt been included.[143] Though the AIDS Quilt has not been exhibited much in the contemporary art world, it has been acknowledged as a spark and resource for contemporary crafters, and many artists, including Josh Faught, have looked to it as a vital precedent for their own textile making.[144] In addition, despite all the vituperation, members of quilting communities admit that if the Quilt has been good at raising awareness about AIDS, it might have been even better, according to quiltmaker McNamara, "for increasing the visibility of quilting."[145] In a moving acknowledgment of the crossing of these spheres—the show quilt circuit of county fairs and the ongoing work of AIDS memorialization—McNamara was the featured keynote speaker at the 2015 Pajaro Valley Quilt Show fair held at the Santa Cruz County fairgrounds, honored by its mostly (but not exclusively) white, straight female members for, among other things, his many finely wrought panels (see figs. 3.18 and 3.19). To see the AIDS Quilt hung in this context was to be reminded of its major impact within the "amateur" craft world.

While black feminists like Ringgold have used quilts in their art for several decades, more recently black male artists have turned to quilting, including Sanford Biggers, who has used textiles in his work to make reference to the Underground Railroad quilt code and the racialization of the quilt medium. So too have queer artists picked up textile techniques as a way to examine sexuality and handmaking, not least the way the fabrics, with their implicit reference to bodies and bedcoverings, connect the private and public. Many queer artists used stitching and mending to figure loss and remembrance during the AIDS crisis of the 1980s and 1990s, including Charles LeDray and Zoe Leonard; the Brazilian artist Leonilson, after learning he was HIV positive, turned exclusively to embroidering. Younger queer artists, too, are not only responding to the ongoing pandemic but reimagining textiles using the techniques of the AIDS Quilt as a resource. Angie Wilson's *Traditional Queer Double Wedding Ring Quilt*, from 2009, for example, turns a classic quilt design (interlocking circles) traditionally given to married couples for their nuptial bed into a sexually suggestive celebration of female anatomy (fig. 3.44). Wilson's topstitching turns the ovals where the rings conjoin into an evocative series of fleshy vulvas. Instead of highlighting the wedding ring as a signifier of heterosexual monogamy, Wilson's quilt focuses on the possibilities of multiplicity found in the negative spaces. The almost florid pinks and darker burgundies of Wilson's design are meant to reflect a range of bodily pigmentation and account for racial difference and variation.[146]

Ginger Brooks Takahashi has also initiated a series of queer quilting bees with the assistance of volunteers and friends, in a project titled *An Army of Lovers Cannot Fail*, named after a 1970s gay liberation chant. Though it is hard to see in reproduction and thematizes that very flirtation with disappearance, the resultant quilt references a flamboyantly perverse queer erotics—the section shown in figure 3.45 features a rabbit having a sexual encounter with a human—using a classic quilt technique of whitework that is associated with the highest levels of skill and refinement and that also hovers on the verge of invisibility. Takahashi's (and Wilson's) work hinges on texture: as you trace the sewn pattern and elaborately cross-stitched letters with your finger, you read it as much by touch as you do by sight. Like the AIDS Quilt workshops of the 1980s, Takahashi's project created a space for communal crafting; photographs of the quilt in process show multiracial, multigendered gatherings of people bent over the fabric to stitch. These projects at-

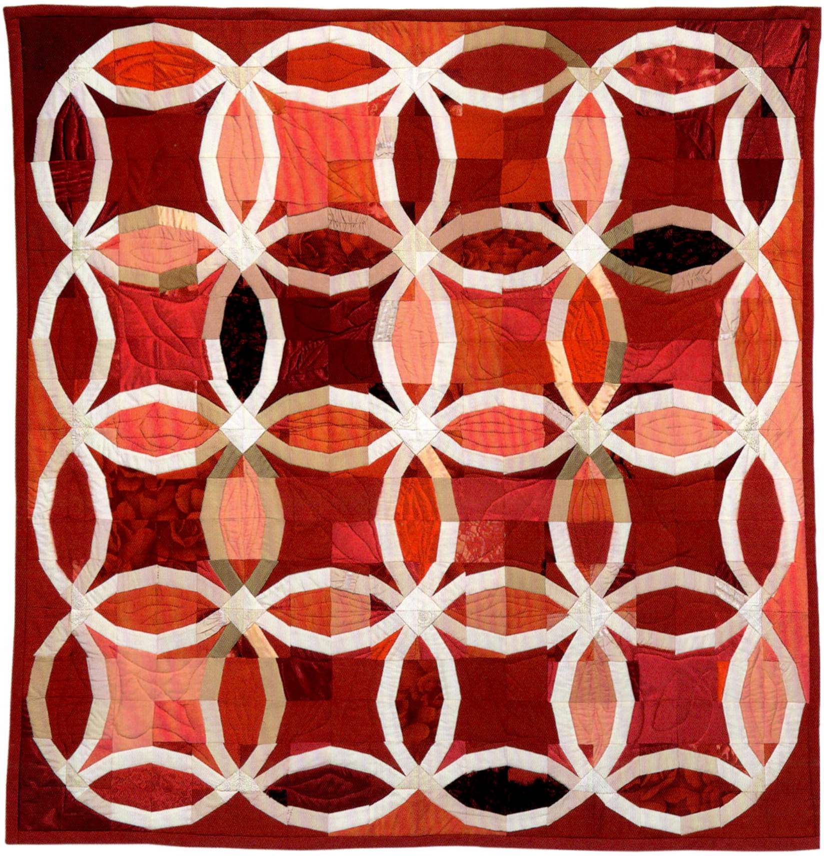

Fig. 3.44. Angie Wilson, *Traditional Queer Double Wedding Ring Quilt*, repurposed garments, fabric, thread, 2009. Photograph by Silbia Savage. Courtesy of the artist.

test to the ways that the motifs of the Quilt have been absorbed and recycled within recent queer needlework by a younger generation, understood not as a sentimental anti-activist blanket but as a launch pad for sly suggestions regarding nonnormative sexuality and collective making made possible by the quilt format.

Other artists beyond the arena of textile handicraft have turned to the Quilt and brought it into spaces it has not otherwise been seen, most notably Andrea Bowers with *The Weight of Relevance*, a multimedia installation produced in 2007 that has been shown in fine art galleries and museums in Vienna and Los Angeles. Bowers is drawn to histories of protest culture, and in this piece she examines the relentless, and feminized, caretaking that attends to the AIDS Quilt. One component of the piece is a video titled *Continual Maintenance and Mending* that portrays Gert McMullin as she works quietly away at the overwhelming, never-ending task of mending the Quilt; the video, shot from above, is projected onto a fabric rectangle on the floor, so that the viewer looks down at the acts of sewing in a way that recalls looking down at the Quilt itself (fig. 3.46). Bowers's piece points back to the early 1970s

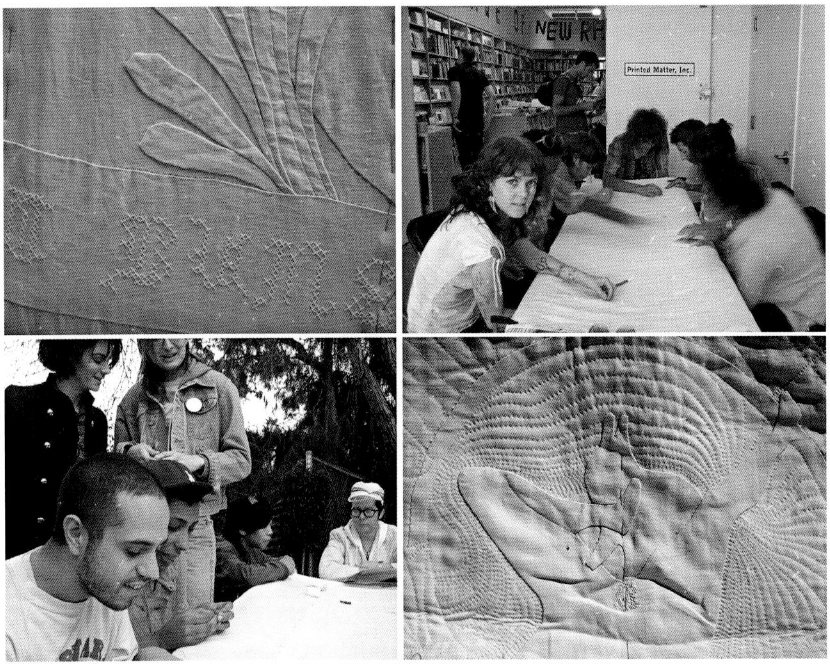

Fig. 3.45. Ginger Brooks Takahashi, *An Army of Lovers Cannot Fail*, detail, group quilting sessions held in multiple locations and completed quilt, 2004–8. Courtesy of the artist.

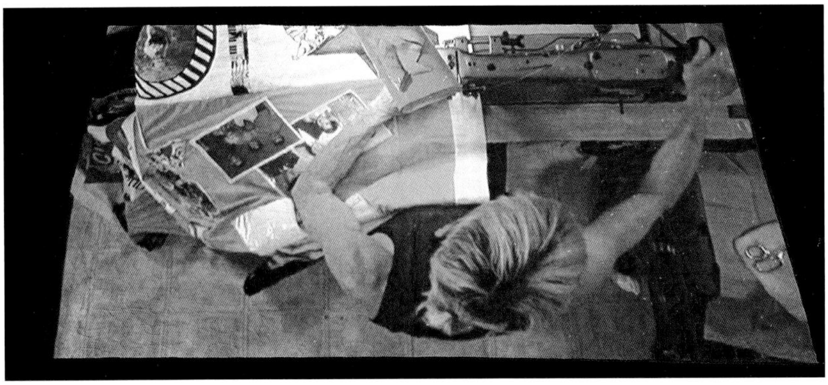

Fig. 3.46. Andrea Bowers, *Continual Maintenance and Mending*, 2007. Single-channel video (color with sound), DVD, DVD player, video projector, speakers, handmade quilt, 54:49 minutes looped, projection 60 × 107″. Courtesy of the artist and Susanne Vielmetter Los Angeles Projects; Christian Wachter, Austria; editor Fil Rüting.

feminist art that sought to make connections between private, gendered female domestic labor and the work of upkeep, such as Mierle Laderman Ukele's *Hartford Wash: Washing / Tracks / Maintenance*, from 1973, in which she scrubbed the floors and dusted the vitrines of the Wadsworth Atheneum.

Bowers's practice is marked by her investment in the handiwork of drawings, and she created a framed black-and-white drawing of one of the cloth panels that bespeaks the ambivalence many feel about the Quilt: "Terry Sutton: he hated this quilt and so do we!" A depiction of an ACT UP T-shirt next to these words seems to confirm the antipathy felt by those in activist groups toward the Quilt (fig. 3.47). Yet the fact of this panel's existence also means that Terry Sutton's friends or lovers, while they "hated" the Quilt, had

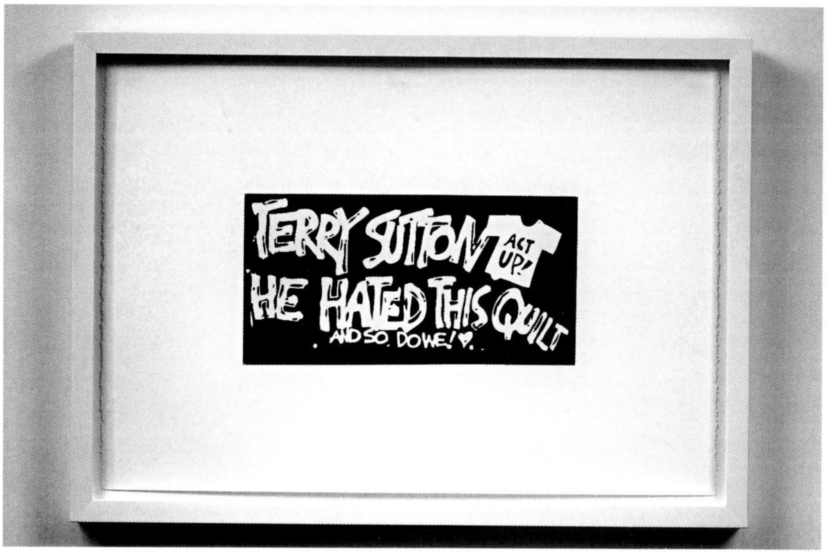

Fig. 3.47. Andrea Bowers, *Excerpts from the AIDS Memorial Quilt (Block 1268)*, powdered graphite and pastel on paper, 15⅛ × 22¼″. Courtesy of the artist and Susanne Vielmetter Los Angeles Projects. Photograph by Gene Ogami.

the urge to contribute to it anyway, to push through or beyond or despite such hate to commemorate their friend with an act of simultaneous anger, grief, hostility, and loss. Bowers has excised Sutton's panel from its block to consider it as a single unit in isolation—but when viewed in relation to its surrounding panels it takes on a slightly different cast (fig. 3.48). In the context of the wider, and complex, grammar of the Quilt, this statement of "hate" is cushioned or queried by the other panels. Another horizontally oriented panel that sits just above it, for Russ Fetters, features a tender queer of color embrace: a man holds another man who wears a checked singlet, exhorting viewers to "love your sisters." On the left side, a redheaded cartoon figure in a photo-collaged dress stares back at the viewer as a kind of saucy rejoinder. The hot pink of the ACT UP T-shirt on Sutton's panel matches the pink of Tom Novotny's panel, which integrates it more fully into the overall pattern and draws the eye away from seeing individual names to grasping all the pieces as part of a larger design.

Looking at such a block, with its humor, its hate, its love—even its Garfield—I think back to Sontag's "Notes on 'Camp.'" She writes: "Camp is playful, anti-serious. More precisely, Camp involves a new, more complex relation to 'the serious.' One can be serious about the frivolous, frivolous about the serious."[147] Beyond its metal studs and leather vests, *this* is the queerest part of the Quilt. It bravely and generously admits just about everything within its scope, what Sontag calls "the equivalence of all objects." Bowers's drawing—divorced from its crafted textures as well as from its larger block—does not quite capture the range of tones and modalities of making that co-exist in this one piece of the Quilt.

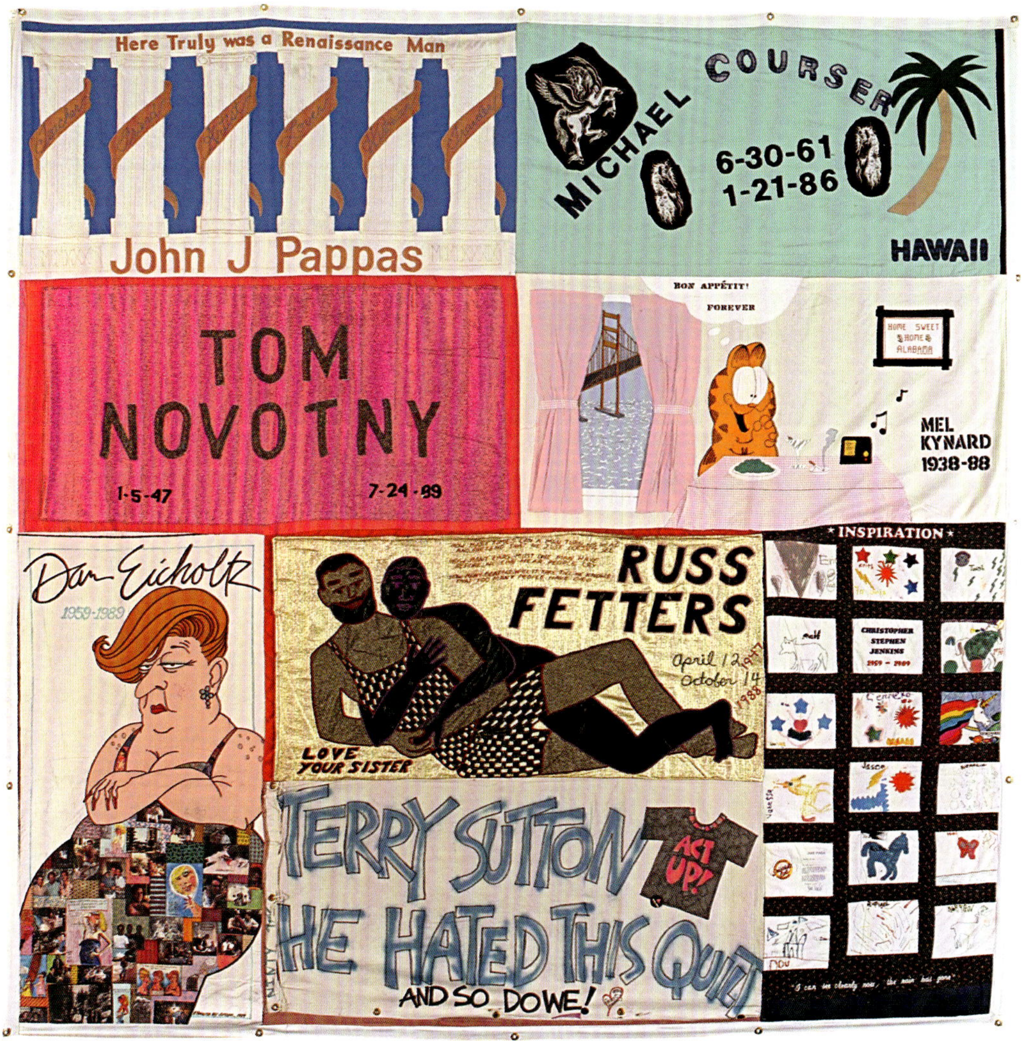

Fig. 3.48. AIDS Quilt block 1268. Courtesy of the NAMES Project.

Because of its memorial language that recounts individual names, and its idealized display location on the Washington Mall, what the AIDS Quilt has most often been compared to in terms of art-historical precedent is not Chicago's *Dinner Party* but Maya Lin's Vietnam Veterans Memorial (a comparison elucidated in Sturken's seminal study). Instead of elaborating the similarities between these two projects, I will point out one major difference: Lin's memorial is a permanent architectural fixture in DC, while the Quilt has been displayed in DC for less than two weeks total over all its displays since 1987. Despite the public attention directed its way, in some vital respects the Quilt has *barely been seen* in its totality. It does not function as a memorial that, affixed to one constant site, serves to remind changing generations in perpetuity. Rather, it is always only a temporary textile gathering place, a substitute, ephemeral graveyard where people come to remember only every so often. One could argue that its many dispersed displays—a block here, a block there, to be viewed for a few days at a time—places it in front of many more audiences than if it were consolidated in a permanent location. But since it has no stable installation location and will perhaps never find one, it renders the national memorialization of those who have died of AIDS vexingly unsettled. Unlike the Vietnam Veterans Memorial's occupation of space, the Quilt flits in and out of the eye of the public, enduring not as a piece of granite but as something else, a cloth "remainder."

As David Eng and David Kazanjian write, "Loss is inseparable from what remains, for what is lost is known only by what remains of it, by how these remains are produced, read, and sustained."[148] With its literal traces of the dead sewn into its fabric, the Quilt is a remainder that has the cast of the abject, something that might need to be expelled, hidden from sight, or let go of for proper mourning to continue and resolve. It might be, in fact, that this abjection *helped* to make it so palatable for mainstream audiences—for it put gay male relations where they already belonged, for many: on the ground, in the dirt, as it were, in the realm of low or base urges, mingling sex, animality, and excretion. Further, its fabric-based pliancy promoted associations with political "yielding." What I am claiming is that the Quilt's peculiar marriage of textile craft and queerness tapped into or exploited a curious affinity—an affinity I explored in depth in chapter 1—that both fueled its success and elicited fervent criticisms.

Decorative arts historian Peter Dormer wrote in a book published in 1997: "Why is craft intellectually inconvenient in modern and contemporary art? Why did it go out of fashion as an interesting concept and activity to argue about and to practice? . . . Craft just seemed so *tedious* because it was almost inelegant in its demands."[149] These words accurately summarize how the AIDS Quilt has over time been seen by activist communities and contemporary art audiences alike: inconvenient, inelegant, and, I might add, collective, amateur, handmade, and queer. One could further say that the academic discourse around the AIDS Quilt is embarrassed by its textile craft, which becomes a code word for the shamefully déclassé, bad taste, kitsch, or middlebrow, with its rough, imperfect assembly, its stuffed animals, its cheesy hot-air balloons, maudlin airbrushing, saccharine rainbows. To give one example, nowhere in the special issue of *Rhetoric and Public Policy* devoted to the AIDS Quilt does the word *craft* appear. Formally, the Quilt has modeled itself after some aspects of high modernism: it is a grid, after all, of identically shaped units placed on the ground, its basic structure akin to a metal plate floor work by Carl Andre. But as with Hammond's *Floorpieces*, its textile nature resolutely distinguishes it from an Andre work. Even more fragile than Hammond's works, the Quilt on display is cloth placed outdoors, directly on the earth, where it can be rained upon, soiled, stepped on, and bleached by the sun. Its fabric is capable of being burned, as Rev. Fred Phelps desired, in a way that Andre's steel plates or Lin's granite cannot be.

I suggest that the forgiving aspect of textiles, the way that they permit a wide spectrum from high to low and back again, means that the Quilt, if it is a "failure" according to some scholars, is also a mourning ritual broad and big enough to accept the anger directed at it, as well as the ambivalence. The Quilt, as a gridded field allowing infinite additions and endless supplements, has a certain resiliency, and its vast and mutable contours make it adept at absorbing or deflecting all manner of statements of hatred, grief, sentiment, or love. As I have argued throughout this book, textile handicrafts are inherently neither "radical" nor "conservative" but are often poised, in tension, somewhere in between. That the Quilt as a textile object has been variously championed as revolutionary and derided as assimilationist is a stark embodiment of this tension.

Coda: Queer Preservation

We should neither overlook the fault lines of the AIDS Quilt nor nostalgically champion it. Instead we must struggle to preserve and complicate these histories; as I have suggested, one way to do justice to it is to attend to its specific formal idiosyncrasies—to take it seriously as a textile that offers a plentitude of visual material, rather than as a monolithic abstraction. The

Quilt is not only an abject object or kitsch creation but also a polyvocal site of conflict—a conflict that plays out across its textured surface. It makes no sense to line up Foucault-reading ACT UP skeptics on one side as definitely anti-Quilt versus uncritical, unacademic unicorn- and rainbow-loving crafters on the other, for as panels to Yowell, Foucault, and Sutton prove, this was always a false binary. The overly limiting categories of hard-edged activist versus nelly crafter fall apart and are threaded together differently within the Quilt's wide, expansive space.

In this chapter I have attempted to describe some of the Quilt's ideological rifts around queerness, gender, race, and nation, in particular as they intersect with questions of textile handmaking. If the AIDS Quilt is fraught with its own contradictions, erasures, and provincialisms, it is also dense with textures—and, following Sedgwick, texxtures—of meaning and valuable provocation; these layers are inextricably linked to its medium, that is, to the very *quiltness* of the Quilt, which is also, crucially, quite unlike a quilt. For though it is a largely handmade object, it disrupts assumptions about quilts and, in doing so, asks questions about the "function" of textiles as it affectively stitches together public art and protest.

How will the AIDS Quilt continue to be preserved, given its fragility and its physical immensity? The foundation has been in conversation with several institutions about forming partnerships to assist in conservation but also to keep it an open archive. As of 2016, the foundation is pursuing the possibility that the Smithsonian or another agency might collect and digitize the more than five hundred thousand letters in the NAMES Project archive, yet the material Quilt itself is not an element in those negotiations. As staff member Roddy Williams told me matter-of-factly, "They absolutely do not want the textile Quilt."[150] Its future as a centralized repository is (as of this writing) somewhat up in the air. Regardless of where it ends up, the Quilt will endure, will persist, as it queerly and craftily holds vital memories. To hold its "failures" together with its achievements, its occlusions alongside its surpluses, we must, as Georges Didi-Huberman reminds us, "think the rend as part of the fabric."[151] Weighted by the burden and the responsibility of the multiple stories it tells, and despite decades of attack and now public neglect, the AIDS Quilt remains.

Afterword

THE CURRENCY OF CLOTH

The small rectangular table is heaped with dark fibers, a cloud of fluff and strands laid out for the viewer's inspection (fig. 4.01). On the left sits a tangle of threads while on the right lies a cluster of balls of fuzz; the two distinct mounds intersect and merge in the center of the table. They are products of artist Angela Hennessy's meticulous handiwork as she unravels black velvet by teasing apart with her fingers the warp from the weft, disarticulating filament from nap. The resultant swells of matter, titled *blacklets: a speck of soot or dirt* (2007), resemble hair mixed with dust, lint, and debris, like sweepings from a barbershop floor. She has heaped these dissected remnants in corners or, as she does here, placed them on a clinical flat surface, contrasting the unstructured material with a rigid architectural geometry. Though contained, the picked-apart velvet fabric—itself the product of an intricate process of double weaving in which the looped fibers are cut to form tufts, causing velvet's signature short dense pile—is intriguing because it is so puzzlingly inchoate, unrecognizable, so distant from intact velvet. This delicate stuff is vulnerable to the viewer rather than protected behind glass; its tactility generates an illicit desire to touch.

Hennessy is interested in blackness as a color, a metaphor, and an identity, and began the project as an etymological investigation into slang for black women ("black velvet" was among the entries she found in the *OED*), conjoining it with a nineteenth-century term for coal dust to invoke the management of black matter and of black bodies.[1] In her *blacklets* series, she uses a cloth with associations with mourning to enact a physical process of undoing. She also materially connects black velvet to its historical associations with expensive finery as well as to more recently maligned amateur artistic practices—black velvet painting is a prototypical example of kitsch—demonstrating how this cloth brings together the most elite and the most denigrated. The accumulated fuzz that she generates is unruly and unusable as she turns functional fabric into "useless" remains (her process cannot be reversed). But she emphasizes that these raced, gendered, and classed mate-

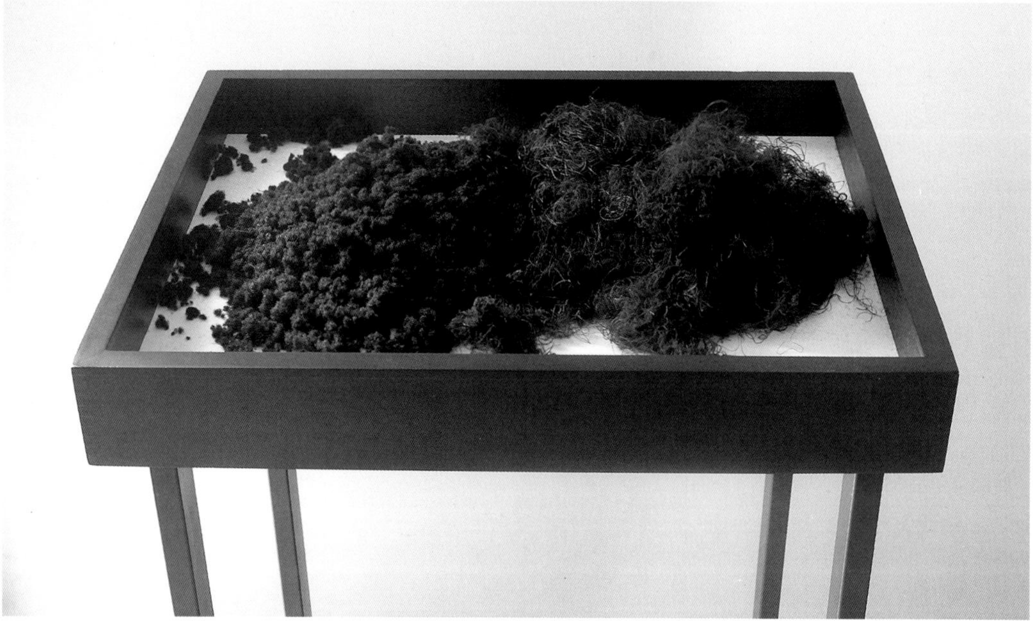

Fig. 4.01. Angela Hennessy, *blacklets: a speck of soot or dirt*, unraveled velvet fuzz and thread, wood and steel table. 42 × 22 × 16″, 2007. Courtesy of the artist.

rials are sites of plentitude rather than deficit. When she has displayed this work, the fuzz leaves a residue, its minuscule fibers infiltrating the gallery spaces and leaving a stain on all surfaces, gesturing to the endurance—the resistance—of blackness in the face of overwhelming whiteness, and of the impossibility of extracting high from low.

As with Hennessy's *blacklets*, Pope.L in his *Trinket* (first created in 2008 and installed at the Museum of Contemporary Art, Los Angeles, in 2015) looks to textiles specifically for their capacity to unravel. For this piece, Pope.L flies a custom-made, 55-foot-long US flag (outfitted with 51 stars), blowing the long length of fabric for the duration of the exhibit by powerful industrial fans until its red and white stripes come apart, whipping in the air like tentacles (fig. 4.02). Like Ringgold and David Hammons before him (both of whom have made work that takes, and critically intervenes in, the form of the US flag), Pope.L activates the stars and stripes as a symbol of the state and calls attention to exclusions around African Americans within national discourse. In addition, the US flag has been a flashpoint of discussion around globalized textile manufacturing, including the passage of a 2014 law that banned the Department of Defense from purchasing flags not entirely made in the United States (the legislation took aim primarily at Chinese imports).

Trinket was on display during summer 2015, a time in which debates around the Confederate flag flying over the South Carolina statehouse raged in the wake of the massacre of nine black churchgoers at Emanuel African Methodist Episcopal Church in Charleston. Thinking critically about flags

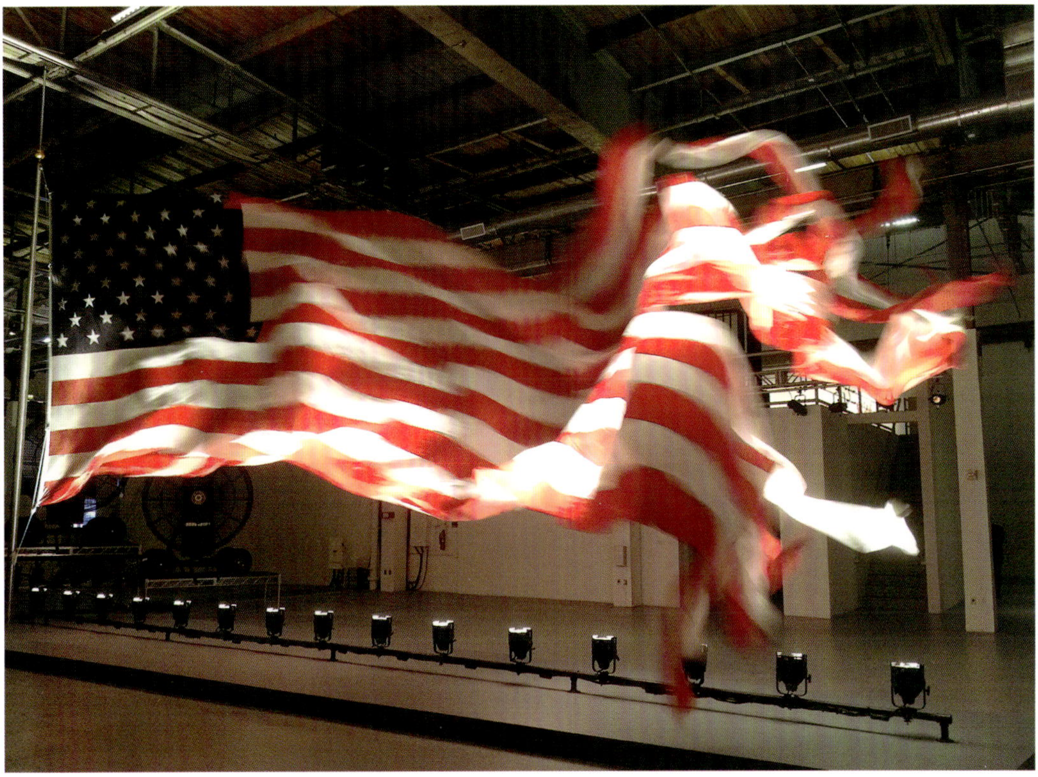

and what they stand for became even more contentious and more urgent. In the aftermath of these events, a reporter, Ed McAllister, visited workers at a South Carolina flag factory, later writing that "employees, most of them African-American, were nearing the end of their nine-and-a-half-hour shift in a hot, low-ceilinged warehouse, sitting at sewing machines standing at cutting tables, or adding brass grommets to nearly finished flags."[2] Using the fraying of flag cloth to comment upon the rending of US race relations, *Trinket* is a durational event as well as a material artifact—it tatters over time, with the constant straining caused by the artificial, but vigorous, winds. Along with the ever-tattering cloth, Pope.L's piece raises questions about visibility and obscurity as a bank of lights trained on the flag turn on and off, plunging the gallery into darkness in one moment and starkly illuminating the flag—and those observing it—the next, triggering associations with the glamour of the stage or movie set as well as the glare of police scrutiny. Though the stripes come loose at the flag's end and flutter wildly, the entire textile is never torn completely asunder; Pope.L uses distressed fabric to assert African American presence as both rupture and resilience. For both Hennessy and Pope.L, textiles enter the fray as manufactured matter, culturally freighted signifier, and raw material undergoing transformation.

Fig. 4.02. Pope.L, *Trinket*, installed at the Museum of Contemporary Art, Los Angeles, 2015. Courtesy of the artist; The Museum of Contemporary Art, Los Angeles; and Mitchell-Innes & Nash, NY. © Pope.L. Photograph by the author.

Craft Cult

I begin this afterword with images of *undoing* to signal a broader loss of confidence in the coherence of textiles as a privileged site for arguments about the politics of handicraft, and to suggest that some of these arguments have been particularly limited with regard to class, race, and gender. In what follows I offer further thoughts that are not meant as a definitive conclusion but as an open-ended engagement with the moment in which I am writing. As I discuss in my introduction, *Fray* evolved along with my increasing reservations about the onslaught of ahistorical claims made in the early 2000s about the progressiveness of handmaking. In this I am not alone: within the short span of a decade, wholly earnest craftivist claims began to give way to gentle parody and more vociferous forms of backlash. A book called *Anti-Craft*, published in 2007, featured patterns aimed at "cynical" people "fed up with syrupy crafts."[3]

And in 2009 metalsmith and writer Gabriel Craig performed his *The Gospel according to Craft*, handing out proselytizing leaflets about craft on the sidewalk in Richmond, Virginia. He wore an all-black outfit—complete with old-fashioned suspenders—as he stood atop a handmade wooden soapbox, calling out: "Excuse me, sir! Have you accepted craft as your road to personal salvation?" In this piece Craig literalizes the evangelistic approach to handmaking taken by educated, mostly white crafters in the contemporary global North, and in particular in the United States, since about 2000. Video documentation of this piece shows some people streaming past Craig without comment, but when the curious stop to listen, he expounds. "Craft," he preaches, is a "twenty-first-century model that will save us from our late capitalist demise. Craft—working by hand for a better tomorrow."

Craig's delivery might be somewhat tongue in cheek, but as a self-described "craft advocate" he is reflective of larger trends within crafting communities of the 2000s. Some of Craig's statements—about craft as a way for workers to reclaim the means of production, or about owning only things that are "beautiful and functional"—are paraphrases of William Morris, the spiritual grandfather of today's craftivism, who influentially wrote about the potentially anticapitalist nature of handiwork in the context of industrialization. As Morris exhorted in 1880, "Have nothing in your homes that you do not know to be useful and believe to be beautiful."[4] Craig's rhetoric echoes the refrain, popularized during the craftivist boom of the 2000s, that handmaking can deliver us from everything from the evils of the alienation of technology to the standardization of culture: a bright craft future. In fact, *Craft Futures* was the subtitle for a 2012 show at the Smithsonian Renwick Gallery titled *40 under 40* that examined the promising new generation of crafters (including Craig) and extolled handmaking in the twenty-first century as a "radical set of practices precisely because most things no longer need to be made by hand."[5] Does engaging in something that is not "needed" necessarily make it "radical"? To extend this logic, we might ask: is analog photography "radical" because most photography is now digital—or is it, on the contrary, more conservative? Is it not more accurate to state, as I have argued, that all methods of making (including textiles) are contingent, that they emerge from and respond to ever-shifting specific political circumstances?

The overheated religious tone Craig enacts in *The Gospel according to Craft* is right on target: in the first decade of the twenty-first century, handmaking inspired a kind of fervor. Witness the loose network of crafters called the Church of Craft, which was founded in 2000 and currently boasts more than a dozen chapters in cities in the United States, England, and Canada. Dedicated to an anticapitalist, do-it-yourself ethos, the website includes a "sermon" by founder Callie Janoff proclaiming, "Making things is our spiritual practice."[6] This unabashedly romanticized vision of craft—as a tool for personal empowerment, as a community builder, and as an alternative to mass production—gained traction during craft's resurgence in the United States in the 2000s, a resurgence that brought together younger artists, hobbyists, activists, and studio makers in an effort to reroute making into an alternative economy rather than one of commodity exchange.

But where some saw spiritual fulfillment, others saw pure neoliberal entrainment and a doctrine of economized individualism. The discourse around textile handicraft in the early 2000s was a manifestation of a wider investment in "folk politics," which, according to Nick Srnicek and Alex Williams, are "saturated with calls for a return to authenticity, to immediacy, to a world that is 'transparent,' 'human-scaled,' 'tangible,' 'slow,' 'harmonious,' 'simple,' and 'everyday.'"[7] These were the "positive" watchwords of craftivism, but Srnicek and Williams write that these imperatives "fetishize immediate results and the concrete appearance of action" that prevents strategic thought toward a more just, postcapitalist world. In addition, there were disconcerting similarities between neoliberal antifeminist "return to the hearth" celebrations of women embracing homemaking and some of the rhetoric of craftivism, as it too trumpeted handiwork as a route to domestic fulfillment. These ideological paradoxes are instructive; as I have detailed throughout *Fray*, the examples that pepper the pages of craftivist manifestos, such as Chilean arpilleras and the AIDS Quilt, are more riven by contradiction—stretched in opposing directions—than has been generally understood. I chose these widely known examples because they are often referred to but rarely examined for how specifically they lend texture to politics.

Fray has attempted to keep those textures tangible rather than to smooth them over; though it would have been possible for me to write a book that aimed above all to undercut the craftivist manifestos of the early 2000s, such a blanket refutation would have erased the historical moments in which textile handicraft has been received as having a meaningful, but by no means uncritical, relationship to the materiality, labor, and affect of social movements. Some of the anticraftivist backlash has been as overgeneralizing and dismissively indiscriminate as the original sunny assertions of its radical potential. Neither uninflected utopian claims nor summary indictments of textile craft will help us understand how procedures of making function in specific situations and might have been understood in their own moment as insurgent or quiescent. Despite the cloying version of craftivism that has been heavily corporatized and marketed by countless fairs and books, some of the impulses behind early twenty-first-century crafting came, at least in part, from those seeking to reroute normative capitalist culture. "If you don't like the culture you're in, you have to create your own." This statement could have been uttered 150 years ago by an acolyte of Morris, or by a member of the 1960s countercultural movement, or by a 1980s punk committed to smashing televisions and the State, or a 1990s riot grrrl starting her own band and making cut-and-paste zines. In fact, it is a quote from a young woman at the Renegade Craft Fair in Chicago, taken from a 2008 article in the *New York Times* (she was not named).[8] In this view, handmaking is a way to bring something into the world in a form that does not yet exist. It is a way of "making something from nothing," to cite the influential text by Lucy Lippard that was quoted in my introduction.[9] In this essay Lippard looks across the high–low taste divide, with all its classed implications, to claim that both in the hobby realm and in the fine arts, crafters (primarily women) have resourcefully remade their surroundings and retooled their environments.

Recent social practice projects have brought different kinds of makers into conjunction through textiles to catalyze conversations across class lines, and can have a measured approach to what such handicraft might offer as they examine its intersection with gendered and racialized labor. These include *The Worker's Rug / La alfombra del trabajador*, a braided rag rug collectively created out of old work clothes by day laborers in Los Angeles in conjunction with the Craft and Folk Art Museum, organizers of the Instituto de Educación Popular del Sur de California, and artists Katie Bachler and Jade Thacker. Hung on the wall rather than laid on the ground as a way to dignify the workers' efforts as precisely not utilitarian, the rug was made by a mixed-gender group who shared stories as they ripped donated clothes and braided fabric strips.[10] In another collective craft project, Ramekon O'Arwisters's ongoing *Crochet Jam*, the artist invites participants to join him in making

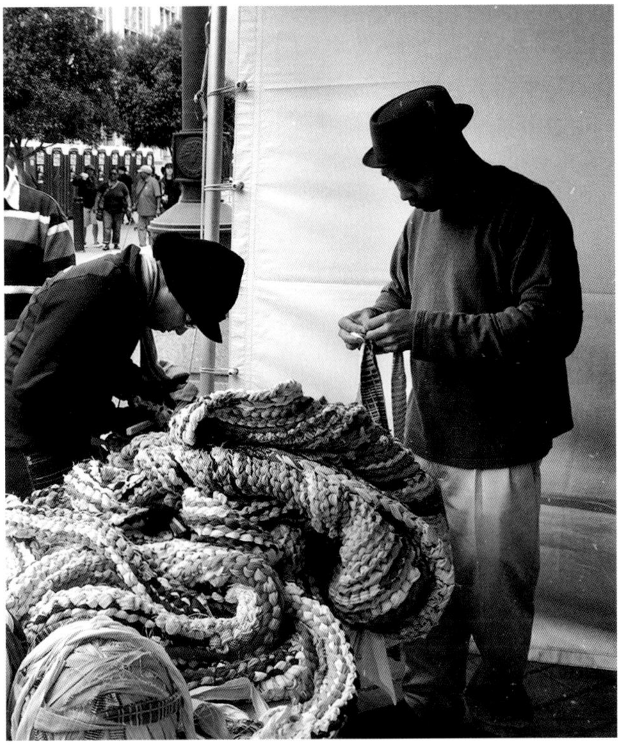

Fig. 4.03.
Ramekon O'Arwisters, *Ramekon's Crochet Jam*, participatory crochet demonstration, Art and Soul music festival, Oakland, 2012. Photograph by Carlo Abruzzese.

large, improvised rag-rug pieces (fig. 4.03). Drawing on his own memories of making quilts with his grandmother, the *Crochet Jam* makes public a version of queer black male textile production that has roots in African American female making. Hosting *Crochet Jam* both at arts events and at non-art venues such as street festivals, O'Arwisters conducts impromptu crochet lessons and invites participants to add to the mound of his ever-mutating whorls. If Hammond's *Floorpieces* effected an inversion of low and high, the *Worker's Rug* and *Crochet Jam*, by including an array of contributors—many of whom are not invested in claiming themselves as artists—aim to eradicate those distinctions altogether.

Indeed, these projects emphasize that there are differences between how textile craft was incorporated into art in the 1970s in feminist works like Hammond's rugs—or Chicago's *The Dinner Party* with its hundreds of skilled artisan-volunteers—and the rhetoric regarding contemporary handmaking. For today textile craft is not only a rapidly institutionalizing artistic trend but also a thriving enterprise that more visibly exists within a larger geopolitical context of mass production. And the lines between manufacture and handiwork are not necessarily clear; journalist and author Leslie T. Chang reports that "it takes two hundred pairs of hands to make a running shoe."[11] (The assertion that most things are no longer handmade is therefore demonstrably inaccurate.) As the photograph from the Reebok factory illustrated in the introduction shows (see fig. 0.09), those hands are disproportionately of nonwhite females. The very notion of "women's work" that compelled Chicago has shifted in light of the feminization of the global labor force. Women's work now registers both as the purview of the female homemaker in the private domestic sphere and also, pressingly, as a factory workforce, where racial, structural, and material oppressions are ever present. This shift means that some earlier feminist art uses of craft—as an institutional critique of gendered hierarchies of formalist quality in art, or as a recuperation of the decorative, for example—are less pertinent today than are considerations of the economics of textile production.

Textile Currents

What was partly at stake in the reclamation of textiles in the early 2000s was a declaration of the contemporary relevance of craft—that is to say, its *currency*.[12] Rather than seen as retrograde, outmoded throwbacks to a previous era, the craftivist movement insisted on knitting, sewing, and crocheting as current, up to date, or even future-looking, with sophisticated digital interfaces for how-to websites and networked tools that link online hackers to textile makers across the globe. Mike Press writes, "Today's quiet revolution of craft is most obviously about technological change; about makers raiding the creative potential of digital technologies for new processes, media and creative strategies. It is also about practitioners defining their practice outside the traditional domain of the handcrafted object for the gallery market—and locating themselves increasingly in new media and other creative practices."[13] Though Press does not mention the large arena of handcrafted objects that were never targeted "for the gallery market," this quote points to the fact that within some of the craft literature in the 2000s the lively dialogues between digital media makers and crafters have become one of the predominant examples of the currency of craft, moving it from its presumably musty or old-fashioned associations squarely into the present. The conjunctions between online communities and handmaking networks (and the dissolution between analog and digital techniques) is also noted by authors like David Gauntlett, who in his book *Making Is Connecting* argues for the growing social value of creating as a mode of community building and a rejection of mass media.[14]

Another proclamation of the currency of craft circulated around the anonymous textile street installations known as knit graffiti, yarn bombing, or yarn storming, in which public fixtures such as bike racks and stop signs are adorned with brightly colored strands.[15] These movements (new media and yarn bombing) are related, for "to record their ephemeral works . . . yarn bombers photograph and videotape their creations and upload them to blogs, social networks, and Web sites for all the world to see."[16] Popularized by a Houston group called Knitta Please around 2005, and since then appearing in many urban centers, yarn bombing—its faux rebellious name nods to both insurrectionary Molotov cocktails and graffiti bombing—has notably *not* come under any systematic legal fire for its sometimes lawbreaking vandalism. Despite the name Knitta Please, which riffs on an affectionate phrase swapped among African Americans, "nigga please," yarn bombers are, demographically speaking, usually white and female.[17] No doubt this fact—along with the presumed unthreatening softness and ephemerality of their chosen medium, which, exposed to the elements, degrades over time—affords yarn bombers safeguards against the criminalization of their actions. Granted legal protections by virtue of white privilege, yarn bombing and its practitioners have not been subject to state surveillance and police scrutiny in the aggressive way that spray-paint tagging by men of color has been. The authors of the book *Yarn Bombing* display little awareness of this imbalance and instead boast about their own presumed invisibility (including their advice to dress in all black for "ninja"-style attacks.)[18]

Though they are sometimes memorial in nature, with sodden strands wrapped around signposts near fatal traffic accidents, yarn bombs are often whimsical, made simply to adorn the concrete landscape with colorful fiber. Rather than decried by angry citizens as evidence of disorderly behavior, or systematically removed as graffiti is, yarn bombs have been embraced by municipalities, which sometimes commission them to produce fanciful civic adornments. For instance, in 2010, in celebration of August Craft Month, the city of Belfast was yarn bombed at the behest of Craft Northern Ireland, a state-sponsored organization that promotes local artisanal goods.[19] But if yarn bombing has been since its inception popular, it has also been attacked—as is the case for much textile craft—*not* for its many privileges but for its persistent associations with the low. The crochet artist known as Olek, according to an article in the *New York Times*, "considers yarn bombing to be the trite work of amateurs and exhibitionists. 'Lots of people have aunts or grandmas who paint,' she said. 'Do you want to see that work in the galleries? No. The street is an extension of the gallery. Not everyone's work deserves to be in public.'"[20]

Olek's assertion assumes that a space such as a street is utterly disconnected from the domain of the gallery but should be governed by its rules of inclusion or exclusion. Yet many yarn bombers move fluidly within and beyond the confining realms of low and high, and approach publicly sited knitting as an extension of their gallery-based work. In a piece from 2013 installed in the rapidly gentrifying Friedrichshain neighborhood of Berlin, a striped pole announced a textile-based art project in an alternative gallery nearby, creating a tactile connection between the two sites (street and art space; fig. 4.04). Strategically placed near scrawled multicolored tags on the walls, the anonymous knitted tube activated a visual relationship to the spray-painted graffiti, perhaps in an attempt to express a fraught solidarity. (Recall other conjunctions between graffiti and textiles in this book, such as the PARO arpillera or Koskovich's AIDS Quilt panel for Foucault.) In addition, the tube's insertion into a construction site that included a ripped-up street, piles of dirt, concrete blocks, and red-and-white hazard signs punctuated the normalized chaos of an urban landscape in transition. But what effect this textile punctuation has is an open question, as it seems not to critique the displacement of communities under way here but rather to prettify it in the name of urban revitalization and advertise its proximity to other realms of cultural production.

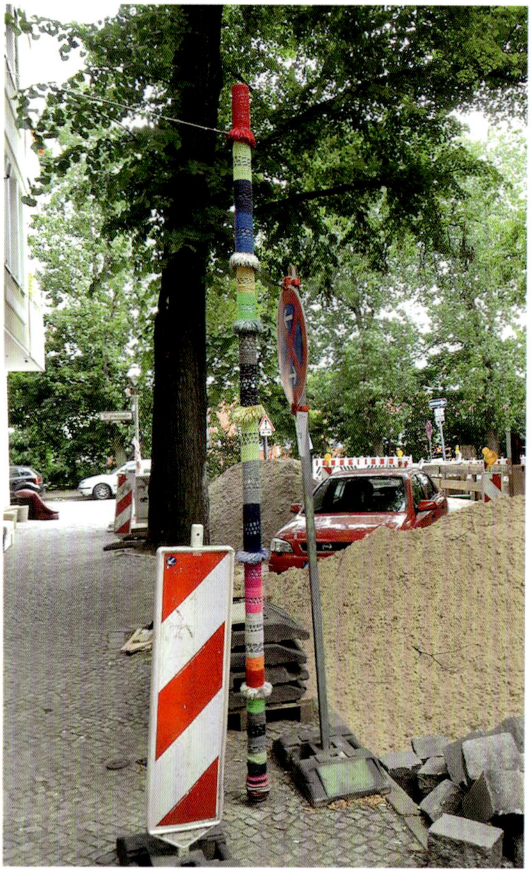

Fig. 4.04. Yarn-bombed street sign, Friedrichshain, Berlin, Germany, 2013. Photograph by the author.

As Olek's comments demonstrate and as the entire phenomenon of yarn bombing makes clear, the eruption of textile making for both self-identified hobby and fine arts crafters generates friction about taste, race, and class. As Lippard famously wrote in 1978, "The greatest lack in the feminist art movement may be of contact and dialogue with those 'amateurs' whose work sometimes appears to be imitated by others."[21] Despite feminist theorizations of such tensions in the 1970s and 1980s, notably by authors such as Lippard, Rozsika Parker, Griselda Pollock, and Freida Tesfagiorgis, the "new wave" of craftivism was less willing to interrogate its own racial and class fault lines. Indeed, the most cogent critique of the economic biases within the early 2000s embrace of domestic handmaking comes not from craftivist blogs but from humor writer Amy Sedaris's parody coffee-table book *Simple Times: Crafts for Poor People*, published in 2010. With its satirical chapter titles such as "The Craft of Crafting Craftingly" and "The Joy of Poverty," Sedaris's book operates as a withering deflation of overhyped claims about the personal comforts and therapeutic benefits of handmaking.[22] The rich white fictional narrator (who has plenty of time on her hands as a direct measure of her wealth) complains, "I don't have the benefit of pauperism. Being poor is a wonderful motivation to being creative."[23]

With its outrageously hokey suggested projects that include making dice out of old bread and belts out of plastic wrap, *Simple Times* satirically takes on, point by point, every recent "radical" promise made regarding craft and dismantles it. Notably, handmaking is offered as a response to trauma and a method of healing for a wide range of physical ailments in the chapter "Handicraftable" (a pun that merges *handicapped* with *handicraft*). Sedaris lampoons craft's grasps at currency as well as its proclaimed forward-looking nature (recall Craig preaching, also somewhat jokingly, that craft is "working by hand for a better tomorrow") by inventing absurd futuristic projects. "Just imagine crafting in a galaxy from out of our craft dreams of tomorrow!" exclaims Sedaris's introductory text for a chapter featuring projects like macaroni alien masks and a rocket made of an oatmeal box. (Sedaris is pictured in a fringed shawl, sniffing glue and looking pleasantly dazed.) "Yarn and beads can take you anywhere you want to go. . . . Yes, crafting is the pastime of yesteryear we do today, but it is also the bygone, achieved in the here and now, that delivers us to the future, presently, and that is out of this world!"[24] Nothing better captures the anxieties about temporality so pervasive in contemporary craft—the bygone that we do now that will take us to the future that is enacted in the present—than this bewildering passage.

Yet there might be something serious at the heart of Sedaris's joke. What is the currency of craft? What is the time, in particular, of textiles? Janus-faced, they have been cast simultaneously as outmoded and reactionary but also as progressive and prefigurative. Textiles warp between the past and the present: relentlessly recruited for pressing contemporary concerns, they are also tasked with reminding us of, and are often pulled back to, the traditions from which they sprung. As much as aspects of their social lives have evolved and changed, the basic actions of hand-stitching and rag-braiding maintain a strong relationship to their own histories; many instruction books from a hundred years ago could be picked up by contemporary crafters and followed today. Even when practiced in the present, textiles are envisioned as perpetually drawn back to history.

Beyond the rhetoric of craft as making a "better tomorrow," since the early 2000s there has been an avalanche of blogs, books, exhibitions, and art projects asserting that handmaking has a special relationship to "slow time," as it helps practitioners more fully inhabit, and decelerate, the present moment.

To cite the project summary from the 2008 exhibit *Taking Time: Craft and the Slow Revolution*: "Slowness is also associated with craft skills: skill which is acquired over time, cannot be rushed and is intuitively learned. Many makers today are developing critical positions in response to our consumer behaviour; questioning modes of production through new processes, looking at issues of stewardship and sustainability, as well as collective making and reworking everyday objects."[25] Similar language was featured in the exhibition *Gestures of Resistance: Craft, Performance, and the Politics of Slowness*, curated by Judith Leemann and Shannon Stratton.[26] I could cite dozens of similar texts and discussions about "slow craft," each of which emphasizes the relationship between the time-consuming skills and methods of working materials by hand and a more deliberately unhurried temporality that flies in the face of pressures to speed up, to produce more, and to consume more.

In these "slow time" writings, handmaking becomes a method for extending, or dragging out, time while remaining insistently present. Sedaris's dizzying discussion of temporality is intentionally nonsensical, to be sure, but perhaps craft time has a peculiar relationship with what has been theorized as *queer time*, for queer temporalities are also nonlinear, looping back between past and present and veering into imagined futures. Theorizations of queer temporality propose that time is not a straightforward progression of *this* follows *this* follows *this*, but rather that past and present collapse when histories erupt in the now.[27] With its anachronistic collisions and unspooling into the future, craft time can intersect with queer time.

From Hammond's rugs laid on the floor to the AIDS Quilt hugging the ground, I am interested in what happens when "low" handicraft procedures are married to spatially low display orientations. With their embrace of lowness, craft and queerness have strong ties to the horizontal, or, better, the horizon, especially as a marker of the passage of time. As Glenn Adamson writes in *Thinking through Craft*, "This book argues that craft should be thought of as a horizon: as a conceptual limit active throughout modern artistic practice."[28] Similarly, queer cultural critic José Esteban Muñoz, in a chapter called "Queerness as Horizon" from his book *Cruising Utopia*, states, "I contend that if queerness is to have any value whatsoever, it must be viewed as being visible only in the horizon."[29] In other words, both are viewed as in process, strategically unfixed—a nascent formation at once impossibly distant and tremblingly about to become.

Thus there are multiple meanings embedded within my question about "currency": in one sense, textiles are in the now, contemporary, alive in the present moment. Yet textiles also *carry a current*—they can convey a charge, an almost electrical ability to act as a temporal conduit as they move us from the past into realms of affective simultaneous coexistence. Textiles also function as literal economic currency, that is, as money or other forms of capital to be exchanged. (This latter function harks back to a fundamental paradox within the career of Morris: his socialist visions did not always square with the realities of the high cost of his luxury commodity objects.) Far from outside a market or resistant to economic pressures, the spate of titles such as *Craft, Inc.: Turn Your Hobby into a Creative Business*; *Grow Your Handmade Business*; and *The Handmade Marketplace* (all published between 2009 and 2012) make clear how embedded handicraft has become within neoliberal entrepreneurial culture.[30] From the founding of the Church of Craft in 2000 to the publication of *Craft, Inc.* in 2009: this rapid absorption could suggest that the sincere, quasi-spiritual strains of craftivism did not last a full decade.

For some makers, setting up booths at fairs or selling their work on Etsy has morphed from what could be considered a meaningful "spare-time" project to the way they pay their rent. It is increasingly hard to reconcile the tension between what is envisioned by many as a grassroots micro-economy of local production with the aggressive small-business model of self-marketing and self-promotion demanded of those who depend upon such exchanges for regular income. There is even a portmanteau, *Etsy-preneurship*, that sums up the way the online craft marketplace Etsy is not only a forum for connecting consumers with hobby makers but a site of enterprising personal branding.[31] Etsy was embraced by some crafters as an engine that might turn self-described hobbyists, who create mostly for themselves, into professionals who craft to make a living.

However, a 2009 *New York Times* article titled "That Hobby Looks like a Lot of Work" outlined how difficult it is to make a decent living wage given the time and materials these crafts demand, as some crafters work over eighty hours a week just to scrape by.[32] (In April 2015, Etsy went public, triggering excitement among some about new profits and derision from others about a loss of integrity; Etsy also launched a wholesale division oriented toward sellers who are scaling up from small-batch amateur making to more large-scale objectives.)[33] As Nicole Dawkins writes in an article on the handmaking collectives in Detroit, the making and selling of craft items "is informed by . . . post-Fordist subjectivities—as a form of highly individualized, flexible, affective work that blurs the boundaries of leisure and labor time."[34] Dawkins grasps how contemporary craft marketplaces embody, rather than resist, current neoliberal pressures. "Decided not to learn to knit, as a resistance to neoliberalism," I recall reading on one cranky anticraftivist blog, an expression of a much broader scorn and cynicism, if not outright hostility, toward the rah-rah craft cheerleading of the early 2000s.

Performing Labors

I now shift to one facet of craft's "currency" that speaks directly to contemporary economic conditions, namely the ubiquity of outsourcing and mass fabrication, by discussing projects by female artists that engage with the histories and present conditions of textile manufacturing. For the state of handmaking today is multiple: it consists of young urban yarn bombers, to be sure, but it is overwhelmingly dominated by women making consumer objects in factories in places like China, Bangladesh, and Mexico. Artists who have provocatively explored multinational manufacturing and its effects on workers' bodies and minds include Margarita Cabrera, who was born in Mexico and currently lives in El Paso, Texas. Cabrera has executed a number of projects that focus on the rise of the US–Mexico border factories known as *maquiladoras* in the wake of the 1994 North American Free Trade Agreement and the subsequent decline of long-established Mexican crafts.

Beginning in the early 2000s, she has created a series of sculptures that replicate everyday objects, like toasters and cars, that are assembled in maquiladoras. She replaces the plastic parts made in these factories under toxic conditions with vinyl, leaving the threads dangling to emphasize the nature of their construction and to emphasize the vulnerability that attends these working environments. In her piece *Pink Blender* (2002), whose pastel tone is offset by shaggy black strands, her use of a clichéd "female" color comments on the gendered population of maquiladora workers and on the brutal deaths of these women in Juárez, where hundreds of *feminicidios* (femicides) have occurred since 1993 (fig. 4.05). (Pink and black are the colors of femicide awareness activism.) Blenders might be ordinary kitchen appliances, but to be "put through a blender" is to be wrecked, ground up, or pulverized. With near-allegorical starkness, the Juárez murders highlight not only the dangers of joining the immense global labor force that produces most of the things that we buy but also the moral implications of participating in the system of purchase and commodity acquisition as a consumer. Importantly, and in contrast to the greatly exaggerated size of Claes Oldenburg's soft sculptures, Cabrera keeps her objects life sized, anchoring them in real conditions of manufacture and risk.[35] Along with the harmful plastic production undertaken in such factories, textile manufacturing (evoked by her use of cloth and thread) involves labor-intensive work, requiring minute repetitive motions and diligent attention to detail that can lead to bodily injury: eyestrain, neck problems, wrist and joint aches, shooting pains in fingers and forearms, damage (including threat of amputation) from malfunctioning machinery, and a multitude of punishing other conditions in which workers are viewed as expendable.

Like Cabrera, Stephanie Syjuco has explored the unsettling triangulation of work, gender, and textiles, recruiting hobbyist makers online to stimulate discussions about issues like global outsourcing and its labor conventions. Hers is among a number of practices that involve artists working with textiles to consciously engage amateur textile handmakers, often mobilizing far-flung communities of crafters via the Internet. In her *Counterfeit Crochet Project (Critique of a Political Economy)* (2006–8), Syjuco invited the contributions of hobby crafters to intervene in the branding and fabrication of desire. Participants hand-replicated designer handbags based on instructions Syjuco disseminated online, such as "How to Bootleg a Chanel Purse" (fig. 4.06). These crocheted knockoffs of goods bearing the logos of Gucci, Louis Vuitton, or Prada, with their lumpy yarn, lowly methods, and off-kilter interpretations of sleekly fabricated designs, are quite obviously not the genuine article. Yet the bags, made by persons with basic crochet skills, extra time on their hands, and access to the Internet, implicitly raise questions about those who make (and are paid wages that are wildly disproportionate to the extraordinarily high prices of) the luxury originals. In effect, Syjuco, like the corporations being bootlegged, "outsources" her artistic labor, as she provides instructions but others produce the retooled objects. *The Counterfeit Crochet Project* is a knowing invocation of how artistic making and distribution are bound up in larger networks of the production and circulation of other kinds of commodities.

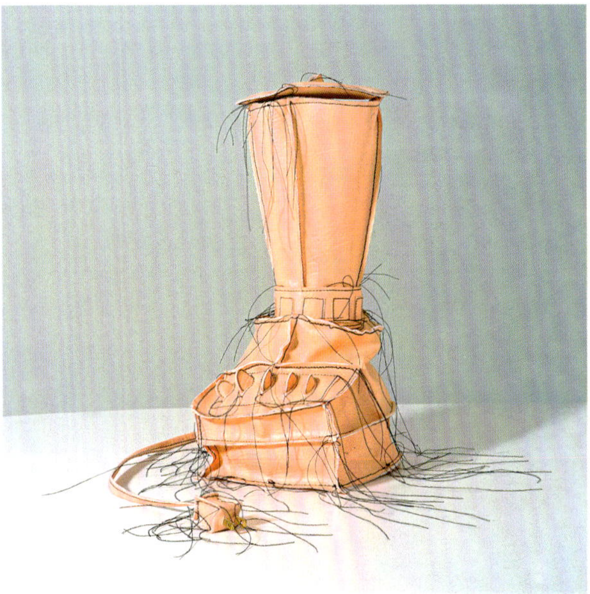

Fig. 4.05. Margarita Cabrera, *Pink Blender*, vinyl and thread, 2002. Art © Margarita Cabrera / Licensed by VAGA, New York, NY.

Further strategically blurring the line between the handmade and the mass-produced textile is Zoë Sheehan Saldaña, whose *Shopdropping* series entailed her purchasing garments from Walmart, meticulously duplicating them, and then returning them to the rack to be bought for their original price. In the instance shown in figure 4.07, from 2003, a checked sleeveless shirt made by the label Faded Glory was purchased by the artist for $9.77. Every aspect, including fabric choice, embellishments, and sewing techniques, was replicated by hand by Saldaña; when complete, the original tag was transferred to the duplicate, which was taken back to the store and "returned" to be sold for $9.77. In each case the artist takes a photograph of the duplicate in order to exhibit the original and an image of its uncanny double. But are

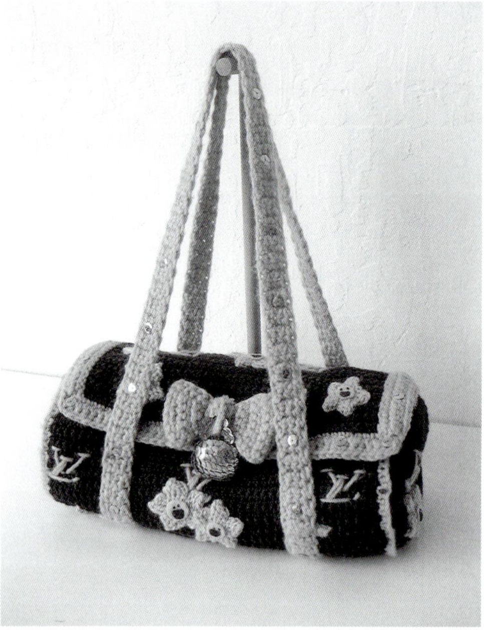

Fig. 4.06.
Louis Vuitton Brown Murakami Papillon Bag, made by Katie Furuyama, London, 2008, for *The Counterfeit Crochet Project (Critique of a Political Economy)*, organized by Stephanie Syjuco. Photograph by Stephanie Syjuco.

these duplicated garments detected *as duplicates* by their new owners? Is there some elusive quality that might distinguish them from the mass-manufactured original? Saldaña's work solicits this ambiguity. Both garments have been hand-worked to some degree, but that making happens under vastly different circumstances, within strikingly disparate systems of value and necessity. Incisively, Saldaña foregrounds the tension between the privilege to craft and the impetus for survival that—for those with few economic advantages—often accompanies textile handmaking.

Cabrera, Syjuco, and Saldaña all embarked on art projects in the 2000s in which textile objects are replicated by hand at their actual scale, firmly situating them in the realm of the everyday. Their acts of remaking ask us to think about how process, remuneration, and physical effort in textile production are wildly variable and remind us that fabrics and fibers have complex stories to tell. Other female artists use the durational performance of handmaking to ask questions about the gendered and raced production of contemporary textiles in an era marked by globalized manufacturing. In 2013 artist Beili Liu sat in an Austin art gallery under a cloud of suspended Chinese-made scissors, hand-sewing scraps of white cloth together with black thread (fig. 4.08). As

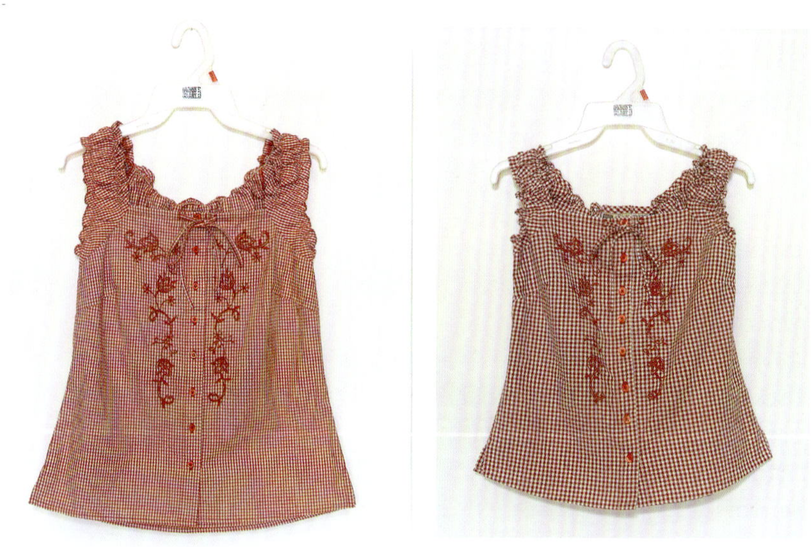

Fig. 4.07.
Zoë Sheehan Saldaña, *Faded Glory Ruched Shoulder Tank (China Red)*, clothing, hanger, photographic print (left: purchased item; right: photograph of duplicate), 2003. Courtesy of the artist.

viewers passed into the exhibition space, they were invited to snip pieces off a large piece of fabric hung by the entrance and hand them to the artist, who was spotlit in the center of the room facing a small table. The fifteen hundred iron scissors glinted as they hung near the ceiling from filaments of fishing line, their blades open and poised; one critic likened them to "the beaks of hungry birds descending on a mess of wriggling worms."[36] As Liu threaded her needle and made small stitches for this performance-based installation, titled *The Mending Project*, the cloth swatches, sutured with their visible dark seams, accumulated like a widening moat around her feet. The title indicates that while the fabric might be sewn together, the body enacting the mending might itself need attention. The piece was site-specific, conceived especially for Austin's nonprofit Women and Their Work gallery, and Liu describes the conceptual fit between the title of the art space and her act of sewing as characteristic of domestic women's handiwork.[37]

Liu's is one of many recent performance-based works enacted by artists mapping the intersections of textiles, gendered bodies, and methods of production. *The Mending Project* echoes precedents within the history of process-based live making such as works by Ann Hamilton (*lineament* [1994], in which female gallery attendants extracted strips of texts from books and wound them into balls) and Janine Antoni (*Slumber* [1994], featuring the artist weaving a blanket out of strips of her nightgown, following the pattern of her rapid eye movements during sleep, among other elements). Beyond these resonances with feminist practices from the 1990s, Liu participates more broadly in the genre of contemporary craft performance which has proliferated in galleries and public spaces since the mid-2000s. Recent exhibitions, including *Out of the Ordinary: Spectacular Craft*, at the Victoria and Albert Museum in 2007, and *Hand + Made: The Performative Impulse in Art and Craft*, at Houston's Contemporary Arts Museum in 2010, have explored these connections.[38] Some artists move beyond the frame of the art institution and take their mending to the streets to help stitch up clothes and coverings in need of repair, including Carole Lung (aka Frau Fiber) and Michael Swaine.

Why perform such effortful labors in public? What do these attempts at transparency and demystification offer us in an age of anxiety about what textile work looks like and where it is located? There are many other artists working at the intersection of performance, work, and craft, among them Gaye Chan, Travis Meinolf, and Anne Wilson, each of whom differently addresses handmaking and its embodiment, labor, and performance-based craftwork in the time of feminized mass manufacturing. In Liu's performance, the specter of Chinese factory work is made visible by the hovering scissors (she pointedly names their national origin). Textiles are utilized because of their visible stitchwork—labor made visible—even as Liu's sewing

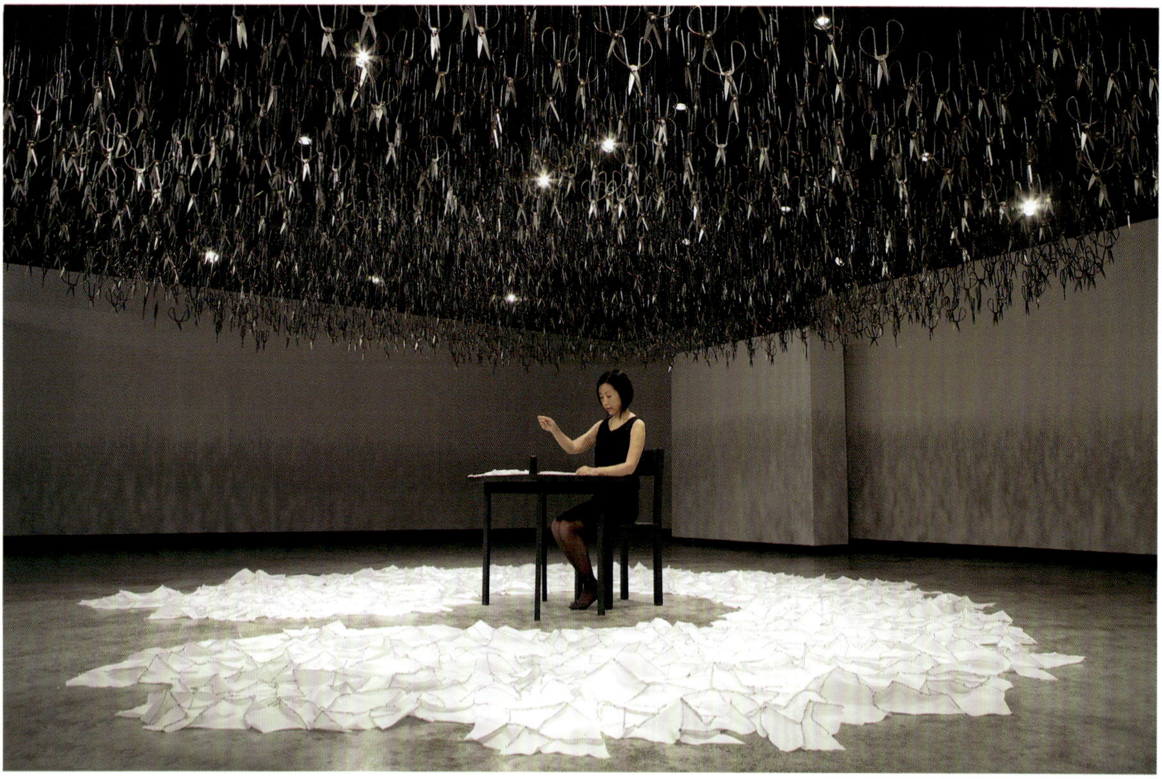

Fig. 4.08. Beili Liu, *The Mending Project*, performance with table, cloth, thread, scissors, Austin, Texas, 2013. Courtesy of Beili Liu Studio.

gestures to other sorts of work, and efforts, and bodies, whose frozen images are made widely available in stock photography of women in factories but are not always accounted for.

The idea of craft as performance is signaled by art historians such as Jenni Sorkin, who elaborates on the "simultaneity of the craft-based performance and its produced object."[39] The phrase "craft as performance" is also discussed within anthropology and environmental policy to describe how local craftspeople are often expected to make their objects in full view of the tourists seeking to make "native" purchases.[40] Buyers from afar demand "authentic" wares—in this exchange, the transparency by which crafting happens before the tourist is folded into the ritual of colonial consumption. The idea of the "demonstration" has a long history within craft institutions and tourist circuits alike, in which makers perform their embroidery, dyeing, weaving, or patchwork, effectively suturing together the object made and the body making it. As Ramón Rivera-Servera's research shows, these exhibitions of handicraft labor are often reliant on bodies of color; in the case of Oaxaca, where his study is based, indigenous crafters are recruited to provide a sense of authenticity for US consumers.[41] Laboring bodies are compelled to make themselves visible so that travelers can witness them at work, a visibility that satisfies the hunger for the "real." Such crafted performance functions as a guarantee that one is not buying mass-produced substitutes for handcrafted goods. Liu's process, by contrast, works via a logic of compensation—she is there, individually and physically in the flesh, sewing fabric together, in effect standing in for countless other racialized and feminized bodies whose physical presence is not rendered entirely visible to the consumer and whose labors are not prized as "authentic."

Liu's process-based performance did not result in a finished object to be sold—though, as scholars of performance have noted, the photographs themselves circulate as a tangible document and as such accrue a kind of value.[42] Instead she emphasized that both performance and craft are operations of the body. How do bodies—most critically, hands, which in discussions of craft metonymically stand in for bodies—shape craft? Crafters across the high–low spectrum often derive great satisfaction from engaging directly with their materials, whether wood or wool or scrapbooking supplies sold in the arts-and-crafts chain store Michaels. *Desire, gratification, release, comfort, security*—for many converts to the "church of craft," these terms describe the immersive corporeal experience of handmaking. But within the context of contemporary culture, there is a spectrum of crafting bodies to consider, ones marked by race, region, gender, sexuality, ability, age, and class, and not all of them revel in the procedures of making by hand. These bodies have vastly unequal levels of access to capital and to power, so that the women hand-sewing uniforms onto action figures in the Pearl River District on a sixteen-hour work shift—workers that I believe Liu, with her Chinese scissors, is gesturing to in their very absence—might have a quite different understanding of the intersection of bodies, production, and textiles.

Artists like Liu participate in the affective labors of body craft—reforming individual desires as well as the body politic. In recent projects that highlight performance and process, the "preachy" aspect of craft is complicated and nuanced; these artists do not shy away from ambivalence. Handmaking has been heralded as a path to personal and social "salvation," as Craig's soapbox speech declared. However, the political and economic realities of textile handicraft in the early twenty-first century mean that any alternative it offers to late capitalism also coexists with its predictably neoliberal encouragements of individual branding—that is, craft does not undercut market exchanges but impels and relies upon their flexible expansion. Here the notion of "craft futures" does not signify utopian promise but keys in to commodity futures trading and speculation—gambling on the uncertainties of the economy to yield large profits. The relentless marketing of the handmade as a way to purchase "unique" objects, coupled with the sometimes high physical costs enacted on the bodies of some makers, means that textiles must always be seen as a mixed terrain, one marked by cares and also exploitations.

Against the paeans to handcrafted textile objects as a savior, then, there is a more distressing side. Some artists have plumbed this more negative cast, turning to textiles as they relate to affective constriction, isolation, difficulty, failure, obsession, shame, trauma, pain. In 2011 artist and fashion designer Liz Collins (who with her *Knitting Nation* series has been at the forefront of textile performance) set up a hand-cranked knitting machine on a city street as part of Allison Smith's broader project *The Cries of San Francisco* and offered, for a fee, a selection of wounds that people could have inserted into their clothes. With *The Walking Wounded*, Collins explored what it meant to perform both labor and commerce, functioning as a vendor of on-the-spot interventions that disrupted the integrity of the garments while also customizing them. Cutting open and then immediately mending these sutures, Collins grafted "sores" and "slashes" into sweaters and shirts, making gashes dripping with red threads, slits, oozing masses, and blooming tumors. This range of options was spelled out on the accompanying fabric banner (fig. 4.09). As Collins indicates, if we examine how bodies and performance shape textiles, it is just as important to consider how textiles shape—discipline, entrain, confine—bodies. Clothes are a social membrane that tells others who we are, and Collins's intervention, however playful, made visible wounds both psychic and physical that would otherwise be covered. "Wear your heart on your sleeve!" it enjoins. One woman asked for a fist-sized pink wound on

Fig. 4.09. (*Facing*) Liz Collins, *The Walking Wounded*, banner from performance at Allison Smith's *Cries of San Francisco*, 2011. Courtesy of the artist.

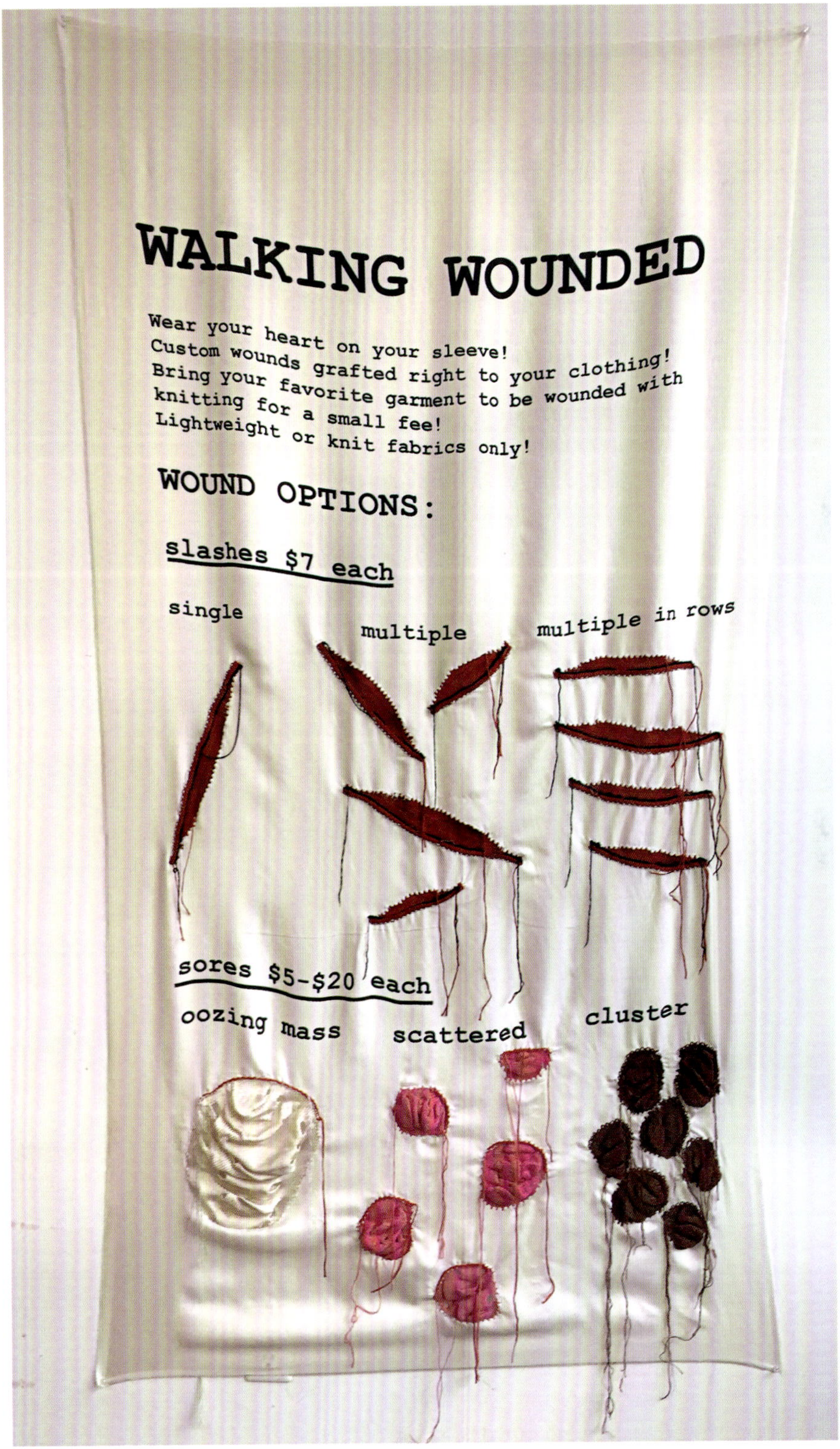
WALKING WOUNDED
Wear your heart on your sleeve!
Custom wounds grafted right to your clothing!
Bring your favorite garment to be wounded with
knitting for a small fee!
Lightweight or knit fabrics only!
WOUND OPTIONS:
slashes $7 each
single
multiple
multiple in rows
sores $5-$20 each
oozing mass
scattered
cluster

her shirt to be worn over an actual cancerous tumor that was growing near her collarbone. In projects like Liu's and Collins's, textile performances work to surface that which can go unseen.

Coda: Circling Back

In this afterword I have returned to and expanded upon some of the themes laid out in my introduction. Throughout this book I have endeavored to think through specific instances of the fraying of textile handicraft (that is to say, their polemical unraveling, as well as the unraveling of their polemics) primarily in the 1970s, 1980s, and 1990s. I have frequently referred to properties such as the malleability of some cloth and the flexibility of some fiber as my case studies reveal moments of contestation and discontinuity generated by those pliabilities. My chapters have explored how handmade techniques, as well as handmade things, have been subject to a great deal of projection and fantasy; such projections manifest in confident assertions about how textiles inherently function. Yet an object heralded by one person as radical (whether it be a Cockette's headdress or a precario by Vicuña) is someone else's regressive relic.

What I call "textile politics" have nothing to do with any stable ideology that might be activated by the procedures of handmaking, but rather with craft's strange, pressured, and contested position within the schematic of contemporary consumption. As I have argued, textiles create a rupture around and through notions of amateur, art, and craft, throwing the words themselves into crisis—akin to an identity crisis. These ongoing fissures have been central to my concerns as I have looked at examples from the United States and Chile in which textiles have been interrogated and redefined within hobby making, theoretical texts, and art institutions. I have also asked how textiles have been believed to *solve* a range of crises—of heteronormativity, of memory, of consumerism, of global capitalism, of femininity. Do textiles emerge with intensity in times of disaster, or do they retreat? It might be better to say that textiles live at the edges of crisis, often creating conflicts or tensions as much as assuaging them.

As this book has explored both collective and individual ways of making, I have considered how textile craft has been variably narrated, defined, and defended. I have speculated about how different spheres of textiles, such as that composed of those who mostly consider themselves hobbyists and that consisting of those who self-identify as artists creating works intended for museums, are often in contact, informing each other. And though these categories are by no means discrete, it is my contention that widespread interest in craft among everyday or amateur makers helps impel art-critical and art-institutional attention. Just as fine-art photography as a genre evolves under constant pressure exerted by the collective expertise of snapshot photographers, textiles as a field draws strength from a wide pool of self-trained makers who not only make up much of the audience for museum exhibits but also contribute to robust discourse around these techniques. This was true during the early 2000s surge in interest around craft, which arguably first gained prominence within the realm of hobby making and only later spread to institutional contexts, as fiber artists like Sheila Hicks have been "rediscovered" and celebrated in exhibitions around the globe. While such shows might be a step in the right direction, many have tended to be highly formalist in nature, erasing the highly contentious, that is to say explicitly feminist, context in which many of these textile-based techniques first made their appearance within contemporary art.

My methodology has been rooted in close looking and, whenever possible, handling and touching, an intimate approach too often neglected in writings about textiles, especially when considering objects that are the products of so-called amateur makers. I examine the material construction and formal effects of these textiles not as a perfunctory aesthetic exercise but because it is through careful observation that we can best grasp how objects have been textured, that is to say worked, and how they work on us. This close looking is not incidental to my arguments but is rather, across each chapter, constitutive of my arguments about textiles as they perpetually transgress lines between high and low and as they are generated "in the fray" of various arguments regarding handmaking.

Indeed, as the case studies of *Fray* have demonstrated, these riotously varied costumes, rugs, yarn-based sculptures, appliquéd tapestries, and quilts do not and cannot function in any singular way; no type of cultural production, whether painting, collage, or poetry, can. Such generalizations do a disservice to the myriad textured ways makers use materials, to fluctuating attitudes toward those materials in different moments and locations, and to materials' promiscuous reinterpretations as objects take on lives of their own and are received by multiple audiences. At the same time, I have been drawn to potent instances in which textiles were explicitly enlisted for reasons beyond simple expediency, when crafted procedures were chosen precisely because of their simultaneous attachment to the past and their ability to speak to the present.

I STILL HAVE the "Ladies' Sewing Circle and Terrorist Society" T-shirt that my mother bought in 1977, the one I discussed in the introduction to this book (fig. 0.01). It is the garment I have owned the longest, by a measure of several decades. It accompanied me to college, to my postcollege years in Oregon temping and working in food service, to graduate school in California, to my first job in Rhode Island, and back again to California. Though the silkscreened logo is now cracked, a visible registration of how often the shirt has been worn and washed, folded and unfolded, packed away and then dug out of boxes over a period of decades, it is in remarkably good shape. But I haven't worn it for years. Not only because I am afraid its joke might be misunderstood in a time when jokes about terrorism are not considered funny, but also because it is too important to me. I don't want to risk more damage, contribute to its inevitable wearing out, or hasten the day when the logo is completely illegible. No matter how sturdy cloth seems, it is usually quite fragile. It is one organizing contradiction of textiles that the more they are cherished, the more they disintegrate.

This book has explored the special persistence of textiles and how their significance endures even as they unravel. *Fray* was written, in part, to pay homage to the challenge provided by the "Ladies' Sewing Circle and Terrorist Society" T-shirt, as well as to the moment of its creation within the liberation movements of the 1970s and to my mother's self-identification as a handmaker and as a feminist. Its hypothetical evocation of women crafters scheming against the patriarchy speaks to a historical moment whose details are fading from our ken; it is in the threads that some of these details can still be found.

Acknowledgments

Emerging from my personal encounters with textile objects, this research project has been an unusually familiar—that is, intimate—one. It feels right, then, to begin these acknowledgments with my family. First, I owe a tremendous debt of gratitude to my mother, Susan Bryan, fierce feminist sewer extraordinaire. Thanks as well to Carroll and Lynda Wilson, Becca and Craig Clark, Darcy Bryan-Wilson and Kevin Murphy, Bryan Poff and Erin Colwell, Jerry Beetz, Ruth and Michael Chen, Derek Chen, and my beloved nieces and nephews Seth, Rosy, Trent, Lulu, and Greyson.

I am particularly indebted to my formative friendship with Liz Collins, who has perhaps above all others modeled for me what it means to think and feel with textiles. Glenn Adamson has been an immensely valued collaborator and was a generous, productive reader of this manuscript. Johanna Burton made crucial suggestions and consistently offered her steadying kindness. Carrie Lambert-Beatty inspired me with her smarts and her care, and whisked us both away for a pivotal writing retreat at the exact right moment. Cristóbal Lehyt went above and beyond in his signature magnanimous fashion. Darby English, ever astute, importantly challenged me to go further with the AIDS Quilt. Richard Meyer's sharp thinking helped me refine my ideas; he is a true and terrific friend. Pamela Lee and Geoff Kaplan have been consistent sources of joy and adventure.

I am grateful for enriching discussions—about textiles and, mercifully, not about textiles—with the following academics, writers, and artists at various stages in my research: Jo Applin, Elissa Auther, Nicholas Bell, Natalia Brizuela, Maria Elena Buszek, Tim Choy, Bridget Cooks, Tom Crow, Josh Faught, Macarena Gómez-Barris, Jennifer González, Sabrina Gschwandtner, Jack Halberstam, Cori Hayden, Sharon Hayes, Lucas Hilderbrand, Shannon Jackson, Arlene Keizer, Rachel Kushner, Thomas Lax, Miguel López, Lilith Mahmud, Cat Mazza, Allyson Mitchell, Mignon Nixon, Tavia Nyong'o, Jeanine Oleson, Trevor Paglen, Ben Piekut, Griselda Pollock, Helena Reckitt, Amy Sadao, Robin Schuldenfrei, Susan Schweik, Ezra Shales, Jenni Sorkin, Allison Smith, Anne Wagner, Anne Walsh, Namita Wiggers, Dominic Willsdon, and Angie Wilson. Other friends also offered abundant humor, advice, and emotional support: Quang H. Dang, Patrick Hazelton, Karin Martin, Amy Yunis, Beth Maloney, Hadas Rivera-Weiss, Margo Rivera-Weiss, Cara O'Connor, Miranda

July, Kelly Quinn, Jon Raymond, and most especially Amber Straus, whose salutary contributions to my life throughout many decades have been immeasurable (not least by bringing the marvelous Matsu Wilson-Straus into the world).

Along the way, I have received vital assistance from many people and institutions. My deepest appreciation extends to those in Chile who facilitated my research: Gabriella Dobo; Carla Miranda at the Museo de la Solidaridad Salvador Allende; Carla Hernández at the Fundación Salvador Allende; and María Luisa Ortiz and Verónica Sánchez at the Museo de la Memoria y los Derechos Humanos. Additional gratitude goes to Winnie Lira, former director of the Fundación Solidaridad, for the time she took to talk with me and show me her personal papers. I thank Roddy Williams at the NAMES Project and Sergio Waksman for their exceptional help with images. I am grateful to the many artists, crafters, and activists I interviewed, including Beaver Bauer, Sally-Jo Bowman, Jessica Copen, Avram Finkelstein, Alexandra Jacopetti Hart, Fayette Hauser, Angela Hennessy, Scrumbly Koldewyn, Rachael Matthews, Mac McNamara, and Faith Wilding. Special relationships are often forged through scholarly inquiry, and this has proved true with Harmony Hammond and Cecilia Vicuña; they endured years of my questions with patience, wisdom, and grace.

At UC Berkeley I have been fortunate to work among great colleagues in the Department of History of Art: Diliana Angelova, Pat Berger, Whitney Davis, Beate Fricke, Darcy Grimaldo Grigsby, Chris Hallett, Elizabeth Honig, Lauren Kroiz, Henrike Lange, Anneka Lenssen, Greg Levine, Margaretta Lovell, Todd Olson, Sugata Ray, Andy Stewart, and Lisa Trever. An extra shout-out to Darcy and Todd for being such perceptive interlocutors and steadfast allies, and to Anneka for our bracing conversations about abstraction. The students in my undergraduate seminars on contemporary art and handicraft at UC Irvine and Berkeley were full of insights and observations, and I thank my graduate students past and present for being such generative sounding boards, especially Sarah Cowan, Ellen Feiss, Jez Flores, and Emma Silverman. Incredible research assistants worked with me through the UC Berkeley Undergraduate Research Apprentice Program: Natalie Christian Cone, Molly Everett, Jana LaBrasca, Fabián Leyva-Barragán, and Pablo Seward. I am forever indebted to those who cheerfully, efficiently, and skillfully assisted with gathering images, secured permissions, and performed other administrative or technical work on my behalf: Lynn Cunningham, Eugene De La Rosa, Jason Hosford, Julie Wolf, John McChesney-Young, and Linda Fitzgerald. At the University of Chicago Press, Susan Bielstein and James Toftness have been a dream to work with, and I am also appreciative of the work performed by Ruth Goring, Jill Shimabukuro, Derek Gottlieb, and the stellar Sarah Cowan.

My research has been funded by grants and fellowships from the Center for Craft, Creativity, and Design; the College Art Association's Millard Meiss Publication Fund; the Sterling and Francine Clark Art Institute; the Henry Moore Institute; the Terra Foundation for American Art; the Townsend Center for the Humanities; the UC Irvine International Center for Writing and Translation; and the UC Berkeley Committee on Research.

Over the past decade, I benefited from questions asked by insightful audiences at invited talks and conversations in which I presented my work-in-progress, including at the California College of the Arts, Columbia University, the Courtauld Institute of Art, Cranbrook Academy of Art, the Getty Research Institute, Goldsmiths University, Harvard University, Humboldt-Universität, Knoxville Museum of Art, the Leslie-Lohman Museum, Leuphana Universität, the Maryland Institute College of Art, the New School for Social Research, the Palais des Académies in Brussels, Reed College, the Royal College of Art, the Santa Barbara Museum of Art, the School of the Art Institute of Chicago, Swarthmore College, UC San Diego, University of Chicago, University of Colorado–Denver, University of Pennsylvania, University of Southern California, Vermont College of Fine Arts, the Victoria and Albert Museum, and Washington University in St. Louis.

My early thoughts about some of these issues appeared, in different form, in the following venues: "Sewing Notions" (*Artforum*); "Queerly Made: Harmony Hammond's *Floorpieces*" (*Journal of Modern Craft*); "Bodycraft: Preaching, Process, and Performance" (*40 under 40: Craft Futures*); "Handmade Genders: Queer Costuming in San Francisco circa 1970" (*West of Center: Art and the Countercultural Experiment in America*); and "Knit Dissent" (*Contemporary Art: 1989 to the Present*).

Finally, *Fray* has been indelibly shaped, very much for the better, by Mel Y. Chen, who provided loving encouragement, wicked laughter, and incisive edits, and with typical brilliance helped clarify its title. Mel, you are my light, my sweet, my miraculous best friend, my most cherished intellectual companion. This book is for you.

Notes

1. Interview with Sally-Jo Bowman, January 2015, telephone. I am grateful to Bowman for the time she took to speak to me about this T-shirt, whose exact history had been obscured. Finding the original maker of this design was no easy feat; I had to draw on all my research skills to track down Bowman by triangulating old classified ads, current phone books, and US copyright records.
2. Classified ad in *New York*, November 30, 1981, 132. While *Ms.* was Bowman's primary outlet for selling the shirt, she also experimented with magazines such as *New York* and *Mother Jones*.
3. Bernardine Dohrn, Bill Ayers, Jeff Jones, and Celia Sojourn, *Prairie Fire: The Politics of Revolutionary Anti-imperialism* ([San Francisco]: Communications, 1974). I put the publishing location in brackets, following the cue of several library databases; in the colophon of the book itself, the location of the press is listed as "underground."
4. Ibid., 125.
5. Karen Beckman has provided a helpful discussion on the relationship between feminism and terrorism in her "Terrorism, Feminism, Sisters, and Twins: Building Relations in the Wake of the World Trade Center Attacks," *Grey Room* 7 (Spring 2002): 24–39.
6. Elizabeth Freeman, "Packing History, Count(er)ing Generations," *New Literary History* 4, no. 31 (Autumn 2000): 727–44.
7. Marcia Stepanek, "Women in Illinois Government: The Power and the Promise," *Illinois Issues* 7, no. 1 (January 1981).
8. Roland Barthes, "Analyse textuelle d'un conte d'Edgar Poe," in *Sémiotique narrative et textuelle*, ed. Claude Chabrol (Paris: Larousse, 1973), 29–54; Theodor Adorno, *Über einege Relationen zwischen Musik und Malerei: Die Kunst und die Künste* (Berlin: Akademie der Künste, 1967), 450.
9. Stephen Knott, *Amateur Craft: History and Theory* (London: Bloomsbury Academic, 2015), xii.
10. For one critical take on the Gee's bend phenomenon, see Bridget R. Cooks, "The Quilts of Gee's Bend, 2002," in *Exhibiting Blackness: African Americans and the American Art Museum* (Amherst: University of Massachusetts Press, 2011), 135–44. See also Anna C. Chave's incisive article, "Dis/Cover/ing the Quilts of Gee's Bend, Alabama," *Journal of Modern Craft* 1, no. 2 (July 2008): 221–54.
11. Laurel Thatcher Ulrich, *The Age of Homespun: Objects and Stories in the Creation of an American Myth* (New York: Alfred A. Knopf, 2001), 183.
12. Ibid.
13. Kirkpatrick Sale, *Rebels against the Future: The Luddites and Their War on the Industrial Revolution* (Cambridge, MA: Perseus, 1995).
14. Friedrich Engels, *The Condition of the Working Class in England* (orig. 1845; Stanford, CA: Stanford University Press, 1958); Karl Marx, *Capital: A Critique of Political Economy* (orig. 1867; New York: International Publishers, 1967).
15. Glenn Adamson, *The Invention of Craft* (London: Bloomsbury Academic, 2013).
16. For more on Morris's theories of labor and leisure, see Ruth Kinna, "William

Morris: Art, Work, and Leisure," *Journal of the History of Ideas* 61, no. 3 (July 2000): 493–512.

17. Darcy Grimaldo Grigsby, *Enduring Truths: Sojourner's Shadows and Substance* (Chicago: University of Chicago Press, 2015), 81.
18. Lisa Tickner, *The Spectacle of Women: Imagery of the Suffrage Campaign, 1907–1914* (Chicago: University of Chicago Press, 1988), 63. For a close look at one embroidered object from this movement, see Maureen Daly Goggin, "Fabricating Identity: Janie Terrero's 1912 Embroidered English Suffrage Signature Handkerchief," in *Women and Things 1750–1950: Gendered Material Strategies*, ed. Maureen Daly Goggin and Beth Fowkes Tobin (Farnham, UK: Ashgate, 2009), 31–50.
19. Rozsika Parker, *The Subversive Stitch: Embroidery and the Making of the Feminine* (London: Women's Press, 1984), ix.
20. Christina Kiaer, "The Russian Constructivist Flapper Dress," *Critical Inquiry* 28, no. 1 (Autumn 2001): 189.
21. Ibid., 225.
22. Abigail McGowan, *Crafting the Nation in Colonial India* (New York: Palgrave McMillan, 2009), 191.
23. For more on Gandhi's undermining of traditional gender roles, see Rebecca Brown, *Gandhi's Spinning Wheel and the Making of India* (London: Taylor and Francis, 2010).
24. Anne Macdonald, *No Idle Hands: The Social History of American Knitting* (Boston: Ballantine Books, 1988), 295.
25. See, for instance, Ariel Zeitlin Cooke and Marsha MacDowell, eds., *Weavings of War: Fabrics of Memory* (East Lansing: Michigan State University, 2005); Deborah A. Deacon and Paula E. Calvin, *War Imagery in Women's Textiles: An International Study of Weaving, Knitting, Sewing, Quilting, Rug Making and Other Fabric Arts* (Jefferson, NC: McFarland, 2014); and Bibiana Obler, "Craft as a Response to War," in *Nation Building: Craft and Contemporary American Culture*, ed. Nicholas Bell (London: Bloomsbury Academic and Smithsonian Renwick Gallery, 2016).
26. Mary C. Beaudry, *Findings: The Material Culture of Needlework and Sewing* (New Haven, CT: Yale University Press, 2006), 149. For more on this evolution, see Laurel Thatcher Ulrich, "Wheels, Looms, and the Gender Division of Labor in Eighteenth-Century New England," *William and Mary Quarterly* 55 (January 1998): 3–38.
27. For one exhibit that situated works such as Oiticica's wearable *Parangolé* capes within the frame of textiles, see *Textiles Art and the Social Fabric*, curated by Grant Watson, Museum of Contemporary Art Antwerp (2009–2010).
28. Joan Livingstone and John Ploof, eds., *The Object of Labor: Art, Cloth, and Cultural Production* (Cambridge, MA: MIT Press, 2007), vii.
29. Janis Jefferies, *The Handbook of Textile Culture* (London: Bloomsbury Academic, 2015).
30. Seth Siegelaub in conversation with Hans Ulrich Obrist, in *A Brief History of Curating* (Zurich: JRP Ringier, 2008), 116–30; Siegelaub, *Bibliographica Textilia Historiæ: Towards a General Bibliography on the History of Textiles Based on the Library and Archives of the Center for Social Research on Old Textiles* (New York: International Gen-

eral, 1997). For more on Siegelaub's relationship with textiles, see Sara Martinetti, ed., *Seth Siegelaub: Beyond Conceptual Art* (Amsterdam: Stedelijk Museum, 2015).

31. For more on Riegl's work on textiles, see Sabeth Buchmann and Rike Frank, eds., *Textile Theorien der Moderne: Alois Riegl in der Kunstrkritik* (Berlin: b_books, 2016).
32. Amalia Mesa-Bains, "Domesticana: The Sensibility of Chicana Rasquache," *Aztlan: A Journal of Chicano Studies* 24, no. 2 (Fall 1999): 157–67; bell hooks, "Aesthetic Inheritances: History Worked by Hand," in *Yearnings: Race, Gender, and Cultural Politics* (Boston: South End, 1990), 115–22; Alice Walker, "Everyday Use," in *In Love and Trouble: Stories of Black Women* (1973; repr. New York: Mariner Books, 2003), 47–59.
33. Glenn Adamson, *Thinking Through Craft* (London: Berg, 2007); Elissa Auther, *String, Felt, Thread: The Hierarchy of Art and Craft in American Art* (Minneapolis: University of Minnesota Press, 2009); Maria Elena Buszek, ed., *Extra/Ordinary: Craft and Contemporary Art* (Durham, NC: Duke University Press, 2011); Cooks, *Exhibiting Blackness*; Jessica Hemmings, ed., *Cultural Threads: Transnational Textiles Today* (London: Bloomsbury Academic, 2015); Laura E. Pérez, *Chicana Art: The Politics of Spiritual and Aesthetic Altarities* (Durham, NC: Duke University Press, 2007); T'ai Smith, *Bauhaus Weaving Theory: From Feminine Craft to Mode of Design* (Minneapolis: University of Minnesota Press, 2014); Michele Wallace, "Feminism, Race, and the Division of Labor," originally published in *Division of Labor* (1995), reprinted in *Dark Designs and Visual Culture* (Durham, NC: Duke University Press, 2004), 390–400; Freida High Wasikhongo Tesfagiorgis, "In Search of a Discourse and Critique/s That Center the Art of Black Women Artists," in *Gendered Visions: The Art of Contemporary Africana Women Artists*, ed. Salah M. Hassan (Trenton, NJ: Africa World Press, 1997); Judith Wilson, "How the Invisible Woman Got Herself on the Map: Black Women Artists in California," in *Art/Women/California, 1950–2000: Parallels and Intersections*, ed. Diana Burgess Fuller and Daniela Salvioni (Berkeley: University of California Press, 2002), 201–16.
34. Janis Jefferies, *Selvedges: Janis Jefferies—Works since 1980* (Norwich, UK: Norwich School of Art and Design, 2000); Rozsika Parker and Griselda Pollock, *Old Mistresses: Women, Art, and Ideology* (London: Pandora, 1992); Lucy R. Lippard, *The Pink Glass Swan: Selected Feminist Essays on Art* (New York: New Press, 1995).
35. The longer passage by Truth from which this is excerpted is quoted in Lisa E. Farrington, *Faith Ringgold* (Petaluma, CA: Pomegranate, 2004), 49.
36. Ringgold, a member of the Art Workers' Coalition, also cofounded Where We At Black Women Artists as well as Women Students and Artists for Black Art Liberation; see her *We Flew over the Bridge: The Memoirs of Faith Ringgold* (Durham, NC: Duke University Press, 2005). Michele Wallace, her daughter, has been at the forefront of the critical discourse about Ringgold's activism and textiles; see Wallace, "*The French Collection*: Momma Jones, Mommy Fay, and Me," in *Dancing at the Louvre: Faith Ringgold's French Collection and Other Story Quilts*, ed. Dan Cameron (New York: New Museum of Contemporary Art and University of California Press, 1998), 14–25.
37. Auther, *String, Felt, Thread*, 107.
38. Jane F. Gerhard, *The Dinner Party: Judy Chicago and the Power of Popular Feminism*,

1970–2007 (Athens: University of Georgia Press, 2013), 227–28.

39. Quoted in Elaine Levine, "Clay: Judy Chicago's Dinner Party," *Craft Horizons*, April 1979, 54.

40. Hilton Kramer, "Does Feminism Conflict with Artistic Standards?" *New York Times*, January 27, 1980, 103, 129. For more on the reception of Chicago's work and its importance for feminist art history, see Amelia Jones, ed., *Sexual Politics: Judy Chicago's "Dinner Party" in Feminist Art History* (Los Angeles: Armand Hammer Museum of Art and University of California Press, 1996).

41. Alice Walker, "One Child of One's Own," *Ms.*, August 1979, 72; see also Helen Molesworth, "Cleaning Up in the 1970s: The Work of Judy Chicago, Mary Kelly and Mierle Laderman Ukeles," in *Rewriting Conceptual Art*, ed. Michael Newman and Jon Bird (London: Reaktion Books, 1999), 107–22.

42. For more on textiles in art by women of color in the United States in the 1970s and 1980s in distinction to Chicago, see Julia Bryan-Wilson, "Fabrications: Race, genre et travail du textile," in *Perspective: Actualité en histoire de l'art* 1 (2016): 210–15.

43. Herbert W. Hemphill Jr. and Julia Weissman, *Twentieth-Century American Folk Art and Artists* (New York: E. P. Dutton, 1974). This institutionalization was mirrored by an increasing academic attention to folk art, including publications by Henry Glassie and others; see Henry Glassie, *Pattern in the Material Folk Culture of the Eastern United States* (Philadelphia: University of Pennsylvania Press, 1969).

44. Jonathan Holstein, *Abstract Design in American Quilts* (New York: Whitney Museum of American Art, 1971).

45. Clustered under the heading "Three at the Whitney," these reviews were Rosalyn Drexler, "Two Hundred Years of North American Indian Art," Marjorie Welish, "Calder's Tapestries," and David Shapiro, "American Quilts," *Craft Horizons*, December 1971, 31–45, 72.

46. Joe Ben Wheat, foreword to Charlene Cerny, *Navajo Pictorial Weaving* (Santa Fe: Museum of New Mexico, 1975), 3.

47. The interest in fiber arts—and their purported separation from phenomena such as postminimalism—in the late 1960s and early 1970s was beautifully documented in Auther, *String, Felt, Thread.*

48. Ann-Sargent Wooster, *Quiltmaking: The Modern Approach to a Traditional Craft* (New York: Galahad Books, 1972), book jacket.

49. Ibid., 93, 95.

50. hooks, "Aesthetic Inheritances," 118. For more on Powers, see also Tesfagiorgis, "In Search," and Gladys-Marie Fry, *Stitched from the Soul: Slave Quilts from the Antebellum South* (New York: Dutton Studios, 1990).

51. See, for instance, Judith Wragg Chase, *Afro-American Art and Craft* (New York: Van Nostrand Reinhold, 1971).

52. John Michael Vlach, *The Afro-American Tradition in Decorative Arts* (Cleveland: Cleveland Museum of Art, 1978), 54.

53. Rozsika Parker, "Portrait of the Artist as a Housewife," in *Framing Feminism: Art and the Women's Movement 1970–1985*, ed. Rozsika Parker and Griselda Pollock (London: Pandora, 1987), 208.

54. Mirra Bank, *Anonymous Was a Woman* (New York: St. Martin's, 1979), 92.

55. Lucy R. Lippard, "Making Something from Nothing (Toward a Definition of

Women's 'Hobby Art')," *Heresies* 4 (Winter 1978): 62–65, reprinted in *Pink Glass Swan*, 138.

56. Simone de Beauvoir, *The Second Sex* (1949), trans. Constance Borde and Sheila Malovany-Chevallier (New York: Knopf Doubleday, 2010), 634.
57. Virginia Harvey, *Macramé: The Art of Creative Knotting* (New York: Reinhold Book, 1967); Dona Z. Meilach, *Macramé: Creative Design in Knotting* (New York: Crown, 1971).
58. Joyce Bennett, *Mad about Macramé* 36 (Rosemead, CA: Hazel Pearson Handicrafts, 1975), 2.
59. One unusual macramé hobby how-to guide, written by two white women living in Flagstaff, Arizona, "literally on the edge of the Navajo and Hopi reservations," features a Navajo woman and her Navajo-Hopi son on the cover and offers a Navajo-language greeting: Jan Inman and Ginger Epperson, *Old Knots and New Ideas* (Flagstaff, AZ: Inman-Epperson, 1976).
60. Rosey Grier, *Rosey Grier's Needlepoint for Men* (New York: Walker, 1973).
61. The process of constructing this project is documented in Ben Van Meter, dir., *The Saga of Macramé Park* (1974), color film, 21 minutes. See also Duncan Campbell, "Early Childhood: Macramé Playground," *Saturday Review of Education*, May 1973, 70; and "Community Action: It's Amazing What You Can Do with a Bit More Than Two Miles of Dacron Rope," *Sunset Magazine*, July 1974, 142.
62. Judith Weston, "End of the Rope," *Pacific Sun*, December 14–20, 1972, 9.
63. "Enterprise: Return of the Guild," *Newsweek*, August 20, 1973, 58, 60.
64. Interviews with Alexandra Jacopetti Hart, July 18, 2014, Oakland, and October 23, 2014, Sebastopol, CA.
65. For more on *Womanhouse*, see Arlene Raven, "Womanhouse," in *The Power of Feminist Art: The American Movement of the 1970s—History and Impact*, ed. Norma Broude and Mary D. Garrard (New York: Harry N. Abrams, 1994), 48–65.
66. Faith Wilding, "By Our Own Hands," in *By Our Own Hands* (Santa Monica, CA: Double X, 1977), http://www.womanhouse.net/related-content/2016/1/24/by-our-own-hands.
67. Interview with Faith Wilding, February 12, 2010, Chicago.
68. For more on the politics of this reconstruction, and a critique of the institutional framing by which it becomes "beautiful but innocuous" in these re-creations, see Miwon Kwon, *One Place after Another: Site-Specific Art and Locational Identity* (Cambridge, MA: MIT Press, 2002), 43.
69. This is a quote from the introductory text of the spring 1969 edition of Stewart Brand's *Whole Earth Catalog* (Menlo Park, CA: Portola Institute, 1969). For the pro-globalization politics and neoliberal business models undergirding Brand's enterprise, see Fred Turner, *From Counterculture to Cyberculture: Stewart Brand, the Whole Earth Network, and the Rise of Digital Utopianism* (Chicago: University of Chicago Press, 2006). See also Andrew Blauvelt, ed., *Hippie Modernism: The Struggle for Utopia* (Minneapolis: Walker Art Center, 2015).
70. Julie Jackson, *Subversive Cross Stitch* (San Francisco: Chronicle Books, 2006); Melissa Alvarado et al., *Subversive Seamster* (Newtown, CT: Taunton, 2007).
71. Betty Christiansen, *Knitting for Peace: Make the World a Better Place One Stitch at a Time* (New York: Stewart, Tabori and Chang, 2006); Katherine Bell, *Quilting for*

Peace: Make the World a Better Place One Stitch at a Time (New York: Stewart, Tabori and Chang, 2009).

72. Betsy Greer, ed., *Craftivism: The Art of Craft and Activism* (Vancouver: Arsenal Pulp, 2014). See also Sarah Corbett, *A Little Book of Craftivism* (London: Cicada Books, 2013).
73. Betsy Greer, "Craftivist History," in *Extra/Ordinary*, ed. Buszek, 174–83.
74. Betsy Greer, *Knitting for Good!: A Guide to Creating Personal, Social, and Political Change Stitch by Stitch* (Boston: Trumpeter, 2008).
75. Renée Green, *Knitting*, video, 35 minutes (2005); my thanks to Green and Javier Anguera for alerting me to this piece and giving me access to view it in its entirety.
76. Nicole Burisch, quoted in Hiroko Tabuchi, "Etsy's Success Gives Rise to Problems of Credibility and Scale," *New York Times*, March 15, 2015.
77. Lisa Lowe, *Immigrant Acts: On Asian American Cultural Politics* (Durham, NC: Duke University Press, 1996).
78. I have been part of a rich set of dialogues around queer craft, including with Jenni Sorkin, who organized a panel at the College Art Association Annual Conference in 2009; with John Chaich, curator of *Queer Threads* at the Leslie-Lohman Museum of Gay and Lesbian Art in 2014; and with Matt Smith, who organized a panel discussion on this subject at the Victoria and Albert Museum in 2016. I look forward to Joseph McBrinn's *Queering the Subversive Stitch: Men and the Culture of Needlework* (London: Bloomsbury Academic, 2017).
79. Carlos Huneeus, *El régimen de Pinochet* (Santiago, Chile: Editorial Sudamericana, 2000).
80. Juan Gabriel Valdés, *Pinochet's Economists: The Chicago School of Economics in Chile* (Cambridge: Cambridge University Press, 1995), 30.
81. Ibid., 227.
82. Wendy Brown, *Undoing the Demos: Neoliberalism's Stealth Revolution* (New York: Zone Books, 2015), 20.
83. Silvia Federici, *Revolution at Point Zero: Housework, Reproduction, and the Feminist Struggle* (Oakland: PM Press; Brooklyn: Autonomedia, 2012).
84. Nancy Fraser, "Feminism, Capitalism, and the Cunning of History," *New Left Review* 56 (March-April 2009): 108.
85. Özlem Aslan and Zeynep Gambetti, "Provincializing Fraser's History: Feminism and Neoliberalism Revisited," *History of the Present* 1, no. 1 (Summer 2011): 130–47.
86. Another text that insists upon the necessity of longer histories, and helpfully focuses on the Greenham Common camp in the early 1980s, is Kirsty Robertson, "Rebellious Doilies and Subversive Stitches: Writing a Craftivist History," in *Extra/Ordinary*, ed. Buszek, 184–203.
87. Faythe Levine and Cortney Heimerl, *Handmade Nation: The Rise of DIY, Art, Craft, and Design* (Princeton, NJ: Princeton Architectural Press, 2008).
88. See a website of pro-life crafters, Handmade for Life, http://handmadeforlife.blogspot.com/p/shops.html.
89. Jean Zimmerman, *Made from Scratch: Reclaiming the Pleasures of the American Hearth* (New York: Free Press, 2003); Shannon Hayes, *Radical Homemakers: Reclaiming Domesticity from a Consumer Culture* (Richmondville, NY: Left to Write, 2010); Mat-

thew Crawford, *Shop Class as Soulcraft: An Inquiry into the Value of Work* (New York: Penguin, 2009).

90. Jenelle Porter, curator, *Fiber: Sculpture 1960–Present* (Boston: Institute of Contemporary Art, 2014). The largely studio-craft range of the exhibit itself was augmented by intelligent catalogue essays by Adamson and T'ai Smith.
91. Gregory Sholette, *Dark Matter: Art and Politics in the Age of Enterprise Culture* (London: Pluto, 2011).
92. Other thinkers in recent years, including Howard Risatti and Richard Sennett, have discussed the philosophical import of forms of handmaking: Sennett, *The Craftsman* (New Haven, CT: Yale University Press, 2009); Risatti, *A Theory of Craft: Function and Aesthetic Expression* (Chapel Hill: University of North Carolina Press, 2007).
93. Rick A. Lopéz, *Crafting Mexico: Intellectuals, Artisans, and the State after the Revolution* (Durham, NC: Duke University Press, 2010).
94. Rike Frank and Grant Watson, eds., *Textiles: Open Letter* (Berlin: Sternberg, 2015).
95. Janet Catherine Berlo, "Beyond Bricolage: Women and Aesthetic Strategies in Latin American Textiles," in *Textile Traditions of Mesoamerica and the Andes*, ed. Margot Blum Schevill, Janet Catherine Berlo, and Edward B. Dwyer (New York: Garland, 1991), 439.
96. I thank Rachael Matthews for discussing with me at length Cast Off's knitting demonstrations on the Circle Line in the mid-2000s.
97. In 2014 the Victoria and Albert Museum held an exhibit that collected many objects of protest cultures, including ones that are textile based: Catherine Flood and Gavin Grindon, *Disobedient Objects* (London: Victoria and Albert Museum, 2014). I contributed to the roundtable discussion published in this catalogue.
98. For more on the gendering of disability, see Alison Kafer, *Feminist, Queer, Crip* (Bloomington: Indiana University Press, 2013).
99. They have also knitted blankets and clothes for Iraqi war orphans. See http://grannypeacebrigade.org/2008/03/21/grannies-times-square-knit-in-for-peace/.
100. See https://www.pinterest.com/homesteadingctg/support-our-troops/ and http://www.operationgratitude.com/blog/tag/knitting/.

CHAPTER ONE

1. Adrienne Rich, "When We Dead Awaken," in *Diving into the Wreck: Poems 1971–1972* (New York: W. W. Norton, 1973), 5.
2. Dorothy Allison, "The Theory and Practice of the Strap-On Dildo," in *Skin: Talking about Sex, Class, and Literature* (Ithaca, NY: Firebrand Books, 1994), 130.
3. John Heidenry, *What Wild Ecstasy: The Rise and Fall of the Sexual Revolution* (New York: Simon and Schuster, 1997), 75.
4. Allison, "Theory and Practice," 131.
5. Ibid.

6. Many in the queer leather community acquire textile skills to make custom pieces; see for instance the hand-knit leather penis warmer in the Peter Thomas papers, ONE National Gay & Lesbian Archives, University of Southern California, Los Angeles.
7. Susan Sontag, "Notes on 'Camp,'" *Partisan Review* 31, no. 4 (Fall 1964): 515–30; reprinted in *Against Interpretation and Other Essays* (New York: Farrar, Straus and Giroux, 1966), 275–92.
8. Alexandra Jacopetti, *Native Funk and Flash: An Emerging Folk Art* (San Francisco: Scrimshaw, 1974).
9. Ibid.
10. Sontag, "Notes on 'Camp'"; Esther Newton, *Mother Camp: Female Impersonators in America* (Chicago: University of Chicago Press, 1979); Judith Butler, *Gender Trouble: Feminism and the Subversion of Identity* (New York: Routledge, 1990). The literature on both drag and camp is vast and includes important more recent work by Jack Halberstam, José Esteban Muñoz, and Ann Pellegrini.
11. Sontag, "Notes on 'Camp,'" 277.
12. Ibid., 282.
13. Ibid., 280.
14. Judith Butler, *Bodies That Matter: On the Discursive Limits of "Sex"* (New York: Routledge, 1993), 231.
15. Nelson Goodman, *Ways of Worldmaking* (Indianapolis: Hackett, 1978), 97.
16. Hannah Arendt, *The Human Condition*, 2nd ed. (1st ed. 1958; Chicago: University of Chicago Press, 1998), 9.
17. Goodman, *Ways of Worldmaking*, 6.
18. Lauren Berlant and Michael Warner, "Sex in Public," *Critical Inquiry* 24, no. 2 (Winter 1998): 558.
19. The David Weissman and Bill Weber documentary *The Cockettes* (2002) is to date the most comprehensive overview of the founding of the group and its demise. Photographic documentation, films, and other ephemera have been displayed in several recent exhibitions, including at San Francisco's Yerba Buena Center for the Arts (2002) and *Dear Cockettes* (2007), curated by Ida Ekblad and Anders Nordby at UKS Gallery in Oslo, Norway. The Cockettes were also featured in the exhibitions *West of Center: Art and the Counterculture Experiment in America, 1965–1977*, curated by Elissa Auther and Adam Lerner (2011), and *Hippie Modernism: The Struggle for Utopia*, curated by Andrew Blauvelt (2015). Though former members are attempting to put images and information online, many of the primary sources exist in boxes in basements, in private collections, or in the homes of the dead members' families. Some archival material can be found in the Martin Wong Papers at the Fales Special Collections of NYU and the Martin Worman papers in the New York Public Library.
20. *Myth Thing* was an Angels of Light show from 1971; as I explain, the Angels were an outgrowth of the Cockettes, and some of the membership of the two groups was shared.
21. A 2015 retrospective included a diverse range of Wong's significant contributions: Antonio Sergio Bessa and Yasmin Ramírez, *Martin Wong: Human Instamatic* (New York: Bronx Museum of the Arts, 2015).

22. Quoted in Mark Thompson, "Children of Paradise: A Brief History of Queens," in *Out in Culture: Gay, Lesbian, and Queer Essays in Popular Culture*, ed. Corey K. Creekmur and Alexander Doty (Durham, NC: Duke University Press), 452.
23. See Christopher Lonc, "Genderfuck and Its Delights," *Gay Sunshine* 21 (Spring 1974), reprinted in *Gay Roots: Twenty Years of "Gay Sunshine,"* ed. Winston Leyland (San Francisco: Gay Sunshine Press, 1991), 223–26.
24. Ibid., 225–26.
25. Robb Hernandez, *The Fire of Life: The Robert Legorreta–Cyclona Collection* (Los Angeles: UCLA Chicano Studies Research Center Press, 2009).
26. Susan Strasser, *Waste and Want: A Social History of Trash* (New York: Metropolitan Books, 1999).
27. Interview with Fayette Hauser, January 2015, San Francisco.
28. Interview with Beaver Bauer, October 10, 2008, San Francisco.
29. Other histories on alternative communities in the United States include Peter Braunstein and Michael William Doyle, eds., *Imagine Nation: The American Counterculture of the 1960s and 1970s* (New York: Routledge, 2002).
30. Interview with Bauer.
31. Interview with Hauser.
32. Thompson, "Children of Paradise," 459.
33. Maitland Zane, "Les Cockettes de San Francisco: Tinsel Tarts in a Hot Coma!," *Rolling Stone*, no. 93 (October 14, 1971), 32.
34. Ibid. Emphasis in the original.
35. *The Official Cockettes Paper Doll Book*, art by John Flowers, photography by Clay Geerdes (San Francisco: Last Gasp Eco-Funnies, 1971).
36. Interview with Hauser.
37. John Flowers, quoted in Pam Tent, *Midnight at the Palace: My Life as a Fabulous Cockette* (Los Angeles: Alyson Books, 2004), 37.
38. Interview with Scrumbly Koldewyn, January 2015, Oakland.
39. Interview with Jessica Copen, October 2008, telephone.
40. However, as the Angels became more confident in their movement and dance skills over the years, their outfits became more body-conscious and form-fitting, though no less extravagant.
41. Tent, *Midnight at the Palace*, 34.
42. Interview with Bauer.
43. Adrian Brooks, *Flights of Angels: My Life with the Angels of Light* (Vancouver, BC: Arsenal Pulp, 2008), 46.
44. Jacopetti, *Native Funk and Flash*, 5.
45. Edward Said was among the most incisive critics of this dynamic, in his *Orientalism* (New York: Vintage Books, 1978).
46. For more on some of these debates, particularly in a Canadian context, see Sandra Alfoldy, *Crafting Identity: The Development of Professional Fine Craft in Canada* (Montreal: McGill-Queen's University Press, 2005).
47. Interview with Jacopetti, October 23, 2014, Sebastopol, CA.
48. Interview with Hauser.
49. Funk artists were gathered under this rubric most prominently in an exhibition curated by Peter Selz; Selz, *Funk* (Berkeley, CA: University Art Museum, 1967).

50. Clayton Riley, "A New Black Magic—and They Weave It Well," *New York Times*, November 7, 1971, 230, 242.
51. David Talbot, *Season of the Witch: Enchantment, Terror, and Deliverance in the City of Love* (New York: Free Press, 2012), 104.
52. Scrumbly Koldewyn, "Artist Mission Statement," 2014, unpublished.
53. Quoted in Joshua Gamson, *The Fabulous Sylvester* (New York: Picador, 2006), 59.
54. Scrumbly Koldewyn, quoted in ibid., 58.
55. Interview with Bauer.
56. Such skills in crafting and design proved useful even after these groups stopped performing; Bauer now works as a professional costume designer. Former Cockette Hauser is also a noted costume and textile designer.
57. Jennie Livingston, dir., *Paris Is Burning* (1990), 71 minutes, color film. Livingston's film was criticized for its portrayal of black and brown gay men and for the absence of the white female director's voice; see bell hooks, "Is Paris Burning?," in *Black Looks: Race and Representation* (Boston: South End, 1992), 145–56.
58. For an excellent discussion of theatricality and its relationship to performativity and gender theory, see Shannon Jackson, "Theatricality's Proper Objects: Genealogies of Performance and Gender Theory," in *Theatricality*, ed. Tracy C. Davis and Thomas Postlewait (Cambridge: Cambridge University Press, 2003), 186–214.
59. Tent, *Midnight at the Palace*, 28.
60. Thompson, "Children of Paradise," 454.
61. Sontag, "Notes on 'Camp,'" 275.
62. Interview with Bauer.
63. Interview with Hauser, October 2008, Los Angeles.
64. Interview with Hauser, January 2015.
65. Ibid.
66. Tent, *Midnight at the Palace*, 30.
67. Interview with Koldewyn.
68. For more on the shifting definitions of craftsmanship, see Risatti, *Theory of Craft*, 2007.
69. Jacopetti, *Native Funk and Flash*, 46.
70. See, for example, Olivia Emery, *Craftsman Lifestyle: The Gentle Revolution* (Pasadena: California Design, 1976); this publication was brought to my attention by Glenn Adamson's "Craft and the Romance of the Studio," *American Art Journal* 21, no. 1 (Spring 2007): 14–18.
71. Theodore Roszak, *The Making of a Counter Culture: Reflections on the Technocratic Society and Its Youthful Opposition* (New York: Doubleday, 1969).
72. Jacopetti, *Native Funk and Flash*, 91.
73. Claudia Levin and Michael Fram, *Telegraph Avenue Craft Market* (Berkeley, CA: Authors, 1984).
74. For instance, the Smithsonian began to heavily promote Native crafts with the inauguration of its 1967 Festival of Folklife and the 1972 opening of the Renwick, which had an exhibition dedicated to Native work.
75. Levin and Fram, *Telegraph Avenue Craft Market*, unpaginated.
76. Zane, "Les Cockettes de San Francisco," 33.

77. Michael Owen Jones, *The Handmade Object and Its Maker* (Berkeley: University of California, 1975), 22.
78. Ibid., 23.
79. Art historian Richard Meyer has also documented another movement that sought to mend this rift, in "Back to the Effeminist Future," presented at the Museum of Modern Art, The Feminist Future conference, January 2007.
80. Interview with Copen, 2008.
81. Jo Lauria and Suzanne Baizerman, *California Design: The Legacy of West Coast Craft and Style* (San Francisco: Chronicle Books, 2005).
82. See Charles Perry, *The Haight-Ashbury: A History* (New York: Vintage Books, 1985).
83. The history of 1960s and 1970s San Francisco–area gay and lesbian scene is documented in numerous books and articles, including Elizabeth A. Armstrong, *Forging Gay Identities: Organizing Sexuality in San Francisco, 1950–1994* (Chicago: University of Chicago Press, 2002); and Susan Stryker and Jim Van Buskirk, *Gay by the Bay: A History of Queer Culture in the San Francisco Bay Area* (San Francisco: Chronicle Books, 1996). For more general histories that touch on the regional differences in the gay rights movement, see John D'Emilio, *Sexual Politics, Sexual Communities: The Making a Homosexual Minority in the United States, 1940–1970* (Chicago: University of Chicago Press, 1983); and David Eisenbach, *Gay Power: An American Revolution* (New York: Carroll and Graf, 2006).
84. Clement Greenberg, "Milton Avery," in *Art and Culture: Critical Essays* (Boston: Beacon, 1961), 200. See also Elissa Auther, "The Decorative, Abstraction, and the Hierarchy of Art and Craft in the Art Criticism of Clement Greenberg," *Oxford Art Journal* 27, no. 3 (2004): 339–64.
85. Adolf Loos, "Ornament and Crime" (1908), reprinted in Bernie Miller and Melony Ward, eds., *Crime and Ornament: The Arts and Popular Culture in the Shadow of Adolf Loos* (Toronto: YYZ Books, 2002), 29–36.
86. Hal Foster, *Design and Crime (and Other Diatribes)* (London and New York: Verso, 2002), 15.
87. Sontag, "Notes on 'Camp,'" 279.
88. Richard Dyer, *The Culture of Queers* (London: Routledge, 2002), 6.
89. See the exhibition *Deeply Superficial: Andy Warhol's "Voyeurism,"* Muscarelle Museum of Art, College of William and Mary, Williamsburg, VA, 2009–10.
90. Zane, "Les Cockettes de San Francisco," 34.
91. Ibid.
92. Joan Didion, "Slouching towards Bethlehem," *Saturday Evening Post*, 1967, reprinted in *Slouching towards Bethlehem* (New York: Farrar, Straus and Giroux, 1968), 122.
93. Ibid., 84.
94. Zane, "Les Cockettes de San Francisco," 35.
95. Christopher Reed, "Design for (Queer) Living: Sexual Identity, Performance, and Decor in British *Vogue*, 1922–1926,"*GLQ: A Journal of Lesbian and Gay Studies* 12, no. 3 (2006): 377.
96. Tent, *Midnight at the Palace*, unpaginated acknowledgments.
97. Brooks, *Flights of Angels*, 63.

98. This includes revivals of the play *Pearls over Shanghai*, screenings of the Cockettes' film *Tricia's Wedding*, and various reunions of former members. Coinciding with the contemporary renaissance in hipster crafting, *Native Funk and Flash* has become something of a sensation as well in recent years, with many do-it-yourself crafters acknowledging it as a major influence; in 2013 it was reissued with a new afterword that includes extra pictures of the Cockettes. Furthermore, Balenciaga designer Nicolas Ghesquiere admitted to copying outright a vest he saw in the book for his 2002 spring collection (Cathy Horyn, "Is Copying Really a Part of the Creative Process?" *New York Times*, April 9, 2002, B10). See also Allison Smith's writing about this book on the blog for the *Journal for Modern Craft*, http://journalofmoderncraft.com/responses/native-funk-and-flash-part-one.
99. Gamson, *Fabulous Sylvester*, 55.
100. Tent, *Midnight at the Palace*, 37.
101. Gordon H. Chang, Mark Johnson, and Paul Karlstrom, eds., *Asian American Art: A History, 1850–1970* (Stanford, CA: Stanford University Press, 2008), 260.
102. Allen Ginsberg, quoted in Tent, *Midnight in the Palace*, 37.
103. Interview with Hammond, 2007, telephone. Much information about these works came from a series of in-person interviews, phone conversations, and e-mail exchanges with Hammond, 2007–16.
104. Harmony Hammond, "Statement Accompanying Exhibition at A.I.R. Gallery, NYC, 1973," reprinted in *Wrappings: Essays on Feminism, Art, and the Martial Arts* (New York: Time and Space Limited, 1984), 9.
105. Leo Steinberg, *Other Criteria: Confrontations with Twentieth-Century Art* (New York: Oxford University Press, 1972).
106. Susan E. Bernick, "A Quilt Is an Art Object When It Stands Up like a Man," in *Quilt Culture: Tracing the Pattern*, ed. Cheryl Torsney and Judy Elsley (Columbia: University of Missouri Press, 1994), 134–50.
107. Elissa Auther, "Fiber Art and the Hierarchy of Art and Craft, 1960–80," *Journal of Modern Craft* 1, no. 1 (March 2008): 13–34.
108. Hammond was particularly inspired by George Wharton James, *Indian Basketry* (New York: Dover, 1972), first published in 1909 by Henry Malkan. She admits this text is "extremely dated" in its anthropological language but notes that it was also "ahead of its time" in its foregrounding of women's creativity (e-mail to the author, February 7, 2015).
109. Rosalind Krauss, "Grids," *October* 9 (Summer 1979): 50–64.
110. See Margaret Chin, *Sewing Women: Immigrants and the New York City Garment Industry* (New York: Columbia University Press, 2005).
111. Immanuel Ness, "Globalization and Worker Organization in New York City's Garment District," in *Sweatshop USA: The American Sweatshop in Historical and Global Perspective*, ed. Daniel E. Bender and Richard A. Greenwald (New York: Routledge, 2003), 169.
112. Jane L. Collins, *Threads: Gender, Labor, and Power in the Global Apparel Industry* (Chicago: University of Chicago Press, 2003), 34.
113. Harmony Hammond, "The Meeting of Passion and Intellect," unpublished manuscript.
114. Harmony Hammond, "Class Notes," *Heresies: A Feminist Publication on Art and*

Politics, no. 3 (Fall 1977), reprinted in *Wrappings*, 36.

115. Philip Leider, "Carl Andre," *Artforum*, February 1968, 46.

116. Carl Andre, "Letter to the Editor," *Artforum*, April 1973, 9.

117. See Jeanne Siegel, "Carl Andre: Artworker," *Studio International*, November 1970, 175–79; and Julia Bryan-Wilson, *Art Workers: Radical Practice in the Vietnam War Era* (Berkeley: University of California Press, 2009).

118. David Bourdon, "Fling, Dribble and Dip," *Life*, February 27, 1970, 62–66.

119. See, for instance, Blake Gopnik, "Stretching the Canvas: At the Katzen Center, Abstraction off the Wall," *Washington Post*, December 25, 2006, C01.

120. E-mail correspondence with the author, January 2015.

121. Hammond discovered—too late to be discussed in this book—one further transitional *Floorpiece* in the series, bringing the total number in the series to seven (two preliminary works and five resolved pieces). She speculates that this piece was made shortly after *Floorpiece I* but has titled it retrospectively *Floorpiece VII* (correspondence with the author, April 2016).

122. Gopnik, "Stretching the Canvas," C01.

123. Harmony Hammond, "Spiral," *New Art Examiner*, November 1982, reprinted in *Wrappings*, 64.

124. Harmony Hammond, *Lesbian Art in America: A Contemporary History* (New York: Rizzoli, 2000), 19.

125. Harmony Hammond, "Creating Feminist Works," in *Creating Feminist Works: A Panel Discussion from The Scholar and the Feminist V* (New York: Barnard College Women's Center, 1978), reprinted in *Wrappings*, 12.

126. Barbara Zucker, "Harmony Hammond at La Magna," *Art in America*, May-June 1976, 106.

127. Carter Ratcliff, "Harmony Hammond," *Arts*, March 1976, 7.

128. Judith Barry and Sandy Flitterman-Lewis, "Textual Strategies: The Politics of Art-Making," *Screen* 21, no. 2 (Summer 1980), reprinted in *Visibly Female: Feminism and Art Today—An Anthology*, ed. Hilary Robinson (London: Camden, 1987), 110, 112.

129. Harmony Hammond, "Lesbian Artists," in *Our Right to Love*, ed. Ginny Vida (New York: Prentice Hall, 1978), reprinted in *Wrappings*, 41.

130. Harmony Hammond, "A Sense of Touch," first version in *New Art Examiner*, Summer 1979, second version in *Heresies: A Feminist Publication on Art and Politics*, no. 12 (1981); reprinted in *Wrappings*, 80.

131. Ibid., 80.

132. Hammond, *Lesbian Art in America*, 10.

133. For more on queer orientation, see Sara Ahmed, *Queer Phenomenology: Orientations, Objects, Others* (Durham, NC: Duke University Press, 2006).

134. E-mail correspondence with the author, August 2007.

135. Paul Eli Ivey, "In the Succeeding Silence," in *Harmony Hammond: Dialogues and Meditations*, exhibition catalogue (Tucson, AZ: Museum of Contemporary Art, 2002), n.p.

136. E-mail correspondence, August 2007.

137. Harmony Hammond, "Spiral" (1982), reprinted in *Wrappings*, 65.

138. Luce Irigaray, *This Sex Which Is Not One*, trans. Catherine Porter with Carolyn Burke (Ithaca, NY: Cornell University Press, 1985).

139. Hammond, "Sense of Touch," 80.
140. Monique Wittig, *The Lesbian Body*, trans. David LeVay (New York: William Morrow, 1975).
141. For more on textiles that signify beyond the gender binary, see Jeanne Vaccaro, "Feelings and Fractals: Wooly Ecologies of Transgender Matter," *GLQ: A Journal of Lesbian and Gay Studies* 21 nos. 2-3 (2015): 273-294.
142. Sigmund Freud, "New Introductory Lectures on Psychoanalysis, 33: Femininity Lecture" (1933), in *The Standard Edition of the Complete Psychological Works of Sigmund Freud*, vol. 22, trans. and ed. James Strachey (London: Hogarth and Institute of Psycho-Analysis, 1964), 132.
143. Ibid., 117.
144. Anna C. Chave, "Outlaws: Women, Abstraction, and Painting in New York, 1967–1975," in *High Times, Hard Times: New York Painting 1967–1975*, ed. Katy Siegel (New York: Independent Curators International, 2006), 134.
145. Sontag, "Notes on 'Camp,'" 280.
146. Helen Molesworth, "Painting with Ambivalence," in *WACK! Art and the Feminist Revolution*, org. Cornelia Butler, ed. Lisa Gabrielle Mark (Los Angeles: Museum of Contemporary Art; Cambridge, MA: MIT Press, 2007), 428–439; Catherine Lord, "Their Memory Is Playing Tricks on Her: Notes towards a Calligraphy of Rage," in *WACK!*, 440–457.
147. Jill Johnston, "Dyke Nationalism and Heterosexuality," October 12, 1972, in *Admission Accomplished: The Lesbian Nation Years* (London: Serpent's Tail, 1998), 173.
148. Malik Gaines, "Through Women's Eyes," *Advocate*, July 4, 2000, 76.
149. Laura Cottingham, "Notes on *Lesbian*," *Art Journal*. 55, no. 4 (Winter 1996): 72–77.
150. "Up from the Kitchen Floor," *New York Times Magazine*, March 4, 1973, 33–34. For more on this conflict, see Lillian Faderman, *Odd Girls and Twilight Lovers: A History of Lesbian Life in 20th-Century America* (New York: Penguin, 1991), 212.
151. Harmony Hammond, "A Lesbian Show," in *Statements by Lesbian Artists* (New York: 112 Workshop, 1978), unpaginated, White Columns Archives, New York.
152. Hammond, "Lesbian Artists," in *Wrappings*, 41.
153. For more on queer gossip, see Gavin Butt, *Between You and Me: Queer Disclosures in the New York Art World, 1948–1963* (Durham, NC: Duke University Press, 2005).
154. Librarian Nancy Silverrod at the San Francisco Public Library did a great deal of etymological work for me on the history of postwar lesbian sexual slang, and I thank her for her incredible thoroughness.
155. Bruce Rodgers, *The Queens' Vernacular: A Gay Lexicon* (San Francisco: Straight Arrow Books, 1972).
156. Julia P. Stanley, "When We Say 'Out of the Closets!'" *College English*, special issue, "The Homosexual Imagination," ed. Louie Crew and Rictor Norton, 36, no. 3 (November 1974): 385. Stanley's article includes many of the phrases still in circulation among all types of queers, including *the closet*, *drag*, *coming out*, and *going down*.
157. Laura Cottingham, "Eating from the Dinner Party Plates and Other Myths, Metaphors, and Moments of Lesbian Enunciation in Feminism and in Its Art Movement," in *Sexual Politics: Judy Chicago's "Dinner Party" in Feminist Art History*, ed.

Amelia Jones (Los Angeles: Armand Hammer Museum of Art and University of California Press, 1996); this is a reading Chicago herself has disavowed.

158. Hammond, "Class Notes," 34–36.

159. Lucy R. Lippard, "Making Something from Nothing (Towards a Definition of Women's 'Hobby Art,')" *Heresies* 4 (Winter 1978): 62–65, reprinted in *Pink Glass Swan*, 130.

160. Sylvia Plath, *The Bell Jar* (1963; repr. New York: Faber's, 1995), 80.

161. See Mike Davis, *Prisoners of the American Dream* (London: Verso Books, 1986).

162. Pen Dalton, "Housewives, Leisure Crafts, and Ideology," in *Women and Craft*, ed. Gillian Elinor et.al. (London: Virago, 1987), 31.

163. Geraldine Johnson, *Weaving Rag Rugs: A Women's Craft in Western Maryland* (Knoxville: University of Tennessee Press, 1985), 137.

164. Anne Louise Kaddy, *The Braided Rug: Our American Heritage* (Auburn, MA: John Hardy, 1973).

165. Gerald W. R. Ward, ed., *Grove Encyclopedia of Materials and Techniques in Art* (Oxford: Oxford University Press, 2008), 581.

166. Shirley Teresa Wajda, "Floor Coverings," in *Material Culture in America: Understanding Everyday Life*, ed. Helen Sheumaker and Shirley Teresa Wajda (Santa Barbara, CA: ABC-CLIO, 2008), 192.

167. For more on needlework in the Colonial Revival, see Beverly Gordon, "Spinning Wheels, Samplers, and the Modern Priscilla: The Images and Paradoxes of Colonial Revival Needlework," *Winterthur Portfolio* 33, nos. 2/3 (Summer-Autumn 1998): 163–94.

168. Rosemary Troy Krill, *Early American Decorative Arts, 1620–1850: A Handbook for Interpreters* (Lanham, MD: Altamira, 2010), 251.

169. Nicholas Natanson, *The Black Image in the New Deal: The Politics of FSA Photography* (Knoxville: University of Tennessee Press, 1992), 216.

170. Carolyn Steedman, *Past Tenses: Essays on Writing, Autobiography and History* (London: Rivers Oram, 1992), 197. She revisits this statement, which importantly concerns British (not American) interiors and textile production, in Carolyn Steedman, "What a Rag Rug Means," *Journal of Material Culture* 3, no. 3 (1998): 260.

171. The Elgin Community College papers at the Illinois State Archives, where I found this photograph, has no date on record; I thank Carma Gorman for her wonderfully detailed expertise as she assisted me in dating it based on the shirt collars and hairdos of the women depicted, and I am grateful to Margaretta Lovell for putting us in touch. Unfortunately, I was unable to secure permission to reproduce this photograph.

172. For instance, see Della Duncan, *How to Make Hand Made Rag Rugs of All Kinds* (St. Louis: Duncan, 1917).

173. Joel Kopp and Kate Kopp, *Hooked Rugs in the Folk Art Tradition* (New York: Museum of American Folk Art, 1974). The rugs on display in this show were mostly pictorial in nature.

174. E-mail correspondence, January 2015.

175. Sontag, "Notes on 'Camp,'" 291.

176. Several such pairings appear under the heading "Couples" in the queer exhibition

and accompanying catalogue *In a Different Light: Visual Culture, Sexual Identity, Queer Practice*, ed. Nayland Blake, Lawrence Rinder, and Amy Scholder (San Francisco: City Lights Books, 1995).

177. E-mail correspondence, January 2015.
178. Interview with the author, May 25, 2007, telephone.
179. Cottingham, "Eating from the Dinner Party Plates," 145.
180. Barbara Hammer, "The Politics of Abstraction," in *Queer Looks: Perspectives on Lesbian and Gay Film and Video*, ed. Martha Gever, Pratibha Parmar, and John Greyson (New York: Routledge, 1993), 70.
181. Hammond, "Creating Feminist Works," 14.
182. Amy Sillman and Gregg Bordowitz, *Between Artists: Amy Sillman / Gregg Bordowitz* (New York: A.R.T., 2007), 9.
183. Conference proceedings first published in *Women Artists News*, Spring 1983, transcript by Gladys Osterman, reprinted in *Mutiny and the Mainstream: Talk That Changed Art 1975–1990*, ed. Judy Seigel (New York: Midmarch Arts, 1992), 213.

CHAPTER TWO

1. Cecilia Vicuña, "24 June 1973," in *Saborami* (Cullompton, Devon, UK: Beau Geste, 1973); u.p.; unless otherwise noted, all translations from the Spanish are mine. This title is sometimes listed as *Sabor a mí* (Spanish for "taste of me").
2. "The End of Allende," *Economist*, September 15, 1973.
3. Macarena Gómez-Barris, *Where Memory Dwells: Culture and State Violence in Chile* (Berkeley: University of California Press, 2008), 8.
4. Rosalind Krauss, "Sculpture in the Expanded Field," *October* 8 (Spring 1979): 30–44.
5. For some influential accounts of the quipu, especially its encoding of linguistic information, see Gary Urton, *The Khipus of Laguna de Los Condores / Los khipus de la Laguna de los Cóndores* (Lima: Forma e Imagen, 2008); Jeffrey Quilter and Gary Urton, eds., *Narrative Threads: Accounting and Recounting in Andean Khipu* (Austin: University of Texas Press, 2002); and Marco Curatola Petrocchi and José Carlos de la Puente Luna, eds., *El quipu colonial: Estudios y nateriales* (Lima: Universidad Católica, 2013).
6. The work might have also consisted of a single thread strung across her bedroom; this is M. Catherine de Zegher's understanding of the piece, though Vicuña has emphasized to me that the work in its original instance did not have a physical incarnation; "Ouvrage: Knot a Not, Notes as Knots," in *The Precarious: The Art and Poetry of Cecilia Vicuña*, ed. M. Catherine de Zegher (Hanover, NH: University Press of New England, 1997), 34. In Vicuña's own archive I have located a journal entry dated 1970 that refers to "a quipu that remembers nothing," including a small drawing that was made in preparation for a exhibit, but this notation came after the piece (which consisted solely of the thought).
7. "Knot a Quipu," video interview by Sabrina Gschwandtner, 2005, New York.
8. Interview with Cecilia Vicuña, October 2013, New York City.
9. For one of the earliest definitions of dematerialization in art, see Oscar Masotta,

"Después del Pop, nosotros desmaterializamos (After Pop, We Dematerialize)," given at the Instituto Di Tella in Buenos Aires, Argentina, July 21, 1967, reprinted in Mari Carmen Ramírez and Héctor Olea, *Inverted Utopias: Avant-Garde Art in Latin America* (Houston: Museum of Fine Arts, 2004), 532–33. I have written about conceptual art's connections to ostensibly "dematerialized" labor: Julia Bryan-Wilson, *Art Workers: Radical Practice in the Vietnam War Era* (Berkeley: University of California Press, 2009).

10. Quipus are now found in Santiago's Museo Chileno de Arte Precolombino, which opened in 1981. Vicuña recalls that she first saw a quipu in a book in 1966 in her aunt Rosa's library; it is possible the book was written in any of several languages, including Spanish, Portuguese, or English, as her aunt had lived in New York and São Paulo and had traveled abroad extensively. Given what was available in the 1950s and 1960s, the book was not likely to have been entirely devoted to quipus but rather some other general-audience text that included an image of a quipu. Overviews of the quipu and its uses that she might have encountered include Carlos Radicati di Primeglio, *Introducción al estudio de los quipus* (Lima: Biblioteca de la Sociedad Peruana de Historia, 1951).
11. See, for instance, Mme de Grafigny, *Letters Written by a Peruvian Princess* (Dublin: Printed for S. Powell by Thomas Moore, 1748).
12. One such account is Marcia Ascher and Robert Ascher, *Code of the Quipu: A Study in Media, Mathematics, and Culture* (Ann Arbor: University of Michigan Press, 1981). My thanks to Lisa Trever for help with the historiography of the quipu since the eighteenth century.
13. Chronology in *Cecilia Vicuña* (London: England, 2013), 17; and interview with Vicuña, April 2015, New York.
14. Gary Urton, "An Overview of Spanish Colonial Commentary on Andean Knotted-String Records," in *Narrative Threads*, ed. Quilter and Urton.
15. Frank Salomon, *The Cord Keepers: Khipus and Cultural Life in a Peruvian Village* (Durham, NC: Duke University Press, 2004).
16. She used an assumed name for this BBC documentary, Maria Santiago (BBC London, 12 minutes, 1973). See also Dawn Adès, "Cecilia Vicuña's *Calcomanías*," in *Cecilia Vicuña*, 5; and Cecilia Vicuña, "The Diaguita Opera Singer," in *Spit Temple: The Selected Performances of Cecilia Vicuña*, ed. and trans. Rosa Alcalá (Brooklyn: Ugly Duckling Presse, 2012), 53.
17. Patricia Richards, *Race and the Chilean Miracle: Neoliberalism, Democracy, and Indigenous Rights* (Pittsburgh: University of Pittsburgh Press, 2013), 66.
18. Vicuña's work within and around poetry is significant, including coediting an anthology on Latin American poetry: Cecilia Vicuña and Ernesto Livon-Grosman, eds., *The Oxford Book of Latin American Poetry* (New York: Oxford University Press, 2009). Many scholarly texts about her poetry mention her visual work, as she works fluidly across and between words and art; see Hugo Méndez-Ramírez, "Cryptic Weaving," in *The Precarious*, 59–71. Her poetry also sits on the page in an insistently visual manner; see for instance Cecilia Vicuña, *Palabrarmas* (Buenos Aires: El Imaginero, 1984).
19. De Zegher, "Ouvrage: Knot a Not, Notes as Knots," in *The Precarious*, ed. De Zegher, 19.

20. For one look specifically at the women's work of the Mapuche in southern Chile, see Angélica Willson, *Textilería mapuche, arte de mujeres* (Santiago: CEDEM, 1992).
21. Blenda Femenías, "Regional Dress of the Colca Valley, Peru: A Dynamic Tradition," in *Textile Traditions of Mesoamerica and the Andes* (New York: Garland, 1991), 188.
22. Willson, *Textilería mapuche*, 11.
23. Vicuña, "El Ande futuro," in *The Precarious*, ed. de Zegher, 98.
24. Vicuña, "The Glove," *The Precarious*, 22.
25. Femenías, "Regional Dress of the Colca Valley, Peru," 180.
26. Vicuña, "Head Net," in *The Precarious*, 27. Vicuña has explained that the title came much later than the piece itself, after she became aware of a Mayan god of the scribes with a similar name. Interview with Cecilia Vicuña, January 2015, telephone.
27. Vicuña, "Knot a Quipu," 2005.
28. One of her notebooks from 1965 lists books she wanted to buy, including William Seitz's *The Art of Assemblage* (New York: Museum of Modern Art, 1961), which includes both Picasso and Schwitters.
29. Interview with Cecilia Vicuña, October 2013, New York.
30. For more on Albers's relationship to Andean textiles, see Virginia Gardner Troy, *Anni Albers and Ancient American Textiles: From Bauhaus to Black Mountain* (Burlington, VT: Ashgate, 2002).
31. The "social life" of Andean textiles is addressed in Denise Y. Arnold and Elvira Espejo, *El textil tridimensional: La naturaleza del tejido como objeto y como sujeto* (La Paz, Bolivia: ILCA, 2013).
32. The economic and social turmoil within Chile after the election of Allende was exacerbated by pressures from the US, which ultimately backed Pinochet and the coup.
33. Quoted in Lucy R. Lippard, "Spinning the Common Thread," in *The Precarious*, 9.
34. Sol LeWitt, "Sentences on Conceptual Art," *0–9*, no. 5 (January 1969): 3–5.
35. Vicuña, *Saborami*, u.p.
36. De Zegher, in *The Precarious*, 21.
37. Vicuña, "24 June 1973."
38. Vicuña, in *The Precarious*, 40.
39. Paulina Varas Alarcón, *Catalina Parra: El fantasma político del arte* (Santiago, Chile: Ediciones Metales Pesados, 2011).
40. Jailee Rychen, "Stitching Together Reality," gallery brochure, Ludlow 38 (New York), 2011.
41. Guy Brett, "Sharing Art," *Times* (London), July 16, 1974, 7.
42. Interview with Vicuña, January 2015.
43. This is the 1974 handwritten version of this text; it varies slightly from the typed statement.
44. In *Saborami* she drew a mummy that is also a puppet, with strings pulled by the CIA. The little figure not only evokes these right-wing "mummies" but could also reference the doll-like mummies found in the Atacama Desert in the north of Chile, though Vicuña feels sure she would not have yet been aware of them.
45. This comprehensive history can be found in Peter Winn, *Weavers of Revolution:*

The Yarur Workers and Chile's Road to Socialism (New York: Oxford University Press, 1986).

46. Ibid., 4.
47. Ibid., 84.
48. Patricia Richards discusses how Chile's neoliberal economic policies have also been undergirded by systemic racism against indigenous populations (Richards, *Race and the Chilean Miracle*).
49. See Cathy Lisa Schneider, *Shantytown Protest in Pinochet's Chile* (Philadelphia: Temple University Press, 1995), 91–92, and Peter Winn, "'No Miracle for Us': The Textile Industry in the Pinochet Era, 1973–1988," in *Victims of the Chilean Miracle: Workers and Neoliberalism in the Pinochet Era, 1972–2002*, ed. Winn (Durham, NC: Duke University Press, 2004), 125–63.
50. Rosa Alcalá, "'Made Not of Words, but Forces': Cecilia Vicuña's Oral Performances," in *Spit Temple*, 119.
51. An overview of the political theater in Chile at this time can be found in Luis Pradenas, "El teatro en la calle," in *Teatro en Chile: Huellas y trayectorias, siglos XVI–XX* (Santiago, Chile: LOM Editions, 2006). For more on the Cordero play, see Catherine M. Boyle, *Chilean Theater, 1973–1985: Marginality, Power, Selfhood* (Cranbury, NJ: Associated University Presses, 1992), 39–40.
52. Interview with Cecilia Vicuña, April 2015, New York.
53. John Dugger, "Notes on the Big Chile Vencerá Banner (Profiles and Analysis)," unpublished manuscript, London, 1976.
54. Guy Brett, "An Energy Runs through It: On the Participation Art of John Dugger," in *John Dugger: Ergonic Messenger* (London: England, 2010), 6.
55. John Walker, *Left Shift: Radical Art in 1970s Britain* (London: I. B. Taurus, 2002), 124.
56. Ann Jones, *No Truck with the Chilean Junta! Trade Union Internationalism, Australia and Britain, 1973–1980* (Canberra: Australian National University Press, 2014), 71–72.
57. Interview with Vicuña, January 2015.
58. Interview with Vicuña, October 2013.
59. More on this work, and others by CADA, can be found in Robert Alan Neustadt, *CADA Día: La creación de un arte social* (Santiago, Chile: Cuarto Propio, 2001), 25–30. In his statement for *Para no morir*, Raúl Zurita, a member of CADA, wrote, "My work is like a glass of milk spilt under the blue sky"; quoted in Nelly Richard, *Margins and Institutions: Art in Chile since 1973* (Melbourne: Art and Text, 1986), 82.
60. Vicuña, quoted in Neustadt, *CADA Día*, 181. The Toronto action was performed by Eugenio Téllez.
61. Vicuña, "Crimen lechero," in *Spit Temple*, 82.
62. Neustadt, *CADA Día*, 29.
63. Ibid.
64. Richard, *Margins and Institutions*, 17.
65. Quoted in *Spit Temple*, ed. Alcalá, 16.
66. Vicuña, "Quipu Menstrual (2006)," www.ceciliavicuna.com.
67. Ibid.
68. Cristina Arancibia et al., *Del otro lado: Arte contemporáneo de mujeres en Chile* (Santiago: Centro Cultural Palacio de La Moneda, 2006).

69. See Richard, *Margins and Institutions*, 57–61.

70. For more on Daniela Rivera's connections to CADA, see Liz Munsell, "Re-enmarcando los muros," in *Muros* (Santiago: Museo de Arte Contemporáneo, 2013), 51.

71. Richard, *Margins and Institutions*, 65.

72. See Silvia Japkin, report on the Encuentro del Comité Nacional de Conservación Textil, *Datatèxtil*, no. 10 (2004): 60–61.

73. Ximena Valdés et al., *Memoria y cultura: Femenino y masculino en los oficios artesanales* (Santiago: CEDEM, 1993), 81–82.

74. Daniela Rivera, artist's statement, 2012.

75. Chilean anthropologist Alejandro Lipschutz coined the term *pigmentocracy* to refer to the collusion between hierarchies of racism and colorism in the Americas; Alejandro Lipschutz, *El indoamericanismo y el problema racial en las Américas* (Santiago: Editorial Nascimento, 1944).

76. The precise number of those arrested and executed during the coup is not fully known; official accounts recognize over 3,000 as missing or killed, with some 38,000 detained and/or tortured. For more on the disappeared under Pinochet, see Elías Padilla Ballesteros, *La memoria y el olvido: Detenidos desaparecidos en Chile* (Santiago: Ediciones Orígenes, 1995).

77. In Chile, *saco* is a more commonly used term for burlap than *arpillera*. Many of the specificities of Chilean terminology have been clarified for me by Cristóbal Lehyt and Pablo Seward.

78. Henry Glassie, "Folk Art," in *Material Culture Studies in America*, ed. Thomas J. Schlereth (Landham, MD: Altamira, 1981), 130.

79. See, for instance, the contributions in Eli Bartra, ed., *Crafting Gender: Women and Folk Art in Latin America and the Caribbean* (Durham, NC: Duke University Press, 2003).

80. Eliana Moya-Raggio, "Arpilleras: Chilean Culture of Resistance," *Feminist Studies* 10, no. 2 (Summer 1984): 281.

81. Néstor García Canclini, *Hybrid Cultures: Strategies for Entering and Leaving Modernity*, trans. Christopher L. Chiappari and Silvia López (Minneapolis: University of Minnesota Press, 1995), 175.

82. For more on the founding of the Vicaría and its role in Pinochet's Chile, see Juan Ignacio Gutiérrez Fuentes, *Chile, la Vicaría de la Solidaridad* (Madrid: Alianza Editoriale, 1986); Jaime Esponda, "Objetivos y criterios estratégicos aplicados por la Vicaría de la Solidaridad del Arzobispado de Santiago en su tarea de defensa de los derechos humanos," in *Represión política y defensa de los derechos humanos*, ed. Hugo Frühling (Santiago: Ediciones Chile y América, 1986), 107–39; and Nubia Becker and Oswald Torres, *Sistematización de la experiencia de defensa de los derechos humanos en Chile* (Santiago: ALDHU, 1992).

83. Interview with Maria Eugenia (Winnie) Lira, January 2013, Santiago.

84. There were many such articles. See, for instance, "Los tapices de la difamación," *La Segunda* (Santiago), April 11, 1978; "La propaganda subversiva," *La Tercera*, April 17, 1980.

85. For a basic account of the fire, see *Memorias para construir la paz (Cronología), 1977–1980* (Santiago: Fundación Documentación y Archivo de La Vicaría de la Soli-

daridad); for more on harassment of Vicaría workers, see Steve J. Stern, *Battling for Hearts and Minds: Memory Struggles in Pinochet's Chile, 1973–1988* (Durham, NC: Duke University Press, 2006).

86. Interview with Verónica Sánchez, conservator, Museo de la Memoria y los Derechos Humanos, January 2013, Santiago.

87. An illustrated catalogue of portions of the museum's collection was published in 2012: *Arpilleras: Colección del Museo de la Memoria y los Derechos Humanos* (Santiago: Ocho Libros Editores, 2012).

88. *Arpilleras: Otra forma de denuncia* (Chile: Agrupación de Familiares de Detenidos-Desaparecidos, ca. 1985).

89. Marjorie Agosín, *Scraps of Life: Chilean Arpilleras*, trans. Cola Franzen (Trenton, NJ: Red Sea, 1987), and *Tapestries of Hope, Threads of Love: The Arpillera Movement in Chile*, 2nd ed., foreword by Isabel Allende (Lanham, MD: Rowman and Littlefield, 2007); Jacqueline Adams, *Surviving Dictatorship: A Work of Visual Sociology* (New York: Routledge, 2012), and *Art against Dictatorship: Making and Exporting Arpilleras under Pinochet* (Austin: University of Texas Press, 2013).

90. Roberta Bacic, ed. and curator, *Arpilleras de la resistencia política chilena* (Brasília: Biblioteca Nacional, 2012). For more on women's workshops and arpilleras of Peru, see Gaby Franger, *Arpilleras: Cuadros que hablan* (Lima: Betaprint, 1988).

91. Guy Brett, "All This We Have Seen," in *Through Our Own Eyes: Popular Art and Modern History* (London: GMP, 1986), 29–54; Lucy R. Lippard, *Get the Message?: A Decade of Art for Social Change* (New York: E. P. Dutton, 1984).

92. I have seen the arpilleras in the collections of the Museo de la Memoria y los Derechos Humanos; Museo de la Solidaridad Salvador Allende; Fundación Salvador Allende; and the private collection of Lira—all in Santiago. I have also consulted the digital archives of the Biblioteca Nacional de Chile, the Fundación Documentación y Archivo de la Vicaría de la Solidaridad (both in Santiago), and the Royal Alberta Museum in Canada.

93. Adams, *Art against Dictatorship*, 74.

94. Some of these precedents are listed in Agosín, *Scraps of Life*, 49–50, and in Adams, *Art against Dictatorship*, 66–68. Panamanian *molas* and patchwork as a "foreign fashion very much in vogue at the time" are described by the testimony of artist and key volunteer Valentina Bonne in Agosín, *Tapestries of Hope*, 96–97. See also the account of Bonne's centrality to the development of arpilleras, August 2007, housed in the archives of the Fundación Salvador Allende. Adams elaborates on the speculative connections with Parra, and those who refuse such connections, in *Art against Dictatorship*, 61.

95. For more on Peruvian arpilleras, see Olga González, "Juana Huaytalla Mendez: Peruvian *Arpillerista*," in *Weavings of War: Fabrics of Memory*, ed. Ariel Zeitlin Cooke and Marsha MacDowell (East Lansing: Michigan State University, 2005), 69–74.

96. Interview with Lira, 2013; and interview with Verónica Sánchez, 2013.

97. Interview with Vicuña, October 2013. She has described her arpillera to me as an embroidered landscape with boats, people, and houses depicted without linear perspective, given to her by a cousin who was friends with Violeta Parra.

98. Peter Kornbluh, *The Pinochet File: A Declassified Dossier on Atrocity and Accountability* (New York: New Press, 2003), 43.

99. For photographic documentation of violent protest, murals, and street art under Pinochet, see Ariel Chabalgoity, Sengo Pérez, and Roger Rodríguez, *Chile: La derrota del miedo* (Montevideo: Puntosur Editores, 1988). See also the articles on populist murals of the Brigada Ramona Parra and other dissident art, including a piece by David Kunzle on arpilleras, in *Chile vive* (Mexico City: Centro de Estudios Económicos y Sociales del Tercer Mundo, 1982), 80–90.
100. "Tapetes interceptados," *La Segunda*, July 26, 1978.
101. See Cynthia Brown, *La Vicaría de la Solidaridad en Chile* (New York: Americas Watch, 1987), and other documents in the Fundación Documentación y Archivo de la Vicaría de la Solidaridad, Santiago.
102. "Vicaría niega que patrocine tarea artesanal politizada," *La Segunda*, April 7, 1978.
103. Interview with Lira, 2013.
104. Agosín dates the first workshop to March 1974, when artist Bonne gave women affiliated with the disappeared cloth and encouraged them to sew; *Tapestries of Hope*, 45. Adams says the first unemployed women's workshops began in 1975: *Art against Dictatorship*, 54.
105. Brett, *Through Our Own Eyes*, 29.
106. This quote comes from the twenty-five-minute documentary *Las partes del todo*, directed by Natalia Arcos and Gabriela Vergara (Santiago: ARTV, 2009), in which a group of nine arpilleristas were interviewed.
107. Agosín, *Scraps of Life*, 79.
108. Ibid., 90.
109. Adams, *Surviving Dictatorship*, 11.
110. Emma Sepúlveda, introduction to *We, Chile: Personal Testimonies of the Chilean Arpilleristas* (Falls Church, VA: Azul Editions, 1996), 32.
111. Agosín, "Arpilleras of Chile: Using Art as a Teaching Tool," *Heresies: A Feminist Publication on Art and Politics* 22 (1987): 33; and *Arpilleras: Lebensbilder aus Chile: Frauenbewegung und Diktatur* (Braunschweig, Germany: Labyrinth, 1989).
112. Agosín, *Scraps of Life*, 14.
113. Elsa Chaney, *Supermadre: Women in Politics in Latin America* (Austin: University of Texas Press, 1979).
114. Adams, *Surviving Dictatorship*, 9.
115. Adams, *Art against Dictatorship*, 141.
116. Agosín, *Tapestries of Hope*, 58.
117. Adams, *Art against Dictatorship*, 13.
118. Adams, *Surviving Dictatorship*, 10.
119. Adriana Rojas, quoted in Agosín, *Tapestries of Hope*, 161.
120. Adams, *Surviving Dictatorship*, 207.
121. Hernán Vera, "Arpilleras: An Iconography of Contemporary Childhood," *Children's Literature* 15 (1987): 162.
122. Quoted in Sepúlveda, *We, Chile*, 110.
123. Interview with Lira, 2013.
124. Interview with Carla Miranda, January 2013, Santiago.
125. For more on the complex ideological role played by CEMA, see Teresa Valdés and Marisa Weinstein, *Mujeres que sueñan: Las organizaciones de pobladoras en Chile, 1973–1989* (Santiago: FLASCO, 1993); and Gwynn Thomas, *Contesting Legitimacy in*

Chile: Familial Ideals, Citizenship, and Political Struggle, 1970–1990 (University Park, PA: Penn State Press, 2011).

126. *Military Ideology and the Dissolution of Democracy: Women in Chile* (London: CHANGE International Reports, 1981), 18.

127. Ibid., 16. See also Norbert Lechner and Susana Levy, *El disciplinamiento de la mujer* (Santiago: FLASCO, 1984).

128. Julieta Kirkwood, *Ser política en Chile: Las feministas y los partidos* (Santiago: Facultad Latinoamericana de Ciencias Sociales, 1986).

129. Camila Fernanda Sastre Díaz, "Reflexiones sobre la politización de las arpilleristas chilenas (1973–1990)," *Revista Sociedad & Equidad*, no. 2 (July 2011): 364–77.

130. Torture is defined as the "intentional infliction" of harm or suffering to someone to obtain information or a confession; see Nubia Becker and Oswaldo Torres, *Sistematización de la experiencia de defensa de los derechos humanos en Chile* (Santiago: Asociación Latinoamericano para los Derechos Humanos, 1992) 34–35.

131. See, for instance, Schneider, *Shantytown Protest*, 86.

132. Nubia Becker, quoted in Mark Ensalaco, *Chile under Pinochet: Recovering the Truth* (Philadelphia: University of Pennsylvania Press, 1999), 93.

133. Price list from the Fundación Solidaridad, Lira personal archive.

134. Marvine Howe, "Chile's Women Sew a Protest Message in Folk Art Hangings," *New York Times*, November 14, 1984.

135. Interview with Lira, 2013.

136. Joel R. Pruce, "Constituencies of Compassion: The Politics of Human Rights and Consumerism," in *The Uses and Misuses of Human Rights: A Critical Approach to Advocacy*, ed. George Andreopoulos and Zehra F. Kabaskal Arat (New York: Palgrave Macmillan, 2014), 198.

137. Agosín, *Scraps of Life*, 48.

138. More on the formation of the folklore groups can be found in Adams, *Art against Dictatorship*; Agosín, *Scraps of Life*; and Sepúlveda, *We, Chile*.

139. A detailed look at the *cueca sola* is in Agosín, "The Dance of Life: Women and Human Rights in Chile," in *Dance, Human Rights, and Social Justice: Dignity in Motion*, ed. Naomi Jackson and Toni Shapiro-Phim (Lanham, MD: Scarecrow, 2008), 296–304.

140. María de la Luz Hurtado, "La memoria en el teatro chileno actual: Subjetividad e historia," in *El teatro y su crítica*, ed. Osvaldo Pellettieri (Buenos Aires: Galerna, 1998), 118.

141. David Benavente, *Pedro, Juan y Diego; Tres Marías y una Rosa* (Santiago: CESOC, Ediciones ChileAmérica, 1989), 176.

142. Alice A. Nelson, *Political Bodies: Gender, History, and the Struggle for Narrative Power in Recent Chilean Literature* (Lewisburg, PA: Bucknell University Press, 2002), 100.

143. Neustadt, *CADA Día*, 153.

144. Interview with Lira, 2013.

145. Eliana Moya-Raggio, "Arpilleras: Chilean Culture in Resistance," *Feminist Studies* 10, no. 2 (Summer 1984): 277–90.

146. Peter Kornbluh, introduction to Agosín, *Tapestries of Hope*, 9.

147. Ruth Robinson, "Needlework Stories Tell of Chilean Life," *New York Times*, October 22, 1989.

148. *Dignidad Hecha a Mano: 30 Años* (Santiago: Fundación Solidaridad, 2005), 57.
149. For more on the March of the Pots and Pans, see Margaret Power, *Right-Wing Women in Chile: Feminine Power and the Struggle against Allende, 1964–1973* (University Park, PA: Penn State Press, 2002).

CHAPTER THREE

1. According to one scholar, *Felix* is a singular instance of a contemporary Canadian art photograph of a deceased person; see Penny Cousineau-Levine, *Faking Death: Canadian Art Photography and the Canadian Imagination* (Montreal: McGill-Queen's Press, 2003), 63–64.
2. AA Bronson, speaking in the short video "Singular Visions" (New York: Whitney Museum of American Art, 2011).
3. Eve Sedgwick, *Touching Feeling: Affect, Pedagogy, Performativity* (Durham, NC: Duke University Press, 2003), 13.
4. Ibid., 14.
5. The statistics of the Quilt are ever-changing; updates can be found on the NAMES Project website, http://www.aidsquilt.org/about.
6. Kevin Michael DeLuca, Christine Harold, and Kenneth Rufo, "Q.U.I.L.T.: A Patchwork of Reflections," *Rhetoric and Public Affairs* 10, no. 4 (Winter 2007): 627.
7. DeLuca, Harold, and Rufo, "Q.U.I.L.T.: A Patchwork of Reflections," in *Remembering the* AIDS *Quilt*, ed. Charles E. Morris III (East Lansing: Michigan State Press, 2011), 78.
8. Milk's political career and his assassination are chronicled in Randy Shilts, *The Mayor of Castro Street: The Life and Times of Harvey Milk* (New York: St. Martin's, 1982).
9. Cleve Jones, *Stitching a Revolution: The Making of an Activist* (San Francisco: HarperSanFrancisco, 2000), 107.
10. David Román, *Acts of Intervention: Performance, Gay Culture, and* AIDS (Bloomington: Indiana University Press, 1998), 31–32.
11. For a close tracking of the Reagan administration's response to AIDS, see Jennifer Brier, *Infectious Ideas: U.S. Political Response to the* AIDS *Crisis* (Chapel Hill: University of North Carolina Press, 2009).
12. Richard Meyer, "Rock Hudson's Body," in *Inside/Out: Lesbian Theories, Gay Theories*, ed. Diana Fuss (New York: Routledge, 1991), 259–88.
13. Cleve Jones, quoted in Cindy Ruskin, *The Quilt: Stories from The NAMES Project* (New York: Pocket Books, 1988), 12.
14. Jones, quoted in Ruskin, *Quilt*, 18.
15. The "SILENCE=DEATH" poster was designed in 1986 but not widely wheat-pasted around New York City until 1987. Avram Finkelstein, correspondence with the author, February 2015.
16. Douglas Crimp and Adam Rolston, AIDS *Demo Graphics* (Seattle: Bay, 1990), 14.
17. Finkelstein, correspondence with the author, February 2015.
18. An immense literature exists on the history of American quilts; for one overview,

see Robert Shaw, *American Quilts: The Democratic Art 1780–2007* (New York: Sterling, 2009).

19. "Textiles," in *Material Culture in America: Understanding Everyday Life*, ed. Helen Sheumaker and Shirley Teresa Wajda (Santa Barbara, CA: ABC-CLIO, 2008), 443.
20. Jones, *Stitching a Revolution*, 108.
21. Patricia Mainardi, "Quilts: The Great American Art," *Feminist Art Journal* 2, no. 1 (Winter 1973): 18–23; reprinted as *Quilts: The Great American Art* (San Pedro: Miles and Weir, 1978).
22. For two examples that bookend the 1980s, see Elaine Hedges, "Quilts and Women's Culture," in *In Her Own Image: Women Working in the Arts*, ed. Elaine Hedges and Ingrid Wendt (Old Westbury, NY: Feminist Press, 1980), 13–19; Faith Wilding and Miriam Schapiro, "Cunts/Quilts/Consciousness," *Heresies: A Feminist Publication on Art and Politics* 6, no. 4 (1989): 6–17.
23. Jones, *Stitching a Revolution*, 108.
24. Miriam Schapiro and Melissa Meyer, "Waste Not, Want Not: An Inquiry into What Women Saved and Assembled—FEMMAGE," *Heresies* 1, no. 4 (Winter 1977–78): 66–69.
25. Penny McMorris and Michael Kile, *The Art Quilt* (San Francisco: Quilt Digest Press, 1986).
26. Kristen McKenna, "Avant-Garde Exhibit Takes Quilt beyond Cozy Image," *Los Angeles Times*, November 5, 1986.
27. Durant's role in the founding of the AIDS Quilt has been debated; I am choosing to name him here as Jones's close collaborator.
28. James L. Ferrigan, "The Evolution and Adaptation of the Rainbow Flag in San Francisco," *Flag Bulletin* 130 (1989): 116–22.
29. Jones, *Stitching the Revolution*, 123.
30. Ibid., 126.
31. Typed flyer, February 1987, NAMES Project ephemera file, GLBT Historical Society archives, San Francisco.
32. Jones, quoted in Ruskin, *Quilt*, 12.
33. Cara O'Connor, e-mail correspondence with the author, April 3, 2016.
34. *NAMESletter* 1, no. 1 (December 1987); GLTB Historical Society.
35. Interview with Mike (Mac) McNamara, March 2015, San Francisco.
36. Mark C. Donovan, "The Problem with Making AIDS Comfortable: Federal Policy Making and the Rhetoric of Innocence," *Journal of Homosexuality* 32, nos. 3–4 (1997): 115–44.
37. For one description of a tradition of community quilt gifting, see Dorothy R. Zopf, "Surviving the Winter: The Evolution of Quiltmaking among Two Cultures in New Mexico," in *Women Artists of the American West*, ed. Susan R. Ressler (Jefferson, NC: McFarland, 2003), 19–36.
38. Katherine Bishop, "Denying AIDS Its Sting: A Quilt of Life," *New York Times*, October 5, 1987.
39. Interview with Julie Rhoad, November 2010, Atlanta.
40. Linda Pershing, *The Ribbon around the Pentagon: Peace by Piecemakers* (Knoxville: University of Tennessee Press, 1996).

41. Don Wilcox, "Peace Ribbon Wraps Washington in Largest Collaborative Craft Event in American History," *Craft Report*, October 1985, 10.
42. Pershing, *Ribbon around the Pentagon*, 3.
43. Jane Przybysz, "Quilts and Women's Bodies," in *Bodylore*, ed. Katharine Young (Knoxville: University of Tennessee Press, 1993), 175.
44. "Quilt of Love: Those Who Had AIDS Remembered," *Austin American-Statesman*, August 2, 1987.
45. NAMES Project website, http://www.aidsquilt.org/about/the-names-project-foundation.
46. Interview with Gert McMullin, November 2010, Atlanta.
47. The National Museum of Funeral Arts has on display a floral ribbon mourning quilt from the 1920s, described as one of "very few floral ribbons [sic] mourning quilts in existence today, because of the deterioration of the ribbon fabric over the years." Wall text, National Museum of Funeral Arts, Houston.
48. For more on passage quilts, see Sabrina Gschwandtner, "Passage Quilts," *Fiber-Arts*, November/December 2008, 48–51; and Carol Williams Gebel, *Passage Quilts: Quilts Wrap the Deceased for Burial and Line Coffins* (San Francisco: Uncoverings, 1995).
49. T. D. Vacalis, P. J. Shoemaker, and A. McAlister, "A Baseline Study of AIDS in Texas: Knowledge, Attitudes, Behaviors," *Tex Med* 85, no. 6 (June 1989): 74–79.
50. Erika Doss, *Memorial Mania: Public Feeling in America* (Chicago: University of Chicago, 2010), 154–55.
51. Jane Bennett, *Vibrant Matter* (Durham, NC: Duke University Press, 2010), 5.
52. Ellen Uzelac, "Patchwork of Memories," *Milwaukee Journal*, June 12, 1988, 4G.
53. Interview with McNamara, 2015.
54. "How to Make a Panel," flyer, GLBT Historical Society archives.
55. Interview with McMullin, 2010.
56. Ruskin, *Quilt*, 27.
57. Robert Epstein and Jeffrey Friedman, dirs., *Common Threads: Stories from the Quilt* (Telling Pictures, 1989).
58. Form letter from the NAMES Project, September 20, 1987, in the GLBT Historical Society archives, NAME Project ephemera file.
59. Schedule of Quilt Readers, October 11, 1987, Richard Chenault Papers, GLBT Historical Society archives.
60. "Entire Quilt Displayed for Nation, " *NAMESLetter* 6, no. 1 (Winter 1992/1993): 1.
61. Jim Fox, "Rain Doesn't Dampen Hawaiian Spirits," *NAMESLetter* 3, no. 1 (Spring 1990): 1–2.
62. *The AIDS Quilt Songbook* (Boosey and Hawkes Music, 1993).
63. "Kansans Add New Panels to AIDS Quilt," *Lawrence Journal-World*, December 1, 1991, 3A.
64. Gary Bauer, "AIDS and the College Student," *Campus Review* 3, no. 8 (November 1987): 1.
65. "'Gerbils' Quilt Sparks Controversy," *Daily Iowan*, July 17, 1991, 1.
66. For more on the mythic lore of gerbiling, see Norine Dresser, "The Case of the Missing Gerbil," *Western Folklore* 53, no. 3 (July 1994): 229–42.

67. Daniel Harris, "Making Kitsch from AIDS: A Disease with a Gift Shop of Its Own," *Harper's Magazine* 298, no. 1730 (July 1994): 55–56.
68. See Van E. Hillard, "Census, Consensus, and the Commodification of Form," in *Quilt Culture: Tracing the Pattern*, ed. Cheryl B. Torsney and Judy Elsley (Columbia: University of Missouri Press, 1994), 112–24.
69. Visual AIDS has also done critical work supporting HIV positive artists and archiving their art.
70. Interview with Julie Davids, March 2011, telephone.
71. Jones, *Stitching the Revolution*, 127.
72. Les Wright, "San Francisco," in *Queer Sites: Gay Urban Histories since 1600*, ed. David Higgs (London: Routledge, 1999), 185.
73. Frank A. Conway, "CS People to Watch: Cleve Jones," *Christopher Street* 11, no. 2, issue 122 (May 1988): 39.
74. Cleve Jones, quoted in Marita Sturken, *Tangled Memories: The Vietnam War, the* AIDS *Epidemic, and the Politics of Remembering* (Berkeley: University of California Press, 1997), 195.
75. "DC96 Drumbeat Campaign," *NAMESLetter* 9, no. 1 (Spring 1996): 6.
76. Cleve Jones, quoted in Ruskin, *Quilt*, 19.
77. Erin Rand, "Repeated Remembrance: Commemorating the AIDS Quilt and Resuscitating the Mourned Subject," *Rhetoric and Public Affairs* 10, no. 4 (Winter 2007): 655.
78. "The NAMES Project: National Tour," 1988, commemorative brochure, GLBT Historical Society archives.
79. Douglas Crimp, "The Spectacle of Mourning," in *Melancholia and Moralism: Essays on* AIDS *and Queer Politics* (Cambridge, MA: MIT Press, 2002), 198.
80. Christopher Capozzola, "A Very American Epidemic: Memory Politics and Identity Politics in the AIDS Memorial Quilt, 1985–1993," *Radical History Review* 82 (Winter 2002): 91–109.
81. Jones, *Stitching the Revolution*, 107.
82. Crimp, "Spectacle of Mourning," 200.
83. Mainardi, "Quilts," 37.
84. This history is articulated in Gladys-Marie Fry, *Stitched from the Soul: Slave Quilts from the Antebellum South* (New York: Museum of American Folk Art, 1990); and Jacqueline Tobin and Raymond Dobard, *Hidden in Plain View: A Secret Story of Quilts and the Underground Railroad* (New York: Doubleday, 1999). Both books have been attacked by critics who discount their reliance on oral histories; defenders of the quilt code point out that African American histories have been so institutionally neglected that such oral histories are in fact vital.
85. Interview with Davids, 2011.
86. Joe Brown, ed., *A Promise to Remember: The NAMES Project Book of Letters* (New York: Avon Books, 1992).
87. Bush's endorsement was printed on other NAMES Project literature for the 1992 display; Crimp makes mention of a brochure that includes this "anodyne and cliché-ridden blurb" ("Spectacle of Mourning," 201).
88. James Wentzy, dir., *The Ashes Action* (AIDS Community Television / DIVA TV,

1995). This was the same display of the Quilt that I saw as a college student, though I was not aware of the protests around it at the time.

89. Tom Roach, *Friendship as a Way of Life: Foucault, AIDS, and the Politics of Shared Estrangement* (Albany: State University of New York Press, 2012), 147.
90. Deborah B. Gould, *Moving Politics: Emotion and ACT UP's Fight against AIDS* (Chicago: University of Chicago Press, 2009), 230.
91. Bob Rafsky, "I'm Not Dying Anymore," *QW*, July 12, 1992, 51.
92. Avram Finkelstein, "The Other Quilt," *QW*, October 25, 1992, 10.
93. Avram Finkelstein, correspondence with the author, March 2015.
94. Finkelstein, correspondence with author, February 2015.
95. Ruskin, *Quilt*, 103.
96. Crimp, "Spectacle of Mourning," 196.
97. Bill Wilson, "Memories of Inaugurals Past," *San Francisco Sentinel*, http://www.sanfranciscosentinel.com/?p=18554.
98. Betty Cuniberti, "Max Robinson's Silent Struggle with AIDS," *Los Angeles Times*, December 22, 1988.
99. For more on the development of red, gold, green, and black as Pan-African colors, particularly via the design of Marcus Garvey's flag, see Neil J. Savishinsky, "African Dimensions of the Jamaican Rastafarian Movement," in *Chanting Down Babylon: The Rastafari Reader*, ed. Nathaniel Samuel Murrell, William David Spencer, and Adrian Anthony McFarlane (Philadelphia: Temple University Press, 1998), 134–35.
100. Sturken, *Tangled Memories*, 5.
101. Anonymous letter, "The NAMES Project Exposed: What Cleve Jones Doesn't Want You to Know," undated, unpaginated, GLBT Historical Society, NAMES Project ephemera file.
102. Ibid.
103. Andrew Sullivan, *Virtually Normal: An Argument about Homosexuality* (New York: Alfred A. Knopf, 1995); Michael Warner, *The Trouble with Normal: Sex, Politics, and the Ethics of Queer Life* (New York: Free Press, 1999).
104. Interview with Jada Harris, November 2010, Atlanta.
105. Centers for Disease Control and Prevention, "HIV among African Americans," http://www.cdc.gov/hiv/group/racialethnic/africanamericans/.
106. For more on African American uses of African kente cloth, see Doran H. Ross, *Wrapped in Pride: Ghanaian Kente and African American Identity* (Los Angeles: UCLA Fowler Museum of Cultural History, 1998).
107. Michel Foucault, *L'archéologie du savoir* (Paris: Éditions Gallimard, 1969); Allan Sekula, "The Body and the Archive," *October* 39 (Winter 1986): 3–64.
108. Patricia A. Turner, introduction to *Crafted Lives: Stories and Studies of African American Quilters* (Jackson: University of Mississippi Press, 2009), 1; see also Fry, *Stitched from the Soul*, and Kyra E. Hicks, *Black Threads: An African American Quilting Sourcebook* (Jefferson, NC: McFarland, 2003).
109. Freida High Wasikhongo [Tesfagiorgis], "Afrofemcentric: Twenty Years of Faith Ringgold," in *Faith Ringgold: Twenty Years of Painting, Sculpture and Performance (1963–1983)*, ed. Michele Wallace (New York: Studio Museum in Harlem, 1984), 17.
110. Lisa E. Farrington, *Faith Ringgold* (Petaluma, CA: Pomegranate, 2004), 71.

111. Eli Leon, *Who'd a Thought It: Improvisation in African-American Quiltmaking* (San Francisco: San Francisco Craft and Folk Art Museum, 1987).
112. Elaine Showalter, *Sister's Choice: Tradition and Change in American Women's Writing* (Oxford: Clarendon; New York: Oxford University Press, 1991), 172.
113. Interview with Harris, 2010.
114. Interview with Roddy Williams, June 2015, Atlanta.
115. Judith Butler, *Bodies That Matter: On the Discursive Limits of "Sex"* (New York: Routledge, 1993), 236.
116. Judith Butler, *Frames of War: When Is Life Grievable?* (London: Verso, 2009), 38.
117. Jasbir Puar, *Terrorist Assemblages: Homonationalism in Queer Times* (Durham, NC: Duke University Press, 2007), 2.
118. *NAMESLetter* 6, no. 1 (Winter 1992/1993).
119. Valjeanne Estes, "Breaking Barriers: A Story of Cultural Challenge for Panelmakers," *NAMESLetter* 8, no. 3 (Fall 1995): 3.
120. Ibid.
121. Max Carocci, "Textiles of Healing: Native American AIDS Quilts," *Textile* 8, no. 1 (2010): 68–85.
122. Several exhibits have paid homage to the influential designers and stylists who died of AIDS, including *Fashion Victims: AIDS in the '80s*, curated by Virginia Heaven at Columbia College Chicago, 2007, and *A Queer History of Fashion*, curated by Valerie Steele, Fashion Institute of Technology, 2013.
123. *Always Remember: A Selection of Panels Created by and for International Fashion Designers*, photography by Paul Margolies (New York: Simon and Schuster Editions, 1996).
124. Anthony Turney, introduction to *Always Remember*, 12.
125. Letter/form by Robyn sent to accompany the panel, excerpted in *Always Remember*, 30.
126. Online searches for this panel came up with nothing, and Rhoad told me in 2010 that it was officially "missing." This was reiterated by Williams in 2015.
127. Patrick Robyn, e-mail correspondence, April 2015.
128. Sturken, *Tangled Memories*, 218.
129. For more on the development of this language, see Robert D. Bullard, Glenn S. Johnson, and Angel O. Torres, "Atlanta: A Black Mecca?," in *The Black Metropolis in the Twenty-First Century: Race, Power, and the Politics of Place*, ed. Bullard (Lanham, MD: Rowman and Littlefield, 2007), 149–72.
130. Interview with Williams, 2010.
131. Ibid.
132. Ann Cvetkovich, *An Archive of Feelings: Trauma, Sexuality, and Lesbian Public Cultures* (Durham, NC: Duke University Press, 2003).
133. Ibid., 91.
134. Interview with Rhoad, 2010.
135. Marjorie Whitehouse, quoted in Scott Williams, "Levi Grant Inspires Generous Donations," *NAMESLetter* 9, no. 1 (Spring 1996): 5.
136. "Archive Project Update," *NAMESLetter* 9, no. 1 (Spring 1996): 4.
137. There are several ways to digitally interface with the Quilt; through the NAMES Project website at http://www.aidsquilt.org/view-the-quilt/search-the-quilt;

through the mobile app developed for the 2012 display at http://aidsquilttouch.org/; and through a Microsoft research project at http://research.microsoft.com/en-us/um/redmond/projects/aidsquilt/.

138. A complete list can be found in the brochure *Quilt in the Capital 2012*.

139. Interview with Williams, 2010.

140. NAMES Project, *Quilt Display Handbook* (San Francisco, 1995), 47.

141. I am grateful to all those who responded to this request and sent photographs, including Bruce Vasbinder, Carol Terry, Diana Chesser, Corey Roskin, Cherie Mitchell, Ginger Hoernig, Kathryn Hedgepath, and Henry Paquin.

142. Interview with Rhoad, 2010.

143. When I asked curator Helen Molesworth about her decision not to include the Quilt in her show *This Will Have Been: Art, Love, and Politics in the 1980s*, at the Institute of Contemporary Art, Boston, she answered that she "never even considered it." E-mail with the author, March 2011. Molesworth does discuss the importance of the Quilt in "The Whole World Is Watching," in *Jim Hodges: Give More Than You Take*, ed. Jeffrey Grove and Olga Viso (Dallas: Dallas Museum of Art / Minneapolis: Walker Art Center, 2013), 171–85.

144. Public conversation with the artist, Josh Faught, n/a art space, Oakland, December 2013.

145. Interview with McNamara, 2015.

146. For more on Wilson, see Julia Bryan-Wilson, interview, *Queer Threads*, ed. John Chaich, forthcoming.

147. Susan Sontag, "Notes on 'Camp,'" *Partisan Review* 31, no. 4 (Fall 1964): 515–30; reprinted in *Against Interpretation and Other Essays* (New York: Farrar, Straus and Giroux, 1966), 275–92, quote from 288.

148. David Eng and David Kazanjian, "Introduction: Mourning Remains," in *Loss: The Politics of Mourning*, eds. Eng and Kazanjian (Berkeley: University of California Press, 2002), 2.

149. Peter Dormer, "The salon de refuse?," in *The Culture of Craft*, ed. Dormer (Manchester: Manchester University Press, 1997), 3.

150. Interview with Williams, 2015.

151. Georges Didi-Huberman, *Confronting Images: Questioning the Ends of a Certain History of Art* (University Park: Penn State Press, 2005), 8.

AFTERWORD

1. Interview with Angela Hennessy, February 2016, Oakland.
2. Edward McAllister, "At Rural South Carolina Flag Factory, Sadness and Pride," Reuters.com, http://www.reuters.com/article/us-usa-shooting-south-carolina-flag-fact-idUSKBNOP421P20150624.
3. Renée Rigdon and Zabet Stewart, *AntiCraft: Knitting, Beading, and Stitching for the Slightly Sinister* (Cincinnati, OH: North Light Books, 2007).
4. William Morris, "The Beauty of Life, " in *William Morris on Art and Socialism*, ed. Norman Kelvin (Mineola, NY: Dover, 1999), 53.

5. Nicholas Bell, "Craft Futures: A Generation at Hand," in *40 under 40: Craft Futures* (Washington, DC: Smithsonian Renwick Gallery; New Haven, CT: Yale University Press, 2012), 14.
6. Church of Craft website, http://churchofcraft.org/a-sermon-simple-and-captivating/.
7. Nick Srnicek and Alex Williams, *Inventing the Future: Postcapitalism and a World without Work* (Brooklyn, NY: Verso Books, 2015).
8. Quoted in Penelope Green, "The Ambassador of Handmade," *New York Times*, September 4, 2008, F1.
9. Lippard, "Making Something from Nothing."
10. Robby Herbst, "The Worker's Rug: Fine Art from Day Labor," August 26, 2012, http://www.kcet.org/arts/artbound/counties/los-angeles/the-workers-rug-fine-art-from-day-labor.html.
11. Leslie T. Chang, *Factory Girls: From Village to City in a Changing China* (New York: Spiegel and Grau, 2008), 98.
12. For more on the contemporaneity of craft, see my brief polemic "Eleven Propositions in Response to the Question: 'What Is Contemporary about Craft?,'" *Journal of Modern Craft* 6, no. 1 (March 2013): 7–10. I originally named this text "Eleven Contradictory Propositions . . ." but feared the "contradictory" was redundant, given the exaggerated and at times absurdly divisive theses I presented. However, some readers have misunderstood my intentionally oppositional juxtapositions as theoretical confusion; their bewilderment has been a good reminder for me of the vagueness of satire.
13. Mike Press, "Handmade Futures: The Emerging Role of Craft Knowledge in Our Digital Culture," in *NeoCraft: Modernity and the Crafts*, ed. Sandra Alfoldy (Halifax: Press of the Nova Scotia College of Art and Design, 2007), 252.
14. David Gauntlett, *Making Is Connecting: The Social Meaning of Creativity, from DIY and Knitting to YouTube and Web 2.0* (Cambridge: Polity, 2011).
15. To date, the major trade books (which are also how-to guides) on this phenomenon are Mandy Moore and Leanne Prain, *Yarn Bombing: The Art of Crochet and Knit Graffiti* (Vancouver: Arsenal Pulp, 2009); and Deadly Knitshade, *Knit the City: Maschenhaft Seltsames* (Hamburg: Hoffmann und Campe, 2011), the latter of which was translated into English as Lauren O'Farrell, *Knit the City: A Whodunnknit Set in London* (Summersdale, West Sussex, UK: Summersdale, 2011).
16. Malia Wollan, "Graffiti's Cozy, Feminine Side," *New York Times*, May 18, 2011.
17. For more on the whiteness of yarn bombing, see Natalie Cone, "Yarn Bombing Oakland," BA honors thesis, Department of History of Art, UC Berkeley. I was Cone's primary adviser for this thesis.
18. Moore and Prain, *Yarn-Bombing*, 118.
19. Maddy Costa, "The Graffiti Knitting Epidemic," *Guardian*, October 10, 2010.
20. Wollan, "Graffiti's Cozy, Feminine Side."
21. Lippard, "Making Something from Nothing," 138.
22. Amy Sedaris, *Simple Times: Crafts for Poor People* (New York: Grand Central, 2010).
23. Ibid., 73.
24. Ibid., 151.
25. *Taking Time: Craft and the Slow Revolution*, curated by Helen Carnac,

Craftspace, Birmingham, UK, 2009; http://www.craftspace.co.uk/page.asp?fn=2&id=57&stp=1&grp=3.

26. Judith Leemann and Shannon Stratton, "Circling Back Into that Thing We Cast Forward: A Close Reading on *Gestures of Resistance*," in *Collaboration through Craft*, ed. Amanda Ravetz, Alice Kettle, and Helen Felcey (London: Bloomsbury Academic, 2013), 219–32.
27. See Elizabeth Freeman, ed., *Queer Temporalities*, special issue of *GLQ: A Journal of Lesbian and Gay Studies* 13, nos. 2–3 (2007).
28. Adamson, *Thinking through Craft*, 2.
29. José Esteban Muñoz, *Cruising Utopia: The Then and There of Queer Futurity* (New York: New York University Press, 2009), 11.
30. Meg Mateo Ilasco, *Craft, Inc.: Turn Your Creative Hobby into a Business* (San Francisco: Chronicle Books, 2007); Kari Chapin, *Grow Your Handmade Business* (North Adams, MA: Storey, 2012), and *The Handmade Marketplace: How to Sell Your Crafts Locally, Globally, and Online* (North Adams, MA: Storey, 2010).
31. Jason Malinak, *Etsy-preneurship: Everything You Need to Know to Turn Your Handmade Hobby into a Thriving Business* (Hoboken, NJ: John Wiley, 2012).
32. Alex Williams, "That Hobby Looks like a Lot of Work," *New York Times*, December 16, 2009.
33. Hiroko Tabuchi, "Etsy I.P.O. Tests Pledge to Do Good," *New York Times*, April 16, 2015, B1.
34. Nicole Dawkins, "Do-It-Yourself: The Precarious Work and Postfeminist Politics of Handmaking (in) Detroit," *Utopian Studies* 22, no. 2 (2011): 263.
35. For more on Cabrera's practice as distinct from Oldenburg's, see Kate Bonansinga, *Curating at the Edge: Artists Respond to the US/Mexico Border* (Austin: University of Texas Press, 2014), 124.
36. Robert Faires, "Flow of Energy: Beili Liu Makes an Art of Channeling the Forces within Objects and Us," *Austin Chronicle*, March 11, 2011.
37. Joao Beira and Fumika Yamamoto, *The Mending Project* (2011), http://www.beililiu.com/10t011/mend.html.
38. Laurie Britton Newell, *Out of the Ordinary: Spectacular Craft* (London: Victoria and Albert Museum and Crafts Council, 2007); Valerie Cassel, cur. and ed., *Hand + Made: The Performative Impulse in Art and Craft* (Houston: Contemporary Art Museum, 2010).
39. Jenni Sorkin, "Constructing Community," in *Anne Wilson: Wind/Rewind/Weave*, ed. Chris Molinski (Knoxville, TN: Knoxville Museum of Art, 2011), 37.
40. For writings on this subject that explicitly use the phrase "craft as performance," see Mary Elizabeth Hancock, *The Politics of Heritage from Madras to Chennai* (Bloomington: Indiana University Press, 2008); and Robert G. Healy, "'Tourist Merchandise' as a Means of Generating Local Benefits from Ecotourism," in *Tourism in Developing Countries*, ed. Twan Huybers (Cheltenham, UK: Edward Elgar, 2007), 304–18.
41. Ramón Rivera-Servera, "Exhibiting Labor: Indigenous Performance, US American Tourism, and Consumptive Intimacies in Oaxaca, Mexico," public lecture, UC Berkeley, March 5, 2015.

42. There is a long literature about the photography of live events. See, for instance, the incisive approach to the camera's mediation of motion taken up by Carrie Lambert-Beatty in *Being Watched: Yvonne Rainer and the 1960s* (Cambridge, MA: MIT Press, 2008).

Index

Italicized page numbers refer to illustrations.